A SCYTHE OF FIRE

A SCYTHE OF FIRE

*A Civil War Story of the Eighth
Georgia Infantry Regiment*

Warren Wilkinson
and
Steven E. Woodworth

WILLIAM MORROW
An Imprint of HarperCollins*Publishers*

HarperCollins books may be purchased for educational, business, or sales promotional use. For information please write: Special Markets Department, HarperCollins Publishers Inc., 10 East 53rd Street, New York, NY 10022.

FIRST EDITION

Designed by Bernard Klein

Printed on acid-free paper

Library of Congress Cataloging-in-Publication Data

Wilkinson, Warren.
A scythe of fire: a Civil War story of the Eighth Georgia Infantry
Regiment / Warren Wilkinson and Steven E. Woodworth.—1st ed.
p. cm.
Includes bibliographical references and index.
ISBN 0-380-97752-4
1. Confederate States of America. Army. Georgia Infantry Regiment, 8th 2. Georgia—
History—Civil War, 1861–1865—Regimental histories.
3. United States—History—Civil War, 1861–1865—Regimental
histories. I. Woodworth, Steven E. II. Title.

E559.5 8th.W55 2002
973.7'458—dc21
2001032654

02 03 04 05 06 QW 10 9 8 7 6 5 4 3 2 1

Contents

Preface

THIS account of the Eighth Georgia Regiment is meant to speak to a far broader audience about far broader issues than what could be strictly described as regimental history. It will no doubt be of great interest to the descendants of the men of the Eighth—I certainly hope it will—but in it I have tried to show in microcosm, as far as the available sources would permit, the experiences, hopes, thoughts, and motivations of the "common" soldiers of the Army of Northern Virginia. If I have done it well, this should tell us things about the Civil War and about the Old South. On the other hand, I have borne in mind that this is, above all, a story, and so I have tried to avoid extensive and obtrusive passages of analysis or discussions of how this or that finding relates to the most recent theories of such and such scholar. Such connections will be apparent to those who take an interest in that sort of thing. There is a place for heavy analysis, and this is not it. A good story ought in some sense to tell itself and suggest its own meanings. I think this one does. So I have taken the risk of disappointing two classes of readers, those who seek a genealogical reference, on the one hand, and those who seek scholarly arguments on the other. But to all readers—professional scholars, descendants of soldiers, and the great mass who are neither—I hope this book will be, above all, a dramatic story to inspire, enlighten, and deepen understanding as it displays fellow human beings—not so very different from ourselves—coping with extraordinary circumstances the like of which we, by the mercy of God, may never see.

A word may be in order as to how this book came to be and how Mr. Wilkinson and I came to be its authors. After his successful book on the Fifty-seventh Massachusetts Regiment, *Mother May You Never See the Sights That I Have Seen,* Warren Wilkinson undertook research in preparation for this book on the Eighth Georgia. He had completed the research, having amassed an amazing amount of material, when his tragic and untimely death intervened. Buz Wyeth, his publisher at Harper-Collins, contacted Keith Bohannon, now of Penn State University, about the possibility of taking over and finishing the task. Keith passed, so Buz contacted Rod Gragg, another Civil War historian. Rod also declined but recommended me, and I agreed. The project was delayed several years while Mr. Wilkinson's will cleared probate.

I would like to express my appreciation to Buz Wyeth, Mike Hamilburg, Rod Gragg, Stephen S. Power, and Sarah Durand for the vital roles they played in making this book a reality. I am also profoundly grateful to Steven Townsend, John Roberts, and Dave Larson for providing information about their ancestors in the Eighth Georgia as well as cordial encouragement. Dave's outstanding website on the Eighth Georgia Regiment (http://home.earthlink.net/~larsrbl/8thGeorgiaInfantry.html) is a vast and constantly growing resource that was of much help to me and will be invaluable to anyone who wishes to pursue the study of the regiment in great detail. Special thanks are also in order to Ethan Rafuse, Keith Bohannon, and David Slay for reading and critiquing the manuscript. They have shown themselves true friends by having the courage to tell me frankly when I had gotten it wrong. I of course am fully responsible for any errors that may remain.

Finally, I have once again the pleasure of expressing my appreciation for my top proofreader and all-around encourager, my wife, Leah.

Steven E. Woodworth
Texas Christian University, May 30, 2001

A SCYTHE OF FIRE

CHAPTER ONE

In Defense of Southern Rights

ANNON roared. Half a mile off came the long rattling volleys of musketry that told where rival lines of desperate men were trying their best to blast the life out of each other. Dense clouds of white, sulfurous powder smoke rolled across an undulating countryside green with clover, golden with ripening wheat, and checkered with patches of woodland. A shouted order from close at hand cut through the roar of distant combat, and a long line of gray-clad men scrambled to their feet in the late-afternoon shadows that reached out from the edge of a forested rise. Like good soldiers they formed their ranks and then, on command, marched forward with steady tread toward the inferno that awaited them across the way. One who saw it wrote that "a more splendid line of brave men never moved on to deadly combat."[1]

Enemy gunners had the range and soon were dropping shells into their ranks. Men disintegrated under direct hits. Shrapnel from other bursts would knock down three or four men at a time, but the gray line closed up its gaps and marched on. Stout rail fences lined a dusty road across their path, and as the men broke ranks to climb them the distant artillery pounded them mercilessly. Smoke, dust, fence rails, haversacks, rifles, caps, and bodies sailed through the air, but even some of those tossed about like rag dolls by the exploding shells scrambled to their feet again and formed up with the others on the far side of the fences to continue their advance.

A few score yards farther and the order came, "Double-quick!" Shoulders hunched forward against the storm of shot and shell, the men in the long gray line trotted toward the far wood line. Somewhere in those woods was the enemy, and as the men ran, shoulder to shoulder, toward the unseen foe, something welled up inside them and broke out in a high-pitched chorus of Rebel Yells—discordant, fierce, and rising above the roar of battle to make the short hairs stand up on the backs of their enemies' necks.

This was Gettysburg, July 2, 1863, and in the center of that long gray line was the Eighth Georgia Regiment, moving forward along with its brigade to join in the battle's decisive struggle—along Bloody Run, across the Wheat Field, and to the Valley of Death.

They came from all over Georgia—these brave men of the Eighth—from every walk of life. Planters, cotton factors, and shopkeepers, lawyers, teachers, and dirt farmers—few could have foreseen the cataclysm that now made them all soldiers, and none could have predicted the winding course of events that had brought them from the peaceful scenes of prewar Georgia to this bloody field and would carry them onward down the long, hard road to Appomattox. They were ordinary people, faced with extraordinary choices and challenges. This is their story.

The Elite of the Town

Flowing west past Cartersville, Georgia, the Etowah River joins the southbound Oostanaula River to form the Coosa River—muddy and slow-moving. The Coosa, in turn, flows south and west through the forests and fields of nearby Alabama and on past Mobile into the far-off Gulf of Mexico. At the confluence of these three streams, Etowah, Oostanaula, and Coosa, in the rich river-bottom land bordered by the low hills at the southern end of the Piedmont of the Appalachian Mountains

in northwestern Georgia, lies the city of Rome, in the ancient Cherokee country of Floyd County—green, shady, and lovely. In 1860, fifteen
thousand people or so lived in the little town and the surrounding
county, with about a third of that number being slaves. Commerce
thrived in the Hill City, as Rome was then known locally, and the town
boasted cotton trading, real estate, hotels, mills, and the Noble Brothers
Foundry, which would later produce cannon for the Confederacy.
Steamboats plied the rivers, their decks loaded with all sorts of goods,
and wagons lined the streets bearing every manner of abundant farm
products, chiefly the bulging white cotton bales, ready to ship to Northern mills and European textile factories. The city was well laid out, with
pleasant houses and handsome red-brick commercial buildings lining its
wide downtown streets. At night, gas lamps glowed along its main thoroughfare, Broad Street, lighting the fronts of grocery stores, livery stables,
jewelry shops, clothing stores, bookstores, and drugstores. A railroad spur,
the Memphis Branch Railroad and Steamship Company of Georgia,
linked the town with the Western & Atlantic at Kingston, Georgia. For
most of its population, Rome was a pleasant and attractive community
in which to live.[2]

To teach school in Rome in 1853 went twenty-eight-year-old
Melvin Dwinnell. Born in the Green Mountains of Vermont, Dwinnell
had taken his A.B. in 1849 at the University of Vermont and then gone
on to earn an M.A. In 1855, two years after coming to Rome, Mose, as
he was known to his friends, took advantage of an opportunity to buy
the local newspaper, the *Rome Weekly Courier*, and soon became its
owner and editor. He also grew to be an ardent and vocal defender of
the Southern cause, completely—and forever—forsaking his Northern
roots.[3]

During the late fall of 1860 and the winter that followed, Dwinnell
found plenty of momentous news to fill the columns of his newspaper.
In November, Republican candidate Abraham Lincoln was duly elected
president of the United States on a platform that pledged him not to
tamper with slavery in states like Georgia, where it already existed, but
not to permit its spread to new territories in the West. In December,
South Carolina responded by declaring itself no longer a part of the
United States. Mississippi, Florida, and Alabama followed the next
month. Georgia was not far behind. Immediately after the November

election, Georgia governor Joseph E. Brown asked the state legislature to call for a convention to debate the issue of secession, and on January 19, 1861, that convention took the fateful step. By February, Louisiana and Texas had followed suit, and the seven Deep South states sent delegates to a convention in Montgomery, Alabama, to proclaim a Southern nation, call it the Confederate States of America, and choose as its first president Jefferson Davis of Mississippi. As spring brightened North Georgia with the blossoms of azaleas, dogwoods, and apple trees, Rome's residents, like Americans all over the country, would read of the culmination of the process in accounts from Charleston, South Carolina. There, on April 12, 1861, Confederate cannon opened fire on the tiny U.S. Army garrison of Fort Sumter, in Charleston harbor, and the nation took the final plunge into civil war. Forced to choose between North and South, the states of Virginia, North Carolina, Tennessee, and Arkansas cast their lot with the latter, and the Confederacy was complete.

Back in Georgia, war fever was high in most parts of the state, and Rome, with surrounding Floyd County, was no exception. During the month of May 1861 the town and county dispatched three companies of volunteers to the expected seat of war in Virginia—three companies that would eventually become companies A, E, and H of the Eighth Georgia Infantry Regiment. Two of those companies had existed as organizations for some time before the war. The phenomenon of the "volunteer company" as a peacetime social club and semimilitary organization was common throughout the United States during the prewar years and especially in the South. It was not so much that the members of such companies anticipated the war that finally came, but rather that having fancy tailored uniforms in which to march around during the drills—and to loiter around in after them—was not only a great deal of fun, but also (or so the members devoutly hoped) highly impressive to young ladies. Status, recognition, male bonding—such groups had much to offer. Admission to membership was by election of those already within that enviable circle. One did not enlist in such an outfit; he applied. If accepted, he had to be prepared to purchase his own fancy dress uniform with his own money. Nevertheless, such volunteer companies were all the rage throughout the country during the years before the Civil War made soldiering serious business. Many Southern communities boasted one or more of them. Floyd County had three: the

Cherokee Artillery, the Floyd Cavalry, and the very cream of Floyd County society, the Rome Light Guards, in which the newspaper editor and erstwhile Yankee Melvin Dwinnell held the proud rank of lieutenant. The last two of these companies were destined for the Eighth.

Throughout the winter and spring of 1861, volunteer companies across the South, anticipating the possibility of something like a war, had stepped up their activities. In January the Light Guards had advertised in the local paper its willingness to receive the "petitions" of any who might wish to join its select society. Some apparently did and were accepted, for an observer was soon noting the "fuller ranks" of the Guards as well as Floyd County's other volunteer companies.[4]

Then there was the drilling, diligent and ubiquitous. The Light Guards' captain, Edward Jones Magruder, was a Virginia native and 1855 graduate of the Virginia Military Institute. His good training apparently served him well, for the Light Guards was by all accounts a well-drilled unit. During the inclement weather of January, it drilled regularly in Rome's city hall. Later, various companies drilled in Broad Street, among other places. Marching in his place as a private in the ranks of the Light Guards, twenty-four-year-old Rome physician George S. Barnsley felt the exhilarating call of imagined military glory. He had to admit that he felt disgusted at the idea of "men shooting each other about questions" he thought could be negotiated. Yet, he wrote, "Marching in the streets filled our bosoms to overflowing patriotism, and especially as the pretty girls threw flowers and kisses to us." The steady, unified tramp of their boots alternately striking the pavement in unison also had a charm for him. For the first time the naturally aloof young physician could feel that he was really a part of some great unity larger than himself.[5]

On Washington's birthday, February 22, all three companies were out in full force and full uniform for the benefit of a large and admiring audience. Lt. Dwinnell's squad won a silver cup for being the best drilled, and later that day, when the Guards held a competitive target shoot, Cpl. John J. Black won the prize for the best shot. A young boy who was present that day remembered years later how politicians made speeches promising the enthusiastic audience that "one Southerner could whip ten Yankees," and that "the war would only be a picnic for the soldier boys who went to the front." In early April, the Guards were at it again, traveling the fifteen miles to Kingston, Georgia, for a grand parade and review with several other companies. Under dark and cloudy springtime skies, spectators once again thrilled to the sight of massed uniform finery and the spectacle of a sham battle between the Guards and another company. In the afternoon, local ladies served a picnic lunch, and gentlemen made speeches. A participant recalled that it was "a good time generally of wit and repartee, conversation, mirth and song."[6]

Yet for Melvin Dwinnell, the lowering skies of that April review in Kingston were a metaphor for "the horrid suspense and dreadful anxiety that, like dark clouds, have overhung our new Republic." Serious business lay ahead. Only a few days after the Kingston review and still before the attack on Fort Sumter, the Confederate government, then based in Montgomery, Alabama, called on the seceding states to prepare volunteer troops and hold them in "instant readiness" to create armies for the new government—should they be needed. Georgia's quota was three thousand men, in "well drilled" companies.[7]

Floyd County's response was immediate and enthusiastic. Dwinnell, for one, had no doubts about the cause for which he and his fellow volunteers were so eager to fight. Referring to Northern opposition to the spread of slavery, he wrote, "The wicked fanaticism of the North by its unjust and unconstitutional aggression with vile taunts and hypocritical sneers compelled us to sever the bands that once bound us together." If any of the volunteers harbored doubts about the cause, none expressed it.

Companies hastened to offer their services. The men of the Floyd Cavalry, under Capt. John R. Towers, had been offering theirs for some time, in fact, ever since Lincoln's election the preceding November. Governor Brown had not accepted the offer then, and now word got around that he was not taking any more cavalry companies. Towers, a thirty-six-year-old, blue-eyed, blond-haired native of South Carolina, was not to be deterred. He had organized the Floyd Cavalry just the previous year, recruiting mainly from the farm boys in the outlying area of the county that lay near his home at Cave Springs. Now he simply reorganized the rustic horsemen as a company of infantry, for which the prospects of state acceptance were much better. He named the newly reincarnated company the Miller Rifles, in honor of prominent local physician Homer Virgil Milton Miller. The erstwhile holiday cavalrymen now gave themselves over to diligent drill in the duties of the infantry.[8]

They were not all country boys in the Miller Rifles. In the ranks marched Charles M. Harper, nephew and close associate of Rome cotton, mercantile, and real estate magnate Alfred Shorter. Harper was definitely a member of Rome's upper crust and had even traveled to Charleston, South Carolina, the preceding December to watch with pleasure as that state declared its secession. Now, however, he was a private in the ranks, doing his best to learn the business of soldiering.

However zealous they might be, the Miller Rifles were not going to get ahead of the pride of Rome, at least not yet. On April 18 the Light Guards took the train to Camp Brown, named for the governor and located on the Western & Atlantic Railroad in Smyrna, Georgia, between Atlanta and Marietta and just sixty miles from home. Established on the old Smyrna Camp Meeting Ground, scene of fervent religious meetings in other times, Camp Brown was to be the place for training and organizing various companies, over twenty of them by this time, coming in from all over the state. Food was plentiful and good, camaraderie the same, and the way the volunteers performed the various convolutions of military drill was most satisfactory, at least to themselves. Morale, already high, was further elevated on April 24 when the Light Guards sat up until one o'clock in the morning making the first Confederate flag at Camp Brown. They proudly raised it the next morning, then invited the rest of the camp to join them in saluting it by marching eight times around it at the double-quick.[9]

April 29, however, brought a rude shock to the proud Light Guards. It had been very much a routine Sunday in camp—inspection, church call, and some leisure time—until the governor himself arrived that evening, and all the companies formed up in line on the parade ground to hear his speech. Brown was a strange character—cantankerous, opinionated, and supremely self-willed—and he got off to a bad start with the Light Guards by announcing that the troops at this particular camp of instruction would not be sent to Virginia in response to the Confederate government's call, a week earlier, to forward two thousand troops to that state. Other Georgia troops would go, Brown explained, but those at his namesake encampment would remain in Georgia as home guards because they were "not sufficiently skilled in the science of war." The troops remained silent and respectful in the face of this blatant insult, but that night the camp seethed. Whatever else the governor was, he was a politician. He could not fail to notice that his remarks had not exactly gone over well, and the very next morning he addressed the troops again, this time changing his tune and soothing the men with a promise that "no doubt all would get service as soon as they could reasonably desire." With that, the men felt almost reconciled to their governor—for the time being.[10]

Meanwhile, back in Rome, twenty-six-year-old John Frederick Cooper was organizing yet another company of volunteers, this one called the Floyd Infantry. As captain of the new company, Cooper succeeded on May 13 in obtaining what Towers, of the Miller Rifles, and Magruder, of the Light Guards, had been awaiting in vain: orders direct from the Confederate War Department in Montgomery to proceed as soon as possible to Richmond, for acceptance into Confederate service. The Floyd Infantry, born less than a month before, set up camp that same day at Sheibley's School House about a mile outside of town and began eager preparations. The Miller Rifles soon pitched their tents nearby, amid reports that they too had been accepted by the Confederate government. About the same time, the Light Guards returned—somewhat crestfallen, one gathers—from Camp Brown and joined the other two companies at Sheibley's. Taking a page from Cooper's book, Magruder decided to bypass the erratic Governor Brown entirely and apply directly to President Jefferson Davis. That brought results, and within days, the Light Guards too had their marching orders for Richmond.[11]

Excitement reigned at the camp at Sheibley's as all three companies hurried to complete their final preparations—and celebrations—before leaving for the expected seat of the war. Although Pvt. Julius Borck drowned in the Oostanaula when he and a dozen or so comrades of the Floyd Infantry decided to go for a late-night swim on May 16, the spirits in camp were otherwise high, the festivities of those weeks joyous. The Light Guards' twenty-five-year-old orderly sergeant, Jim Tom Moore, married Miss Letitia Hutchings that same week, and on the 14th, Capt. Magruder himself wed Miss Florence Fouche at Rome's First Baptist Church. It was an impressive ceremony, with bride and groom walking up a long archway formed by the upraised sabers of eighty members of the Light Guards.[12]

What those infantrymen were doing with sabers—an article of cavalry equipment—remains a little obscure, but it was typical of the equipment situation in Rome's volunteer companies: showy uniforms and nonregulation paraphernalia, but a glaring shortage of the necessary standard equipment needed to make them effective soldiers. All three captains were spending a good deal of their time during this final week or two of preparation scrambling around trying to equip their companies with such mundane items as knapsacks, haversacks, canteens, and blankets. With the Light Guards scheduled to board the train for Richmond at 11:30 A.M. on Monday, May 27, Capt. Magruder, on Saturday, the 25th, sent a man to Louisville, Kentucky, to purchase tents—the large, conical Sibley tents then favored by the U.S. Army. They would just have to catch up with the company in Virginia.[13]

Yet the most glaring gap in the volunteer companies' equipment involved rifles: they had none. Incredibly, after months of drilling, mid-May 1861 saw Rome's three infantry captains desperately seeking firearms to put into the hands of their troops, almost on the eve of their departure for the front. On Thursday, May 23, Magruder traveled to Augusta, Georgia, to visit the state arsenal there and draw seventy U.S. Model 1841 rifles. The model 1841 had been made famous in the Mexican War by the First Mississippi Rifles Regiment, under the command of its colonel, Jefferson Davis, and so the weapons were often called Mississippi rifles. By 1861 they were far from being state-of-the-art. Like nearly all weapons of the prewar period, they were muzzle-loaders, but unlike the most modern rifles, these had been designed not for the recently invented conical minié bullet but for the old spherical lead ball, rammed down the barrel wrapped in a leather patch. Still, their new recipients in the Light Guards thought the Model 1841 a beautiful rifle, and so it was. At .54 caliber its bore was slightly smaller than that of the most modern designs. It was forty-eight and a half inches long and weighed nine pounds, twelve ounces. The stock was black walnut and the steel barrel and its fixed iron sights were lacquer-browned on the outside. Barrel bands, trigger guard, butt plate, and patchbox (the oblong hinged plate on the side of the stock covering the receptacle for the soldier's supply of leather patches) were gleaming brass. So too was the handle of the twenty-seven-and-one-quarter-inch-long saber-bayonet that went with it. It looked fine and formidable. The Light Guards lovingly handled their new weapons and reflected on the large stride they were making toward becoming real soldiers.[14]

The rifles, however, were to become a serious problem for the Light Guards, as for the various other Georgia companies, during the coming days. At the heart of the matter was the fact that in the midst of a war being waged ostensibly for "state rights," Georgia's Governor Brown actually believed the concept—or at least acted upon it. The weapons issued by the state arsenals of Georgia were, he maintained, the property of the state, not of the Confederacy. They must be used only for the defense of Georgia, not of the Confederate States as a whole, and, above all, they must not leave the boundaries of the state. He therefore had the state adjutant general issue an order on May 18 specifying that no company could take its state-issued arms, or any of the associated trappings, out of Georgia. If any company were to ignore this order and take its weapons with it to the front anyway, the order specified that the company officers be held personally financially liable.[15]

The order was not popular among Georgia troops pining for the opportunity to demonstrate their martial prowess as soon as possible lest peace break out suddenly and their chance be forever lost. In the columns of the *Courier,* Dwinnell raged against Brown's "exhibition of arbitrary power and spiteful arrogance." For him and his fellow volunteers, there were more important things than state rights. "We have common interests, common hopes and common dangers with the other seceded States," he wrote, "and our efforts should be for the common cause without factious stickeling for the rights of States." But argument and invective were equally lost on Joe Brown, who steadfastly did whatever suited him with stubborn disregard for reason or good policy. The Southern states had banded together to wage a war, but Brown was determined that Georgia would contribute no weapons, even if that meant the state's contingent should march off to battle with empty hands.[16]

The Rome companies found various ways to cope with this absurd situation. Most successful was Capt. Towers of the Miller Rifles, who traveled to Montgomery, Alabama, to meet with Maj. Josiah Gorgas, chief of the Confederate army's Bureau of Ordnance. Gorgas was to become the most efficient of the Confederate army's bureau officers, and though the central government was itself experiencing severe shortages of weapons, he nevertheless managed to provide enough Mississippi rifles to outfit Miller's whole company. Neither of the other two Rome captains chose Towers's solution. Cooper's Floyd Infantry would hope to draw what weapons it could from Confederate sources once it got to Richmond. Likewise, Magruder's Rome Light Guards sadly turned in their beautiful Mississippi rifles, as they prepared to leave, and looked forward to the new weapons—rumor said Harpers Ferry rifles—"Jeff Davis" would provide in Richmond.[17]

Then after months of anticipation and increasingly frenzied preparation, the departures came, all in a rush, during a single week in late May. Thursday morning, May 23, the Floyd Infantry marched to the depot, through streets thronged with citizens despite the early hour. The Light Guards and the Miller Rifles marched along to see them off, and the Cherokee Artillery was on hand to mark the event in style. There were tears among the mothers, sisters, and sweethearts being left behind, emotional leave-takings, and then the train was rolling out of the station amid the cheers of fellow soldiers and the thunders of the artillery salute.[18]

The following Sunday, May 26, was a bright and pleasant Sabbath morning in Rome. At the large Presbyterian church downtown the Light Guards and the Miller Rifles filed into the pews in silent ranks and took their places. The choir sang several pieces dwelling on the theme of parting, and then Pastor John A. Jones stepped into the pulpit to preach the farewell sermon, as the men of the two companies had requested. Jones had addressed the subject of the war the previous two Sundays, dealing with what he held to be the causes of the conflict and what the South's position was and then proceeding to what he called "the evidences of God's favor to the South as manifested during the Revolution to the present."

Now he looked out over a packed house—the nearly two hundred uniformed members of the two companies filling the nearest pews and some eight hundred civilians crowding the space behind them—and thought that this was the most trying moment of his career. In the ranks of the Light Guards the minister could see nineteen-year-old Pvt. James Dunwoody Jones, his son, "looking very solemn and attentive," and felt that he could understand the deep, silent emotional tension that filled the atmosphere in the packed but quiet church that morning. He took his text from the sixteenth chapter of the First Epistle to the Corinthians, ". . . quit you like men, be strong," and spoke of the soldiers' duty to be manly and show fortitude. Then he warned that some of them might not be coming back and they must be prepared for what would come after death. That opened the emotional floodgates, and one who was present recalled, "There was just one convulsive sob from one end of the church to the other, for the congregation was composed of the mothers and wives and sisters and daughters of the soldiers who were marching away." Somehow Jones got through the rest of his message and hoped "that some impressions were made by the Holy Spirit upon the unconverted soldiers."[19]

The next day the Light Guards marched jauntily down to the railroad station, cutting a fine figure in their tailor-made uniforms, each gray coat marked with ten horizontal black stripes across the front, and each stripe having a bright brass button at each end and in the middle. Elaborate patterns of gilt embroidery trimmed their collars and cuffs, along with still more brass buttons, and large epaulets sat on their shoulders fringed with even more gilt thread, while their gray trousers had a wide black stripe running down each outside leg seam. Topping off the outfit was a jaunty gray forage cap.

It looked as if the whole town had flocked down to the station to see them off, and one of the many bystanders thought how young the departing soldiers looked and reflected that only five men in the whole company were married, including the newly hitched captain and first sergeant.[20]

Certainly no more than four wives were left behind. The newly wed Florence Magruder had no intention of parting with her husband of two weeks, and, presumably with the captain's approval, she was with the company now, bags packed, clad in a brown traveling dress crossed with a broad scarf on which was inscribed "The Rome Light Guards." On one hip she wore a pistol and on the other a dagger, and altogether the captain's young bride made a more remarkable appearance than any other member of the company that day. Despite her warlike garb, however, Florence would spend the duration of the conflict with her husband's family in Orange County, Virginia.

Loading the train took time, for the Light Guards were not traveling light. Most of the young men had a trunk or two each, in which they had packed fatigue uniforms, spare clothes, "any quantity of fine linen," and such necessities as silverware, so they could live like civilized gentlemen when they were in camp. Then, as they prepared to depart, their

sweethearts gave them such parting gifts as they thought would be useful to soldiers in the field: "embroidered slippers and pin-cushions and
needlebooks, and all sorts of such little et ceteras." They also loaded the
departing young men with parcels of food to eat on the trip. Then at last
the tearful goodbyes were said, and the soldiers and the young slave men
who accompanied them as personal servants—one observer thought
nearly every member of the company had one—all got aboard the cars.
Amid puffing steam and waving handkerchiefs and final shouted
farewells, "the elite of the town" began their long journey to war.[21]

The departure of the Miller Rifles two days later was almost anticli-
mactic by comparison. Towers marched his country boys down to the
station—cheering crowds, tearful farewells, and another train clattered
off along the twin rails that led to Kingston, Richmond, and the war.[22]

A week previous, Rome had seemed an armed camp full of naive
young men in uniform disporting themselves about the streets and
yearning to be off to prove their valor. Now the town felt quiet and
empty to those who stayed behind—no more drills on Broad Street, no
more finely dressed soldier boys. "The town seemed to be clothed in
sack-cloth and ashes," recalled Mrs. George A. Ward, as those who stayed
behind settled down for the long and anxious wait.

I Go to Illustrate Georgia

One by one the Rome companies arrived in Richmond after unevent-
ful trips. The most striking—and enjoyable—aspect of the journey was
the adulation of the populace of the towns they passed through. Cheers
and fluttering handkerchiefs met them at nearly every station. They arrived in the capital of Virginia just as that city was becoming the capital
of the CSA. The Light Guards entered town May 30, the day before Jefferson Davis and the rest of the Confederate government, and the Miller
Rifles the day after Davis. The city was rapidly becoming the center of
a veritable constellation of armed camps. Confederate military authorities directed the three Rome companies out the east side of town on the
Mechanicsville Turnpike to what Melvin Dwinnell called "a beautiful
pine grove," just on the city's outskirts. The locals called the place
Howard's Grove, but the troops were soon referring to it as Camp Geor-

gia. It was to become a rendezvous for troops from that state. The Rome boys found, however, that they were not the first Georgians to pitch their tents and unpack their trunks at Howard's Grove, and what was waiting for them camped among the pines may have given some, especially the Light Guards, pause to think: a company whose finery exceeded even their own.[23]

The Oglethorpe Light Infantry hailed from Savannah and made a striking appearance as they paraded in their long blue frock coats with fancy gilt embroidery on the collars and cuffs and buff-colored bib fronts secured by two vertical rows of nine big brass buttons each. Heavy gilt-and-fringe epaulets sat on each shoulder. Trousers were blue, trimmed with a broad buff stripe up each outer seam. Crowning the whole uniform, and making the wearer look larger than he really was, perched a tall shako topped with a plume of white feathers and sporting front-and-center a brass nameplate whereon a large wreath encircled the letters "OLI" in old English script. Buff-colored waist and cross belts and white gloves completed the outfit. The company was indeed a sight to behold.[24]

The Oglethorpe Light Infantry had begun back in 1856, when John N. Lewis organized a volunteer company in Savannah and named it after Georgia's colonial founder. The following year the OLI made an important upward leap in social importance when Lewis resigned as captain and the company elected Francis Stebbins Bartow to replace him. Born in 1816 to a distinguished Georgia family, Bartow graduated first from the University of Georgia and then from Yale Law School. He came back to his native state to practice law, and like other Southerners who found success in that profession—or any profession—he used his wealth as a springboard to the pinnacle of Southern occupations and became a planter. In 1844 he married the daughter of a prominent Savannah judge, and his rise in society continued apace. He served a term in the state senate and two in the United States House of Representatives, an ardent Democrat and defender of what were then called "Southern Rights." When in January 1861 Georgians elected delegates to the state convention that would take them out of the Union, Bartow represented Chatham County and vigorously backed secession.[25]

When secession became a reality, it was Bartow who led his Oglethorpe Light Infantry in occupying, without opposition, Fort Pulaski, the U.S. Army's outpost on Cockspur Island at the mouth of the Savannah River, protecting the city from attack by sea. Almost immediately thereafter, Savannah's most prominent son was again called upon, this time as a member of Georgia's delegation to the Montgomery, Alabama, convention that would create the Confederate States of America and become its "Provisional Congress." Bartow believed war with the United States was inevitable and, as chairman of the Military Affairs Committee, threw himself into making preparations for the impending conflict, working closely with Jefferson Davis. He resisted Davis's argument that volunteers should be enlisted for three years, urging instead that six months would be long enough. They finally compromised on a one-year term of enlistment. Stories also had it that although Bartow was captain of the blue-uniformed OLI, it was he who successfully advocated gray as the standard color of Confederate military uniforms. Perhaps, but more likely Davis had the deciding say on that question.[26]

If their uniforms were not standard, the OLI could certainly boast of being exemplary in practically every other way, partially thanks to their own wealth and social standing and partially thanks to the interest and energy of their prominent captain. They carried state-of-the-art .58-caliber Harpers Ferry rifle-muskets, and their drill was superb. They were well known in southeast Georgia, as often as not simply as "Bartow's company," and it came as no surprise—though it was certainly a cause for much excitement and jubilation—when they were among the first of the area's many companies to receive from the Confederate government a summons to duty in Virginia.

From neighboring Effingham County, nineteen-year-old Berrien M. Zettler had gone over to the county seat that day but forgot his errand when he learned the secretary of war had ordered the OLI to Virginia. Zettler set out for home on the run, bursting in all hot and breathless, calling out to his mother that he could not stay for the noon meal. As soon as he could throw a few things together he was leaving for Savannah on the off chance of finding a vacancy in Bartow's lucky and select company. His mother managed to get him to stand still long enough to remind him that it was twenty-six miles to Savannah. That caused him to stop a moment. He should wait until his father got home, his mother urged, and then Mr. Zettler would take him by wagon to the train station, whence he could ride the cars to Savannah. If they caught the early train next morning, he could be on the streets of the port city before eight o'clock. That made sense, but all day and night, as he did a more thorough job of packing, young Zettler was tormented with the thought that he might be too late for the last vacancy in the company.

He was in luck, though. The night before he arrived in Savannah, while he had fretted back at the farm, the membership of the OLI had met and passed a resolution that for the serious business they had ahead of them, only unmarried men were proper candidates. With that, the married members of the company—Bartow himself excepted—were discharged. Their loss, as they perceived it at the time, was pure gain for the likes of Berrien Zettler. Not only did he find a vacancy, but one of the expelled married men gave him his expensive uniform. The excited nineteen-year-old soon found himself armed and fitted out as a soldier and awaiting imminent departure for Virginia.[27]

On May 21, 1861, "Bartow's Beardless Boys," as the now overwhelmingly youthful company was nicknamed, formed ranks in heavy marching order at the parade ground on the corner of South Broad and Whitaker Streets. Nine of Savannah's other volunteer companies turned out in full dress to see them off and snapped to "present arms" as the nattily dressed Oglethorpes marched past in review. Then the other companies swung into column behind them and the whole force tramped off down South Broad Street while the various companies' brass bands all struck up "Bold Soldier Boy." Down Bull Street to Gaston, then on to Whitaker, the sound of boots slapping the cobbled streets in unison and the jaunty music of the bands reverberated from the buildings on either side.

At Whitaker Street a large crowd of ladies and gentlemen were on hand to greet them, and several prominent young women presented Capt. Bartow with a handsome silk Confederate flag—the "Stars and Bars"—which he turned over to the company color-bearer, Fifth Sgt. Charles H. Daniel. Then, of course, he made a speech. Fine oratory, even badly overheated oratory, was much appreciated in those days, as political communication, art form, and entertainment. Bartow rose to the occasion: "I pledge to you this day in their behalf," he declaimed, speaking for the company, "that should they fail to bring back to you this flag it will be because there is not one arm left among them to bear it aloft." He went on to speak of the hardships and dangers that lay before them and to exhort any man not willing to face such trials to step out of the ranks at once. Not surprisingly, no one did, but none probably would have even if he could have done so discreetly. They were in their glory, and listening from the ranks of soldiers standing under full pack and field gear, young Pvt. Billy Dasher thought he was "enjoying the proudest honor that could be conferred upon any man—that of being among the first to go to the front to drive back the hostile invasion of the south."

With the ceremonies concluded, the column took up its march again, back to South Broad Street and so on to the Central Railroad Depot. All along the way the sidewalks were lined with people, and the windows and balconies seemed crowded with spectators, all cheering and many of them waving scarves, while the companies' drummers beat out a staccato accompaniment to the tramp of boots. At the station the OLI boarded its train and rolled off for Virginia amid more shouts and cheers.[28]

The way to Richmond included an early detour for a strange reason. The most direct rail route would have taken the Oglethorpes through Augusta, Georgia, but they believed they had good reason for not wanting to visit that town just then. The fine Harpers Ferry rifle-muskets they carried with them on the train were just what the governor aimed at with his decree about state-issued arms, but the Oglethorpes had not the remotest intention of leaving them in Georgia. They were, after all, the Oglethorpe Light Infantry and had one of the state's most prominent politicians for their captain. Who was going to stop them? Still, when word made the rounds that Brown had telegraphed to Augusta to have the company halted and disarmed there, the Oglethorpes prudently changed their itinerary and took the shortest route to the state line.[29]

They made it out of Georgia without incident and soon found that the welcome they received along the way was no worse for being outside their native state. Pvt. Zettler later recalled how "at every station there were crowds of people, among them ladies with dainty little rosettes that they pinned on the lapels of our coats." At first the officers tried to make the men stay on the train during stops, but this proved to be a losing battle, especially since some of the halts proved to be rather lengthy. Making a virtue of necessity, Bartow and his lieutenants gave permission, and as a soldier recalled, "generally when we reached a station the boys rushed out and mingled with the people."[30]

Their route took them through Charleston, that most enthusiastically secessionist of Southern cities, and there, predictably, the locals called upon Capt. Bartow to make a speech. He responded and in explaining what he and his men, as Georgians, were doing in going to Virginia to fight there he uttered words that his soldiers remembered long after they had forgotten the rest of his speech: "I go to illustrate Georgia."[31]

They arrived in Richmond at noon on May 25, and after a splendid meal at the Exchange Hotel, they marched to the quarters allotted to them by the local Confederate military authorities, several houses of uncertain age. Upon inspecting the premises, Bartow became furious. The buildings were flea-infested, he claimed, and stank to high heaven. He raised such a fuss that he got the orders changed. Instead of bedding down in the foul buildings in town, the Oglethorpes marched to the eastern outskirts and pitched their tents in Howard's Grove.[32]

A Report That Would Be Heard

They soon had company. In fact, another company or two seemed to arrive almost every day. The Oglethorpes found that the occupants of the neighboring camp were fellow Georgians and had arrived that very day. They were the Atlanta Grays, from Fulton County, and they told the OLI boys that they had heard Bartow was going to be organizing a regiment out of the various Georgia companies around Richmond and had been eager to be part of any outfit commanded by that illustrious Georgian.[33]

The Atlanta Grays had been organized in 1859, and the citizens of Fulton County considered them a "very select band." In the spring of 1861, twenty-nine-year-old Atlanta attorney Thomas L. Cooper became their new captain, in the midst of preparations for wartime service. Cooper was also the older brother of Floyd Infantry captain John Frederick Cooper. The Grays marched to their farewell ceremonies on May 22, a "bright spring morning," and Atlanta "gave the company a royal send-off." The citizens had gotten up an amateur entertainment in order to raise money for the company's needs, and the resulting purse was handed to Capt. Cooper at the ceremony. A delegation of ladies presented a fine silk flag, and then the captain's father, Mark A. Cooper, delivered a farewell address, charging the men to do their duty and commending them to the care of God. At the conclusion of his speech, the elder Cooper went down the company's line handing a New Testament to each soldier. When he finished, Capt. Cooper stepped up and thanked him and the ladies in what one observer rapturously described as "bursts of patriotic sentiment."[34]

Then they were on their way, and two days later found themselves camped on the Fairfield Racecourse, east of Richmond and adjacent to Howard's Grove and the camp of Bartow's newly arrived Oglethorpe Light Infantry. The Grays made a striking contrast to the OLI, for their uniforms were as simple as the Oglethorpes' were elaborate. They wore gray trousers and a nine-button, tight-fitting gray shell jacket with dark blue edging around the stand-up collar and three more brass buttons on each cuff. Instead of a jaunty forage cap or tall shako, the Grays wore a plain broad-brimmed slouch hat. They lacked something else that the OLI possessed, and that was rifles. Back in Georgia, the Grays had carried first-class 1855 Harpers Ferry models, just like those the Oglethorpes still sported. The Atlanta boys, however, had complied with Governor Brown's order, turned in their fine rifles, and gone to war unarmed. From the Confederate States arsenal in Richmond they drew weapons to replace their rifles, but these were old .69-caliber Springfield Model 1822 smoothbore muskets. They had been converted from flintlock to the more modern percussion firing mechanism but were still a long way from being modern weapons.[35]

If the Atlanta Grays had to make do with substandard weapons, they could at least take consolation in knowing they were far from being the only unit in that fix. Two days after their arrival at Howard's Grove the Grays and the OLI welcomed the Floyd Infantry, who also duly drew 1822 Springfields from the Richmond arsenal. Another two days' time brought the Pulaski Volunteers.

While many Southern communities, especially towns like Rome and Savannah, possessed well-turned-out volunteer companies, the majority of localities in the predominantly rural South did not. One such was Pulaski County. On the banks of the Ocmulgee River, bang in the middle of the state, Pulaski lay on the northern edge of the less prosperous pine barren and wire grass region. The county's citizens had shown little interest in things military during the decades before the Civil War. Once

Georgia declared itself out of the Union, Pulaski residents, at the urging of physician Thomas D. L. Ryan and several other local leaders, formed the Pulaski Volunteers and elected Ryan their captain. In fact, the response to Ryan's appeal was so strong that a number of eager volunteers had to be turned away after the company had reached its full organizational strength. The initial meeting took place at the Methodist church in Hawkinsville, the county seat. Shortly thereafter the company went in to camp in a nearby grove of trees, and got an elderly veteran of the Mexican and Seminole wars to start giving them some instruction in the rudiments of drill.

As with all the other companies, there was a presentation of a flag by the local ladies, with a speech to the soldiers by one of the ladies—"Take it, soldiers! And return with it to your homes with honor, or die beneath its folds in defense of Southern Rights and the independence of the Confederate States"—and an equally florid oratorical reply by a member of the company.

In due time, Capt. Ryan offered the services of the Pulaski Volunteers to Governor Brown. The governor accepted but sent word they would have to go into the "preparatory camp" at Big Shanty (present-day Kennesaw). This was not at all to the liking of the Pulaski Volunteers, who considered that they had signed up to fight, not to camp out in Georgia. They voted to have Ryan try a direct appeal to the Confederate government, then still located in Montgomery, Alabama. The Pulaski boys too had heard the report that Bartow was to form a regiment out of Georgia companies that went to Richmond, and they wanted to be part of it. In the meantime, they decided to disperse to their homes while they waited to see whether Jefferson Davis had any employment for them. A prearranged signal would call them back to Hawkinsville if the good news came that they could go to war.

The signal was to be the firing of an old cannon that the town owned—no one could remember where it came from—and the man entrusted with handling the gun, when the time came, was seventeen-year-old Sam Stephens. Stephens's fellow soldiers would one day describe him as "a whole-souled man and brave soldier" but also as "the mischief man of the company." He had requested the honor of firing the signal shot with a promise "to give a report that would be heard by the members in the remotest corners of the county, even those who were asleep."

In mid-May, about the same time that the other companies around the state were getting their summons, word came to Capt. Ryan from the Confederate government that the company's offer had been accepted and it should start at once for Richmond. Ryan told Stephens to go ahead and fire the cannon. Afterward Sam never would tell his friends in the company just how much powder he had used. He carefully placed the gun next to a very large tree and somehow contrived to stand behind the tree and reach around it to apply the slow match to the touchhole of the cannon. The report was indeed heard for a considerable distance, and one of the Pulaski boys later reported, "It is said that only one small portion of the cannon could be found, and that was in the rear of Manning's store . . . a distance of three or four hundred yards, where it had fallen and killed a hog." Sam was unhurt, though the tree was much the worse for wear.

Within hours every member of the company was present and earnest preparations were under way for the trip to Richmond. May 23 was departure day, and Hawkinsville gave the Volunteers a sendoff in the style in which such larger towns as Rome, Savannah, and Atlanta were that week bidding farewell to their companies. The boys ate a fine dinner and heard a farewell sermon from the Rev. George R. McCall out in the open grove in front of the Methodist church. Then about three o'clock they marched off, not to the train station, for Hawkinsville had none, but to the ferry that would carry them across the Ocmulgee, where wagons were waiting to take them to the nearest railhead, a place called Buzzard Roost.

Their trip to Richmond was enlivened by a train wreck near Branchville, South Carolina, in which no one was hurt. There was also a squabble over transportation in Petersburg, Virginia, involving the Pulaski Volunteers and two other companies. Through the mismanagement of the railroad, all three companies had been promised transportation though cars were on hand for only two. The other two companies, the Butler "Van Guards" and the Chattahoochee "Beauregards," were destined for other Georgia regiments and, of immediate importance, had possession of the railroad cars. Things were tense for a few minutes, as the men contemplated the possibility of being left in Petersburg another day or two and missing the war, but the three captains finally figured a way to seize an additional railroad car, and did so, and the crisis was averted. The Pulaski Volunteers arrived at Howard's Grove and went into camp on May 28.[36]

And so they came in day after day, and the fields around Howard's Grove sprouted tents as additional Georgia companies arrived. The Echols Guards, of Warm Springs, came in about the same time as the Pulaski Volunteers. Two days later the Rome Light Guards marched into camp in their natty gray uniforms. On the last day of May came the Oglethorpe Rifles, from Oglethorpe County, in the uniforms of "gray cassimere," a point of pride to some, though Pvt. W. H. Maxey, in the ranks of the Oglethorpe Rifles, thought they were "not fit for a dog to look at."

That same day came the Macon Guards, from the city of that name, also in the middle part of the state. The prosperous town of Macon, seat of Bibb County, was situated on the fall line, at the head of navigation of the Ocmulgee, forty miles or so upstream from Hawkinsville. Macon was a thriving community in the heart of Middle Georgia's cotton belt. Bibb County boasted an 1860 population of 8,838 whites and 7,030 slaves. The town itself counted no less than ten sawmills, a cotton gin, four printers, four blacksmiths, two dentists, and two saddle and harness shops. There were three ironworks, two marble works, and sundry factories making everything from guns to machines to finished clothing. Citizens and visitors could have their tintypes made at any one of several studios—or their ambrotypes or daguerreotypes. J. W. Babcock, the carriage dealer, had an establishment at the corner of First and Mulberry Streets, and J. B. Allgood, "negro dealer," hung his shingle at Fifth and Plum. Three other slave depots served the demands of the thriving cotton fields of Bibb County.[37]

The Macon Guards were organized under the command of Capt. Joel R. Griffin in 1859. By that time, Bibb County already had three other volunteer companies and was soon to have a fifth. Throughout 1860, with the John Brown scare fresh in everyone's mind and the national election looming on the horizon, Macon's various companies drilled and paraded with enthusiasm. The guards turned out along with an artillery company and a hired band on March 28. They paraded before the Wesleyan Female College "to allow the young ladies to admire their martial bearing and gay feathers, as also to hear a few pieces played by the band." Then they tramped out to the old railroad depot to fire a few blank rounds from their brass cannon.

As they marched back into the downtown, the cry of fire went up, and the militiamen set off double-quick to lend their assistance. By the time they got to the scene the fire was under control, and Capt. Griffin was about to dismiss them when the sound of their drums spooked the horses hitched to a carriage full of female spectators. Off went the horses. Somehow the driver managed to rein in the frightened beasts anyway, though the pedestrians on Cherry Street had had to step lively for a few seconds. One man was nearly run down. No sooner was that crisis past than another horse bolted, taking its buggy careening wildly several blocks before striking a lamppost, demolishing the buggy and not doing the post much good either. All in all, it had been quite an exciting day for the Macon Guards.[38]

Spring passed with more of the same. There were drills, sponsored dinners, and parades through Macon and the small towns around with refreshments for the soldiers afterward. There were target shoots, and there were "collations"—which meant more good things to eat and drink. Cpl. Thomas Hodgkins won a shooting match, and afterward the whole company dined at the home of First Lt. Lucius M. Lamar. Culmination of the spring campaign was a four-day joint encampment with a number of other Georgia volunteer companies at Fort Valley, where the guards cut a fine figure in their bearskin hats. The militiamen attacked a barrel of lager beer, maneuvered on the dance floor at a grand ball— ladies came from all the surrounding country—and returned home with "any quantity of mementos in the shape of curls, billet-doux," and other tokens of success in what a newspaper editor called "the Court of Cupid."[39]

With the election of Lincoln and subsequent secession, things got a little bit more serious, but only a little bit. Macon was, for the most part, enthusiastically pro-secession and celebrated joyously when the state declared itself out of the Union. Even the prospect of impending war was only moderately sobering. When the guards held a recruiting rally on April 12, they easily got fifty-seven new recruits. Several days later, now under the command of Lamar, who had been promoted to captain, the guards got orders to proceed to the Georgia coast. After a few weeks there, new orders set them on their way to Virginia, and they arrived at Howard's Grove on the last day of May.[40] They were the eighth company to encamp there. Rome's Miller Rifles made their arrival the next day.

Within the space of little more than a week, nine companies had taken up residence at "Camp Georgia."[41]

One more was still on the way. Greene County, Georgia, lay right in the plantation belt in the center of the state and boasted a white population of 4,200 as compared to some 8,400 black slaves. A fair number of Greene County's young white men had not really thought much of enlisting until after the Confederacy had already launched its war at Fort Sumter in April 1861. At that point they made all the haste they could, organizing three companies of volunteers. One of those took the name Stephens Light Guards, in honor of Confederate vice president Alexander H. Stephens of Georgia.[42]

The Stephens Light Guards' first problem was acquiring weapons of any sort. Many companies had already equipped themselves by this time, and the Greene County boys, blithely ignorant of the governor's strange policy regarding arms, feared that no weapons would be left in the state arsenals to equip them. Reckoning that what was needed was fast traveling and fast talking, twenty-four-year-old lawyer John Calvin Reed saddled up his horse and rode off to catch the train for the state capital at Milledgeville. The young Princeton graduate galloped through the night at breakneck speed to the nearest town on the railroad, took the first train he could get, and "by the exercise of some address and great importunity," succeeded in getting the governor to release enough Model 1822 muskets to arm the whole company. Brown apparently cared little if such old weapons left the state, and Reed, apparently unaware that the state's arsenals bulged with fine modern rifles surrendered by troops departing the state, was delighted to have even the muskets.

His comrades in the company were delighted too, and promptly elected him first lieutenant. He declined on the reasonable basis that he knew nothing of drill, so they made him second lieutenant instead. The slot he thus gave up went to Thomas J. Blackwell, a young man from Cobb County who had once been a student at the Georgia Military Institute in Marietta, though he had not graduated. Blackwell began to drill the new company, and they soon fancied, perhaps a bit prematurely, that they knew all there was to know on the subject.

They "longed and prayed" for marching orders, and in mid-May they got what they wanted: a call to Virginia. Reed rode back to his parents' plantation to tell them the good news, but was nonplussed at their sad reaction. Calvin's younger brother was even then in the war zone as a member of the Sixth Georgia. "It pains me now," he wrote years later, "to recall how hopeless and stricken my mother looked as she could not speak her goodbye." There followed tearful farewells to his sweetheart and then to the slaves.

At last the day of departure, June 3, arrived. Reed carefully shaved and told one of his comrades that he would not shave again until the South had won its independence. The company marched down to the depot and, like the others before it in various places around the state, received a rousing send-off. Women waved handkerchiefs and men cheered, but Reed noticed that the older a spectator was, the more likely he or she was to be crying rather than cheering.[43]

With their late start, the Stephens Light Guards, destined to become Company I of the Eighth Georgia, did not catch up with the rest of the regiment until after the other nine companies had already moved on from their camps around Richmond. Three of the boys from Greene County never made it to Richmond at all. Pvts. C. Maloy and T. O'Brien died in a train wreck as the company made its way toward Richmond, June 4, 1861.[44]

Important Movements Are on Foot

The men of the nine companies at Howard's Grove readily settled into camp life on the eastern outskirts of the new Confederate capital. They were a diverse lot of men, all coming from a single Southern state. George Barnsley, of the Rome Light Guards, soon to be known as Company A, took stock of his new comrades shortly after arriving at Howard's Grove. The Savannah contingent, the Oglethorpe Light Infantry soon to be known as Company B, he reckoned to be the descendants of both English settlers and French Huguenots and to be "sons of wealthy and prominent citizens, and well educated, charming young men." The Middle Georgia companies, of which the regiment had three, he held to be mostly English stock that had drifted down from Virginia and the Carolinas. The two companies that came from the hilly fringe of the lower Appalachians were Scots-Irish who had moved southward down the long valleys of that system, opined Barnsley. Finally, the men of his own and the other two Rome companies as well at the Atlanta Grays were a mixture of all three.[45]

Barnsley was probably not too far off in his estimates. At any rate, service records reveal that the companies differed markedly in the sort of men who filled their ranks. Savannah's OLI included lawyers, clerks, planters, students, professional military men, physicians, carpenters, printers, engineers, photographers, merchants, machinists, and even one man, Pvt. James Potter Williamson, who listed his occupation as "loafer." Only young B. M. Zettler, from neighboring Effingham County, claimed to be an ordinary farmer. They were far from being the band of young aristocrats that Barnsley thought them, but they were definitely dwellers of towns or large plantations. On the other hand, in the Middle Georgia companies, nearly everyone except the officers listed his occupation as "farmer." The experiences of war would soon mold this disparate collection of companies into a unified group.[46]

Within days of their arrival at Howard's Grove the companies officially became a new regiment, the Eighth Georgia, the first of the Georgia regiments, at least, to enlist not for the initially standard one-year term but rather for duration of hostilities. Company B's twenty-four-year-old Pvt. Pierce Butler Holmes, of Savannah, was first to sign the articles of enlistment, and thus his comrades liked to point out that he was "the first Confederate to enlist for the war." The regiment's present-for-duty strength on mustering in was just under eight hundred. Including replacements who would join it in future years, a total of 1,378 individuals would serve in the ranks of its ten companies, though regimental strength at any given time would rarely be above one-third that number.

As expected, Bartow became the new regiment's colonel. The second ranking spot went to former U.S. Army major William Montgomery Gardner, a Mexican War veteran and 1846 graduate of the U.S. Military Academy at West Point. He now became lieutenant colonel of the new regiment and the true source of its military training, for Gardner had his men drilling constantly, while Bartow, who nurtured high ambitions of having a fine regiment, looked on approvingly. The men idolized Bartow, writing home about his "lofty character," but Gardner was "the thorough drill master and disciplinarian" of the regiment. Thomas Cooper, who had come to Richmond as captain of the Atlanta Grays, became the Eighth's major.[47]

Life at Howard's Grove was not bad, by soldier standards, and most of the boys enjoyed themselves. Confederate authorities dealt out camp equipment freely, including substantial wall tents big enough to stand up in. Food was plentiful too, if not always up to the judgment of refined palates. There was beef, bacon, flour, cornmeal, rice, hominy, coffee, sugar, and salt, but one of the Oglethorpes of Company B complained that "our fare is not the best" and alleged that the cabbage served them was really "last year's pea-vines painted green."[48]

If the food they found in Virginia was not always to the men's liking, the society definitely was, and Pvt. John L. Martin wrote home to his mother, "We have crowds of ladies out to see us every afternoon," and Berrien Zettler later recalled, "In the afternoons the ladies of Richmond by hundreds would visit the camp to see 'dress parade.' " At this event Martin and Zettler were among the privileged, the Oglethorpes of Company B, who, with their showy uniforms, were favorites at such events. They enjoyed thrilling the onlookers with their fierce "Zouave bayonet drill," named for French Algerian colonial troops who had performed well in recent European wars. Quite a bit of socializing seems to have gone on before and after the parades and drill demonstrations, for Zettler fondly recalled that "more than one Oglethorpe took with him when he left for the front a tiny photograph or card with a name on it." Over in Company K, twenty-year-old Pvt. William H. Maxey wrote his father, "Thare is more prity Girls in the city of Ritchmon than thare is in the [whole] of Georgia."[49]

May 26 was a Sunday and a reminder that the men of the Eighth Georgia, like most Americans of that day, were by and large a fairly devout lot. Only two companies were in camp by that time, and a soldier of one of them wrote home that "the most part of us were invited to church on Sunday and heard a good sermon from a Georgia preacher, Rev. Dock Stiles."[50]

And despite dress parade and social visitors, weekday life in camp was not, after all, merely a fancy-dress tea party. John Martin told his mother that he had been "in camp most of the time and working pretty hard," and Pvt. Vardy Sisson of Company F, the Atlanta Grays, remembered that "the daily drills were severe, and rigid military discipline was exacted by the gallant Gardner." Still, "enthusiasm ran high," for soldiering was a new and exciting adventure, and the men were tolerably well fed and rested. And never far from their minds was the coming test of prowess against the contemptible Yankees.[51]

Whether spent in hard work or shy flirtations, the time encamped near Richmond did not last long. On Monday, June 3, just ten days after the Atlanta Grays and the OLI had been the first companies to make camp at Howard's Grove, word came that the brand-new Eighth Georgia was to take to the road. That evening, after dark, sentinels spotted the figures of two men approaching camp along the road from Richmond, shouted their challenge, and called the sergeant of the guard, twenty-seven-year-old Fred Hutchings of Rome. Hutchings saw that the two men looked respectable and important, but he was determined to fulfill his duty to the letter and made the two stand in the road until he was completely sure of their identity. They were, as it turned out, President Jefferson Davis and Secretary of War Leroy Pope Walker. Davis was no doubt impressed with Hutchings. A stickler for duty, the West Point–trained Confederate president would undoubtedly have done the same himself had their positions been reversed.[52]

After much saluting, the excited sentries showed their high-ranking guests through the shadowy encampment to Bartow's headquarters tent. In those early days the war had not yet gotten big enough to rule out a very direct and hands-on approach by the Confederate commander-in-chief, and that just suited Jefferson Davis, who with at least half his mind would rather have been a general anyway. Now he instructed Col. Bartow in person to get his regiment ready and hold them prepared to march on short notice. That notice was not long in coming, taking the form of a written order the following morning at ten o'clock directing Bartow to march for Harpers Ferry, Virginia.[53]

Harpers Ferry was the location of a prewar U.S. arsenal, the scene of John Brown's shocking 1859 antislavery raid, and one of the most strategic points of the great Valley of Virginia. It was the place where the Shenandoah River joined the Potomac and their united stream plunged through a gap in the mountain rampart of the Blue Ridge. Best of all, it was a place that the enemy were rumored to be threatening very seriously. A more exciting place for the fresh volunteers from Georgia could hardly be imagined. Amid the bustle of collapsing tents and scrambling men as Company A, the Rome Light Guards, broke up their camp of only five days, an eager Lt. Melvin Dwinnell wrote to the readers of the *Courier* back in Floyd County: "Important movements are on foot." So was the Eighth Georgia.[54]

CHAPTER TWO

&

To Belong to the Southern Army

Daughter of the Stars

THE Shenandoah—"Daughter of the Stars" in the local Indians' tongue—is born of the marriage of the North and South rivers at Port Republic, Virginia, and flows due northeast some ninety miles to meet the Potomac at Harpers Ferry. For the whole of her journey the Shenandoah is cradled in a broad valley between the misty Blue Ridge, on the east, and the rugged Alleghenies, to the west, a valley that stretches on to the southwest far beyond the headwaters of the Shenandoah, and in the opposite direction, across the Potomac, through Pennsylvania and Maryland. The portion of the valley that holds the Shenandoah is naturally known as the Shenandoah Valley. During the nineteenth century it might also be known as the Valley of Virginia or, especially during the war, simply the Valley.

Tranquil and verdant with its golden expanses of wheat and corn and its fragrant meadows thick with clover, the Valley in 1861 was a land of fertile fields, homey country towns, and dusty fence-lined roads. The rich farms that dotted its broad floor made it the breadbasket of Virginia and also harbored abundant horses, cattle, pigs, fowl, goats, and sheep. Large and comfortable two-story farmhouses of red brick, stone, or painted white clapboards, with steeply pitched roofs and large open porches shaded by ancient oaks, chestnuts, and walnuts, sat at the edges of the neatly fenced fields, the center of clustered outbuildings and smaller structures, from the huge barns with lofts richly weighted with sweet-smelling hay to springhouses for cooling the fresh milk, eggs, and butter to wells of crystal water, chicken houses, hog pens, and beehives.

Throughout the Valley, in its acidic soil, the wild evergreen mountain laurel grew, its buds blossoming into delicate white flowers in early May, their sweet fragrance drifting over the tilled earth on the wind. On lands untouched by human endeavor, patches of oak, elm, hickory, maple, ash, and conifer blanketed the lowlands and slopes of the mountains, adding their deep greens to the panoply of color. And in farmers' fields apple and peach orchards gave forth, in season, their delicious red and yellow fruits.

At the far northern, or in local parlance lower, end of this abundant land, the Potomac River caps the section of Valley belonging to the Shenandoah. On the spit of land jutting between the broad, sparkling waters of the two rushing rivers just before they join sits the town of Harpers Ferry in a deep mountain basin bounded on the west by Bolivar Heights, on the southeast and across the Shenandoah by Loudoun Heights of the Blue Ridge, and to the north and over the Potomac—in Maryland—by Maryland Heights on Elk Ridge Mountain. These three prominences well shielded the village, which sloped steeply down to both rivers' stony banks. However, the capture of those hills by hostile forces would reverse their significance, rendering the small town helpless in the face of a commanding and threatening foe.

When Virginia seceded in April 1861, the state's militia had seized Harpers Ferry. The valuable rifle-making machinery from the U.S. arsenal there was soon on its way to a more secure location in North Carolina, while first Virginia and then Confederate troops continued to hold Harpers Ferry as the gateway to the rich Shenandoah Valley.

During May 1861 a Union force began taking shape around Chambersburg, Pennsylvania, threatening the Confederate position at the mouth of the Shenandoah. About eighteen thousand Pennsylvania militia with a few U.S. Army Regulars formed the command of the aged Union general Robert Patterson. In response, the Confederate government opted to reinforce its small force—about ten thousand men—under Gen. Joseph E. Johnston guarding the Shenandoah. That was the decision that brought President Davis and Secretary of War Walker to the Eighth Georgia's camp on the evening of June 3, and had the soldiers all in a frenzy the next day in their anxious preparations to be off.

"We leave for Harpers Ferry this afternoon," scribbled Pvt. Ham Branch of Company B to his mother back in Savannah, adding that "we can stand a pretty good chance of getting in a fight." To that heady thought he added with pride a compliment that Davis had paid them when he had visited their camp the night before. "The president says we are a fine body of men," Branch wrote, "and he will rely on our courage Strength and readiness." They were eager to prove his faith well founded.[1]

But for the immediate future at least, they were doomed to frustration. The immediate cause of delay was by now an old and festering source of vexation, their weapons. Nearly every one of the nine companies had been well armed with either Mississippi or Harpers Ferry rifles back in Georgia. Only two of them had carried those weapons to Virginia—the Miller Rifles, whose resourceful Capt. Towers had secured Mississippi rifles from the Confederate government, and the politically powerful Oglethorpes, who had carried their Harpers Ferry rifles out of Georgia in defiance of Governor Brown. The other seven companies all depended on Confederate arms supplies in Virginia. While Jefferson Davis's government did succeed in putting arms in their hands within a reasonable time, those arms were not rifles but Model 1822 .69-caliber smoothbore muskets, and the process of providing them took several days. When the orders first came for Harpers Ferry, several of the Georgia companies had been in Virginia only three or four days and were not yet armed. Staff officers hurried to get the necessary weapons out of the Richmond arsenal and issued to the troops, but the movement was delayed all the same.

The problem compounded the soldiers' bitterness against Brown. "Every member of this company mourns the loss of his rifle," wrote an anonymous member of the Atlanta Grays in a letter to a Georgia newspaper about this time. "This act of Joseph E. Brown, of taking our guns from us, was descending below the dignity of the Chief Magistrate of the Empire State of the South." The soldier went on to complain that the governor seemed willing to have inadequately armed Georgia troops slaughtered in unequal combat purely "in order to gratify his hatred to President Davis."

The problem extended even to one of the companies ostensibly equipped with rifles. Floyd County's Miller Rifles had been the last of the companies to reach Howard's Grove, arriving just the previous Saturday, June 1, the very day the regiment had officially been organized. Towers had not in fact managed to get quite enough Mississippi rifles for all the recruits he was rapidly signing into his company during the days before leaving Rome, but apparently Confederate authorities in Montgomery had led him to hope that he could obtain the necessary additional weapons once he arrived in Richmond. He had therefore given the new recruits his personal guarantee that they would be equipped with rifles, not muskets, or else their enlistment would be void.

When the company arrived in Richmond, however, Towers soon learned that the Richmond arsenal's scant supply of rifles was long gone. Weapons he could have, but only the hated smoothbores. Fifteen of Towers's men could not be given rifles and refused to carry muskets. Keeping his word to his men, the captain granted them discharges and paid their expenses home. Not everyone in the regiment was quite as understanding as Capt. Towers, particularly fellow soldiers who were resigned to going into battle with Model 1822 muskets. The departing recruits' "*pluck* was seriously questioned by the other companies," wrote Melvin Dwinnell in the columns of the *Courier,* immediately under a list of the men's names, "and they left the camp amidst taunts, jeers and groans." As far as the other members of the Eighth were concerned, the quitters were "entirely too fastidious in regard to the kind of arms furnished them." Two of the discharged soldiers thought better of their action and immediately answered the questioning of their courage by enrolling in the Rome Light Guards. By the middle of July, three more had rejoined the regiment.

And so the Eighth waited while staff officers tried to make sure that each soldier had a weapon—a musket at least.

By the evening of June 4, the necessary arms had been issued, and the regiment was scheduled to depart the next morning at eight o'clock. In fact it did not get off until 1:30 P.M., and even then one company—H, the Floyd Infantry—was left behind to depart the following morning. The other eight marched down to the Broad Street station and piled into two trains for the first leg of their trip to Harpers Ferry. They rode the Virginia Central as far as Gordonsville, then transferred to the Orange & Alexandria for the ride to Manassas Junction. They got there at 3:00 A.M. on June 6, but a problem with one of their locomotives held them up until two o'clock that afternoon. Finally, they rolled out of the junction on the Manassas Gap Railroad, over the Blue Ridge, down into the Shenandoah Valley, and to the town of Strasburg. That was the end of the line, so next morning they set out down the Valley Pike, a fine macadamized road that in peacetime carried a brisk traffic in stage-coaches and Conestoga freight wagons, serving the commerce of the Valley in place of a railroad. For the trip down the pike from Strasburg to Winchester, five companies rode in wagons and coaches, but when transportation ran short, Companies A, B, and C—Rome Light Guards, OLI, and Macon Guards—volunteered to walk. It was an eighteen-mile hike, and Melvin Dwinnell characterized it as their first hardship. They camped that night and the next day at Winchester and continued their journey on Sunday, June 9, this time by means of a spur line of the Baltimore & Ohio Railroad, which carried them in much greater comfort the last thirty miles or so into Harpers Ferry, where they marched through the village and made their camp on Bolivar Heights.[2]

They enjoyed the next six days among scenery that Thomas Jefferson had said was worth a voyage across the Atlantic to see. They also gazed long at the man-made improvements. "From Bolivar Heights," wrote Berrien Zettler, "we could see the splendid railroad brigade of the Baltimore and Ohio Railroad that spans the river here." They could also see the carriage bridge spanning the Shenandoah and, on the far bank of the Potomac, the Chesapeake & Ohio Canal.[3]

While the regiment was camped at Bolivar Heights its two detached companies joined up—H, which had been delayed in leaving Richmond, and I, Greene County's Stephens Light Guards, which had been late in getting to Virginia. The regiment's organization was now complete, with all ten of the component companies it would carry through the entire war.

They Would Rush into Danger

Confederate general Joseph E. Johnston had long been discontent with the position of his force at Harpers Ferry. It was on the eastern edge of the Valley, and he feared a Union thrust farther west, perhaps through Martinsburg, near the Potomac at the northern terminus of the Valley Pike. That would flank him and possibly make his position very difficult. As he was to do again and again throughout the war, Johnston decided that the situation was not quite right for meeting the enemy where he was but would be better some miles to the rear. Specifically, he had in mind Winchester, the crossroads of the lower Valley, where the Valley Pike running south from Martinsburg met the railroad spur running southwest from Harpers Ferry. After several weeks of haggling with the authorities in Richmond he finally succeeded in getting them to take the responsibility for his decision to retreat—and none too soon, as far as he was concerned, since by mid-June he had decided that he could wait no longer. Rumors had it that Patterson was advancing toward Martinsburg, and Federal scouts had been sighted and fired on some six hundred or seven hundred yards from the B&O bridge on the far side of the river.

Thus on Thursday, June 13, after just four days in camp on Bolivar Heights, the Eighth got orders to prepare to break camp and march back southward. The destination was to be Winchester, and this time they would be marching the whole way. The camp once again bustled with hasty preparations, and then, in true army style, they finished hurrying and started waiting. After striking their tents and packing up their excess baggage and cooking utensils at midday Friday, the men of the Eighth had to sit around waiting until almost noon Saturday before their march finally got under way, sleeping in the open and eating cold food. While they prepared to go, Pvt. Sid Goodwin of Company B became the first in the regiment to shed his blood in the field. In the tangle and rush of packing up, he managed to get scratched by a bayonet. The wound was not serious.

During the long wait, the men had time to reflect on the army's movements. They were eager for a fight and even more eager to be seen as such by the folks back home. Regimental adjutant John Branch wrote his mother to say that Harpers Ferry had no importance anyway and that he was "surprised that it was held so long." Just in case some back in

Rome might hear of the move and misconstrue it as a retreat, Melvin Dwinnell wrote to the readers of the *Courier*, "We do not *flee from* the enemy, but *go to meet them*." Since the Yankees were thought to be getting around their flank by moving through Martinsburg, then marching back to block such a move was not a retreat but an advance toward the enemy. It had a certain logic to it, but Dwinnell also noted proudly that the Eighth had been accorded the role of rear guard, the place of honor on a retreat. At any rate, the men of the Eighth were quickly learning that soldiers had no part in the counsels of their commanders; theirs was simply to march, camp, and, perhaps fight where and when their generals ordered.[4]

Along with other troops, the Eighth helped burn the red-brick armory and arsenal buildings, as well as other structures in the village. Johnston had his engineers blow up both the railroad and carriage bridges. The work of destruction was thorough and remorseless, and when Johnston's men had finished, a substantial portion of a Virginia town was a smoldering waste. Then at eleven o'clock on Saturday morning, June 15, the Eighth joined the rear of the long column and turned their backs on Harpers Ferry.[5]

An eight-mile march took them through the village of Charlestown, where old John Brown had been hanged a year and a half before. The Eighth would remember it nearly as well for the fine hot supper the citizens served them there, the first proper meal they had eaten in two days and the last they would enjoy for several days to come. Another four miles or so of marching and they camped for the night.

Next morning, while the camp seethed like a beehive with preparations for another day's march, many members of the Eighth noticed something that seemed to strike nearly all new Civil War soldiers, North or South. It was Sunday, but it did not "feel" like Sunday, or the Sabbath, as they often called it. America in the nineteenth century was an overwhelmingly Christian society, and as such believed that one day in seven was to be kept holy and reserved for rest and worship. Fond memories of bright, peaceful Sunday mornings, worship alongside friends and family, and quiet, restful, contemplative Sunday afternoons and evenings were among the most common reflections of homesick soldiers as they dwelt on the aspects of home life they missed most. The men of the Eighth were no exception. "This does not seem like Sunday morning,"

Dwinnell wrote, "as all hands are busy packing up for the march," a march they fully expected would take them the remaining twenty miles into Winchester.

As usual, however, the hurried preparation led only to tedious waiting, but this time the men of the Rome Light Guards made the most of their time and formed a Sunday school. They went through all the organizational steps popular at the time, electing G. T. Stovall superintendent, Dwinnell secretary, and L. T. Mitchell chorister. They had finished the reading of the Scriptures and were singing hymns when the order came to fall in for the march.[6]

The Rome Light Guards were of course far from the only company in the Eighth to have a large majority of devout men. In Company D, the Echols Guards, Jim Martin wrote his parents, "Every boy in our company has a Bible," and went on to state that the boys could frequently be seen reading their Bibles around camp. Their first lieutenant, twenty-nine-year-old Hugh E. Malone, Martin considered "a great man," because he "talks to the boys frequently, how religious they ought to be & how brave they ought to be."

Still the army was not always—or even usually—an easy place to maintain a careful Christian manner of life. New situations presented new temptations, and moral choices that were settled matters back home now appeared with every imaginable complicating factor to confuse young soldiers. Even more important, those who had previously been more concerned with respectability than with true heart-religion now found themselves far away from the constraints of community opinion.

Or perhaps not so far. Company D's captain was Columbus W. Howard, a farmer who also sometimes served as a Methodist preacher, and before the regiment left Richmond he had fallen into a shocking lapse. He had drunk whiskey, apparently quite a lot of it—enough that his dismayed soldiers noticed his condition. He had also been seen playing billiards. In those days a good many Christians, especially in fervent evangelical denominations like the Methodists, took their faith very seriously and carefully avoided activities that smacked in any way of idleness, gambling, or dissipation. Billiards was then one of those. It did not take long for word to get around the company, and since everyone was more or less from the same hometown—or at least home county—it took only a few days longer for it to get back to Meriwether County.

Howard heard of the talk and apologized to the men. The liquor, he explained, he had taken as medicine for an attack of diarrhea—something just possible in those days when beverage alcohol was still thought to have some therapeutic value. As for the billiards, well, he promised not to let that happen again. As Jim Martin explained to his parents, "The boys drew up some resolutions & told him if he would never do so anymore they would forgive him."[7]

The next several days were tense and trying ones for the soldiers of Johnston's small army. Instead of marching directly to Winchester as they had expected, the column turned northwestward toward Martinsburg on an old market road and finally made camp at Bunker Hill, on the Valley Pike just south of Martinsburg. They were near the western edge of the Valley now, and Apple Pie Ridge, the first range of the Alleghenies here, loomed up just beyond them. Everyone from Johnston down to the privates in the ranks expected a battle at any moment, as rumor had it that a Union army of 25,000 or 30,000 men was present in Martinsburg and preparing to advance. Johnston even asked the regimental commanders to announce the impending clash to their men, and Bartow did so to the Eighth in fine style, assuring them, as one recalled, "that he did not doubt the courage of his men, but on the contrary he was afraid that they would rush needlessly into danger."[8]

"Some of our boys looked pretty pale in the face when we expected an attack," Pvt. Richard Watters explained in a letter to his sister the next day, adding, "but most of them were lively as ever." Whether eager or nervous, the men of the Eighth would have to cope with their anticipation for some time yet. A day of waiting failed to bring the Federals advancing out of Martinsburg—for the excellent reason that they were not there—and when the question became one of whether the Confederates ought to attack, Johnston decided against it. His force was badly short of ammunition. The Eighth had only twenty rounds per man, and the other regiments were no better off. In a dispatch to Richmond that day, Johnston complained, "These troops have not a supply for half an hour's fighting."[9]

So they turned southward once again, this time up the Valley Pike bound for Winchester. The road was good, but the men had been without tents and without any food but cold meat and hardtack for several days. The Eighth was also learning how much more fatiguing a route march could be than simply walking the same number of miles alone. Reveille sounded at 3:30 A.M., but preparations for marching lasted till seven o'clock. Then, when the march did commence, "instead of being allowed to step off at a smart walk," Dwinnell explained, "we were continually being stopped in the hot sun, from two to five minutes at a time, just a little too long to stand in such a situation, and not long enough to break ranks and sit." It was vexing, and Pvt. Richard Watters expressed the feelings of many when he wrote, "I am tired of toting my knapsack over this country."[10]

Watters had to admit, though, that he "never saw finer country." The fields of wheat and clover were the richest he had ever imagined. The bounty of the Valley became a temptation for at least three hungry men of the Eighth, tramping along wearily near the tail end of the column. Berrien Zettler and two of his friends in Company B, Savannah's high-class Oglethorpe Light Infantry, Pvts. John Webb and Henry Parnell, began reflecting on how their supply of cooked rations had given out and how, as they exaggerated their plight, they "had not 'had a mouthful for three days.' " They agreed to fall out of ranks, hide in some bushes until the provost guards at the end of the column were safely past, and then "see what could be done" about getting something to eat.

The plan worked, and the three soon found themselves alone on the road. Casting about for a likely source of food, they spied a nearby farmhouse that, much to the delight of the three Oglethorpes, had several beehives sitting among the grass and clover of the front yard. Eagerly, the hot, tired, thirsty, and hungry soldiers strode up the path to the back door of the large brick house. Their knock brought the farmer to an upstairs window, where he stuck his head out and asked what they wanted. They told him to come downstairs, and he did. Then they explained that they were hungry Confederate soldiers and wanted to buy some of his honey. To their surprise and dismay, he flatly refused. Again they explained their situation, adding that they had not had anything to eat for two days save green apples and that he really ought to *give* them the honey instead of selling it. This was too much for the farmer, who, like many inhabitants of the upper South, was a Unionist and resented the fire-eating hotheads of the cotton states for bringing on the war. The farmer told them as much and suggested that a little starving might do them some good.

"You know, my friend," Webb remarked ominously, "some soldiers don't ask people to give or sell them things when they are hungry."

"Yes," replied the farmer stoutly, "I've heard of such, and I'm ready for them," and with that he reached back inside the door and pulled out a double-barreled shotgun, announcing that anyone who tampered with his property would do so at hazard of his life.

"Oh!" exclaimed Zettler. "You wouldn't kill a man for a few pounds of honey?"

"Yes, I would," replied the farmer.

"But we are willing to buy the honey; sell us that or something else to eat."

But the farmer did not want to aid the cause of secession, and steadfastly maintained that he would not sell and would defend his property with lethal force if necessary. A double-barreled shotgun is a fairly authoritative piece of equipment, and that might have been the end of the matter if the farmer had not been all this while committing a serious tactical error. He was standing there with the butt of his shotgun sitting on the ground and the palm of his hand resting over the muzzle. Without warning, Webb leveled his Harpers Ferry rifle at the farmer's chest, snarling, "If you move I'll kill you." Parnell did the same. "We sure will," he agreed. The farmer took them at their word and stood as still as a statue.

"Well, boys," said Zettler, "if you hold him that way, I'll get the honey." He hurried down to the hives, lifted the honey box off one of them, tied it up in his handkerchief, and hurried back. They marched the farmer several hundred yards down the road without his gun and then turned him loose. The unfortunate man lost no time in making his escape.

The three Oglethorpes now contemplated their booty with relish mixed with a certain amount of guilt. As Zettler later admitted, "We were private soldiers doing a thing which we knew our officers disapproved and for which we would be severely dealt with if found out. We were . . . wrong."

Still the thought of eating all the honey they could hold was an alluring one, and finding a shady bank beside a little rippling brook, they addressed themselves to the honeycomb. "It was delicious," Zettler recalled, "and we thoroughly enjoyed it." They had been hot and dry when they began their repast, and getting their bellies full to bloating with sweet, sticky honey had intensified their thirst. Crawling over to the stream, they lay on the bank and greedily gulped down large amounts of the cold, clear water.

Presently John Webb stopped, sat up, and got a peculiarly serious look on his face. "Boys," he said, "I believe mine is coming ba—, ba—, back," and began vomiting. Parnell and Zettler took one look and headed into the bushes themselves. A few minutes later, relieved, they set out to catch up with their regiment, perhaps reflecting on some of the newly discovered moral ambiguities of soldiering.[11]

Those Halcyon Days in the Valley

On June 20 the Eighth Georgia reached Winchester and camped a little over a mile southeast of town at a place called Hollingsworth Grove. One soldier described it as "an island of shade and a sea of clover." Rolling grassy fields surrounded the site, and nearby, the waters of Town Creek turned the wheel of Hollingsworth's grist mill, a substantial building of native limestone. A little over half a mile away was Shawnee Spring. With its cool, clear water, the spring was a favorite place with the local population, whom some members of the Eighth lost no time in getting to know. On the regiment's first day at Hollingsworth Grove, Hamilton Branch of the OLI went for a stroll up to the spring with a Miss Jennie and a Miss Ella, explaining in a letter to his mother, "They say if you drink this water you are obliged to come back here." The tents and cooking utensils finally caught up with the regiment, and life began to become more comfortable. Few members of the Eighth Georgia would have denied that camp at Winchester in high summer was very good duty indeed.[12]

The abundant clover of the Shenandoah Valley was something many of the Georgia boys had never seen before, and this led to some humorous behavior on the part of members of one of the other regiments in Johnston's army. Coming upon a field of clover one day, the Georgians mistook the luxuriant plants for a growth of peanuts, or, in Georgia parlance, "goobers." Now, the Georgia boys knew what to do with goobers, and in a flash they had broken ranks, run out into the clover field, and begun pulling up plants, only to gape disappointed at bare clover roots where they had expected to find the delectable "goober peas." All they got out of it was a good laugh from the Virginia troops, in which they and their fellow Georgians of the Eighth readily joined. The clover-pullers got the nickname "goober grabbers" that day, and it soon spread to include all the Georgia troops serving in Virginia.[13]

The troops at Hollingsworth Grove continued their drilling, four hours a day, which they considered "pretty good work." They also continued to impress civilian spectators. As at Richmond, many local ladies came out to witness the drills and socialize with the soldiers afterward. The soldiers admired them in turn and wrote of their beauty in letters home. George Barnsley of the Rome Light Guards later recalled that "it was a pleasure to strut about when one could get a leave." Meanwhile Hamilton Branch continued apace and by the third or fourth day at Hollingsworth Grove, Sanford, his brother, noticed that he came to dress parade "with five young ladies, some quite handsome." Sanford also noted that John Branch, his and Ham's older brother and the regimental adjutant, attended a ball on June 26 and "had a very nice time."[14]

In these circumstances, military life was not always a very serious undertaking, and the many gaffs and blunders in protocol and procedures during these weeks were reminders of just how green these newly sprouted soldiers still were. Company I's Lt. John Calvin Reed drew the good-natured laughter of Lt. Col. Gardner, an old army man, by confusing the role of "orderly," a soldier detailed for menial duty, with that of "orderly sergeant," a Civil War company's first sergeant, who was never to be detailed for such duty. Reed, in turn, was highly amused at watching a captain of the neighboring Seventh Georgia try to drill his company. The captain was a tall, thin, stooped man about sixty years of age who had mild blue eyes and a quiet, gentle manner that seemed thoroughly unmilitary. He would lounge against a fallen tree trunk, adjust his spectacles, thumb through his tactics manual, find the command he wished to give, close and set down the manual, place his spectacles up on his high balding forehead, and in a kindly and barely audible voice give his order. Then while his company waited, often in some awkward position halfway through a movement, he repeated the process in searching for the next step in the drill.[15]

Then of course there was the story of the sentry who challenged an approaching figure one night with the warning that he would not be allowed to pass the sentry post unless he said "Potomac," the secret password of the day. Finally there was Pvt. Leonidas Howell, of Company I, who decided to wash his clothes. He was having a fine time splashing his soiled garments in the creek, and he explained in a letter home, "Perhaps I would have remained there all day, but Col. Bartow sent to the creek, and had me arrested for having all my clothes off except my shirt." The colonel let Howell off with an admonition to be more careful about what he wore on his wash days.[16]

Many of the soldiers chose not to do their own washing. Those who had brought along black servants could have them do the job. Those who had not hired whomever they could get, often another soldier's black servant. John Reed had brought along as his servant a free black from Greensboro, Georgia, who went simply by the name of Lit. Lit was much in demand to do washing, and Reed gave him permission to take as many jobs as he could handle. His payment for these jobs was often in the form of the local Shenandoah Valley currency, notes issued by a private bank in absurdly small denominations. These "shin-plasters," as they were called, circulated freely and were tattered and worn in appearance. The soldiers somehow obtained them and then used them to pay Lit for his washing service. The black man was good-natured but had his doubts about this form of cash. "Mas John," he said to Reed one evening, contemplating a pile of the strange bills, "did these people here make this money because they heard that we were coming, or did they always have it?"

As Johnston's small army marched down to Winchester, the general had organized it into brigades. The Eighth Georgia he brigaded with the Seventh Georgia, the Ninth Georgia, and two battalions of Kentuckians and a battery of artillery. Johnston selected Col. Bartow to command the brigade, and that meant that Lt. Col. Montgomery Gardner took over the reins as commander of the Eighth.[17]

Bartow continued to be a favorite with soldiers and civilians, though some began to notice a contrast between his mood and that of the soldiers he commanded. Cornelia McDonald was one of the ladies of Winchester who came out to the camp to see the troops drill. Bartow invited her and the others up to his tent to watch the festivities, and she was not disappointed in the show. It was "a beautiful sight," she wrote in her diary that night. "The men went through all their maneuvers with perfect order." Once the dress parade was over, the soldiers began playing games like schoolboys, for, as Mrs. McDonald noted, "boys most of them were," and the fields around the camp were filled with nattily uniformed soldiers playing at leapfrog and other favorite activities of the schoolyard.

Bartow himself, however, presented a striking contrast to the exuberance of his soldiers. Mrs. Campbell "could not help contrasting their happy looks with the melancholy face of their commander." He stood and watched the capering soldiers with a look of "deep sadness" on his face. To Mrs. Virginia Mason Ambler, who stood nearby, he said, "I cannot drive from my mind the thought of the terrible struggles in which they will have to bear their part."[18]

Bartow already had reason for concern, for the lives of his men were already in imminent danger. Not all the struggles they would face as soldiers would be with human enemies, and by far the greatest toll of deaths would be exacted not by Northern lead and powder but by tiny microbes. This was not a new thing in the history of warfare, for in every conflict from that time back to the earliest recorded history, disease had always been a more efficient killer than human enemies. Nor was lethal disease any stranger to nineteenth-century Americans, who often saw it carry off their loved ones well short of their threescore years and ten. Still, when they went to war, they might talk and think of the possibility of dying at some disputed barricade but never of wasting away in a foul-smelling hospital tent. Yet tens of thousands of young Americans did just that during the Civil War, and the boys of the Eighth Georgia were about to make their acquaintance with this phenomenon.

Nearly every Civil War regiment went through a period of seasoning not long after being organized and taking the field. Some time during the first six months or so of active duty, communicable diseases would sweep through the camp, killing and disabling to such a degree that it was an unusual regiment that carried much more than half of its prescribed numbers into its first battle. Losses to disease would continue throughout the unit's career, but these early months would see the greatest percentage fall to sickness. This time of winnowing might come in winter or summer, but it usually raged worst while the regiment remained some time encamped in one place. Ironically, a settled camp, even if far from the smell of enemy gunpowder, was one of the most unhealthy places for a Civil War soldier to be. In the case of the Eighth Georgia, the seasoning time was interrupted by an interlude of active operations, but it began right here in the idyllic surroundings of Hollingsworth Grove, just outside the picturesque town of Winchester in the lush Shenandoah Valley. "This was one of the most pleasant places we visited during the war," noted Pvt. David Green Fleming of Company G, the Pulaski Volunteers, "but here began the test of the constitutions of our soldiers."[19]

One of the first diseases to sweep the camp was measles. A childhood disease to which many of the men had never before been exposed, it laid low nearly half of regiments at some times. While it was not usually fatal, it could lead to complications that were very deadly indeed. Chief of these was pneumonia. On Saturday, June 29, Pvt. John D. Williams of Company I, the Stephens Light Guards, became the first member of the Eighth to succumb to it at Winchester. Six days earlier, Pvt. William F. Heard of the same company had died in Richmond, where he had been left, too sick to accompany his comrades to the Shenandoah. On July 7, Pvt. B. J. Strickland of the Oglethorpes of Company B succumbed to pneumonia. In the week and a half that followed, three members of Company G died at Winchester, either of measles or of pneumonia, as did at least two members of Company E, the Miller Rifles. The other companies fared about the same, and the regiment was by no means finished with its epidemic when it left the Valley.

Another deadly disease was typhoid fever, which men generally contracted in the summer months when contaminated water or unpasteurized milk from local farms introduced the typhoid bacillus into their systems. Typhoid fever was virtually untreatable in those days before the discovery of penicillin, and one suffered with it until he either died or got better, more often the former. Besides these illnesses there was also the ubiquitous "camp fever," as well as a lengthy catalog of more obscure ailments.

Confederate army physicians, including the Eighth's own surgeon, Dr. H. M. V. Miller, gave the sick what little care they could and shipped the most severely ill to general army hospitals in rear areas. The most serious cases might receive furloughs or even discharges for disability. Others might be transferred to less strenuous duty. In all, during the last three weeks of camping at Hollingsworth Grove, twenty-one members of the regiment died; forty-four more were mustered out of the service, and six were packed off to easier assignments in the quartermaster, commissary, and medical departments. Others were furloughed, and of them, not all lived to return to the ranks. Those who did were often gone for months. In short, the sojourn in the pleasant environs of Winchester nevertheless cost the Eighth casualties to sickness at a rate that would have annihilated the regiment in well under a year—and its seasoning process was not yet complete when it left.

Still, despite the problems of sickness, many members of the Eighth remembered fondly their days near Winchester. Remembering that time with an awareness of the much greater hardships that had followed, Company I's Lt. John Calvin Reed wrote, "O, those halcyon days in the Valley, smiling its last beautiful smile! Every morning we found the camp more lively, the old people around us more like parents, and the girls dearer and fairer. How romantic and sweet it was to each of us to belong to the southern army and be petted by such people."[20]

We Knew Where We Were a Going

Pleasant the situation might be, but the men of the Eighth could not forget that they had come to Virginia to fight and had not done so. Prospects of doing so seemed poor, and the specter loomed of sitting out the war in some inactive sector without the chance to prove their valor. The thought marred the soldiers' enjoyment of the beautiful Shenandoah. "There is any amount of grumbling very generally expressed," Melvin Dwinnell wrote, in regard to Johnston's decision not to retire to Winchester and not to force a battle near Martinsburg. "We all now think," Dwinnell continued, "that we then lost our only *immediate* and perhaps the only *remote* chance also for a fight." He thought there never had been an army "more eager for the fray," but throughout the rest of the month of June it would be disappointed.[21]

Then on Tuesday, July 2, word reached camp that the Federals were on the move. Confederate forces under Brig. Gen. Thomas J. Jackson were skirmishing and falling back before a large Union column that had crossed the Potomac at Williamsport, in the far northwestern corner of the Valley. The bluecoats continued to press southward, and despite a sharp little fight at Falling Waters, Virginia, continued on another eight miles to Martinsburg. Jackson, with orders from Johnston to avoid bringing on a general engagement, fell back before the advancing Federals.

Johnston immediately gave orders for the rest of his army to march northward in support of Jackson. Excitement ran high in the Eighth as the army swung northward along the Valley Pike in light marching order, tents and heavy baggage left behind at Winchester under a small guard. Six miles short of Martinsburg, at the little hamlet of Darkesville, Johnston deployed his army to face Union general Robert Patterson's larger force. For the next four days, the Confederates waited eagerly, but Patterson would not move. The aged Pennsylvania general was acting on orders from Union general-in-chief Winfield Scott in Washington. Scott wanted Patterson to keep Johnston occupied in the Valley so that he could not take his force to aid the Confederate army of Gen. P. G. T. Beauregard at Manassas Junction, well to the east and on the direct route from Washington to Richmond. Never one to be overaggressive, Patterson was content to sit in Martinsburg and try to appear threatening, and he was more than content to have Johnston sit and watch him from Darkesville. Johnston soon tired of the game. Unwilling to sit idle any longer but even more reluctant to attack Patterson's force, ensconced as it was in the town of Martinsburg, he ordered his army back to their camps at Winchester.

The march took place on Sunday, July 8. The Eighth Georgia brought up the rear once again, and a tiresome business it was under the hot sun of one of the warmest days yet that year. Straggling, a constant feature of Civil War armies on the march, was much in evidence, and members of the Eighth guessed they must have passed perhaps as many as a thousand men who had fallen out of ranks during the course of the day. They arrived back at Hollingsworth Grove at eight o'clock that evening and were very glad to see their tents, baggage, and cooking utensils again after five days without them. Interestingly, despite the fatigue and exposure of active operations, the regiment was in better health upon its return than it had been for some days before or would be for some days after. Johnston had an order read in all the camps explaining his reasons for pulling back again, and the men had to be content with it. Adjutant John Branch explained in a letter to his mother that the common soldiers and low-ranking officers referred to their recent maneuver as "retreating," but the high brass called it "resuming our former position."[22]

At least one soldier managed to ease his lot during the Darkesville excursion, though not by honest means. While the army waited at Darkesville to see what the Yankees would do, Sanford Branch, younger brother of the regimental adjutant, borrowed his brother's horse and rode over to the town of Bunker Hill, about four miles from the regiment's camp that night. Carefully selecting the finest house in town, Branch dismounted and walked up to the door. A black house slave answered the door, and Branch asked for the lady of the house. Moments later, "a beautiful creature made her appearance," as Branch later recounted it, and he introduced himself to her as the adjutant of the Eighth Georgia Regiment. The showy uniform of the Oglethorpe Light Infantry offered plausible support for any claim of rank, and she readily believed his lie. He then inquired the way to a tavern or hotel in town where a tired and hungry officer could get a good meal. He knew full well that Bunker Hill boasted no such amenities, but that was part of his plan. As if on cue, the lady replied that there was no public house in the village but that she would be glad to have him join them for dinner. After feigning reluctance, Branch agreed, and, in his own words, "had turkey & green corn for dinner while my mess mates feasted on boiled beef and half baked bread."[23]

The Confederates had taken a number of Union prisoners in the skirmishing during the first few days of July and set them to work building fortifications for the Confederates at Winchester. The captive Yankees soon became an item of interest—a sort of sideshow curiosity—to numerous members of Johnston's army. Stories quickly made the rounds about what poor specimens they were—"mostly small, dried up Pennsylvania Dutchmen"—and how perfidious. A favorite tale had it that when one prisoner was asked what he was fighting against the South for, he replied, "For eleven dollars a month." That the story was false was amply demonstrated by the fact that eleven dollars per month was a Confederate private's pay. Their Union counterparts made thirteen dollars per month. Still, the boys of the Eighth did not know this, and they found it encouraging to reflect that their foes were a "mercenary horde" who would hardly prove resolute in battle.[24]

Camp life at Hollingsworth Grove returned more or less to normal after the early July scare, and yet things were not quite as carefree as before. The possibility of an imminent armed clash kept the Eighth in a state of tense but hopeful expectation. On July 10, Johnston gave orders for the troops to cook their rations in advance—sure sign of an impending movement—and be ready to march at a moment's notice. A morning of frenzied preparations gave way to an afternoon of anxious waiting and fevered speculation about where they were going. In the end, they went nowhere.[25]

Then at 1:00 P.M. on Monday, July 15, the preparatory order came again: cook three days' rations and put them in the haversacks, then strap up blankets and oilcloths for handy carrying and pack everything else to be left behind with the tents. The men hurried to comply. Then six hours later the order was changed; they were to strike tents and pack up everything to go along. Everything, however, was not going to be as much as it had been in previous movements. A recent order from the Confederate Adjutant and Inspector General's Office in Richmond had wisely stipulated that excess baggage was to be curtailed, and the preparations for the movement coincided with preparations to ship off or store the regiment's huge amount of extra truck. Somewhere in the confusion, Company A, the Rome Light Guards, misplaced its fine silken banner, and it was never found again. In any case, company banners were superfluous in the real army, where regiments were the units accorded the honor of carrying flags.[26]

At 7:00 P.M., Bartow's brigade, including the Eighth Georgia, moved out to the north side of Winchester, and the word was that they would be staying there until the arrival of the enemy, then rumored to be advancing. Tuesday brought renewed reports that Patterson was finally stirring from his position at Martinsburg, and throughout that day and the next the Confederates continued to wait. Wednesday afternoon, orders came down to dismantle all the fences in the fields north of Winchester so as to facilitate maneuvering when the big battle finally opened, but by now even the private soldiers were beginning to wonder if Patterson was any more in earnest this time than he had been before.

On Thursday morning, July 18, Melvin Dwinnell wrote at seven o'clock, "Orders have just been issued to pack up baggage, strike tents, cook two days rations and be ready to march immediately, we know not where." He supposed it would only be two or three miles to a somewhat more advantageous position. Others in the regiment had a much different hunch about the object of this movement. Over in Company E, the Miller Rifles, Pvt. Henry C. Harper and his friends believed they were headed for Beauregard's sorely threatened army at Manassas Junction. In his diary he wrote, "We knew where we were a going."[27]

CHAPTER THREE

⌘

Never Give Up the Field

You Must Get There

AT 2:00 P.M., Thursday, July 18, the long-awaited order finally came, and the regiments of Johnston's command fell into line and marched out of their camps around Winchester. If Dwinnell and his comrades in Company A, the Rome Light Guards, could not guess their destination, they were far from alone in their ignorance. The Oglethorpes of B Company were equally puzzled. "Another trot toward Martinsburg all for nothing," quipped several of them when the march order arrived, suspecting it portended nothing more than the hesitation waltz Johnston had been dancing with Patterson for the past fortnight in the Valley.[1]

They loaded tents and the recently reduced baggage onto the wagons; the men would carry nothing but blanket rolls, rifles, ammunition, and haversacks. That turned out to be enough, however. The records and recollections vary as to whether it was two or three days' rations that commissary officers issued that morning, but according to regulations, a day's ration weighed several pounds. Clearly the haversacks were heavy as the men marched out of camp. To the perplexity of those who looked for another gingerly probe toward Martinsburg, the column marched south, through Winchester, and then turned eastward at the crossroads and swung along the open road under a blazing midsummer sun with the long line of the Blue Ridge shimmering through the afternoon haze in front of them.[2]

To Berrien Zettler of Company B it seemed as if all of his companions were asking each other at once, "Where are we going?" But no one seemed to know. Apparently E Company's astute guessing had not made it up to the head of the column where the Oglethorpes were marching. Then, once they were well out of town, Bartow rode along the regimental column, reined in his horse near where Company I was marching, and shouted exuberantly, "We are marching to succor General Beauregard, who is now fighting the enemy at Manassas." The men responded with "deafening cheers." Elsewhere in the Eighth's column, R. H. Cole remembered other field officers riding along making much the same announcement, adding that hardships, privations, and a long, hard march lay ahead and suggesting that any man who did not feel equal to the challenge had better fall out and get back to Winchester. There the sick had been left behind with a few detailed men. Here too the soldiers responded with "cheer after cheer." No one turned back.[3]

The delayed announcement was by Johnston's order, and was occurring successively in each brigade as it got well clear of town and, theoretically, of any chance of the word leaking back into Winchester and finding its way to Patterson. The bit about reluctant men turning back would not have pleased Johnston at all, and it was probably just as well for Lt. Col. Gardner and Maj. Cooper that no one took them up on what was no doubt a purely rhetorical suggestion.[4]

Union strategy for Virginia called for Patterson to keep Johnston entertained in the Shenandoah Valley while another Union army under Maj. Gen. Irvin McDowell marched southwest from Washington toward Richmond. All that would then stand in McDowell's way was a force of about 25,000 men under Confederate general P. G. T. Beauregard at Manassas Junction. McDowell would outnumber Beauregard—unless Johnston's 10,000 men from the Valley managed to join the "Hero of Fort Sumter" at Manassas. Beauregard had been begging for weeks to have Johnston's force sent to him, but Jefferson Davis had wisely reckoned that having Johnston move too soon would only invite a corresponding move by Patterson, thus leaving the odds at Manassas unaltered and unfavorable to the Confederacy. Only when he was sure that the two Union armies had committed themselves to their offensive movements would he authorize Johnston to move. That assurance came on July 17. Both McDowell and Patterson had begun moving forward a couple of days before, but Patterson had stopped and was obviously bluffing. McDowell kept coming. Late that evening, Davis had word telegraphed to Johnston to give Patterson the slip if he could and march for Manassas with all possible speed. True to form, Johnston vacillated, but repeated urging over the wires from both Beauregard at Manassas and the president's assistant, Adjutant and Inspector General Samuel Cooper in Richmond, finally compelled him to move.[5]

By this time a badly frightened Beauregard was petulantly complaining to Richmond that the move was too late. It very nearly was. McDowell's troops marched like the raw levies they were and took several days covering the thirty-five or so miles from Washington to Manassas. If they had marched like veterans, they would have been at Beauregard's throat long before Johnston could have come to his aid. As it was, though, no one was a veteran in this first summer of the war, and the Union march was slow. Still, even as Johnston's troops were packing up and marching out of camp, two of Beauregard's brigades won a brief skirmish against a reconnaissance by McDowell's forces at Blackburn's Ford on Bull Run, a stream flowing from west to east just north of Manassas Junction. Bartow was right in his announcement that Beauregard was then engaged. There was little time to lose.[6]

Through the late-afternoon hours the Eighth Georgia and their comrades in Johnston's Valley army swung along the road under bright sunshine toward the deceptively close-looking but persistently distant slopes of the towering Blue Ridge. When Lt. Col. Gardner announced the destination to the Oglethorpes, all Berrien Zettler heard was that they would probably stop for the night on the top of the Blue Ridge. Zettler thought the yelling that followed, in which he joined right heartily, was due to the fact that the mountains ahead of them "looked to be only three or four miles distant" and the men anticipated a short march and an early halt.[7]

Throughout the afternoon, the misty, towering range did not seem to get much closer, but the soldiers—those who had heard the announcement, at any rate—were almost giddy with the thought of finally seeing battle, proving their courage, and striking a blow at the "mercenary hordes" of the North. The woods and fields along their road rang with the shouts, laughter, and songs of exuberant young men. Officers had no difficulty keeping the column closed up; everyone seemed eager to get to the destination of this march. In the ranks of Company K, Thomas Gilham thought they were moving "almost in a double-quick step," not for fear that Beauregard would be defeated but that he would rout the enemy without their help.[8]

The sun sank low near the tops of the Alleghenies behind them. The shadow of its setting fell upon the column from back to front, and the men marched on through the dusk, while the tree-clad slopes of the Blue Ridge still glowed a golden sunlit green ahead of them. The shadows crept up its slopes more slowly, until the ridge became a black shape against the dark gray sky. The stars came out. And Johnston's troops kept marching. From time to time, Lt. Col. Gardner would dismount and foot it alongside his men. The shouting, singing, and laughter gradually died away along with the fading light, and soon all that could be heard was the murmuring tramp of thousands of boots shuffling along a dusty Virginia road, the clink of arms and accouterments, and the chirping chorus of the crickets in the surrounding woods and fields. Hour after hour they marched on through the darkness.

It was getting close to midnight and Berrien Zettler had the distinct impression that he had nodded off while he was walking when the men in front passed the word down the column, "Get ready to wade the river." River? The only rivers Zettler could think of just then were ones like the Savannah as it flowed past his native Effingham County. The thought of wading clear across something like that seemed like a joke. Thinking the hour and the circumstances hardly appropriate for humor, he paid no attention and plodded wearily on. Sure enough, however, a few more minutes of walking brought him to the bank of the shallow, fast-flowing Shenandoah, and he saw the troops ahead of him wading into the waist-deep water with their clothes bundled up and held with their rifles and accouterments above their heads. Zettler sat down on the bank, half in a daze, and tried to convince himself that it was all a dream.

Failing, he got up, rigged up his clothes and shoes on the end of his musket, and waded in. He soon found out another way in which the Shenandoah differed from the rivers of south Georgia. Georgia river bottoms were sand and clay, while the Shenandoah's seemed to be covered completely with stones. To Zettler's already sore feet, all the stones seemed to have sharp edges. Somehow he made it across.[9]

Most of the boys had a far better time crossing the river. Thoroughly awakened by their midnight wade in "the cold, icy water," as one member recalled it, they began to joke and laugh again. Someone had built up a bonfire on the far shore to light them across, and by its glow hundreds of men could be seen wading through the rushing river, their "clothing and accouterments hung to their guns, and that high over the shoulder." Some of the taller soldiers, glancing back and seeing shorter comrades coming along behind them, would crouch down so as to make the water look much deeper than it was, then laugh uproariously at the concerned looks of the smaller men, already pushing along through water above their waists.[10]

The Shenandoah in this part of its course lies close under the mass of the Blue Ridge, and from its east bank the land rises steadily to the slopes of the mountainside. The soldiers trudged grimly upward. About an hour beyond the river they passed the crest of the Blue Ridge and came to the tiny settlement of Paris, Virginia. There, true to Gardner's word to the Oglethorpes, they stopped for rest. Few of the bone-weary soldiers bothered to hunt up soft ground for sleeping. Most just staggered a few feet into the woods or else sank down in the road where they were standing when the order came to halt.[11]

Berrien Zettler had fallen well behind the regiment while sitting on the riverbank and thinking about wading, and he now had to catch up, working his way through the long impromptu encampment of sprawled soldiers, stumbling over sleepers and asking if this was Company B, Eighth Georgia. The stock answer seemed to be "No, you fool," for quite a long time. At last he found his comrades and settled down to try to get some rest.[12]

Soldier recollections, both in the days that followed and years later, differed as to when they halted—sometime between midnight and 4:00 A.M.—and how long they rested—estimates ranged from one to four hours. Both factors probably varied according to one's position in the column. All

agreed, however, that they were up very early the next morning, pushing forward on legs still stiff and weary from yesterday's marathon
march.[13]

As they swung down the long eastern slope of the Blue Ridge and
the sun rose over the lowlands ahead of them, those who had not already
been thinking of it began to contemplate the subject of food. This was
strange for men who were supposed to have been issued two or three
days' rations less than twenty-four hours before, but somehow the issue
of hunger is a theme in numerous soldier recollections. In the bustle of
preparations for the march the previous midday, no one had gotten any
dinner. Possibly some of the companies had not received their rations as
ordered. Lt. John Reed believed that many of the men had decided the
three days' rations weighed too heavy in their haversacks during the grueling march of July 18 and had lightened their loads by throwing food
away. If so, it was a habit they would learn to break. At any rate, the boys
were very hungry that morning.[14]

As they marched along they came in time to a large, imposing brick
plantation house with a long veranda across the front. A broad circular
drive curved down to dual carriage gates on the road along which the
troops were marching. A black house servant wearing a white apron
stood beside the nearer gate. With "intense earnestness" he was saying
again and again, "Missus says come up to breakfast. Come right up, Missus says, all of you come right up." This brought hoots and laughter from
the men of the two leading companies, A and B, the Rome Light Guards
and the Oglethorpe Light Infantry. Their uniforms were the showiest in
the regiment, and even included epaulettes. "The fool thinks we are officers," shouted one of them, to renewed laughter.

The slave, however, remained steadfast, and the boys decided it was
worth a try. So the head of the column turned in at the gate and
marched up the long circular drive. As they got near the house they saw
a refined-looking lady standing on the front veranda. "Glad to see you,
dear boys," she said. "Just pass round the house to the dining room."
They passed, with much doffing of kepis and shakos, and the very
thought of what they found in that dining room was still making some
of their mouths water fifty years later: "biscuits by the bushel, sliced
bread and ham in stacks two feet high, cakes and doughnuts of all sizes
and shapes, and on each side of the exit door innumerable tubs and

cans of hot coffee." One after another, gray-jacketed Rome Light Guards and Oglethorpes in their tall white-plumed shakos stopped as they entered and gaped at the feast before them. At least a half-dozen ladies stood at various posts around the room ready to serve out the eatables to the salivating soldiers. "They literally passed us along, at the same time stuffing our haversacks as we proceeded," recalled a soldier. "You haven't time to stop to eat," they admonished the men, "you are going to Manassas to help Beauregard; the Yankees attacked him yesterday and were repulsed. You must get there to help him." For those who had not heard Bartow's announcement the afternoon before, this was the first news of the purpose of the march, and they swung down the other side of the circular drive and back onto the road with renewed energy—and pockets and haversacks stuffed with good things to eat—while the tail end of the long column kept right on coming up the nearer drive on their way to the dining room.[15]

Battle and Fighting Mean Death

And that was only the beginning of that memorable day's march. Along the whole route, "at every village, the ladies were out handing edibles and water to the boys," recalled a soldier. About noon they reached Piedmont Station on the Manassas Gap Railroad, where they were to board trains for Manassas Junction. The long, hard march was over, and the footsore soldiers gratefully stacked arms and sprawled out to rest.[16]

The rest at Piedmont proved longer than they had expected or hoped. The South's rail network in 1861 left much to be desired. Though it had grown rapidly during the 1850s, it remained both less extensive and less efficient than that of the North, being built mostly for the purpose of carrying local farm produce to port cities on rivers or the ocean. Its locomotives were both too few and too small, its roadbeds and rails weak, and it lacked sufficient rolling stock to carry large numbers of troops rapidly across country. Besides that, Johnston, who never really understood railroads, had not made adequate preparations for this movement. The result was a long delay at Piedmont while the troops waited for the only available locomotive to shuttle back and forth, hauling one train at a time over the relatively short distance to Manassas Junction. For men who feared they might miss the war during the extra hours of delay thus occasioned, it was hard to take, though their misery was eased somewhat by the continued kindness of the local population, who brought in "wagons of cooked provisions, barrels of milk, water, etc.," all served out by "fair hands."[17]

The Eighth Georgia, along with their comrades of the Seventh Georgia, finally got their chance to board a train at nine o'clock that evening. If they thought the remaining trip to the prospective battlefield would now go quickly, they were in for a big disappointment. The wheezy old engine and the dilapidated roadbed meant that their progress was very slow, and stops were so frequent that the boys began to wonder if the train crew was in cahoots with the Yankees.[18]

The train they rode on was composed of boxcars and stock cars. Berrien Zettler, with his knack for getting into trouble, decided that the top of the car would be the best place to be on a hot summer's evening. This was not so unusual, as another member of his company recalled that there were about as many men on the roofs of the cars as inside them. However, a short ride on the roof convinced Zettler that it was not the place to be. The metal and boards had gotten very hot in the July sun and still were. Then the engine covered him in a cloud of smoke and cinders. Wisely waiting until they reached the next station, he climbed down and got inside. The packed interior of the boxcar was little improvement, and Zettler was soon thinking about the "Black Hole of Calcutta," the notorious guardroom where in 1756 a local Indian potentate had suffocated a number of British prisoners by packing too many of them in too tight a space. Zettler began to wonder if a similar fate awaited him. "I felt that I was being cooked alive." The men back out on the roofs of the cars at least had plenty of air, even if it was full of smoke and cinders. Not long into the trip a good rainstorm came up and lasted all night, so they had the enjoyment of that too.[19]

The eastern sky was just beginning to lighten on the morning of Saturday, July 20, 1861, when their train at last pulled into Manassas Junction. They piled out, marched a short distance, and fell out in an open field to boil coffee and get what rest they could.[20]

Bartow spotted a short, dapper, and very important-looking officer and recognized him as Gen. Beauregard. Riding up to the general, Bartow saluted. "General, I am here with my boys, the Eighth Georgia Regiment," he announced, "and I have promised them they shall be in the opening of the fight."

"They shall be gratified," replied the general and then proceeded to tell Bartow where he wanted the regiment positioned, on the right end of the Confederate line. For those soldiers who were paying attention, it was an exciting moment. Few if any of them had previously seen Beauregard, the South's first great military hero.[21]

Much sooner than the bone-weary soldiers would have liked, the officers again called them to form ranks and prepare to march. Morale was still high, though, and the men fell in without delay. The march that followed, though a matter of only four miles, was as grueling in its own way as the twenty-seven-mile tramp on fresh legs the first day. The clouds had cleared off, and the sun beat down on them through a haze of heat and humidity, causing one soldier to write four days later that these were "the hottest, dustiest, most fatiguing" miles he had ever walked. At length they arrived at their designated campsite, in some woods not far from Bull Run, and settled down for some much-needed rest without tents or baggage, neither of which had yet come up. Some at least of the companies had even left their blankets back at Manassas Junction and now had to lie on the bare ground.[22]

Whatever else they had left behind, they had taken the measles epidemic with them. W. H. Maxey broke out with them on Friday while the regiment was awaiting transportation at Piedmont, and Will Leigh came down with the disease on Saturday at Manassas Junction. The microbes would continue their inexorable campaign regardless of enemy action.[23]

That evening after dark, Bartow came over to the camp of the Oglethorpes, his old company from Savannah. Their nickname had been "Bartow's Beardless Boys," and several of them recalled his fatherly manner that night as he chatted with "his boys." Beauregard was planning a battle for the morrow, he told them, and he had gotten the general to promise that they, the Eighth Georgia, would have the honor of opening it. "Remember, boys," he added before heading back to his own quarters for the night, "that battle and fighting mean death, and probably before sunrise some of us will be dead." That gave nineteen-year-old Berrien Zettler something to think about as he lay looking up at the stars that night and remembering home. Still, he was young and had labored hard the last few days with little rest. He slept soundly.[24]

Get Ready, Men!

Dawn found every man of the Eighth Georgia still alive, and no sign of the much-heralded battle was to be seen or heard. Bartow's prophecies appeared to have been all disproved together. Yet even as the Georgians rubbed their eyes and stretched their stiff limbs in the first gray light, momentous developments were afoot.

Beauregard had intended a grand assault for the morning of Sunday, July 21. He planned to advance his forces on the right, cross Bull Run, crush the Union left, and cut off McDowell's retreat. For that purpose he had massed the bulk of his troops, including the Seventh and Eighth Georgia, the only two of Bartow's regiments that had yet arrived, on the right, or east, end of his line. Like many of the plans Beauregard would make during the war, this one was overelaborate and unrealistic. Even the best and simplest of plans would have been difficult to execute in an army in which everyone, from the general to the lowest private, was new to his job. Mistakes and misunderstandings were bound to occur, and Beauregard's grandiose plan tended to maximize them. So thorough was the muddle in the upper echelons of Confederate command that morning that no significant part of Beauregard's program actually got carried out at all, which was probably just as well.[25]

What finally forestalled Beauregard's design was action on the part of his opponent, Irvin McDowell. McDowell too had a plan, remarkably similar to Beauregard's but more practical. McDowell figured to send the bulk of his forces marching upstream, to *his* right, have them cross Bull Run by Sudley's Ford, beyond the Confederate position, and then turn back downstream and strike the Confederate left flank and rear. The Union movement had started at 2:00 A.M., but McDowell's army was just as green as Beauregard's, and the inevitable confusion and bungling had slowed the operation. As the men of the Eighth Georgia and thousands of other Confederates began sitting up and yawning their first yawns on this quiet Sunday morning, powerful Union formations were already bearing down on the extreme left of the Confederate line.[26]

Bartow was on edge. No orders had come from Beauregard, and clearly things were not progressing as planned. The colonel paced restlessly back and forth. Finally he mounted and rode off into the woods in search of some answers. Some time later—one observer thought it

was about eight o'clock, though in this as in all Civil War battles matters
of time are sketchy and confused—Bartow rode back at a gallop yelling,
"Get ready, men! The battle has been raging for two hours on our extreme left, and we must go there at once."

Indeed, the advancing Federals had encountered Confederate videttes
upstream and exchanged the first shots at about 6:00 A.M. By 8:30, Confederate signalmen grasped the import of the Union movement and
alerted their superiors. Commanding the Confederate brigade first in
the path of the oncoming Union flanking column, Col. Nathan G.
"Shanks" Evans reacted aggressively. His undersized brigade had been
watching the stone bridge that carried the Warrenton Turnpike over Bull
Run. Now he took most of them to Buck Hill, farther upstream, to confront the advancing Federals. He was soon fighting a desperate delaying
action to cover the army's flank until reinforcements could come up.
And reinforcements were on the way. Beauregard reacted to the new situation by ordering the brigades of Bartow and Brig. Gen. Barnard Bee
to march to reinforce Evans.[27]

Bartow's urgent order stirred the drowsy camp into feverish action,
but a regiment of over six hundred men could not simply get up and
walk away without a few minutes to get ready. For one thing, Company F, the Atlanta Grays, had spent the night on picket duty down along
Bull Run, and they had to be recalled and double-quicked back to camp.
As the Grays fell into ranks for the march, each man was handed a sand-
wich and a cup of coffee to gulp down on the way. While waiting for
the completion of final arrangements and the order to fall in, the men
of Company D gathered around and Capt. Howard led them in prayer.[28]

Then they were off. Some soldiers who had heard Bartow's expression "our left" thought he meant to go only a half mile or so. They soon
knew better, but they did not know exactly where Bartow was taking
them. Neither did he. He knew nothing of the terrain or the army's dispositions in that direction, and it seems not to have occurred to Beauregard to assign a staff officer to guide him. To make matters worse, Bartow
was nearsighted. Again and again during the march he would gallop up
to the troops behind which his column was passing and ask, "It this our
extreme left?" With each disappointing answer the column would march
on. By all accounts their route was not as the crow flies or anything like
it, and it is hard to say just how far they went. The soldiers' own esti-

mates ranged from "four or five miles" to well over twelve. Hamilton Branch told his mother, "We marched about 15 miles in all directions." Others too noted the meandering nature of the march, an officer recalling, "We went about and about, sometimes almost countermarching," At least some considerable portion of the trip they covered at the doublequick, and all agreed that it was tiring and hot, "a long weary, woody, hilly, circuitous tramp." "How the perspiration oozed from every pore!" recalled Berrien Zettler.[29]

During the march they could hear the dull boom of distant cannon, and the excitement this produced renewed their energy. As they drew closer to the battlefield, John Reed saw for the first time a shell exploding in the distance. It was not only a novel sight but a novel sound as well. The sound of the shell's detonation reached his ears a split second after the gun's report and sounded like a strange sort of echo that was louder than the original sound: boom-BOOM. Strange things impressed a man at a time like this.[30]

Finally, about 10:00 A.M., they drew near to the scene of the fighting and halted. The artillery firing had been growing louder and more frequent, but now they heard a new sound: the crackling, rattling sound of thousands of muskets and rifles being fired as fast as excited soldiers could ram new loads down their hot barrels. Bartow, who had gone off to bring the Seventh Georgia along behind them, now came galloping back up the road. Nearsighted as ever, he called out, "Boys, what regiment is this?"

"Eighth Georgia!" they called back.

"My God, boys, I am mighty glad to see you."

They were glad to see him too, and cheered vociferously. "We all loved him like a father," recalled a member of Company F.[31]

Bartow gave Lt. Col. Gardner his orders. The Eighth was to move up in support of a Virginia battery that was dueling with several Union batteries. The column swung into motion again and marched up a long, gradual slope. The sounds they had heard and the occasional sight of a distant bursting shell had not prepared them for the scene that greeted them as they crested the rise. Evans's and Bee's brigades were hotly engaged with several Union brigades. Thousands of troops blazed away at each other from various positions in view from the hilltop. "We saw long lines of the enemy, with their bayonets glistening," recalled a Georgian. "We came . . . all at once, into the midst of a fight," wrote another. "The shock was stunning."[32]

They stood in the Widow Henry's cornfield, the stalks about waist high, and formed line of battle. They "dressed right" as if on parade, each man looking to his right and edging over to feel the touch of his right neighbor's elbow against his own. From his position in Company A at the far right of the regimental line, George Barnsley, ever the individualist, glanced back to his left down the long ranks and felt proud of his regiment's precise formation. Then Lt. Col. Gardner, a Mexican War veteran, calmly ordered, "Let the men load their guns and lie down." The clatter of steel ramrods in musket and rifle barrels soon joined the other sounds on the hilltop. Once the men had finished loading, the officers gave the word to lie down in ranks.[33]

The more circumspect were only too happy to do so, but some of the boys had noticed an apple tree on the left of the regimental line, and the thought entered their heads of getting some of the fruit. Breaking ranks, they ran over to the tree and started throwing rocks and dirt clods to try to knock down apples. Seeking a surer way to get better fruit, others started climbing up the tree. Their company officers, meanwhile, were yelling themselves hoarse with orders to get back in line, but from his position placidly sitting his horse, Brimstone, near the other end of the line, Gardner quietly remarked, "I see a battery taking position over yonder; they will not need orders in a few minutes." Berrien Zettler, on the ground in the ranks of Company B, heard the remark but did not know what it meant. For one thing, he did not know what a battery was, and for another, Gardner had spoken so nonchalantly that Zettler hardly thought he could have been referring to anything very serious.

He soon found out what a battery was and just how serious. It seemed only seconds later he heard the boom of a cannon. They were blasting away regularly now, of course, but this report was different because it was immediately followed by a certain indescribable sound that even the most naive member of the regiment at once recognized as that of a shell in flight—coming toward them. "You have no idea," Company B's James Grant explained in a letter to his family the next day, "what a peculiar noise and at what a distance you can hear a ball passing through the air." The fruit-gatherers heard it too. "The boys dropped from the apple tree like shot bears," recalled Zettler, "and scrambled on hands and knees for their places in line." The sight was ludicrous, but Zettler did not feel like laughing just then. "This is unfair," his mind screamed irrationally to itself, "somebody is to blame for getting us all killed. I didn't come out here to fight this way; I wish the earth would crack open and let me drop in."[34]

With a noise something like the whickering of a frightened horse, the shell passed overhead and then exploded with a deafening report. "To say I was frightened, is tame," Zettler recalled of that moment. "The truth is, there is no word in Webster's Unabridged that describes my feelings."

"That went a hundred feet over us," quipped the unimpressed Gardner, still sitting his horse nearby with unruffled dignity. "But the next one will come closer," he added.

Another cannon boomed. "Here it comes!" warned Gardner. "Lie low!" In the bottom of one of the corn furrows nearby, Zettler did his best to obey, though he was already so flat that going lower would have meant getting underground, which he tried to do. The shell sounded much closer. "What a fool!" he thought to himself. "I'm gone! I'm dead!" It struck the earth with a thud, ten feet in front of him, then exploded with an ear-splitting crash, "throwing a wagonload of earth and clods into the air." A big chunk of dirt landed squarely between his shoulders, and, for a moment, he thought he must be dead. Somehow, through it all, Gardner still sat imperturbable on Brimstone, coolly, even leisurely, walking the magnificent white horse along the front of the regiment, "as if he wished to find out what a Yankee battery on another elevation meant by shelling us," recalled an admiring member of Company A.[35]

The third shell, traveling from the right of the line, passed clear over Companies A and B before coming to earth. This time the thunderclap report was followed by loud yells from Company C, the Macon Guards. Two of its members, John C. Howell and George F. McLeod, became the Eighth Georgia's first casualties to enemy fire.[36]

"This was the most trying part of the day," a participant later wrote. Another called it "the most tantalizing." Lying there under the shelling, wondering if the next one would be the fatal shot, and unable to do anything in return, tested the men's nerve in ways that active fighting would not do. "If there be anything which can try the courage of men it is to be in such a position as to not be able to see the enemy, and yet to know that you are being shot at," wrote R. H. Cole two days later. Vardy Sisson of Company F recalled that "never before had I embraced mother earth so affectionately," while George Barnsley contemplated a shell hole a few feet in front of him and wished that he were a ground squirrel or a 'possum so that he could climb into that hole.[37]

In their different ways, they coped with the situation. For Barnsley a few minutes under fire were sufficient to "baptize" him and relieve his fears. "I never had any more fear, keeping cool and in some dim way enjoying the sport or excitement." Lt. John Reed of Company I, Stephens Light Guards, found that action brought relief to his nerves. A brush fence ran between his company and the next company on the right. Maj. Cooper gave an order to pull down the fence. Glancing up from where he was ardently embracing the ground, Reed saw that the fence was ten or fifteen yards away and that another officer was closer than he was. He stayed where he was. So did everyone else, however, and Cooper repeated the order. Shame finally moved Reed. He jumped to his feet and, summoning a dozen of his men, quickly got the job done. "I think that with my springing up went the last of my nervousness that day," he later explained. After lying back down he could coolly study the scene in front of him and locate the battery that was firing at them, some three-quarters of a mile away, and count the seconds between the puff of smoke at a gun's muzzle and the sound of its report.[38]

Remarkably, the regimental band—Bartow's Brass Band, as it had inevitably been nicknamed—was on hand all this time, tooting away gamely on their horns. As the roar of battle rose steadily in front of them, Chief Musician G. G. Merck and his dozen or so plucky bandsmen stepped up their own volume to try to play over it. Their job was to encourage the troops, and in this their first battle, they wanted to do their part. But their brass instruments proved no match for the fifteen-hundred-pound brass tubes of the Federal battery across the way, either in noise or effectiveness, and presently the musicians gave it up.[39]

The regiment lay there for some time, and during that period any soldier who cared to take note of it could have learned something else that would have helped his nerves at least in dealing with artillery. That truth was that long-range artillery fire in the Civil War was not particularly lethal. In fact, the two men in Company C were the Eighth's only victims of a great deal of firing as they lay on the hilltop, though nearly everyone got showered with dirt at least once. At ranges like this, the cannon of the 1860s were better at jangling nerves than at shedding blood.

Rifles and muskets would do most of the killing.

I Could Hear the Bullets

After the Eighth had lain about half an hour under fire on the hilltop, Bartow galloped up to Gardner shouting, "They have your range, Colonel, charge them!" The Eighth was to advance to Matthews Hill on the right of Bee's brigade, with the Seventh Georgia in reserve behind them.[40]

"Rise, Eighth Regiment," shouted Gardner, flourishing the old cavalry saber he had carried in Mexico. In moments every man was on his feet. "Attention," came the next command. "Right face, double-quick, *march!*" Rapidly he moved the regiment up to what would be its jumping-off point for the attack. He halted them then, faced them to the front, and gave a few words of encouragement to the men as they took their courage in their two hands and steeled their minds for their first combat. "Men, I am no orator," he told them. "I shall not attempt to make you a speech. Keep your ranks, do your duty, and show you are worthy of the State from which you came! Right face, double-quick, *march!*" Once again the regiment went trotting off by the right flank.[41]

Their objective was a battery of Union artillery, and the plan for taking it, apparently Bartow's since he accompanied the regiment, was to move forward and to the right and get into a patch of woods that seemed to offer some cover on the battery's flank. From that position they could take the battery under fire and shoot down the horses and gunners preparatory to pressing home their attack.[42]

As they double-timed down the slope a shell burst cut down another soldier, as the Union artillery continued to pound them. "Gracious! How the shot came," one member of the regiment wrote afterward. Keeping as much as possible behind swells of the earth that might give some cover, they moved on across the turnpike, then up Buck Hill, where they formed up briefly in line of battle. Some thought Bartow was expecting a Union counterattack. Actually Bee met them there and, as a brigadier general and Bartow's superior, directed their deployment. Soon they were off again at the double-quick, marching by the right flank.

They passed around the back side of a patch of oak timber, using it as cover, and had only one more large open field to cross to reach the flank of the enemy battery. An old fencerow grown up in brush provided partial concealment as they moved out into the field. As they did so, several more men were hit, but this time by rifle fire from Union positions along another fencerow about three hundred yards away. Their double-quick got quicker and soon became a run. It was hardly 350 yards now to the Federal guns, almost point-blank range. As Company I, near the end of the column, swung away from the woods and out into the field, a shell knocked down three men at once. A few steps behind, another one bowled over Company K men like ninepins. Potentially far more deadly, though, was canister, the short-range ammunition that turned Civil War cannons into gigantic sawed-off shotguns able to heap battle-fields with mangled bodies. John Reed heard a load of the small iron balls rattle through the bushes just above his head. The gunners were aiming high today, and many a Georgian could be thankful for it.

Now only a short slope, sort of a gully or washout about sixty yards broad, lay between them and the dense patch of woodland that was their goal. For some reason—Reed thought it was abject foolishness—Bartow led the head of the column in front of rather than behind the sheltering fencerow for this distance, presenting a fine target to Northern rifles. The Georgians were now at a dead run. "I could hear the bullets zipping and zeeing among us like angry bees," recalled Reed, who saw two more members of his company shot down in this last rush. Others were dropping too. Up near the head of the column the men of Company A were already scrambling up the side of the washout. They were in quite a hurry and the bank was steep. A couple of times George Barnsley stepped on the heels of his file leader, Pvt. Scofield. Scofield became so irritated that in the midst of his scramble he turned his head and shouted that if Barnsley stepped on his heels again he would knock him down with the butt of his musket. To Barnsley this seemed curiously comical at a time when sore heels might soon be the least of their worries.[43]

In Company B, just a few yards farther back in the column, Hamilton Branch saw another Oglethorpe about ten feet in front of him suddenly drop to his knees and duck his head down all the way to the ground. Branch had seen soldiers trying to dodge shells that way, and thought it was a very foolish place to try to duck. "As I passed him I thought I would look and see who it was and tell him to come on as the balls were raining all around us." He looked and saw that the soldier was his friend Tom Purse. But Purse was dead.[44]

As the head of the column entered the thicket, for that is what the woods patch turned out to be, the regiment slackened pace from a run to standard quick time, and Reed was amazed to see that its ranks were still relatively neat despite the quick passage, rough ground, and casualties. In fact, their neat line was end-on to the battery and could now have been raked with canister. Yet they were on rising ground, and that saved them. A multigun volley of the deadly balls whirred by harmlessly overhead.[45]

Glancing behind him across the deadly ground they had just crossed, Reed saw Jesse Dalton, one of the members of his own Company K, hurrying after them as best he could. Reed had an acquaintance with Dalton because the lieutenant, then a lawyer, had once been counsel for the plaintiff in a slander suit brought against the private, when a private citizen. Now, however, Dalton was in much more serious trouble. He was over sixty years of age and the physical demands of the day were obviously telling on him as he wheezed along, trying to run but too exhausted to keep up with the regiment. As Reed watched, bullets kicked up spurts of dust all around the slow-moving target. To his amazement, none of the shots found their mark, and the elderly soldier stumbled on to within a few yards of the thicket. Then a bullet cut him down. A lawyer through and through, Reed could not help thinking of the legal rule "under which a personal action dies with the party."[46]

That Place of Slaughter

The thicket was what George Barnsley called an "old sedge-field, grown up in young pines and thick blackberry bushes." Getting through it was not easy. To make matters worse, an old snake-rail fence ran right through the middle of it. Leading the column, Company A ran up against the fence at an angle. Barnsley stopped and tried to tear the fence down, but the crush of men pressing blindly through the dense foliage behind literally lifted him off his feet and tossed him into a blackberry patch. Struggling up out of the tangled vines and clinging thorns, he found he could not get back into his own place in the ranks and so decided to climb the fence and catch up on the other side of it.

Clambering over the rails, he noticed another member of his company beside him trying the same approach. The other man, "Coon" Mitchell, was "short, chunky, red-faced and freckled, with hair of flaming red," a good-natured fellow much liked in the company. Simultaneously, each man threw a leg over the top of the fence and momentarily sat poised astraddle, preparing to climb down the other side. They never got the chance, however, for at that moment the rail broke under them with a loud snap, throwing both men back into the blackberry briers. Barnsley scrambled out of the brier patch a second time and again clambered up the fence. Looking behind him as he swung over the top, he saw Coon's head slowly rising out of the green, leafy blackberry patch, looking considerably dazed. Apparently he had either landed on his head or been hit in the head by the recoil of one of the ends of the broken rail. Staring around at his rapidly passing comrades, he shook himself and called out, "Boys, where was I hit?" Shouts of mirth greeted the question, and Barnsley trotted off, still laughing, to try to resume his place in the ranks.[47]

Once the regiment was fully inside the pine thicket and far enough in to suit Bartow, he had Gardner halt them and dress up their files. Then, "quivering with rage" at the punishment they had taken in crossing the fields, he shouted, "By the left flank, *march!*" Everyone in the long column now turned and strode to his left, placing the regiment once again in line of battle, two ranks deep and moving directly toward the foe. "Everybody understood that it was now our time," John Reed wrote, "and there was a wild rush to the edge of the thicket."[48]

On its fringe they halted. The scene before them was startling. There in the broad open field were the guns they had come to take, but all around the edges of the field, less than one hundred yards away and often sheltered behind rail fences, straw stacks, barn, and other outbuildings of the Matthews farm, were the battery's supports, a solid line of Union infantry. Above the blue-clad lines waved several of the flags that, until recently, these Georgians had revered. "I looked toward the enemy and for the first time since we left home I saw the once glorious Stars and Stripes floating over the enemy," Thomas Lowndes Wragg wrote to his father two days later. But the presence of those flags had a concrete as well as emotional significance for the men of the Eighth. Perhaps the nearsighted Bartow had not seen these supporting infantry from a distance. Perhaps he had thought them contemptible and easily routed. At any rate, the Eighth would now have to defeat them before it could take the guns.[49]

All along the Eighth's line, men cocked their weapons. Companies B, E, and K sighted their rifles; the others leveled their muskets, and in a long, rattling volley they squeezed off their first shots in anger. In return they received a veritable hurricane of fire. Bullets scythed through the thicket, smacking into the trunks of the young pines, spattering sap and splinters. Enough Federal shots went high to ensure a steady shower of pine twigs and blackberry leaves fluttering down on the embattled Georgians. But not all of the shots went high.

The position from which the Eighth was to fight its battle was actually only a corner of the pine thicket that protruded toward the enemy and thus narrowed the area in which the Georgians could fight. The breadth of this area was only about 110 yards. The length of the regimental line of battle, properly deployed, was nearly 200 yards. The result was that the regiment bunched up massively on the center as the flank companies crowded in to try to get what cover they could. Some could not find any position in the thicket from which they could still engage the enemy, and therefore much of Companies K and I wound up standing out in the open to fight their battle. Inside the thicket, however, men stood in some places seven or eight deep and looked for a opening to use their weapons. Some of the men in the front rank firmly believed afterward that those behind them had not always had completely clear fields of fire when discharging their pieces. Pvt. Simeon Culpepper glanced to the side just in time to see an extremely excited comrade about to fire his musket even though the gun's bayonet was nearly poking the back of another Eighth soldier standing at Culpepper's side. Hastily Culpepper reached over and jerked up the muzzle of the excited soldier's weapon, warning him to be more careful, and a look of something like sanity came back into the man's eyes.[50]

Years later, John Reed remembered that the first volley from the Federals at the rail fence opposite them "roared more loudly than any I ever heard afterwards." He thought it did remarkably little damage for the noise it made, but in the thick underbrush he could not see down the line as far as Company D. The Echols Guards had not fired yet, and Capt. Howard was dressing up his company's line. Several paces in front of the men, he faced toward them with his back to the enemy and looked sideways down the line to see that every man was in his place. They were his last sight on earth. As his men looked on in horror, a Yankee bullet struck him in the left ear, traveling through his head and exiting at the right temple. He dropped his head, "just like one who was disappointed," thought one of his soldiers. His arms shook convulsively for a moment, and then he toppled over backward like a felled tree, his sword still grasped in his right hand. James P. Martin stepped forward from his place in the ranks just about four feet away and leaned over the prostrate form. The fallen captain gazed sightlessly at the blue Virginia sky, and Martin thought "his eyes was as bright as they were when he was alive." But clearly Howard was dead. Turning back toward his gaping comrades, Martin announced the fact to the company. The air now seemed alive with the hissing and humming of bullets. A few yards down the line, "little Billie Godbey," as his comrades called him, took one in the chest and fell to the ground gasping, "Lord, have mercy on me." Lt. Hugh Malone picked up Godbey's musket and cartridge box and, as the company finally opened fire, began loading and shooting as methodically as any private in the ranks.[51]

In Company A, Pvt. Virgil Stewart was kneeling to fire when someone landed heavily on top of him. Struggling out from under, Stewart saw that it was his friend Charlie Norton; Norton had just become the first member of the Rome Light Guards to die in battle—the first of many that day. Moments later, George Stovall fell dead not five yards away. "It was a horrible sight," Stewart recalled, "men falling all around, some dying quickly and the others making the day hideous with their groans. Considering that so many were our boyhood friends, it was all the harder to bear." It was much the same for Jim Martin of Company D. "My friends fell on both sides of me," he wrote home a few days later. "You never hird such groans from the people in your life."[52]

Lt. Col. Gardner, who had dismounted before going into the thicket, did not want the regiment to halt at the edge of the tangle of pines and blackberries but to charge right on all the way to the guns, realizing that was their only hope. Yet in the sudden din he could not make himself heard by more than a few men, and presently he took a bullet in the lower leg and crumpled to the ground. Berrien Zettler stooped over the wounded lieutenant colonel and asked if there was anything he could do for him. "No," replied Gardner, "shoot on." So he did. To his left and right he could hear bullets hitting his comrades and see the men fall. In front of him, a small sapling near which he was standing seemed to be hit every few seconds, and he wondered how long it would be before he too was shot. Frantically he kept on loading and firing as fast as he could. Gardner, meanwhile, crawled to a tree stump, pulled himself up to sit on it, and went on shouting encouragement to the men.[53]

The Eighth's bandsmen were there as well. Having discarded their instruments and taken up the muskets of wounded men, they were making a much different sort of music from their usual repertoire as they blazed away along with everyone else.[54]

George Barnsley, upon catching up with his company, found that he was among the men who had been squeezed out of their places in line and were milling around behind the firing line looking for a place to fight. Like most of the others, he concluded to "go to shooting on my own private account." Finding a gap some distance from his company, he opened fire using the "Zouave drill" they had learned in many long and tiresome sessions. Firing from one knee, he would roll over onto his back to reload, holding the muzzle of the gun up above him at arm's length while the butt rested on the ground between his feet. Then he would roll back up onto one knee to get off his next shot. He lost count of how many times he fired, but he noticed that the barrel of his Model 1822 musket was getting very hot.[55]

John Reed noted with satisfaction that his men were loading and firing vigorously, but also observed that the trunks of the pines around him were showing more and more white as stray shots knocked off more and more of their bark. Again and again came cries of pain or a simple "O, Lord!" which Reed thought the most common exclamation by a man that was shot. A soldier approached him, his head and face a bloody mess, and Reed was appalled to recognize him as Jim Lewis, a member of his company. Lewis had come to tell the lieutenant goodbye before starting for the rear. As Reed walked slowly along the rear of his firing line, he stumbled over a body lying partially hidden in brush. It was Gus Daniel, another Company I man, and Reed marveled that a body could become pale and stiff so quickly.[56]

George R. "Tony" Lumpkin, junior second lieutenant of Company A, was not even supposed to have been there at all. He had been having very serious problems with his lungs for several weeks, coughing up blood. The surgeon had advised that he remain in camp, on the sick list, until his discharge could be put through. Lumpkin had agreed, but when he heard the sound of distant firing that morning, he could not resist and took his accustomed place with the Rome Light Guards. Now he was in the hottest of the fight in the pine thicket, calmly doing his duty, even when a Yankee bullet cut his sword belt in two without injuring him.

One of the Union regiments firing on them was armed with smooth-bore muskets, like most of the Eighth. These Federals, however, were using a highly effective load known as "buck and ball" in their weapons, an ordinary musket ball and three buckshot. As Joel Yarbrough of Company F finished reloading and rose to shoot, a nearly spent buckshot struck his forehead, and he toppled over unconscious. Nearby, Lt. Seymour B. Love felt one smack into his thigh. It drew no blood but hurt considerably. Moments later, Love had an even more unnerving experience when a Northern bullet shot off his cravat and scored a path along the outer layer of skin on his throat. Unharmed, save for a stinging raw streak on his throat to match the purple welt on his thigh, Love bent down, picked up and pocketed his cravat, and carried on.[57]

James Grant of Company B also encountered a low-velocity Federal projectile, whether buckshot or musket ball. Like the one that hit Love's thigh, it hurt a good deal but drew no blood, so Grant went on firing. Lying on his back reloading, he could feel his right arm brush against his friend George Butler, lying beside him and also reloading. Suddenly, Butler jerked with the impact of a bullet, then jumped up and ran for the rear, but collapsed and died within minutes. Grant continued to blaze away with his Mississippi rifle. Rolling onto his back to load again, he saw his friend Bob Baker running up. "Hello, old fellow," called Grant, "is that you?"

"Yes, Jim," replied the grinning Baker. Dropping to one knee beside him, Baker leveled his rifle for a shot, but a bullet slammed into his arm before he could pull the trigger. Blood sprayed over Grant as the stricken

Baker rolled over groaning. Doggedly, Grant kept on while several other members of the company fell around him. The boom of a rifle behind him and the breath of the passing bullet nearby convinced him, however, that he would be safer, at least from his own comrades, if he pulled back another ten or twelve feet into the thicket.[58]

The bullets whizzing and buzzing through the pine brush took some men and left their neighbors with almost capricious unpredictability. In Company B, a bullet struck Julius Ferrill squarely in the chest, and he fell dead without a word. Beside him, Lewis Lippman went down with a bullet in his ankle. Lying on the ground, he asked Tom Wragg, another Company B soldier, for a drink of water. Wragg lent him his canteen, but within the next few minutes the prostrate Lippman was hit again in the leg and a third time in the arm, while Wragg, still standing nearby methodically loading and firing, remained unscathed.[59]

Sanford Branch, who had finagled a dinner at the finest house in Bunker Hill just two weeks ago, was now bent on making good use of his Harpers Ferry rifle. As many others were doing, he left his place in the ranks and worked his way to a more advanced corner of the thicket where he could get a clear shot. He fired, reloaded, then chanced to look back toward B Company. He was just in time to see his brother John, the regimental adjutant, reel and fall. A bullet had torn through his left arm and still had force enough to drive deep into his body. Sanford dropped his gun and ran to him. Company B's Capt. Joseph J. West, a physician in civilian life, got there at about the same time and took a quick look at the wound. John, who was still conscious though in great pain, asked if there was any hope. West shook his head. "Very well, I will die like a soldier and a man," John replied firmly. With the help of several friends, Sanford carried his brother to lower and somewhat more sheltered ground to the rear of the regiment. They had hardly gotten him settled there before they had to face another crisis. The regiment was retreating. Moving John a long distance was out of the question, so Sanford urged his friends to go on and leave him with his brother. Reluctantly, they all did, save for Lewis Eastmead, who steadfastly refused to go. Sanford and John's other brother, Hamilton, did not see his brother fall and learned of his wounding only after the retreat. As Eighth Georgia men streamed past toward the rear, the three waited quietly for the Federals.[60]

Bartow had realized fairly quickly that he had made a terrible mistake bringing the Eighth into "that place of slaughter," as one of the soldiers called it. Already Union troops were closing in on both of the regiment's flanks. Indeed, by this time it was remarkable that Bartow was still unscathed, or nearly so. The only officer to ride his horse through the pine thicket—a wonder in itself—Bartow had then had the animal, a big, impressive cream-colored mare, shot out from under him. The falling beast almost landed on Capt. G. O. Dawson of Company I, and actually did crush Pvt. J. E. Lachlison, dislocating his shoulder and putting him not only out of the battle but out of the war as well. Springing clear of his falling mount, Bartow continued to do his best to inspire the troops, but it did not take an experienced warrior to see that the cause was hopeless. The bullets flew so thick that one of them snapped off the blade of Bartow's sword as he brandished it above his head. Turning to Capt. J. T. Lewis of Company F, Bartow shouted, "We must get these men out of here." Yet though he several times gave the order to withdraw, the smoke, noise, and underbrush, and the fact that the regiment was already losing its cohesion, made it almost impossible to convey that order to the men. Most of them had to figure it out on their own.[61]

George Barnsley, the young Rome physician who had once felt disgusted at the idea of "men shooting each other about questions" he thought could be negotiated, was still sturdily loading and firing. As he lay on his back just completing the loading process yet again, a bullet buzzed past his head, and he had the chilling realization that someone had tried to kill him personally. Swinging up into firing position with his loaded musket, he saw a large Federal who had stepped out in front of the rest of his unit, apparently to get a better shot—at Barnsley. Without hesitation, Barnsley brought up his gun and leveled his sights on a bright brass button halfway down the man's blue uniform coat. He squeezed the trigger, the musket bucked and belched white smoke, and as the wind spun the smoke aside, he could see that the Yankee had fallen and was lying very still. It was not a bad shot for an old Model 1822 smoothbore, and Barnsley was elated at having been shot at and missed and then felled his assailant. Rolling back over to load again, he waved his hat and shouted, "Boys, I got one anyway." No one answered. He looked around and was appalled to see that he was all alone. He lost no more time in plunging into the pine brush after his comrades.[62]

The Federal who had shot at Barnsley and paid for it with his life was part of a Union regiment that was pressing in close on the Eighth's right flank. Berrien Zettler was also near that end of the line. Sensing a commotion on his right, he looked that way and "saw a line of Federal soldiers coming through the thick undergrowth not more than fifty steps distant." The Federals loosed a volley right down the line of the Eighth, and one of the bullets in that volley struck the stock of Zettler's Mississippi rifle, burning the little finger of his right hand, and then passed so close in front of his chest he thought he could feel it. Looking around, he saw that all the other Confederates around him seemed to be wounded or dead, and he decided it might be time to go. "I had no order to retreat," he explained, "but I felt that was the thing to do." With the Yankees closing in, he plunged into the thicket behind him.[63]

Some members of Company A had an even more disconcerting experience with the Union force that was crushing the regiment's right flank. Virgil Stewart was another of the many who never got the word to retreat. Like Zettler, he found himself suddenly alone with the dead and wounded and scrambled back into the heart of the thicket as quickly as he could. He had not gone far when he met Company A's first sergeant, Jim Tom Moore, but Moore had no idea where the rest of the company had gotten to. The two men stood amid the pine and blackberry brush in some perplexity until they heard big, strapping Ike Dankle sing out, "Rally, Rome Light Guards!" Pushing through the brush to where they heard the sound, Stewart and Moore were relieved to see Dankle and about a dozen more of their comrades of Company A. Dankle was the son of a real Pennsylvania Dutchman, a blacksmith, and a hulking muscular fellow over six feet tall—at a time when the average man hardly reached five feet, seven inches.[64]

Together the little knot of soldiers began working their way back through the thicket with Dankle in the lead. Just as the big blacksmith burst out of an especially dense clump of bushes he ran head-on into the color-bearer of a Union regiment that was moving in the opposite direction in as close an approximation of line-of-battle as could be maintained in this tangle of growth. Never at a loss, Dankle knocked down the color-bearer with his fist, grabbed the flag, turned, and made off. The Federals were not to be so easily robbed, however, and the color guard surged after the fleeing blacksmith. All around that area of the thicket men convulsively jerked up their rifles and muskets and blazed away at each other—or at the bushes in which they presumed each other to be lurking. As some of the boys of the Eighth later told the story, the Yankees were laughing so hard at Dankle's sudden exploit that they could not shoot straight. Others theorized that the Federals must have greatly overestimated the number of Confederates in the bushes, not realizing they were up against fewer than twenty men. At any rate, when the smoke had cleared, the Yankees had their flag back and had Dankle too, a prisoner, but the rest of the Company A men made their escape and hurried off to rejoin the regiment as best they could.[65]

Not all the encounters in the pine thicket were bloodless. The Sixty-ninth New York, most famous of the North's Irish regiments, was part of the force bearing down on the Eighth's right flank. Spotting some Rebels fleeing ahead of him on the fringe of the pine thicket, the Sixty-ninth's Lt. Col. Haggerty spurred his horse forward in pursuit. He came suddenly upon Pvt. Peter Brennan, an Irishman of the Eighth's I Company, stooping over the body of a fallen comrade and all but invisible among the scrub growth. Haggerty demanded his surrender, but at point-blank range Brennan leveled his musket and shot the Federal officer out of the saddle, dead on the spot. Charles Godfrey of Company B (the companies were hopelessly mixed by this time) dashed over and grabbed Haggerty's revolver before the two Georgians made off into the bushes. The Sixty-ninth blasted a volley at them and the other scattering gray-clad figures they could see on this side of the thicket, and at least some of the Georgians fired back.[66]

At the opposite end of the Eighth's firing line, Lt. Reed thought the regiment was holding its own. The Union regiment that had been applying pressure to the left flank had drawn back somewhat, and Reed even thought hopefully that the fire from the opposing fence line might be slacking off a little. Then one of his soldiers motioned him to look to either side of the platoon under his immediate command. "Nearly everybody was going back at about quick time," Reed recalled. Naturally he and his men would have to go too, though they were reluctant and did not feel whipped. Slowly, pausing to fire whenever the opportunity offered, they fell back toward the rest of the regiment.[67]

The disorganization of the regiment that had begun with the advance through the thicket, the crowding into too narrow a front, and the high casualties it had suffered was now completed by the trip back through the thicket. For practical purposes, the Eighth Georgia temporarily ceased to exist as a regiment-sized fighting formation. For one thing, it had left nearly half its men lying on the ground dead or wounded on the far edge of the thicket. For another, the men became scattered and scrambled as they fell back through the woods and could not—or sometimes would not—find their places in the ranks again. Many could not even find the regiment, and a handful attached themselves to other regiments and fought on for the remainder of the day. Others succeeded in rejoining what was left of the Eighth.

We Have Whipped 'Em

Elsewhere in the thicket, various clumps of men tried to join up into organized units. Lt. Hamilton Couper of Company B gathered a group of about fifty men from several companies with no officers and was wondering what to do with them when several more officers came up. A hasty conference of officers soon determined that it would be impossible to form the men into line here, but that they should fall back to the next open space and form up there. With that they pushed on into the brush.[68]

As John Reed, leading his platoon, reached the fence that divided the pine thicket from the wheat field behind it, he found Bartow, dismounted, dashing about trying to get the men of the Eighth to regroup and form a line. "He was greatly excited," Reed recalled, "and he implored his men to rally." He had just had the color-bearer plant the regimental colors near the fence when he saw Reed and his group come out of the bushes, and Reed thought he looked pleased to see them still keeping a semblance of military order. Quickly Reed asked where he wanted the line formed, and Bartow pointed out a little corridor of open space running off diagonally into the pine thicket. "Just there," he directed. Reed, who still did not realize that orders had been given to fall back from the opposite side of the thicket, was sick at heart with the thought that the regiment had disgraced itself. He did his best to get the men into the new position.

Meanwhile, Bartow noticed a large swarm of Eighth survivors already making off to the rear across the wheat field. "Who is the officer that is leading off these men?" he raged. No officer was, of course, but Lt. Jake Phinizy of Company K was doing his best to get them to stop and come back. Reed stood at the fence and shouted for the men to come back, calling by name every one he could recognize. A few returned; by one account Bartow managed to get a total of eighty-four men back into line, though who had time to count at this juncture is unknown. The survivors of Company G later claimed that with sixteen men they were the best-represented company in this rally. At any rate it did not last long. Bartow at last saw that the attempt was useless and gave the order to continue the retreat. All semblance of organization vanished, and the group became a large flock of survivors headed for the rear and looking for a place to regroup. Apparently about that time Bartow himself, having found another horse, rode off to the rear to bring up the Seventh Georgia, the only other regiment of his brigade on the field.[69]

With Gardner's wounding, command of the regiment fell to Maj. Thomas L. Cooper. Under his orders, the color-bearer, Pvt. William Charles "Charley" Daniels, picked up the colors and marched off in the direction from which the regiment had come in its advance. Daniels was the Eighth's second color-bearer that day, after Company E's Sgt. Frank Lathrop, who lay dead back in the pine thicket. Impossible as it may have seemed, less than twenty minutes had passed since the Eighth Georgia, in neat column of twos, had double-timed forward across those fields.

For the men of the Eighth, the whole duty of the soldier now consisted of staying with the colors. The number of those who did so seems to have varied almost constantly. The group of about fifty that Lt. James Cooper rounded up in the thicket apparently emerged and joined the colors, but quite a few of its members must have drifted off on their own. Berrien Zettler emerged from the pine thicket about this time. He spotted "a body of men crowding around a flag, but moving along quite rapidly," and ran to catch up with them. When he got close enough to recognize the flag, he was overjoyed almost to the point of tears to see that it was his own Eighth Georgia. Hurrying on, he finally overtook them, but by that time an overwhelming weariness had set in. "I could scarcely put one foot in front of the other," he recalled. Unable to keep up, he dropped down into a shallow gully to catch his breath. There he lay, gasping, while above him the air buzzed with passing bullets so that he thought that if he raised his hand it would surely be struck.[70]

As the remnant of the regiment marched out, a nearby regiment of Virginians cheered them for their courage in the fight. A bit farther on, however, they got a much different reception from their comrades in arms. In what was one of an extraordinary number of cases of mistaken identity this day, other Confederate forces mistook the retreating Eighth Georgia for an advancing Union regiment and poured deadly volleys into it. The Seventh Georgia was one of the culprits in this mishap, along with the South Carolinians of Hampton's Legion and, probably, the Zouaves of the First Louisiana Battalion, the famous "Tigers." Surviving members of the Eighth left no record as to who, if anyone, was hit by these volleys, but did remember them as "galling."[71]

The cluster of men around the flag reached Young's Branch, a tiny and very muddy stream they had crossed in their advance. "The men leaped into the water like thirsty oxen," Reed later wrote. Another soldier called it drinking "a mouthful of mud" but said he was too thirsty to care. While they knelt, lay, or squatted on the banks and gulped down the brown liquid, up rode a finely uniformed officer who exclaimed, "Why, the Georgians are running while the South Carolinians are still fighting." The color-bearer, Daniels, and several others cursed him roundly and threatened to shoot him. As other members of the regiment came running up shouting wildly, the officer said with a dignified bearing, "Oh, I must admit that you are ready enough to fight; I withdraw the words that I should not have used." With that he rode away. Only several days later did the men realize that the officer with whom they had spoken at Young's Branch was Brig. Gen. Barnard Bee, commanding on that part of the field until Johnston and Beauregard arrived personally.[72]

In fact, none of Bee's troops were faring particularly well. The defensive stand by his own, Bartow's, and Evans's brigades the Federals had crushed with heavy casualties. The Eighth, on the right of the Confederate assault, had taken the heaviest punishment, but Bee's whole force was in desperate trouble. It was near noon, and Union victory seemed near. Beauregard and Johnston arrived at the scene of action and went to work rallying the shattered regiments and bringing up others so as to form a new line of resistance on Henry Hill and prevent the entire Confederate army from being rolled up and destroyed.

Bartow got the Seventh Georgia up to a position near the Warrenton Turnpike in the vicinity of the Robinson House and tried hard to get the remnant of the Eighth to rally beside them. They did so, firing several volleys at the advancing Federals. Pvt. Anderson Orr of Company F had just fired his musket and was kneeling, reloading, when a bullet tore through his throat. As blood gushed from the wound, his brother George Orr leaped to his side, but he had time only to take the dying man's hand and exchange a last look before he was gone. Shortly the line was forced backward again, and what was left of the Eighth had to fall back with the rest.[73]

Other members of the Eighth were scattered about the field far from the little group that clustered around the retreating colors, and each one of them had his own battle to fight that afternoon. As George Barnsley had made his way back through the pine thicket in the wake of the rest of the regiment, he heard his friend Jett Howard calling for help. Indeed, at that point the thicket was full of badly wounded men groaning and calling out for help, but Barnsley knew Howard and went to see what he needed. He found him, unwounded, bending over the fallen Lt. Col. Gardner. Gardner's men had carried him a few yards to the rear after he was wounded, but now it would be necessary to get him away entirely before the Yankees came up. That was what Howard needed help with. Horace Heidt, of Company B, was also there, and Jim Grant, another Company B man, soon came along and joined the group. Grant had left the thicket but been sent back by Company A's Capt. Magruder, himself bleeding from a buckshot wound in the arm, to find and help the lieutenant colonel. Soon the four of them prepared to move Gardner, who insisted that they leave him and join the colors. Ignoring his orders, the four privates placed Barnsley's musket under the lieutenant colonel as a sort of seat, with Barnsley holding one end and Howard the other. Grant carefully held Gardner's wounded leg to prevent jarring, and Heidt supported his back and upper body.

Thus they set off, but it was rough going. Bullets still whizzed around them, the ground was rugged and sometimes steep, and Gardner was in a great deal of pain, despite all they tried to do to minimize movement and bumping of his injured leg. Worse, they could not keep up with the rapidly retiring Eighth, and the Yankees were advancing equally rapidly behind them. After covering about a quarter of a mile, they dodged into a gully, where they would be safe from the constant gunfire, and set Gardner down. Barnsley took his musket out from under the lieutenant colonel, silently looked at it, and blanched. The musket was loaded and cocked. Turning a bit so the others could not see him, Barnsley carefully uncocked the hammer. He thought it best not to mention the fact to Jett Howard, who had been carrying the business end of the weapon.

The next problem was what to do about the lieutenant colonel. Grant made it clear that he would not leave him, but Gardner urged them all to go on and rejoin the regiment. The matter weighed all the more heavily since apparently all five men had come to believe Confederate propaganda about what sort of people the Yankees were. They were convinced that when the bluecoats arrived they would bayonet all five of them without ceremony. Barnsley and Howard took the lieutenant colonel's urgings as an order and left. Grant and Heidt, however, remained unwilling to leave their commander thus to the Yankees and determined to stay with him. Grant told the colonel that he would take the one gun they had with them—Barnsley had taken his loaded musket—load it, "and fight it out, that we might as well kill as many as possible." Gardner, however, forestalled him. "No," he countered, "if we keep quiet we might not be observed." For a time it worked, but then a Union regiment advanced to within twenty feet of where they lay. A soldier saw them and raised his rifle. Waving a white handkerchief on the end of a ramrod, Grant called out, "We surrender."[74]

Meanwhile Barnsley and Howard were trying to rejoin the regiment. They were both in a daze of weariness and emotional letdown and hardly knew what they were doing. "The fact was," Barnsley explained, "I had lost all consciousness of danger." Together the two plodded doggedly across an open field swept with gunfire. As they were crossing a fence, Howard was hit and toppled over. Barnsley offered to stay with him, but Howard insisted he go on. When Barnsley finally rejoined the colors, what was left of the regiment was preparing for another stand. A young man of Company B, Chisholm, was loudly calling on the men to rally. Barnsley went up and shook hands with him, and, after the fashion of those times, they swore to each other that they would die by their banner. "As I recollect," Barnsley later wrote, "it seems to me that I woke up or got enthusiastic." He and the other members clustered around the colors, which seemed the properly heroic thing to do, but it also drew an uncomfortable amount of enemy fire. They decided to lie down.

Presently a young man lying near Barnsley in the vicinity of the colors commented that "the balls were getting too frequent for comfort." Getting up, he moved down the line a bit and lay down again in a position farther away from the flag—and was promptly hit by enemy fire. "Put down that flag," yelled some of the boys, but Pvt. Daniel was adamant. "They told me to hold it up when they gave it to me," he replied, "and I'll do it." "Put down that flag," came renewed shouts, "They'll know we are here." "That's what we want," replied the steadfast Daniel and kept the flag flying. He paid the price for his courage, though, when he suffered a leg wound some minutes later. Daniel escaped amputation, but the lingering effects of the wound would leave him unfit for future military service.[75]

Eventually someone, probably Beauregard, gave Maj. Cooper orders to withdraw the regiment behind the lines to rest and regroup. As they marched off the field they happened to pass Gen. Beauregard, sitting his horse and watching the progress of the battle. Seeing them, Beauregard raised his hat and called out, "I salute the gallant Eighth Georgia Regiment," or "I salute the Eighth Georgia Regiment with my hat off," or one of several other versions, depending on whose account one chooses to believe. Whatever his exact words, it was a very proud moment for the men who heard it.[76]

John Reed with his little squad was reluctant to abandon the fight and thought of getting back into action if they could just get another drink of water first, for the march and the hot day and their combat had all combined to produce a persistent and overpowering thirst. Once they had gotten water, however, Reed could see little opportunity to engage in the struggle, and, finally overcome by weariness, he sank down on a large rock and there sat as in a daze watching as the battle was played out before him. Oblivious of the bullets and shells that still whickered and buzzed over and around him, he watched as the Confederate line stabilized on the slope of Henry Hill, anchored by a steady Virginia brigade under the command of Brig. Gen. Jackson, who had also come over from the Shenandoah Valley, and that day earned the nickname "Stonewall."[77]

Gen. Bee fell in the thickest of the fight, and Bartow was there as well, a frenzy of enthusiasm, leading regiments forward, rallying troops, waving the colors of the Seventh Georgia. He had just handed the flag back to the Seventh's color-bearer when a bullet struck him in the left chest and he toppled from his horse. Men gathered around him, and he gasped, "Boys, they have killed me, but *never* give up the field." Some remembered the words slightly differently, but the gist was the same. Within a few minutes, the ambitious lawyer, politician, and amateur soldier from Savannah was dead.[78]

Back behind the lines, George Barnsley was one of hundreds of soldiers from several more or less similarly torn-up regiments who were resting near a cool brook. Unaware of what was going on at the front, they were startled to hear an officer announcing that Confederate cavalry had finally driven the enemy back and that they must all rally and go forward again, charge the enemy, and win the day. "We were candidly told that we had to win the fight or die," he recalled. Eagerly he and about five hundred others jumped up and got into line, a sort of composite ad hoc battalion from several different states. Barnsley had been terribly hungry and tired, but all sense of that was gone now. "It was one of the proudest moments of my life. . . . It seemed to me as I marched forward that I was treading on air—I was so proud and delighted to die for my country."[79]

Onward they marched, back the whole long way they had come in retreat, a mile, more than a mile, and no Union soldier did they see—at least none with a weapon in his hands. The Yankees were in retreat! The day was won! A loud cheer went up from the Confederate troops on Henry Hill and spread along the lines in a prolonged chorus of yells. John Reed always thought that moment was the birth of the Rebel Yell. Confederate officers literally jumped up and down in their excitement, including a gray-haired fellow who kept clapping his hands and repeating over and over, "We have whipped 'em! We have whipped 'em!"[80]

For George Barnsley and the men with him in the stragglers' battalion the reality finally dawned when they reached the hastily abandoned Union camps and found campfires with kettles over them and in the kettles—O joy! O rapture!—boiling ham. Barnsley fished out a piece and was about to eat it when his comrades cried out that it might be poisoned. He paused, considered the odds, and wolfed down the ham voraciously. The other men watched, decided that whatever poison the

diabolical Yankees had put in their ham certainly did not take effect inside the first minute, and went for the ham themselves. In the end,
Barnsley complained, he got only a very small piece. The brave battle
line that had been about to march out to victory or death now disintegrated, and the men drifted off to find their own regiments.[81]

The Confederate victory brought a sudden and agreeable change of
status for most of those members of the Eighth who had been taken
prisoner during the course of the day. Jim Grant had already been agree-
ably surprised when the Federals who captured him, Lt. Col. Gardner,
and Horace Heidt, did not bayonet them but instead treated them kindly
and saw that Gardner got medical attention right along with the Union
wounded. "They all treated us honorably and as prisoners of war," Grant
wrote the next day, "Never was I more surprised; the physicians exam-
ined the Colonel's leg, had a litter brought for him, gave us water, and in
all respects treated us with every kindness." Other Confederate wounded
lying nearby "received the same kind attentions," while still others, taken
on other parts of the field, had an equally enlightening experience.[82]

When Joel Yarbrough of Company F first woke up after losing consciousness in the midst of the fight in the pine thicket, three Union doc-
tors were examining the wound in his forehead made by the nearly
spent buckshot. "We have got your Colonel," they informed him, and
after treating his wound, took him to where Gardner and the other
Eighth Georgia men were.[83]

Several unwounded Confederates, led by Charles M. Harper of Company E, the Miller Rifles, succeeded in getting the drop on their Union
captors and taking them prisoner in turn. The trusting Northerners had
neglected to relieve Harper and his fellow prisoners of their weapons.[84]

When the Union army retreated it simply left behind many of the
wounded Confederate prisoners, and some who were not wounded. At
the field hospital where Lt. Col. Gardner, Yarbrough, and the others lay,
Grant and Heidt had some anxious moments trying to make sure their
building was not taken under fire by Confederate artillery during the
Union retreat. The shells were getting pretty close, and Gardner ordered
them to raise a white flag. That was not such a straightforward matter
under the circumstances. All their handkerchiefs were far too badly
soiled, mostly with blood, to have any chance of passing for white.
Grant tried tying a piece of an undergarment to a length of bedpost and

sticking that out a window, but to no avail. The incoming rounds were landing closer still. Next they went out in the yard, Heidt boosted Grant up onto the roof of an adjoining building, and he tied his white shirt to its chimney. While he was doing so a cannon ball passed close—he thought not more than three feet—above him. "I was rather scared," he laconically explained. Clambering down off the roof, he found yet another piece of more or less white cloth and erected it as a flag out in the yard. That seemed to do the job, and the firing ceased. Grant and Heidt spent the rest of the day helping the wounded of both sides there at the abandoned Union field hospital and that evening got an ambulance to carry Gardner back to the camp of the Eighth Georgia.[85]

What an Insignificant Creature One Man Is

As the retreating Northern army, briefly pursued by a few Confederate cavalry, receded into the distance, a tall, thin, ramrod-straight man galloped onto the battlefield from the direction of Manassas Junction looking commanding but somehow incongruous in a suit of plain gray civilian clothes. President Davis had arrived, having come up that day by train from Richmond, and was disappointed at having missed the fight. The troops saw him riding across the field and cheered loudly.[86]

While president and generals surveyed the field and discussed what to do next, the first thought in the minds of most of the common soldiers, including those of the Eighth Georgia, was to see what had become of their fallen comrades and try to help the ones who were still alive. Ed Hull of Company C, the Macon Guards, found himself particularly well placed to begin this task as soon as the fighting ended. During the desperate fight in the pine thicket, a shell had burst near him, and one of its fragments had torn off his cartridge box and belt without actually putting a wound on his body. The concussion of the shell, however, knocked him out cold, and when he came around he was surrounded by Federals. A captain asked if he was wounded. "I think not," he replied, but when he tried to get up he found he could not move. The captain told him to lie still until the ambulances arrived to carry him off. As the fortunes of the day developed, the Federals retreated, and Hull was left a free man again. By this time he found that the effects of the shell burst were wearing off and that he was once again able to move about. Wounded men were all around him, moaning and crying for help, and Hull began to do what he could.[87]

Aside from pain—and sometimes, at least initially, instead of pain— the most intense feeling experienced by wounded soldiers in the Civil War was an overpowering thirst. Even the unwounded grew parched from the heat, exertion, and stress, and, George Barnsley thought, from tearing open paper cartridges with their teeth as part of the loading process. Wounded men had the additional factor of massive loss of blood to compound their thirst, and of course most of them were unable to fetch drink for themselves. Thus cries for water were among the most frequent from a field or thicket full of badly wounded men.[88]

So Hull, though still quite shaky himself, began going back and forth between the pine thicket and a nearby stream, carrying canteens full of water to the wounded men. He kept it up all the rest of the day until nightfall. As he was staggering along under a load of water-filled canteens, a man on horseback approached and asked for a drink.

"No," Hull replied flatly, "I am carrying this water to those who cannot walk. You can walk, and you may go to the branch and help yourself." With that he was about to turn away when someone nearby spoke up and told him he was speaking to President Davis. Much taken aback, Hull insisted that the president take a drink from Hull's own canteen.

After Davis had ridden on, Hull completed his errand and then tramped back down to the stream with a load of empty canteens. There sitting beside the stream he found Capt. John Frederick Cooper (not to be confused with his older brother Maj. Thomas L. Cooper or with Lt. James H. Cooper, of Company B; the Eighth had its share of commissioned Coopers) of Company H, the Floyd Infantry. The twenty-six-year-old commander of the first of the Rome companies to get its orders for Richmond had been shot in the knee, not too seriously he thought, and was pouring creek water over the wound to cool and wash it. Lt. Hull offered to examine the wound, and Cooper consented. Using his pocket knife, Hull enlarged the hole in Cooper's trouser leg through which the bullet had entered until the knee was fully exposed. The wound looked more serious than the captain had seemed to think, as the knee appeared to be shattered. There was little Hull could do about it now, though, except make Cooper as comfortable as possible until others arrived who could help get him to a surgeon.[89]

George Barnsley, after easing his hunger with a chunk of Yankee ham, borrowed a horse from an acquaintance who was adjutant in another regiment and did not seem to need the animal just then. Thus mounted, he rode for the pine thicket at the best pace the very tired horse could manage. He found other unwounded comrades had got there before him, and together they did their best to help their wounded friends. Besides bringing water to the injured, Barnsley visited a nearby house to get some honey and rifled the haversacks of fallen Federals for hardtack, which he then distributed to the wounded. He found his friend S. J. McDonald, of Company B, badly hit with a bullet in his thigh and another that had lodged in his abdomen after striking his arm. Barnsley and the others made McDonald as comfortable as they could. He also found the dead Federal whom he had shot just before fleeing the pine thicket. "I was sorry then and afterward," Barnsley later wrote, "but consoled myself from the fact that he almost hit me, and he shot first."[90]

John Reed got back to the pine thicket as soon as he could. One of the first sights he saw in it appalled him. There, lying on his back just on the edge of the pine thicket, was "the handsomest man in our company," Pvt. Thad Howell. "A bullet had struck the top of his forehead, and the brains were oozing out." To complete the horror of the situation, Howell's heels kept up a constant drumming against the ground, though the dying soldier remained completely unconscious. Reed had to shake off the shock of the sight, for there were plenty of others who still needed his help. He helped some into ambulances, though those vehicles were far too few for the number of wounded. He carried water to those that remained. "Some drank as though they would burst," Reed recalled, but he felt certain the copious amounts of water would do no harm. One wounded soldier was so desperate for water that as Reed started off to refill his canteen for him a second time, the soldier begged him to swear that he really would. At last every soldier whom Reed could find in and around the pine thicket seemed to have gotten all the water he wanted, but for Reed there was no rest.

Darkness fell. The wounded men's teeth began to chatter convulsively. Reed gathered blankets wherever he could, often from dead Federals, and did his best to keep the men warm. Hour by hour the men's friends straggled into the thicket, looking for their comrades. Around midnight it started to rain—hard—but by that time the wounded had other care-takers and Reed felt he could return to camp. Taking an oilcloth from another dead Yankee, he walked back to the camp of the Eighth, lay down in the mud, and slept soundly.[91]

Elsewhere that evening, members of the Eighth thought over the events of the day and tried to grasp the meaning of the horror they had seen. To young George Whitefield Stevens, of Company B, it all spoke very clearly. The son of devout Methodist parents, "Whit" Stevens had not yet embraced his parents' faith. Now, however, reflecting on the carnage all around him that day and how so many had been struck down around him, he "felt that the Almighty had been very merciful to protect my unworthy life." A little after sunset he sought out a place where he could be alone and found it in an open and airy grove of mature pine trees. There, kneeling on the grass, he thanked God for sparing him in the battle he had just been through, and, as he later explained, "I gave him my word that I would try and serve him as long as I lived."[92]

That night was a very long one for regimental surgeon Homer Virgil Milton Miller and the others who were in the grove of willows where Miller had established the regimental hospital, near a stream, that evening. Chief Musician Merck and his bandsmen, incredibly unscathed after their participation in the battle, were there serving as orderlies. For all of them, especially the wounded, it was a night of horrors. Civil War medicine was still relatively primitive, knew nothing of antisepsis, and could often do little for the wounded, particularly if their wounds were in the head or torso. Surgeons could probe for bullets with long steel instruments and perhaps remove them if found, but even the most skillful surgeons could also inadvertently finish off a wounded patient in this way, doing with their probes what the enemy had failed to accomplish with his bullet. Yet in all fairness, the task these surgeons faced was awful beyond belief. A relatively low-velocity .58- or .69-caliber soft lead slug made a ghastly wound, particularly if it struck bone. The bone would shatter, driving splinters into the surrounding flesh, and the wound would also be contaminated by bits of clothing the bullet carried into it. Such a wound had a very low probability of healing properly and a very high one of becoming infected

with gangrene, blood poisoning, or any number of other highly efficient killers. Civil War medicine knew only one remedy for that type
of wound, and it explains why the bone saw was the most prominent
piece of equipment in the Civil War surgeon's tool kit. The surgeon
would amputate the limb somewhere above the devastating wound.
The resulting scenes in hundreds of field hospitals were indescribably
grisly.

"All night long Miller and his assistants amputated arms and legs, and
probed for balls, and used bandages and splints and other appliances," a
soldier recalled, "and as fast as one man was fixed up he was taken away
and the doctor said 'Next!' like in a barber shop." The fortitude of the
soldiers was amazing. Jett Howard limped up on his own, suffering from
the wound that had felled him when he and George Barnsley were making their way back to the regiment. "What's the matter with you, Jett?"
asked the doctor. Howard showed Miller where a bullet had struck him
in the hip. Quickly Miller poked a probe into the wound and pulled it
out again, found where the ball was lodged farther back in the side of
Howard's hip, grabbed his knife, made a quick incision, and pulled the
bullet out. "Here's your diploma, Jett," Miller said, handing him the bullet. "Next!" Howard hobbled off. God had been merciful to him; the
bullet had glanced along the side of his hipbone instead of striking and
shattering it.[93]

In worse condition was Company H's Capt. J. Frederick Cooper, who
also took his turn on Miller's table that night. Miller took one look at
the smashed knee that Lt. Hull had looked at down by the creek that
evening and knew what had to be done. "Fred," he said, reaching for his
knife and saw, "this leg must come off immediately."

"Stop, doctor," gasped Cooper. "Can't you save my leg?"

"No, it is impossible," Miller replied. "It must come off, I tell you."

"Doctor, is there a possible chance for me to save this leg?"

"Perhaps," the surgeon said thoughtfully, "one chance in a hundred,
but I warn you now that if it is not speedily cut off you will be a dead
man in two weeks."

"Doctor," the captain replied without hesitation, "I will take that
chance."

"Next!" shouted Miller, and orderlies lifted another shattered body
onto the table as other strong hands lifted Cooper off. Miller's predic-

tion proved false, though not by much. Cooper lived almost another seven weeks and died September 9.[94]

Berrien Zettler stood by that evening watching Dr. Miller's proceedings in the willow grove, already in full swing well before sundown. He watched surgeons sawing off arms and legs while a squad of soldiers nearby buried those who had died before they could receive such medical attention as the surgeons could offer. Then Zettler walked on to the infamous pine thicket, drawn like so many of his comrades to the ground where they had fought so desperately for fifteen minutes that morning. He walked among the dead and saw the bullet-scarred saplings—one not more than eight inches in diameter had received over twenty balls—and wondered again how he or any of his comrades had escaped. "Surely, surely," he thought, "there will never be another battle." Like George Barnsley before leaving Rome, he thought it was barbarous for men to try to settle their disputes in this gruesome and destructive manner. Surely, now that there had been a battle, all the world should know what *he*, Berrien M. Zettler, now knew, and such a thing could never be again. Yet deep down he knew that it *would* happen again, and he would be in it when it did. "I have often thought that one on a ship going down at sea must have the most helpless feeling possible," he reflected years later, "but I think a battle not only makes one feel perfectly helpless, but also impresses on him as nothing else can what an insignificant creature in an army one man is. I believe, too, no soldier in the ranks ever wanted to go into a second battle. Of course he was willing to go, but only as a duty that pride and honor would not let him openly avoid."[95]

CHAPTER FOUR

All Quiet Along the Potomac

I Have Missed It

EORGE Barnsley awoke to find himself lying several inches deep in a fast-flowing muddy stream. It was early morning, Monday, July 22, 1861. It had been nearly 3:00 A.M. when he had finally found his way to camp after spending half the night trying to help the wounded. Almost asleep on his feet, he had staggered to the nearest open spot he could find in the inky darkness of the encampment. A heavy overcast had moved in, and neither moon nor star was to be seen. The spot he found happened to be the bottom of a shallow but very muddy gully, but he lay down, pillowed his head on his knapsack, and knew no more. As he lay there sleeping the sleep of utter exhaustion, the rain came.

Civil War soldiers would later say that the smoke, or maybe the noise, of a great battle actually caused heavy rain to come within the next day or two. Certainly a great many of the war's major battles, though by no means all, were indeed followed by downpours. Such, at any rate, was the case with the battle of July 21, 1861, which Northerners were already calling the Battle of Bull Run and Southerners would call Manassas, though for now Barnsley and his comrades thought it should be called the Battle of Stone Bridge, for the span that carried the Warrenton Turnpike over Bull Run near the heavily contested Confederate left. The rain gushed down in torrents during the small hours of the 22nd, and the roiling brown run-off water gurgled around the slumbering Barnsley, who in his exhaustion was oblivious both to it and the heavy downpour that had already soaked him to the skin.

It was when the muddy water started to splash into his mouth sometime after daybreak that he finally awoke. Sitting up and taking stock of his condition, Barnsley had to admit, "I was a fine sight for a tea party." But there was consolation to be found in the fact that all of his comrades of the once nattily uniformed Rome Light Guards looked more or less as bad as he did. Relieved that the ordeal of the day before was over and happy to be alive and able to look up and see the sky, even if rain was falling from it, they looked at each other in their mud-soaked finery and laughed heartily. Once the rain stopped, Barnsley decided that since his entire (admittedly rather limited) wardrobe was soaked and filthy, he would wash it and himself at the same time. Accordingly he plunged into the waters of Bull Run clothes and all and spent a good deal of time sitting in the creek, washing off the grime and perhaps some of the horror of the preceding twenty-four hours. Whether the sluggish and not particularly clear waters of Bull Run actually made him or his clothes any cleaner may be open to question, but he emerged after some time, satisfied with the results, and, as he put it, "hung myself out to dry."[1]

Like Barnsley and his comrades in Company A, the rest of the Eighth's unwounded survivors were euphoric at having passed through the battle unscathed. "You never saw boys as glad to see one another in your life," James Martin wrote in a letter home a few days later. Grinning all over their faces, they shook hands with each other again and again, laughing and saying things like "Old fellow, I thought you was gone," and assuring each other that they were indeed still alive.[2]

At the same time, their delirium was tempered by the memory of those they had lost the day before. All of them missed Bartow, who had been almost like a second father to the mostly very young men in the regiment, especially to his "Beardless Boys" in the Oglethorpe Light Infantry. Along with their common bereavement, each of them had sad memories of individual friends whom they would see no more on earth. Hamilton Branch, so recently the social lion of Winchester, had lost one brother killed and another taken prisoner. Men of Company D remembered "little Billie Godbey" and their captain, C. W. Howard, with whom they had gathered for prayer just twenty-four hours before. Over in Company F, George Orr and the wounded Joel Yarbrough remembered George's brother Anderson, and how he had been a devout Christian and had often led religious meetings in the company. Things like that were especially comforting to think of at times like this, for the realization that this earthly life was not the end of their human existence, that through the merits of Jesus Christ they could be reunited with their loved ones in heaven someday, was one of the most important factors that helped Civil War soldiers cope with the horrors of that conflict.[3]

These horrors, the enormity of it beyond all their previous experience, the excitement, and the lack of solid factual information all fed a tendency for the creation of outlandish rumors that bounced and reverberated their way through the army, accepted by the men as solid fact. The most exaggerated of such rumors tended to be those that described the force against which they had fought and the amount of damage they had done to it. The line they assaulted from the pine thicket they pegged at 6,000 or more—too high by a factor of at least four. Total Union numbers on the field they estimated all the way from the true figure of 35,000 men, comparable to the Confederate force, up to 60,000 or more. Federal casualties had been 8,000 killed and wounded, or so the scuttlebutt said, while the Southerners had lost only about 2,000 or perhaps 3,000. Best of all, according to the rumors that the boys avidly repeated in their letters home, the Confederate army had captured sixty-one or sixty-two pieces of Union artillery, not only a massive boon to the industrially deficient South, but also proof positive that the Union army was soundly whipped.[4]

The true figures were considerably more modest. Union losses had come to 470 killed, 1,071 wounded, and 792 captured and missing for a total of 3,334. Confederate losses, according to Beauregard's own report, were 378 killed, 1,489 wounded, and 30 missing. Of the Confederate killed and wounded, 208 were from the Eighth Georgia. In the overall totals killed and wounded, victor and vanquished had fared almost exactly the same, but the hasty Union retreat had increased the number of Northern prisoners and decreased the number of Southern. As for pieces of artillery captured, Beauregard claimed only twenty-eight. The First Battle of Manassas may not have been the overwhelming statistical triumph that the Confederate camp grapevine made it in the days that followed, nor against such long odds, but it was an undisputed victory just the same, and the men had fought well to win it.[5]

That it had been a great battle, perhaps *the* great battle of the war, and a great victory too, was painfully obvious to the several dozen members of the regiment who arrived too late to have a part in the glorious event. Most of the companies of the Eighth received a handful of much-needed recruits from Georgia within a few days to a week or two of the battle, and the new men were dismayed at having missed the great adventure.[6]

Yet even more intense was the chagrin of those soldiers who had been left sick in Winchester. Gradually recovering, they reached the regiment's camp by twos and threes over the next couple of weeks, almost beside themselves at the thought of what they had missed and openly expressing their hope that another great battle would take place, and soon. Their worst fear was that the war would end without such a conflict and they would have to go home never having seen the face of battle. Joseph Gnann of Company B had heard in Winchester that the regiment was about to go into battle and had actually set out to join them with or without orders. He arrived two or three days after the battle and could only listen, in tears, as the boys told of their experiences in combat. "The only battle that I came out here to be in has been fought," he sobbed, "and I have missed it." The newly wise veterans of Manassas could only shake their heads. They would be happy just to know that they would be going home at all someday, and they were content to see as little additional fighting as honor permitted until that day.[7]

The Eighth Georgia Is Known

Meanwhile there was stern duty to be done. One of the first and most pressing unpleasant ones was the burial of the dead. The army had no graves and registration service to deal with the remains of the fallen. That task was left up to whoever would do it, and the victor, who retained possession of the battlefield, often as not had it to do for the bodies of his foes as well. Of especial importance to Civil War soldiers was seeing that insofar as possible the members of their own company, their friends from back home, received at least some semblance of a decent burial. It was a task that could not be put off. In the absence of embalming, decay could set in with astonishing rapidity and appalling results, especially under the hot skies of Virginia in July. So it was that early on Monday, July 22, the men of the Eighth performed the last sad duty for a number of their fallen comrades. James Grant recorded in a letter to his mother how B Company interred its dead. The men dug a single long grave and laid their comrades' bodies in it side by side, "brothers in arms, brothers in death," Grant wrote. First there was John Branch, once a lieutenant in the company, who had died as regimental adjutant. Beside him they laid George Butler, who had been lying beside Grant himself when he was killed. Then came the bodies of four others, with Grant carefully noting their names and their places in the grave. Sadly, the Oglethorpes closed the grave and marched away, leaving all that was mortal of six young men who had come a very long way from Savannah to lie in the soil of Virginia. They would not be the last.[8]

Especially in this early period of the war, however, the families of fallen soldiers often chose to bring home the bodies of their dead loved ones for burial in familiar ground. This would be done either by getting word to some reliable person in Virginia to make the necessary arrangements—embalming, purchase of a coffin, and so on—and send the body home, or else, more frequently, by some member of the family, often a bereaved father, coming in person to bring the body back. So it was that a veritable procession of family members visited the camps of the Eighth during the days after the battle.

Back in Rome, Georgia, Reuben S. Norton had just returned from Virginia a few days earlier, having visited his son in Winchester and parted with him in front of the hotel in that town ten days before, when on July 24, he had to write in his diary, "Received the news that Charles B. Norton was among the killed." The elder Norton immediately began making preparations to return north to retrieve the body of the Rome Light Guards' first combat fatality. From Atlanta, former state school commissioner Gustavus J. Orr came for his brother, Anderson Orr. From

Savannah came John Ferrill for his son Julius, Dan Purse for his son Tom, and several others. They usually wanted to know how it had happened, and the dead men's friends supplied information and helped them gather up personal effects.[9]

Occasionally a sad errand of this sort could take a bizarre and surprising twist. Hearing that his son Andy had perished in the great battle in Virginia, Major Beardon set out from Savannah. Since coffins were likely to be at a premium in Virginia, he brought with him a fine metallic model. He was totally unprepared for what he actually found when he reached Manassas, for, as Andy's friend Richard Watters put it, "Andy didn't quite care about going into" the fine metallic coffin "just now." It turned out that Andy had been slightly wounded and taken prisoner but was among the many who escaped in the confusion at the end of the battle. He was in camp when his father arrived, and, needless to say, the two were very pleased to see each other.[10]

Another mistaken death report involved Joel S. Yarbrough of Company F. Perhaps the confusion arose from the similarity of his name to that of Lewis G. Yarbrough of Company E, who was mortally wounded in the battle and died on July 24. On August 6, the *Atlanta Southern Confederacy* reported the death of a "Mr. Yarborough" of Floyd County. Perhaps readers overlooked the reported place of residence in the home county of Company E's Miller Rifles as well as the misspelling of both men's names. At any rate, a number of Atlantans got the wrong idea. At the engine house of the Atlanta Hook and Ladder Fire Company, where Joel Yarbrough had served before the war, the firemen sadly hung out black bunting as a display of mourning, and Yarbrough's fellow members of the First Methodist Church did the same at their building. A Mr. Chandler, with whom Joel had boarded before going off to war, telegraphed to Virginia to have his remains returned to Georgia. To his surprise, the reply came back, as Yarbrough recalled it years later, "that I said I was not ready to send my remains home yet, that I was then sitting in a tent singing 'Dixie.' "[11]

By far the most famous member of the Eighth to return to Georgia in death was, of course, Col. Francis S. Bartow. A small escort of his old company, the Oglethorpe Light Infantry, traveled with the casket of their beloved commander, arriving by train in Savannah on July 26, and then proceeding through the streets in solemn procession while crowds looked on and a volunteer artillery company fired minute guns. The body lay in state at Savannah's City Exchange building until the funeral, on Sunday, July 28. The *Savannah Daily Morning News* called the funeral "the most solemn and imposing spectacle we ever witnessed in Savannah." More artillery salutes boomed, and the bells of the city tolled mournfully as the black hearse, drawn by four gray horses and followed by a vast procession, made its way slowly to Laurel Cemetery, where Bartow was buried. Already there was talk of erecting a suitable stone monument at the place where he had fallen back in Virginia.[12]

No dead bodies returned to Oglethorpe County, in Middle Georgia, during the weeks following the battle. Nor did any of the county's Oglethorpe Rifles sleep under the Virginia sod. Alone among the ten companies of the Eighth Georgia, the Oglethorpe Rifles, Company K, suffered not a single fatality. In the weeks after the battle, the soldiers learned of a circumstance that they believed accounted for this fact. On that Sunday morning, July 21, when the battle had been fought, a number of citizens of rural Oglethorpe County had gathered at Atkinson's Church to hold a special prayer meeting on behalf of the boys in the company. Several weeks later, with a quiet, sober awe, the men of Company K worked out the times and realized that while they had been passing through the bloody carnage of the pine thicket, their friends and loved ones had been gathered on their knees in the old country church house back home, beseeching God to spare their lives.[13]

Meanwhile, at Manassas the seamier side of war was more notable that week. The necessity of burying the 470 Union dead was more a sanitary than a sentimental one. Ugly bitterness was already putting down deep roots in many on both sides, and one member of the Eighth wrote home that as far as he was concerned the vultures could eat the dead Northerners. The vultures, however, were not fast enough, and neither were Confederate burial parties. James Grant saw numerous dead lying unburied two days after the battle, and already the stench was "intolerable." Slowly, and often in a careless manner, the gruesome job got done.[14]

Several days after the battle, George Barnsley got leave to go out and tramp the field again to try to understand where the different units had been and what had happened. Across the battlefield he saw another soldier, moving along quickly and carrying a bundle of something. Barnsley had been in the Confederate army long enough by now to be more or less perpetually interested in food, and he thought this man had the look of someone who might have something good to eat, probably peaches or potatoes. Hurrying to meet the other man, Barnsley asked if he had anything of which he would like to sell a part. The other soldier was friendly enough but explained that this was not something to eat. Instead it was a "great curiosity" that he had found on the battlefield and was taking back to his regiment to exhibit. Would Barnsley like to see? "Of course." So the man set down his bundle and spread out the cloth covering to reveal a human skull, which, as Barnsley noted with revulsion, was "not quite clean of flesh." With a wise look, the soldier vouchsafed that this was in fact the skull of a Yankee. It took the nonplussed Barnsley a few minutes to comprehend that this backwoodsman had accepted current Southern propaganda at face value and actually believed that a Yankee was not human at all but rather "a sort of devil with a tail." The amazing discovery that a dead Yankee had the skull of a man was the evidence with which he planned to reveal to his equally rustic messmates the humanity of their enemies. Barnsley persuaded him to bury the skull instead.[15]

The great majority of those hit by enemy fire during the battle were not dead, however, but wounded. The need to care for them was as urgent as the burial of the dead and went on after the fallen comrades' remains rested under the sod. After a few days, most of the more serious cases, at least those that were able to travel, were shipped off to large, makeshift Confederate hospitals in places such as Richmond, Orange Court House, Culpeper Court House, and Charlottesville. In the latter town, the stately buildings of the University of Virginia, designed by Thomas Jefferson, were filled with wounded Confederates and such volunteer surgeons and nurses as the surrounding area could provide.[16]

George Hammond, of Company F, took bullets in the left shoulder and right leg during the fight in the pine thicket, and his comrades had no choice but to leave him behind when they retreated. The advancing Federals took him up and sent him to their field hospital, where the surgeons dressed his wounds just as they were doing for hundreds of others, Union and Confederate alike. In the Union retreat that evening, his captors left him and the other severely wounded behind, and late the following day, Capt. J. T. Lewis and Lt. Seymour Love of his own company, along with the Eighth's assistant surgeon, Dr. Alexander, came by the hospital, now abandoned by its staff, to see if any of their men were there. Finding Hammond as well as James R. George, they gently placed them into a wagon to take them back to the care of the Confederate physicians at Manassas. The trip quickly turned into a nightmare. The dirt roads were much the worse for the recent traffic and heavy rains, and the wagon jolted mercilessly even at a walk. Night fell long before they reached their destination, and they had no lantern. From time to time, Capt. Lewis would look back into the wagon and ask, "How are you, George Hammond?" or "How are you, Jimmy George?" The boys were not too well at all, but they gamely answered, "Fine," or "All right." Finally, an inquiry to Jimmy George went unanswered. The captain asked again, but silence and the creaking of the wagon were the only reply. At last George Hammond found his voice. "Captain," he said weakly, "he is dead."

The trip wound up taking most of the night, and it was near dawn when they reached Manassas Junction. There they met Hammond's father, an officer in the Seventh Georgia. Hours earlier he had heard a false report of his son's death and was overjoyed to find him alive. Gaining leave for both of them, Hammond's father conducted him back to Georgia, where he spent months recovering from his wounds; he was never able to return to duty with the regiment.[17]

The inadequacy of the facilities for caring for the wounded was partially because of the South's paucity of resources but much more because of the fact that no one expected the kind of massive bloodletting that the Civil War had already unleashed. The overworked Surgeon Miller on the night after the battle was all too typical of what wounded Confederates would have to face—at best. Medical science was fairly primitive, but to their credit, the surgeons and other medical personnel, as well as the folks back home, did the best they could. From Savannah, Mr. David R. Dillon sent a sixty-pound sack of "superior Bermuda Arrow Root" for the relief of the wounded. Whether or not it ever cured anyone, at least it reminded the boys that someone back home was thinking of them.[18]

One thing that the Eighth had gained in being so fearfully cut up in the fight was fame, and the boys reveled in it. To all who would listen and in their letters home they repeated again and again Beauregard's words about saluting them with his hat off, though with increasing variations of wording, since most of them had not actually been able to hear Beauregard and had to rely on the way the story was repeated around camp. Decades later, some of them were still repeating those words in their memoirs. There were other sayings as well that the men seized upon. Johnston was reputed to have called their advance the most gallant feat of arms he had ever witnessed, and Maria Key Steele of Maryland even celebrated their bloody exploits in a poem, "The Charge of the Georgia Eighth":

> *The morning sun shines gaily*
> *On proud Manassas' height.*
> *Six Hundred gallant Georgians*
> *Are ready for the fight.*

—and so on through another twelve stanzas.

Praise came from high places. Lt. Ed Hull, recuperating in Richmond from a bout of illness, chanced to encounter President Davis, whom he had initially refused a drink of water on the evening of the battle. Davis at once recognized and warmly greeted the embarrassed lieutenant, asking to what regiment he belonged.

"To the Eighth Georgia," Hull replied.

"To belong to that regiment is glory enough," declared Davis, and his words were soon the talk of camp. To another member of the Eighth that summer, Davis was reported to have said, "The Eighth Georgia is *known.*" For the boys in their camp near Manassas, such bright flashes of military glory were some compensation for both the horrors of battle and the everyday miseries of camp life.[19]

He Caused Them to Have Some Serious Thoughts

Several days after the battle, the Eighth Georgia moved to a more permanent location about four miles northeast of Manassas Junction, which they promptly named Camp Bartow. There they spent the remainder of the summer. It was an unavoidable letdown after the previous few months of excitement—the news of war, the preparations to go to Virginia, the trip, the organization of the regiment, the anxious ma-

neuvering in the Shenandoah, the desperate march and train ride to
Manassas, and the incredible experience of battle there. Later genera-
tions might refer to their condition as "post-traumatic stress," but as the
men of the Eighth explained it, they were tired, bored, and depressed.
Sometimes they took their frustrations out on each other, as on the
morning when the regiment saw three fistfights before breakfast. Sometimes came rations; sometimes the men had to make do on scanty fare.
Payment of their wages seemed abominably overdue, though they
would see much worse in years to come. Occasional rumors that the
Yankees were coming out to have another try at the Manassas lines
were greeted by the soldiers with relief, despite their newfound distaste
for combat. "I had sooner fight than be here in the fix we are in now,"
one of them wrote his wife.[20]

Conditions compared poorly with their almost idyllic encampment at
Winchester. "The water—if you get it at all—is very bad," wrote
Richard Watters. "Such dirt—You can't see the bottom of a bucket. I fear
such water as this is not the best for one's health." So he took to mixing
a little wine in his water in hopes of staying healthy.[21]

Sickness was a very real concern for the men of the Eighth during
those weeks, for the epidemics that had begun in Winchester had not yet
run their course, and in any case, a settled encampment was usually not
a very healthy place for Civil War soldiers. "We have some very sick Boys
heare at the Horse Pittle," wrote Sgt. A. D. Craver, of Company D, in a
letter to a furloughed comrade, using a variant spelling of the word *hospital*. Craver then went on to list comrades, one after another, "got the
fever," "realapes of the Measles," "chills & some little Fever." Lt. Tony
Lumpkin survived the battle he fought contrary to the surgeon's advice,
unscathed save for a severed sword belt, but his lung ailment continued
to grow worse, and he finally had to go home in mid-August. Even that
would not cure him, however, and he eventually succumbed in 1864.
Another of the sick was George Barnsley, who came down with double
pneumonia after a long stint of sentry duty in a heavy storm. They sent
him home with a raging fever, delirious, and though he recovered, he
never carried a musket into battle again. Many others fared still worse,
dying in the camp, far from home.[22]

Above all, the men were homesick. Most of them had never been
away from their homes and families before, and now they had been gone

well over two months and, worse, had time sitting around camp to think about it. For some, bodily illness intensified the sorrow of missing family members. "My dear wife," wrote Samuel Brewer after a bout of sickness, "I can not tell you how bad I have felt for the last two weeks; not able to wait upon myself and so far from you all. It almost breaks my heart." Healthy men felt the tug of home as well and frequently coped with it by writing letters and hoping to receive letters from the folks back in Georgia. "Write soon," Richard Watters begged his sister repeatedly in pleas that were typical of most soldiers. "Write often. Write all you can." "The happiest moments I enjoy in camp are those spent reading letters from you and thinking of you and my little boy," Brewer assured his wife, "and the next are those spent writing to you."[23]

But letters could only do so much. These soldiers wanted to go home. "Our President says our regiment has done their part in the war and thinks we ought to come home," wrote one member of the Eighth. Of course, Davis had not said anything of the sort, being one of the few Americans who had anticipated a long war from the very outset. Yet other members of the Eighth (and other regiments) entertained similar thoughts. The great battle was won, and they had done more than their share in winning it. Why could they not go home now? Some thought perhaps furloughs might be issued on a generous basis, but continued fears of another Union advance meant that such furloughs as were granted went only to the very sick or very badly wounded. By one report, at least one member of the Eighth decided to grant himself a furlough during this period. "One of our men is a deserter," James Martin, of Company D, wrote his parents on August 6. "I am sorry for him for deserting," Martin continued, noting mistakenly that the man had come through the battle unscathed. "Poor fellow, he is to be pitied," Martin concluded firmly, "but he brought it upon himself." In fact the deserter was eighteen-year-old Pvt. Thomas J. Barber, of Company H, the Floyd Infantry. He had been sick in the hospital, had missed the battle of Manassas, and had rejoined the regiment July 31. Apparently his disappointment and chagrin were so intense that he deserted the following day. Thereafter, he disappears from the records. Apparently he was never apprehended.[24]

Much as the men of the Eighth might have wished to get away from Camp Bartow, at least for a few weeks, there was one group of them who wished very much to be there but could not. Assuming that all of the Confederates captured in the battle and carried off as prisoners to Washington were included in the category that Beauregard called "missing" in his report, then more than half of the thirty men he listed in that category were members of the Eighth Georgia who were captured and subsequently neither escaped nor had the good fortune to be left behind by the retreating Federals. In all, seventeen members of the regiment were in Washington that summer as unwilling guests of the United States government. Twelve of them were confined in the Old Capitol Prison, site of the present-day Supreme Court building, whence Sanford Branch wrote his mother to break the sad news of John's death. He continued to send and receive letters during the whole period of his captivity. The prisoners fared about as well as the soldiers in camp, if not better, with soup for supper every evening, hardtack for other meals, and plenty of water to drink. U.S. general J. K. F. Mansfield had charge of them, and while he did not allow them to receive visitors, he did permit pro-Confederate women in Washington to bring them parcels of food. "We are well fed & clothed," Sanford Branch explained to his mother, "and hope for exchange." Exchange was long in coming, but in late August the prisoners were paroled—released on their promise not to take up arms again until properly exchanged. By September 1, Branch was in Orange Court House, Virginia, preparing to wait out his exchange in less constricted circumstances.[25]

Back at Camp Bartow, several members of the Eighth Georgia noted another change that the battle had made in the regiment in the form of an increased interest in religion. Company D's Pvt. Benjamin Garrett "has changed considerably," a fellow soldier wrote a week after the battle. "Says he will praise God the ballance of his days." The prospect of imminent death had turned many men to contemplation of their own eternal destinies. Noting that enemy bullets had fallen "as thick as hail nearly" where the regiment had stood in the pine thicket, James Martin wrote that God had protected those who survived. "He caused many a one of us to be saved from being shot & no doubt He caused them to have some serious thoughts." Martin felt that there had been a certain amount of insincere last-minute praying done during the battle. "When they get into battle," he explained of such soldiers, "they then pray to the Lord to save them, after kicking & abusing His name all over the camp."

Yet he also believed there were many who were honest in their desire to seek God. "They prayed . . . for the Lord to spare them this time & they would be better men the ballance of their days," he explained. "And now you can scarcely hear an oath about the encampment uttered & we have prayer meeting every night & some of the best singing you ever hird in your life."[26]

The Rev. John Jones, the pastor of the First Presbyterian Church in Rome, Georgia, who had preached the farewell sermon for the Rome Light Guards back in May, had been in Richmond on the day of the battle and arrived at Manassas the next day seeking news of his son Dunwoody Jones. The younger Jones was unscathed save for a bruise on his foot where a spent ball had struck his shoe. The happy John Jones remained with the regiment for several months as chaplain. "We have a good Presbyterian preacher to preach for us," Martin, a good Methodist, wrote to his parents. He noted that Jones would go through the camp every evening, talking to the boys and asking them to come to the preaching services "in such a way that they are obliged to go." He handed out Christian tracts as well. He preached outdoors, to large and appreciative crowds, and on those Sundays when the Eighth happened to be deployed out of camp on picket duty, he found equally ready listeners in neighboring regiments. Jones's friend the noted Presbyterian minister Joseph C. Stiles visited the regiment in October and preached at a Sunday service as he passed through on his way to hold a "protracted meeting"—a series of nightly services—in another brigade.[27]

The good news of forgiveness of sins and acceptance by God through Jesus Christ was of immediate, intense importance to men who knew they might die in the very near future. The threat of renewed battle hung over them constantly, and the slower but far more efficient killing processes of disease never really stopped. When death was imminent, a man needed to settle the matter of what would come after. Such was the case at a private home in Orange Court House where in mid-August several members of the Eighth lay in the throes of various diseases. James Martin was among them, but had passed the crisis of his illness and was beginning to mend. On the evening of August 19, he sat writing a letter to his mother, while just across the hall a fellow member of D Company, Tom Render, struggled with a very serious case of typhoid fever. "I think he will die before night," Martin told his mother, "but pray that he may be spared because he can't say that he is willing to meet his Savior." Martin did more than pray. Pausing in his letter writing a few minutes later, he and several other members of the company went next door to talk to Render about being reconciled to God, and this time the dying man proved receptive. Returning to his letter later that night, Martin happily informed his mother that Render was now prepared to die. And the record shows that Pvt. Thomas C. Render succumbed to typhoid fever, August 19, 1861.[28]

Nothing Unusual

As the weeks passed after the Battle of Manassas, the fame of Bartow grew. Along with Barnard Bee, who had also fallen at the crisis of the battle, he became recognized across the South as a martyr to the cause of Confederate independence and a symbol of Southern courage and dedication to that cause. It was thus fitting that Bartow became the subject of the very first Civil War battlefield monument to be erected. With relatively little to do at Camp Bartow, the men of the Eighth gave much thought to the memory of their first colonel and how they might create a lasting memorial to him. Somehow they got a slab of white marble and had it engraved as a monument to their fallen leader. Then they planned a dedication ceremony to erect the stone on the place where Bartow fell.

At the date and time appointed, 2:00 P.M., September 4, 1861, the full brigade marched out to the site—Seventh, Eighth, and Ninth Georgia, along with the First Kentucky, and their new brigade commander, Brig. Gen. Samuel Jones, and his staff. Numerous civilians gathered in as well, and estimates of attendance were well over a thousand. Someone had apparently arranged—or thought he had arranged—for Vice President Alexander Stephens and Brig. Gen. Robert Toombs, Georgia's two most prominent politicians in Virginia, to attend and offer some appropriate remarks. What went wrong is not quite clear, but the two august personages never showed up. An embarrassing wait ensued, and finally it was decided to go ahead without them. A brass band played Confederate airs while each regiment of the brigade formally saluted the colors of the Eighth. Then a chaplain led in prayer.

Still, this did not make up for the lack of oratory. Casting about hastily, officers spied Louisiana attorney general Thomas J. Semmes among the civilian attendees and quickly pressed him into service. It all came as quite a shock to Semmes, who, in a situation perhaps unique in his life as a politician, found himself with nothing to say. Mrs. Semmes, however, had plenty to say, and in the brief moments before her husband was to take the platform, gave him a few ideas for a speech. Years later she modestly recalled his subsequent effort as "the grandest speech he ever made in his life."

That done, several officers of the Eighth followed up with remarks of their own. Then eager hands lifted the monument, a marble obelisk, from where it lay on the ground and held it in an upright position. On its side was chiseled "Francis S. Bartow" and the inscription "They have killed me boys! Never give up the field," the accepted version of the colonel's last words. Then the officers present filed past the monument and each threw a handful of earth at the base of the monument. Following them came Charlotte Branch, mother of Hamilton, Sanford (now a prisoner), and the Eighth's late adjutant, John. She too cast a bit of dirt at the base of the shaft, and then, in a long procession, the enlisted men passed by to pay their respects and add their handfuls of earth to the small mound growing around the monument's base. That concluded the ceremony. The soldiers marched back to their camps, and the civilians made their way to their various lodgings.[29]

Back in camp, on this as on every day, the Eighth had to deal with more practical matters. With Bartow dead, the Confederate War Department promoted Gardner to the rank of full colonel and nominal command of the regiment. Yet the doughty old regular's wound still forbade any hopes of an early return to duty, and acting command of the Eighth fell to the next-ranking officer. Following routine procedures, the War Department filled the position of lieutenant colonel, vacated by Gardner's promotion, by moving up the next most senior officer in the regiment, Maj. Thomas L. Cooper. Despite Cooper's unquestionably gallant conduct at Manassas, his promotion was not welcomed by the Eighth. It "created a great deal of dissatisfaction among the soldiers of the Regiment," Company A's Richard Watters wrote his sister. "There are not, I don't think, a dozen men in the Regiment in favor of the appointment." Watters and others who disapproved of Cooper's promotion gave as their reason the claim that Cooper was simply unqualified for the position. "The office that he held before as Major was a degree or two higher than he was capable of filling," Watters wrote. An anonymous letter-writer in Company B complained—in print in the *Savannah Republican*—that the new lieutenant colonel "has no military ability naturally, no military skill or experience, no talent for managing men." They had high regard for him as a man, the critics insisted, but they maintained that as a military leader "the men have no confidence whatever in him."

Most of the other commissioned officers of the regiment got together and held a meeting to discuss the situation. They appointed several of their number as a committee with the task of approaching Cooper and suggesting that "in consideration of the condition of the regiment after its terrible mutilation in the battle of Manassas" it might be well "to appoint an able and experienced regular army officer to command it until Col. Gardner's recovery." The idea was to give the lieutenant colonel the broadest of hints and the easiest of ways to hand over top leadership in the regiment. Cooper, however, somehow got wind of what was afoot, and when the officers' committee reached his quarters he told them he knew why they had come and preferred to receive their message in writing. So the officers wrote out their suggestion, but Cooper wrote back to say that he believed it was his duty to retain command of the regiment.

This enraged those who had wanted him gone, and in response, the captains of the regiment got up a petition to President Davis, asking him to sack Cooper. If they had known the president better, they could have spared themselves the time and trouble. Such a thing was against proper army procedures, and Davis would hear none of it. Indeed, from his response, the officers got the distinct impression that "Davis now thinks the Regiment in a sort of rebellious condition." That was no doubt exactly what he thought. At this point, the enlisted personnel of the regiment got involved, and all but a few of them signed a petition directly to Cooper, calling on him to resign. Again, the lieutenant colonel refused. There the matter rested, after a fashion, with Cooper steadfastly in command of a regiment seething with discontent.[30]

Less controversial was the appointment of the new lieutenant colonel's brother, Capt. James Frederick Cooper of Company H, the Floyd Infantry, to move up into the newly vacant position of major. "He will never be able to fill it," wrote Richard Watters, and indeed, Fred Cooper received his new commission on September 5, the day before he finally succumbed to the effects of his Manassas wound.[31]

Happy with its officers or not, the Eighth was soon on the advance again and facing the prospect of imminent battle. All across the South, civilians and soldiers alike had expected a triumphant advance after the victory at Manassas. The Southern temperament demanded aggressive actions, taking the offensive and taking the fight to the enemy. With a great battle fought and won, they had all the more reason to chafe at the army's inactivity and desire a furious onward rush that would win the war at once. Already, in the highest echelons of Confederate command, men such as Beauregard, Johnston, and Davis were beginning the recriminations as to whose fault it was that an effective pursuit had not followed the battle. In fact, it was no one's—no such pursuit had been possible. However, desire was strong, on the part of generals and public, to advance and force the issue.

Beauregard had made a beginning in this direction when early in August he had shifted several brigades to positions much closer to Washington and sent his cavalry pickets so far forward as to be within sight of the capital city. In the weeks that followed, he and Johnston, who as senior was now the overall commander of the two small armies that had combined on the eve of Manassas, edged their forces farther and farther north. On September 10 came the Eighth Georgia's turn to move up. Packing their baggage into the wagons again—it was amazing how much impedimenta the regiment still had even after winnowing their baggage when leaving Winchester that summer—the soldiers prepared to march. The wagons were overloaded, and soldiers were told that they had the choice of carrying their knapsacks on their backs or leaving them behind. Many chose the latter option, rolled up their blankets, tied them over one shoulder and across the chest, slung haversack and cartridge box with forty rounds, and marched out of Camp Bartow.

After a tramp of about a dozen miles, they encamped again about two o'clock that afternoon near the army's new headquarters at Fairfax Court House, Virginia. Washington itself was only another fifteen or so miles farther up the road. Things got off to a rough start there for the Eighth, though by now the men at least had a summer's experience with the lot of a soldier. About an hour and a half after their arrival, a heavy rain shower soaked them. The baggage wagons came up about six o'clock, and they finally pitched their tents and made camp in a low and soggy place that headquarters had assigned them. Night brought more rain, a downpour with howling winds, but the men were tough and took it in stride, rolling tighter in their blankets. When the following day offered enough sunshine to dry out their things they counted themselves well off.[32]

The following Sunday morning, September 15, the Eighth moved out for its first four-day stint along the Confederate advanced picket line on Mason's Hill and Munson's Hill, near Falls Church, Virginia, about eight miles in advance of the main camps. The Eighth's sector was Mason's Hill. Here they were a scant half-dozen or so miles from the Potomac and, beyond it, the city of Washington, and they could see both. For most of the boys it was their first glimpse of the unfinished dome of the U.S. Capitol building, and they gazed at it with wonder, excitement, and expectation. "The senery from this hill is sublime," wrote one of them. "It commands a view of the dome of the great capitol of the old United States." The men also found that they could hear the sound of drums and bands from the Union army camps, and one day they watched the ascension of one of the hot-air balloons that the Federals were using to observe Rebel positions. A battery of Confederate artillery nearby opened fire on the balloon, and when two shells in rapid succession exploded near it, its Union operators reeled it in with frantic haste. The Eighth was even close enough to Union lines that some of the boys remembered hearing the burst of laughter from the Yankee soldiers at the fright of their comrades in the balloon detail.[33]

In their letters home the Georgians wrote eagerly of how they would soon be crossing the Potomac and then fighting and winning the great climactic battle of the war. Company B's Tom Wragg told his father that a neighbor who was trying to raise a company of troops had better hurry. "If he don't make hast and come on," Wragg warned, "he will be too late for the taking of the great city of Washington." Richard Watters was more terse: "We are daily expecting a row of some sort."[34]

The constant expectation of the showdown battle was exciting, but it made picket duty at times an unpleasantly serious affair. Watters pulled picket duty the regiment's first night at Mason's Hill and heard several gunshots during the night—probably from nervous sentinels firing at phantoms of their imagination, but one could never be sure.[35]

A few nights later, Berrien Zettler was among those detailed for picket duty at some of the very most advanced outposts. The officer posting the guard led his party of sentries along an old road and dropped off two of them at each post, instructing them that they must both remain awake but make no noise. Zettler and his friend Henry Parnell drew a post near an old barn. It was an uncommonly dark night, and Zettler and Parnell stood for hours straining their eyes into the inky blackness, wondering how it would be if Union scouts tried to creep up on them unawares. Then in the dead stillness they heard a low noise. It seemed to come from the loft of the nearby barn. The two nervous sentinels drew closer to each other and listened harder. Zettler felt the hair rising on his scalp. The noise came again, louder. In a whisper, Zettler asked Parnell what he thought it was. "Man, I think," came the other's shaky reply. They waited longer, and then the noise came again. This time it sounded as if there might be more than one man in the loft. Zettler decided it was time to act. "You go around that side of the house," he whispered to Parnell, meaning the barn, "and I'll go on this side." Stealthily they crept to their positions. On Parnell's side of the barn was a window, devoid of glass; on Zettler's side, a door. He took a moment to steel himself, then, one hand tightly gripping his rifle, he gently eased the other hand onto the doorknob. With a rush he burst into the barn, only to hear Parnell scream from the other side. Before he could reach his comrade, however, Zettler heard him exclaiming, "It's a cat! He jumped right into my breast." The remainder of the night passed quietly, and when the corporal of the guard arrived just before daylight to relieve them, Zettler and Parnell reported, "Nothing unusual observed."[36]

Picket duty could vary greatly depending upon the specific sector of front that fell to one's lot. One company of the Eighth would occupy a section of outposts along which the opposing Confederate and Union pickets made informal truces and met between the lines to chat and swap pocketknives and overcoats. Yet at the same time, other companies would find themselves opposite Yankees of far more hostile bent, where firing went on more or less all the time and a man had to lie on his belly sometimes for twelve hours at a stretch.[37]

Completing its first tour of duty at Mason's Hill, the Eighth returned to the camp of the main army near Fairfax for a few days before its next stint at the forward outposts. That came October 1, and the regiment marched out of camp just in time to miss an august visitor whose passing acquaintance some of them had already made. President Davis arrived that day from Richmond to discuss strategy with the army's top generals, Joseph E. Johnston, P. G. T. Beauregard, and Gustavus W. Smith. The generals had written Davis urging that the army be reinforced so that it could take the offensive before snow flew. At their suggestion, Davis had come to Fairfax to discuss the possibilities, but the meeting did not go well. Davis was surprised to find the army's numbers as depleted as they were—disease was still doing its work—and the generals' demands for reinforcements were far beyond anything he was prepared to consider. Though neither president nor generals desired to surrender the initiative and wait for the Federals to move in the spring, they reluctantly decided they had no choice.[38]

If Fairfax Court House was not to be the jumping-off place for an offensive, it was certainly an ill place for Southerners to defend. The Potomac swept around it in a broad curve from northwest to southeast, and the Potomac's far bank was enemy territory. Johnston and his lieutenants therefore determined to pull back to Centreville, just north of the old Manassas battlefield. On October 5, just two days after the president's departure to return to Richmond, Johnston ordered the withdrawal to begin, starting with the sick, who would be cleared out to rear areas first, before the rest of the army began its pullback. Before the end of October, the withdrawal was complete.[39]

Even in the camps at Centreville, both officers and men continued to wonder if they might fight another battle before winter brought an end to active campaigning. They knew that Union general George B. McClellan was training and equipping a large army in the camps around Washington, and the question was simply where and when he would use it. The Indian summer of 1861 stretched unusually long, with mild, dry, sunny weather lingering all the way into December. "If McClellan thinks of advancing on us this winter," a member of the Eighth wrote on December 8, "he certainly will not get a prettier spell of weather. I

don't think I ever saw a prettier day in Ga. For this time of year. It is perfectly still and the sun is shining beautifully." But McClellan's army
stayed in its camps, and the autumn finally came to an end amid continued absence of major military action in Virginia, a situation that
prompted Ethel Lynn Beers to pen her plaintive song "All Quiet Along
the Potomac Tonight," about a fictional picket killed by an enemy sharpshooter in an insignificant and meaningless nocturnal encounter. Young
women played and sang it with feeling in many a Virginia parlor that
winter, but for the Eighth Georgia, the only losses of that autumn came
not from the likes of Beers's "rifleman hid in the thicket" but rather from
the even more anonymous, inglorious, and relentless workings of disease
germs.[40]

One of those who succumbed to the ravages of sickness that autumn
was Whit Stevens, who had promised on his knees to try to serve God
the rest of his life, there under the pine trees on the evening of the great
battle of Manassas. He had done his best to keep that promise, but
clearly the life of service he had promised would now be tragically
short. Sent back to Richmond to recover, he lodged in the Columbia
Hotel, in far nicer quarters than his comrades enjoyed back in camp. Yet
he only grew worse, and the prognosis was all too clear. He was dying,
and he knew it. Late one November night he sensed that the end was
near and sent for the Rev. James A. Duncan, a prominent Methodist
minister in Richmond.

Duncan rose at midnight, hurriedly dressed, and made his way
through cold, dark streets to the Columbia. He found Stevens in his
dimly lit room, stretched upon his bed, and failing. By the bedside sat a
matronly old lady, his nurse. At the foot of the bed stood the Eighth's
new regimental adjutant, Lt. Armistead R. "Alex" Harper. Both, in their
separate spheres of duty, were keeping this last vigil with the dying man.
Whit explained that he had sent for Duncan to pray with him and talk
to him. Duncan asked if he was a church member, and the young soldier
explained that he was not but told of his commitment on the battlefield
four months earlier.

"Then, Whitefield, you are not afraid to die?" Duncan asked.

"No, sir," came the young man's reply, "I have been a faithful soldier
and a dutiful son . . ."

Here the nurse, fearing that he was trusting in his own good works to win acceptance with God, broke in, "Whitefield, my son, you know all that won't save you."

Something like a smile passed over his pale, drawn face as he finished the thought he had been expressing: ". . . but my trust is in Jesus Christ, the Savior of men." That was what mattered—to Duncan, to the nurse, and especially to young Whitefield.

As they continued to watch by his bedside, Whit spoke again. "Sing to me some of those good old hymns I used to hear at home," he requested. They could hardly refuse, so Duncan and the nurse sang some of the old familiar hymns, while Lt. Harper, overcome with emotion, leaned on the footboard of the bed and wept quietly. "Father, I stretch my hands to Thee," they sang, and "Amazing grace, how sweet the sound, that saved a wretch like me." These were not just sentimental tunes for young Whit, who knew the words by heart and knew what they meant. Duncan could see that he was moved by the hymns and occasionally he could see the young man's lips moving as he tried to join in the singing. Then they sang, "Jesus, lover of my soul, Let me to Thy bosom fly," and the young soldier became obviously excited, even animated. As they reached the words ". . . Cover my defenseless head, With the shadow of thy wing," he burst out, "Adjutant! Adjutant! Is not that grand?" Harper gazed blankly at him.

"Ah!" cried Whit. "You don't know what that means! I will tell you what it means. At Manassas, when the bullets were whistling around us like hail, and our boys were dropping in the ranks, and poor Bartow fell, then the Almighty covered my defenseless head with the shadow of His wing!" Then Whit had not been ready to die; now he was. Then death had loomed as the ultimate catastrophe for him; now he had confidence in the One to whom he had committed his future. "Cover *my* defenseless head," he repeated more quietly but with increased emphasis, "With the shadow of *Thy* wing."

His head sank back on the pillow, and he rested quietly. In the hours that followed, he gradually grew weaker. His father, Thomas F. Stevens, arrived that morning by the early train, having come all the way from Savannah when he heard that his son was desperately ill. He was too late to see Whit alive, but Duncan told him the story of his son's passing, and the elder Stevens smiled through his tears. "I am satisfied," he said. "Whitefield died as I would have him die—died for his country; died honorably; and, above all, died in the faith of the gospel. It will comfort his mother. I shall return to my home and praise God for his goodness in the midst of our sorrows."[41]

Moped Up in a Tent

The cold winds finally came, and the men began to feel keenly their lack of adequate clothing for the season. They had not left home equipped for a winter in Virginia, and what they had taken with them had suffered a great deal from eight months' hard service. By the end of October the crisp autumn nights had prompted the Atlanta Grays, Company F, to appeal to the people of Atlanta to provide them with new uniforms. "The coat should be a heavy frock, with military cape attached," read their notice in the *Atlanta Daily Intelligencer,* "out of *any kind* of material, so that it is *warm.*"[42]

The men's thin tents also offered little protection against the chill, and the weather was already colder than many of those from Middle and especially South Georgia were commonly used to seeing it. "Ice is common with us," Tom Wragg wrote his father. "It is always on the ground, never melts." And he complained, "It is so cold that I can not hold my pen." To try to cope with the weather, most of the men built sod fireplaces at one end of their tents. They made a good deal of smoke and none too much heat, but they were better than nothing.

Clearly it was time for the army to go into winter quarters. At this point another of the seemingly perennial misunderstandings between Davis and his generals intervened to make the situation more difficult. Each side had somehow gotten the idea that the other was going to take care of hiring barracks—or huts or something—built to shelter the men that winter, though why Johnston and Beauregard imagined that Davis would handle such a detail is hard to fathom. At any rate, the plan to have civilian builders construct housing came to nothing, and the cold blasts of winter caught the soldiers in mid-December with no shelter and no prospect of any but what they could build for themselves. On orders from Johnston, the various regiments got to work. About December 18 the men of the Eighth began felling trees in preparation for going into the house-building business. They spent more than a week lumbering, and then the plan was for them to erect houses—one soldier called them "stables"—six to a company, built of logs, each with a roof slanting only one way. It would be crowded in those tiny huts, and Tom Wragg thought the cramped quarters would create more sickness that winter.

On December 24, Lt. Col. Cooper, accompanied by regimental quartermaster Lt. E. A. Wilcox, rode out to look over some likely sites for erecting the winter quarters. They wanted someplace with good access to both wood and water. No one ever explained exactly why except that he was riding a "very fiery" steed, but for some reason Cooper's horse spooked and bolted in the woods. Wilcox lost sight of him almost immediately as the lieutenant colonel's frenzied mount plunged through the thickets. When the quartermaster caught up with Cooper—and it took quite a while—he found him lying on the ground up against a tree. The lieutenant colonel was unconscious, but it was fairly obvious what had happened. Thrown from his horse, Cooper had hit the tree, breaking several ribs and his back and apparently injuring his head as well. Wilcox quickly summoned an ambulance and they carried Cooper back to camp, but he never regained consciousness and died about two o'clock Christmas morning. It was a shock to the men. "He was an awful sight to look at," wrote Tom Wragg a few days later. "His face was so swollen that you could not recognize him at all. Although he was not well liked in the regiment," Wragg added, "we all were very sorry when he died."[43]

That Christmas would not have been a very festive occasion anyway, and the gruesome death of Lt. Col. Cooper only deepened the soldiers' gloom. "I have spent a very poor christmass," Wragg admitted, adding that all he wanted was "a box of eatibles." Samuel Brewer found some "eatibles" but had only a marginally better time. Purchasing two dozen eggs and a quart of peach brandy for five dollars, nearly two weeks' pay, he had "two good drinks of egg-nog" and then "sat moped up in a tent all day" thinking about how much he missed his family back home. It was bitterly cold.

So passed the Eighth Georgia's first Christmas of the war. The year 1861 passed into history, with all its bloodshed and momentous changes. The new year promised more of the same. The winter months dragged by with little to differentiate one day from another. Frost, snow, sleet, and mud alternated from day to day through the dreary weeks, while men struggled through bouts of illness, boredom, and loneliness. Some wrote letters to relieve their homesickness, and nearly all wished devoutly that the folks back home in Georgia would send more letters to them. It was not a glamorous war, and they had already had all the adventure in it that they desired. Yet most of them determined to stay as long as duty demanded.[44]

CHAPTER FIVE

✄

We Must Not Let the Yankees Take Richmond

The Blighting Effects of War

THE spring of 1862 brought dark clouds on the horizon of the Southern Confederacy. The winter had brought Confederate defeats in the West almost as frequently as it had sent snowstorms howling down out of the North. In January, Southern forces fell at Mill Springs, Kentucky, opening East Tennessee to Union troops. In February, devastating twin defeats at Forts Henry and Donelson, on the Tennessee and Cumberland rivers, opened up the rest of Tennessee as well as northern Mississippi and Alabama. The following month, Confederates in Arkansas took a drubbing at Pea Ridge, destroying forever Southern hopes of adding Missouri to the Confederacy, and all the way out in New Mexico Territory a Union victory at Glorieta Pass meant the South could bid farewell to that region as well. A combined Federal army-navy expedition was on the move down the Mississippi River, and another hovered on an offshore island in the Gulf of Mexico, threatening New Orleans. Meanwhile, on the Virginia front, McClellan lovingly prepared every detail of his magnificent army around Washington, readying it for the day when it would finally march out to crush secession, while the nation waited, North and South, almost with bated breath, to see when that day would come and the final blow would fall that would finish the failing Confederacy.

In command of the Confederate army at Centreville, Gen. Joseph E. Johnston had no intention of waiting to receive that blow. During the months in Centreville an assessment of Johnston's fighting qualities had come from an unusual quarter within the Eighth Georgia. A major review was scheduled, but John Reed was unable to attend because of sickness. He asked his servant, Lit, to watch the show and tell him about it afterward. When the time came to recount the grand spectacle, Reed asked Lit how the various generals had impressed him. "Mr. Beauregard" looked brave enough, replied the servant, himself notorious for his freely confessed lack of courage, but "Mr. Johnston" was a different matter. "Ah ha, Mas John," said Lit knowingly, "that man looks too cunning. He's never gwine where he can git hurt." Lit was slightly off the truth in his estimate of Joseph Johnston. The general would readily risk his own person but never his reputation.

Never one to fight a battle if he could retreat instead, Johnston made plans to withdraw from Centreville to a position behind the Rappahannock River, some thirty-five miles farther south. True to form, Johnston kept his own counsel about his intended move, even concealing its full extent and timing from President Davis, but by the beginning of March his preparations were in full swing, and the men knew something was up.

"I don't know what to say we are going to do," Richard Watters wrote his sister from the camp of the Eighth Georgia, and then added, "It seems very evident that the intention is to fall back." So much for all of Johnston's carefully guarded secrecy. Indeed, Watters continued, "Tis reported that we will fall back to the Rappahannock river."

He did not say the origin of the report, and he probably did not know, but the evidence of some impending movement, and a backward one, was on every hand. Headquarters issued orders to have the sick at the railroad depot first thing in the morning on February 27 for shipment south. They were there as ordered, but the trains to carry them were not, and the suffering men had to wait in the cold wind until eight or nine o'clock that evening, while comrades wrapped them in blankets and tended campfires nearby to try to keep them warm. Next day came orders to ship all the extra baggage and ammunition to the rear as well.[1]

Yet the preparations were still far from complete when Johnston decided he could wait no longer. Afraid an early Union advance might catch him in his position at Centreville and force him to fight, Johnston fretted at the time the army took packing up and finally decided to abandon and burn large amounts of baggage as well as vast stocks of cured meat and put the troops in motion at once. As the often underfed soldiers marched away, they could smell the tantalizing odor of sizzling bacon from the heaps of burning meat, and the rising clouds of greasy black smoke were not exactly a monument to good management.

"The blighting effects of war are sadly apparent, in this beautiful section where we now are," wrote Lt. Melvin Dwinnell of Company A, the Rome Light Guards, as the Eighth Georgia marched southward through northern Virginia along with the rest of Johnston's retreating army. Depressing was the sight of fine plantations, obviously carefully tended, now ragged, their gardens and shrubs trampled, fences gone, beautiful groves cut down. Doubly vexing was the realization that it was not the Yankees who had wrought this destruction. The army was passing through a part of the country that had yet to feel the tread of a Union soldier's boot—but soon would feel them in abundance. Confederate soldiers had burned the fence rails and shade trees for their campfires, and their officers' horses had chewed and trampled the shrubbery. It was the very presence of an army—the Southern army—that had given houses, grounds, and all "a sort of dissipated look . . . a haggard appearance."[2]

It was a hard time for the soldiers too. Their route took them to Orange Court House. There, on March 17, Sgt. Hamilton Branch celebrated his eighteenth birthday by walking the mile and a half from camp into the town and buying two dollars' worth of candy. It was the best he could do. Then on April 7 the regiment marched for Fredericksburg, through a steady rain and cold driving wind. For B. P. Barker of Company E, the elements were too much, and he died along the road of congestion of the lungs. Two mornings later, W. M. Settle of Company K also succumbed to the fatigue and exposure. Yet the regiment had not even reached Fredericksburg when the order came to march right back to Orange. Snow, sleet, and rain fell alternately much of the time, and the roads were ankle-deep or worse in mud. Sometimes their tents arrived several days after them, leaving them to camp in the open under the harsh elements as best they could. Days of idleness, huddled against the cold and wet, alternated with brutal forced marches that might continue until three o'clock in the morning. Yet even then the soldiers might wind up doing more standing in ranks, waiting for the column to get moving again, than they did actual walking.[3]

Meanwhile, more and bigger campaigns were in preparation. Far to the north, the Union commander McClellan had a plan. No more eager for a fight than was Johnston, McClellan hoped to avoid the necessity of cutting his way to Richmond through Rebel opposition by carrying his army by ship down the Chesapeake to land at the tip of the peninsula between the James and York rivers. Then, with no need to cross major rivers such as the Rappahannock, he would advance directly up the Peninsula to Richmond. With luck, he might beat Johnston there and thus win the war without having to fight a battle at all. Or so he hoped.

On March 17, while Ham Branch was eating his birthday candy at Orange Court House, McClellan began shipping his army down the bay. Ten days later, Jefferson Davis in Richmond was certain enough of what was going on to be ready to react vigorously. Reports from Maj. Gen. John B. Magruder, commanding the small Confederate force on the Peninsula, indicated a massive increase in Federal troop strength there. Davis responded by ordering Johnston to leave only a small covering force on the Rappahannock and take all the rest of his army in a quick movement down to Richmond and then eastward along the Peninsula to confront McClellan's army where Magruder now faced it near the old Revolutionary War battlefield of Yorktown.

That movement included the Eighth Georgia. Their turn to board the train for Richmond came on Friday evening, April 11, and after riding the train all that night, they arrived in Richmond the next morning and marched out to camp on the outskirts of town. The people of Richmond had been painfully aware of the danger posed by the Union army in their vicinity and lined the streets to cheer the arrival of the Confederate troops, whom they regarded as rescuers. On Sunday, April 13, the Eighth, with its band playing lustily, marched across town to the James River docks to board a miscellaneous flotilla of canal boats and schooners, drawn by steam tugs, that would depart the docks at nine o'clock that evening, carrying them down the James to the lower Peninsula, already desperately threatened by McClellan's rapidly arriving host. Once again the Richmond populace turned out in force to cheer their march.[4]

Company E's Capt. Dunlap Scott had in recent weeks been serving as commander of the division's provost guard detachment, a small number of troops whose job it was to follow along at the rear of the column sweeping the woods and fields for any stragglers who had fallen out to rest or slunk away from their units to pilfer food from civilians. By all accounts, Scott was both diligent and skillful in this job. "Right well he performed his duty," recalled a Texan in a neighboring brigade. The great mass of rank-and-file soldiers as a general rule did not appreciate the diligent efforts of Scott and his guardians of military order, but they took it all with fairly good humor, making a joke out of it. "Old Scott," they called him, "that viper-eyed enemy of straggling humanity," and later, "the Provost Fiend of Longstreet's Corps." Whenever the men in ranks would spy one of their number sneaking off into the woods, they would shout, "Scott! Scott!" Likewise, the captain's appearance in any of the camps was usually sufficient to trigger a waggish cry of "Scott!" that was sometimes taken up by others until a whole brigade was at it. The men were, after all, often very bored.

Capt. Scott had been on sick leave during the days immediately preceding the Eighth's transfer to the Peninsula, and he planned to rejoin the regiment as it passed through Richmond. Thus, as the Eighth swung down Main Street in Richmond, Scott stepped out of the Spotswood Hotel. Seeing him for the first time in a number of days, the men of the regiment and others up and down the column soon set up their chant, "Scott! Scott! Scott!" and the Richmond citizens along the sidewalks looked around to see just who that might be. The captain, however, proved equal to the occasion. Coolly, as if it were an everyday occurrence, he climbed onto a carriage step, a raised platform a couple of feet higher than the street and used to help people clamber into carriages. Prominent atop this pedestal, he stood waving his cap and smiling his acknowledgment of what the civilians all took to be an admiring ovation.[5]

The Occasional Crack of a Rifle

Dawn on Monday, April 14, found the Eighth still gliding down the James River, and those who were awake at that hour watched the sun rise above the glassy surface of the river stretching eastward ahead of them. The river was broad, a mile and a half to two miles in width, and the land on either side seemed as flat as the surface of the James and almost as low-lying. About nine o'clock that morning they passed Jamestown, site of the first permanent English colony in North America, founded back in 1607. It was mostly ruins now, but some of the men, at least, looked with awe upon the traces of the beginnings of their civilization on these shores, over two and a half centuries earlier.

An hour or two later they landed at King's Point, fifteen miles from Yorktown and, by the meanders of the river, just over ninety miles from Richmond. They marched all afternoon and reached their assigned position at five o'clock. The mood of the soldiers was expectant, and they looked for the great battle of the campaign, perhaps the great battle of the war, to be fought there, around Yorktown, within the next few days.[6]

In fact, it was only two days later that they experienced combat on the Peninsula. Their brigade, now commanded by George T. Anderson and composed of the First, Seventh, Eighth, and Eleventh Georgia, moved up as ordered to support the right, or southern, end of the eastward-facing Confederate defenses. Maj. Gen. John B. Magruder had begun the fortifications on the Peninsula before the arrival of Johnston's army, and in the desperate situation he had faced had made the most of whatever advantages the terrain offered. That, as it turned out, was little enough. On the left, extensive fortifications at Yorktown anchored Confederate lines on the York River. On the other side of the Peninsula a small and sluggish stream known as the Warwick River wandered briefly across the Peninsula and emptied into the James River. Magruder took what advantage there was to be had of the Warwick and laid his defensive line behind it, but it was a flimsy obstacle at best, and the best part was near its mouth beyond the Confederate right. Farther into the

Peninsula it became a pitifully small stream that would hardly slow a wading Union column. Magruder therefore aided nature in aiding his cause by having his men construct several small dams to impound the Warwick's waters into ponds that he hoped might prove more effective obstacles. The Eighth's position was in reserve behind the Confederate lines at the first of these dams, what Magruder called Dam Number One.

On the morning of April 16 they got orders to move up into a supporting position directly behind the front lines. They had no more than completed their movement when the patch of woods they were in came under heavy artillery bombardment. The steady skirmishing and desultory cannonading that had gone on for days rose in an unexpected crescendo. Smoke filled the air, some from the burning woodlands and some from the gunpowder of the artillery. The Yankee batteries were busy, and the shells bursting frequently in the forest canopy overhead gave the men an unpleasant reminder of the first phase of their experience at Manassas the summer before. Limbs and leaves fluttered down around them. At the head of the Eighth, twenty-seven-year-old Col. Lucius M. Lamar considered the situation. John Reed thought Lamar "the handsomest man in the army," and of fine bearing, gallant in the extreme but not ostentatious. He had brought the Macon Guards, now Company C, north to Virginia as their first captain and had led them through Manassas, where the experienced Lt. Col. Gardner had bid the men take shelter as best they could on a bare hillside. Lamar now followed Gardner's example by directing the men to make use of the woods. "They are shooting as if they know we are here," he called out. "Break ranks and take care of yourselves behind the trees." The men of the Eighth were not usually slow to obey orders, and this time their promptness was downright exemplary. Sheltering as best they could, crouching behind the mossy boles of the old forest oaks, they listened to the thundering guns interspersed with the occasional rattle of musketry. In Company A, William Aycock felt a sharp sting on his shoulder and found that he had been hit by a piece of shrapnel from an exploding shell. The piece of metal was moving too slowly even to penetrate the fabric of his jacket, and he got off with no worse injury than a bruise. Others had similar experiences.[7]

Suddenly, about 3:30 P.M., the guns fell silent. "All was quiet except the occasional crack of a rifle," a Georgian recalled. Then they heard a sound that told them what was happening in the woods beyond their sight in front of them.[8]

The shouts of the opposing armies were sharply distinct. Southern troops moving forward to the attack gave the "Rebel Yell." It could be a discordant chorus of keening wails or yipping cries—it was not the sort of thing even an army could standardize—but it was always high-pitched and blood-curdling. The Yankees, by contrast, gave organized, unison cheers, in a deep, roaring baritone. Northerners thought the Rebel Yell sounded unearthly, inhuman, demonic. Southerners thought Yankee cheers sounded ridiculous.

Berrien Zettler described the sound they heard, as they waited there in the suddenly quiet woods, as "a sort of 'Hoo-raw.' "The Yankees were coming. Next came the crash of real, serious musketry. "Into line!" shouted Lamar, and the Georgians needed little prompting to scramble back into their places in the ranks. Then the colonel had them lie down and wait to see if they would be needed. They did not have to wait long. The sounds of battle in front of them soon gave way to a tremendous crashing in the undergrowth out in front, "as if ten thousand Texas steers were coming toward us," Zettler thought. Then, bursting out of the brush came a large number of Confederate soldiers. Some carried rifles. Some carried shovels, with which they had until recently been working on the still-incomplete entrenchments. Some carried nothing that would impede their flight. Soldiers hastening to the rear in no particular order are not an impressive sight, and Zettler rather uncharitably described these men of the Fifteenth North Carolina as "a mob of panicky soldiers." But then he may have been influenced against them by the fact that one of them tripped over his head and fell heavily on him and his neighbor, prompting the neighbor to say things to the unfortunate North Carolinian that two soldiers on the same side should not say to each other.

The Fifteenth had been caught in a bad way. They had been working on the fortifications and had their rifles stacked nearby. The Union assault caught them by surprise, apparently before many of them could reach their weapons. Their colonel had tried to rally them but had been shot down in front of the regiment. Those circumstances, coupled with the approaching bluecoats, four companies of the Third Vermont, already splashing across the impoundment, bayoneted rifles above their heads, were too much for the Carolinians, and they headed for the rear. Stopping the Union assault would now be up to the supporting troops, especially the two lead regiments of George T. Anderson's brigade, the Seventh and Eighth Georgia.[9]

"Attention!" shouted Lamar. "Forward!" The Eighth rose, even as the Seventh was doing the same to their left. Their brigade commander, Anderson, galloped down the line shouting that he did not want his men to fire a shot: "Give them the cold steel!" he roared. Then the brigade charged forward toward the works the Federals had just taken. They emerged from the cover of underbrush to see the Union line less than fifty yards ahead. Berrien Zettler recalled the regiment pausing to fire a volley at that point. J. H. Brightwell of Company K was sure they did not. At any rate they plunged forward with the bayonet as ordered. The Federals were disorganized after their charge through the pond and over the Fifteenth North Carolina's position. Their ammunition had gotten wet, and they were surprised by the sudden appearance close in front of them of an enemy line of battle where they thought none could be. Now it was their turn to run, and the Georgians ran after them, loading and firing as they went. Some even splashed out into the pond after the retreating Yankees, wading out waist deep.

Officers called them back and ordered them to "get down" in a shallow trench on the Confederate side of the pond. There they took shelter from the renewed Union artillery bombardment. Zettler thought it lasted another hour, and it was distinctly "uncomfortable" for the Confederates in the trench. The discomfort was compounded by the fact that the trench had fifteen inches of water standing in the bottom of it. Still, no one seemed tempted to get out while Union shells whistled and burst nearby.

Again the bombardment lifted, and again the Federal troops, now two full regiments of Vermonters, marched forward to the assault. This time, however, the Confederates were ready, and the attack had no chance of success. Still the Federals came on valiantly, sometimes wading through chest-deep water, and John Reed, who mistakenly thought the attackers were from Maine, had to admire "the bravery of the men of Maine who made this desperate trial with resolute manhood." But despite Northern courage, the Confederate lines held, and the surviving bluecoats swarmed back to their starting point. Brightwell remembered vividly the blue-clad bodies floating in the pond. Some of the members of the Eighth and their sister regiment the Seventh waded out into the pond to retrieve Union rifles to replace their own inferior weapons. None of the Georgians was hurt in this second phase of the Battle of Dam Number One.[10]

Though the Union attack had actually been a mere probe of the Confederate position, the Georgians were enthused about their victory, one considerably less expensive than Manassas. Not surprisingly, they were also happy with their brigade commander. The former colonel of the Eleventh Georgia, George T. Anderson had served as a lieutenant in a Georgia regiment during the Mexican War. Then he had held a commission in the regular U.S. Army for several years during the 1850s. Early in the war the men had noticed a certain tan-colored pair of pants he wore that looked almost yellow, and they had nicknamed him "Old Yellow Dog." On this day, however, after the fight at Dam Number One, they called him "Tige" instead. One of the members of Company G, the Pulaski Volunteers, claimed to have been the first to do so. That nickname stuck to him for the rest of the war, and the Eighth would be known as part of Tige Anderson's brigade.[11]

The Eighth now had itself a front-line position in the operation known as the siege of Yorktown. For days they took their turn, on a twenty-four-hour rotation, sitting in trenches knee-deep in water. "These trenches are very small and slight," Melvin Dwinnell explained, "2½ feet deep, same width at bottom, and evidently thrown up in a hurry." The pathologically cautious McClellan slowly edged his army forward in regular siege operations, laboriously digging emplacements for heavy guns while desultory artillery and sharpshooter fire forced the defenders to keep their heads down. J. H. Brightwell recalled that in the sector his company held the water was hip-deep "when we squatted down, which we were obliged to do nearly all the time night and day" because of the enemy sharpshooters. The Union sharpshooters were very good at their job, as John Reed recalled: "During the day light, if you exposed but a finger it would be hit by a bullet." "The federal sharpshooters were up in the trees of the swamp in our front," Brightwell remembered, "and to expose a head above the low embankment was certain death." That was just how McClellan wanted it. The danger of sudden death from a sharpshooter's bullet was one of the chief things that forced the Confederates to keep down in their soggy trenches and prevented them from interfering with the Union general's slow but methodical siege operations.[12]

Sometimes those operations included additional probes at one part or another of the Confederate lines. Two or three of these probes struck the section of line held by the Eighth. They were not generally very serious affairs, no one emptied his cartridge box, and once the defenders had fired, on average, about five or six rounds each, the Yankees would fall back, satisfied that this part of the Confederate line was still strongly held.

During one of these brief engagements, a member of Company G became convinced that he had shot a Union color-bearer and excitedly boasted of this accomplishment to his comrades. The constant damp conditions in the trenches meant that black-powder weapons, left loaded for any length of time, might well prove unusable when needed in an emergency. A regiment with wet charges in its rifles and muskets would be helpless in the event of an enemy attack. It was therefore a very routine matter, a couple of days after one of the Union forays, when the Eighth's officers directed their men to "draw" the charges from their weapons—carefully remove the loads with special tools—and then load them with fresh charges so as to be ready in case of emergency. When the proud soldier who had boasted of winging a color-bearer went to work on his weapon, he was chagrined to draw out a second load after the first, then a third, fourth, fifth, and sixth—all six loads rammed into the gun and none of them fired.

The phenomenon was surprisingly common in Civil War battles. A soldier would load his weapon, aim, and pull the trigger, but for some reason the weapon would not discharge. In the noise and tumult of battle, the man somehow would not notice the absence of recoil or smoke (from his own gun) or the fact that with each successive load his ramrod traveled a shorter distance into the barrel. The usual cause was the soldier's forgetting to insert the necessary percussion cap at the breech of the gun, but in this case the reason may have been dampness in the first charge the soldier attempted to fire. Once a man had double-loaded his gun, it was just as well for him if the weapon continued to misfire at every subsequent attempt until the charges were drawn. The embarrassed Company G man had a different analysis, however, and vowed never to shoot at a color-bearer again.[13]

Human nature is such that even grave dangers, after long exposure, can come to seem mundane or even, in some cases, to become the very elements of humor. One man who never got used to the danger, however, and never thought it funny was John Reed's black servant, Lit. A big strapping fellow six feet tall, Lit saw no sense in taking risks, whether of shells, bullets, or fists, and he was always the first to back down in any encounter with the regiment's other black servants. He was also notorious for an episode back at the battle of Manassas, when a shell landing in safe but disturbing proximity to the field hospital where he was working had launched Lit into a truly impressive athletic performance, sprinting across the fields and hurdling amazingly tall fences to put more of Virginia between himself and the Yankee cannon.

Here on the Yorktown lines some of his fellow black servants decided to have a bit of "fun" with the large but unwarlike Lit. One of them decoyed him out into a field behind the lines known to be watched by the gunners of a Union battery across the way and where any moving figures were sure to draw a few rounds from those guns. True to form, the distant Federals opened up on the tiny human shapes moving in the field, but they were not fast enough to hit Lit, who turned in another impressive track and field performance, amid howls of laughter from the other blacks. Back in camp that night, Lit angrily asked Reed, "What good would it do a yankee to kill a nigger?"

For the men in the trenches, where real dangers lurked, comradeship was one of the things that made the hardships of war bearable. A favorite comrade of Reed's was Sgt. Frank Cone, also of Company I. The son of a prominent judge, Cone was "the most vivacious and enchanting talker." "Handsome, all-accomplished, magnetic, lovable and gallant," Cone was universally well liked. One evening in early May, he entertained Reed and several other members of the company with an impressive recitation of Falstaff's soliloquy on honor, a bravura performance by all accounts and none the easier to carry off sitting in a foot or so of muddy water while bullets whistled overhead.

The next morning the Confederates in the Dam Number One sector found themselves severely annoyed by a particularly skillful Union sharpshooter. A little way down the line, a couple of members of the Texas Brigade pitted their skill and cunning against his in a dangerous game of concealment and marksmanship—one man decoying the Yankee while the other drew a bead on him—but the Northerner was too good for them. Refusing to buck a stacked deck, he slipped ghostlike down the battlelines toward the Eighth's section of trench. The Confederates could not see him, but over time he revealed his progress as he gradually shifted the sectors of the Confederate line he worked over. Soon several members of I Company felt the breeze of his bullets a fraction of an inch from their heads.

John Reed was enjoying a delightful section of relatively dry trench, and stretched out at full length he was lying well out of the way of the pestilent sniper's bullets, contentedly reading his Shakespeare, when another of the unwelcome missiles smacked into the trench parapet, throwing sand into the eyes of several men. Reed heard Cone exclaim, "Well, Cone rises to the question," and rolling over to look in the direction of the voice, Reed saw his orderly sergeant pop up, head and shoulders above the rim of the trench, intently searching the terrain out front for the sniper's lair. But the Union sharpshooter found him first. Reed was about to "rebuke his exposure and order him down" when Cone dropped his musket, threw up his arms, and toppled backward into the trench. Reed and the others rushed to him and found him dead, a bullet hole square in the middle of his forehead.

That same day, orders came down from headquarters to abandon the position at Dam Number One and pull back. Johnston was retreating again, leaving the Yorktown lines and withdrawing to a position closer to Richmond. The men of Company I had to rush their burial of Sgt. Cone, but there was nothing else to do. They could not bring his body with them. Lt. Reed packed up Cone's effects and sent them to his family back in Georgia. Then, looking at the notebook in which Cone had kept some company records, Reed found something different. A day or two before, Cone had written on an empty page in the back of the notebook farewell messages to his sister back in Georgia and his sweetheart in Winchester. The sergeant had apparently believed that his own demise was imminent. Reed forwarded the messages and mused on soldiers' premonitions of death. "I noticed," he later wrote, "that such a presentiment of death never deceived one in the army who was in good health."[14]

The Idol of His Regiment

That night, May 3, the army began to pull out of its positions secretly, lest McClellan discover that his enemy was fleeing and pursue too quickly. The heavy cannon in the Confederate fortifications at Yorktown fired a last grand cannonade, partially to cover the withdrawal and partially to use up remaining stocks of heavy ammunition that could not be brought along. While the guns thundered and rumbled to the north of them, the men of the Eighth Georgia filed out of the by now unspeakably rank trenches they had held for the past eighteen days. Their canteens were muffled to avoid any clatter that might give away the movement. Brightwell thought that in their sojourn in the trenches they had "suffered to the full extent of our endurance."[15]

They marched all night, through a more or less constant drizzling rain. By the next day the troops and wheeled vehicles had churned the roads of the Peninsula into a seemingly bottomless quagmire, but the army had to keep moving; Federal patrols discovered the empty Confederate fortifications that morning and the Union army moved forward in pursuit. Teams strained to pull heavy supply wagons through the mire, and infantry slogged wearily onward through the sucking, squelching mud, stacking arms occasionally to help haul a stuck wagon or gun out of a morass, then taking up their weapons again and plodding on.

The retreat lasted several weeks and included a number of pauses. The Eighth halted several days at Savage's Station on the York River Railroad, then broke camp and trudged on toward Richmond, their backs to the enemy. They next paused near Meadow Bridges on the Chickahominy, not far from Mechanicsville.

There a handful of new recruits arrived from Georgia, as other small contingents had been arriving all spring, in the charge of some of the several officers and sergeants who had been dispatched for that purpose the previous winter. Their numbers were few, however. Dozens of new regiments were then forming up back in the home state, and somehow a new company always had more appeal to recruits than a veteran one.

The sum total of the new contingents was little more than half of the number needed, and the regiment had a present-for-duty strength between half and two-thirds its nominal full compliment of one thousand men, depending on how many were sick in the hospital on a given day.[16]

Also at Meadow Bridges, the regiment fought a small skirmish with the pursuing Federals, losing one man wounded. Companies A, B, and K, who were deployed as skirmishers, lost their knapsacks in this fray. They had stacked them in the rear before going out onto the skirmish line, and the tide of the fight had carried them away from their cache. It was all part of the vicissitudes of soldiering for the increasingly campaign-hardened men of the Eighth. Downstream from Meadow Bridges, Union troops took another member of the regiment prisoner near Bottom's Bridge, a few days later. Finally, in early June, the army reached the position that Johnston had always wanted it to occupy, a defensive line on the very outskirts of Richmond. There they settled down for another and even longer period of holding static defensive positions against light but almost constant enemy pressure. Soldiers and camp conditions became filthy, and the vicinity in which both contending armies were encamped, the bottomland of the Chickahominy River, tended in any case to be swampy and not very healthy. Sick lists continued to grow. Back in Richmond, three members of Company G and four of Company E died of disease that month. It was about the same in the other companies.[17]

The filthy conditions also brought another affliction upon the men, though no one liked to talk about it: lice. Reed noticed a very uncomfortable itch not long after they got into the lines at Yorktown. He had heard that some of the less clean men in the regiment were infested with "vermin," but he could not remember coming into close contact with any of those soldiers of late. He finally could not stand it anymore and "retired to an obscure place" where, upon examining his clothing, he found—he could not bring himself to name them. The shame was almost overwhelming. In fact, Reed thought it would have overwhelmed him if not for the fact that a friend of his, over in the Fifteenth Georgia, told him not long after that the Fifteenth's colonel had been lousy for weeks. The colonel of the Fifteenth was a man of good reputation, known for his courage, good nature, popularity, and, more to the point, cleanliness. That made Reed feel better. Perhaps, under the circumstances, it was not an unendurable disgrace to be afflicted by—"vermin."

Still, like everyone else in the regiment, he kept his affliction a careful secret from the others. This could not go on very long, of course, in a military camp. Eventually people were going to find out about each other. Soon after the Eighth had moved into its lines near Richmond the unfortunate Sgt. Harrison, of Company K, became the first to go public with the universal problem. As the others in the regiment were doing, and as indeed officers and enlisted men in probably every regiment on both sides were compelled to do, he sneaked out of camp one morning to find a secluded place where he could remove his clothing and hunt over the interior surfaces, finding and killing all the lice he could. The place he found for that purpose was sitting down in a field of tall green wheat. His head was well below the level of the gently waving immature heads of grain as he sat bending over his shirt, which he had spread on his knees, but unfortunately he had not taken into account the fact that a path, frequented by members of the regiment, ran over the hill just behind him. His white back, contrasting with the green of the field, was dotted with red welts left by his unwelcome guests, and in this position he was spotted by several members of the regiment, including some from his own company. One of them called out to him, "Hello, Harrison, what luck with your fishing." The embarrassed soldier quickly ducked down into the wheat and answered that he had caught nothing, but his comrade was not fooled. "The devil you haven't," he replied, "with so many bites."

It did not take long for the men to come to accept the fact that they all had lice. No secret was made of it anymore, and the men compared notes about the creatures and their ways. It became their settled belief that the louse preferred a clean man to a dirty one. "As soon as one of the mess changed his clothes," Reed recalled, "they deserted all the others and concentrated on him." In Company I of the Eighth at least, the troops combated this tactic of the lice by agreeing that the entire mess—six or eight men—should put on clean clothes at the same time, thus in theory offering the lice no especially enticing target. Lt. Reed held that the only good thing about the lice was that they motivated the soldiers to boil their clothes frequently.[18]

They might grow accustomed to the lice, but they never got over their loathing of them, and the insects remained one of the more severe trials of soldiering. "I never saw the like before," wrote Lt. Tom Hodgkins of Company C. "You may wash and put on clean clothes all over & in half a day you will find some on you. No wonder I am sick, disgusted too, of the war."[19]

Duty on the lines near Richmond was much like that near York-town—filth, discomfort, and long periods of boredom during which death could still strike occasionally with shocking suddenness. One day a group of men from Company G, the Pulaski Volunteers, were sitting around under a tree when a shell burst in their midst, mangling four of them, three of whom died within a few hours.[20]

Federal artillery practice was not always that lethal, but it did make the boys jump at times. The irrepressible Berrien Zettler was away from the regiment on detailed duty one day when in passing along behind Confederate lines he came to a cherry tree loaded with cherries. That was unusual, since in such proximity to sixty thousand more or less per-petually hungry Confederate soldiers, fruit was likely to be picked the moment it got ripe—at the latest. Zettler asked some nearby soldiers why the tree had not been picked over and was told that it was within sight of the Federal batteries just over the crest of the hill. Since scouts and pickets often resorted to climbing into trees to spy out their ene-mies' dispositions, neither side would tolerate a distant enemy climbing into one. In this case, the Federals were using their highly accurate rifled artillery to make sure that no one stayed long in the cherry tree. Zettler decided he would try anyway. Climbing into the cherry tree, he stood up on a branch about ten feet off the ground and reached up to grab a handful of the enticing red cherries. All the while, however, he kept an eye cocked at a Union battery he could see several hundred yards away. When he saw a flash at the muzzle of one of the cannon, that was enough for him. He jumped and dropped clear to the ground, just as a shell crashed through the branches over his head. Giving further thought to the matter, he decided that the cherries were probably sour and went on his way back to the regiment.

Payday did not come very frequently for Confederate soldiers, so when it did come it was a memorable affair. The regiment received a portion of the wages due it while encamped near Richmond that spring. The men were giddy at possession of the vast sum of twenty dollars. Not all the members of the regiment had been devout men to begin with, and army life was often corrosive of good morals. Thus it was not too surprising that a number of them chose to employ their newfound wealth in gambling. One day a group of gamblers sat under an apple tree behind the lines, sheltered from Federal eyes by the brow of a nearby hill. The game was "an unusually interesting" one, and the players sat hunched over their cards, their "chips," actually grains of dried corn, piled on a board between them that constituted the pot. Fascinated spectators stood all around them. Perhaps the heads of the spectators came into the Yankees' line of sight just over the top of the hill, or perhaps what happened next was a mere random shot. At any rate, a shell crashed through the boughs of the apple tree above their heads. Instantly the whole assembly went diving for cover, scattering cards and "chips" in all directions. "An ill shot," one of the soldiers concluded, "that did somebody good."[21]

Another temptation the soldiers did not always resist was Richmond itself. The city had everything to offer that their comfortless camps did not, and many sneaked out of camp of an evening to enjoy the metropolis of Virginia. Berrien Zettler, of course, would be one of them. He had a particularly favorable situation for making such excursions, an assignment to Company B's cook squad. It was good duty. Since the trench lines were too close to the enemy and too exposed to allow the kindling of fires, Zettler and the other members of the cook squad were detailed to remain safely in the rear, rise at dawn, cook the day's rations, and then carry them out to the company. It was hard work for most of the morning, but in the afternoon the members of the cook squad lolled around camp reading books or papers, or playing cards or marbles. Best of all, "there was no standing guard" and "no picket duty" for them.

One evening Zettler proposed to his comrade and occasional partner in crime Billy Dasher that they sneak into Richmond. Sentinels guarded the roads to prevent just such excursions, but the soldiers usually succeeded in evading them. That night was no exception, and the two country boys from south Georgia soon found themselves inside Richmond and ready to sample the forbidden fruits of the great city. Zettler knew just what to do. He led Dasher to the house of his friends Mr. and Mrs. W. W. Yarrington, where they were kindly received and fed a hearty meal. There followed an evening of pleasant conversation with the Yarringtons and their niece, and then the boys explained that they had to be back to camp by dawn. Mr. Yarrington showed them how to let themselves out in the morning and then showed them to the guest room. The beautiful white sheets looked too good to sleep on, so the boys lay down on the floor and fell right to sleep.

Early next morning, haversacks loaded with good things to eat that the Yarringtons had insisted they take, they set out for camp. In theory this was much easier than the journey into town, since the sentries had orders to let pass any men who were returning to their regiments. Unfortunately, Zettler and Dasher got on the wrong road and had to cut through a woodlot to get back on course. As they came out of the woods, a sentry nabbed them and refused to buy their tale about being on their way back to camp. Following orders, he marched them off to see the colonel of their regiment. They tried various angles of persuasion to get him to let them go, all to no avail. Even the suggestion that he sit down and take a rest while they went down to the spring for a drink of water got no result. Finally they approached Col. Lamar's tent.

"Good morning, Colonel!" Zettler burst out. "Here is a *Richmond Dispatch,* and see what our Richmond friends gave us on our way to camp," as he and Dasher set out some particularly appetizing delicacies on the colonel's camp chest.

Lamar seemed impressed. "Yes, yes, yes, boys!" he replied. "Those Richmond ladies are the finest in the world. We must not let the Yankees take Richmond, boys, never never!"

"But, Colonel," Zettler added meekly, "we are prisoners. This man arrested us on our way out and insisted on bringing us to our colonel."

"Ah," Lamar replied, turning to the sentry, "and were you instructed to bring them to their colonel? Well, I'm Colonel Lamar of the Eighth Georgia Regiment, and these are my men, so you have done your duty. You may go." Then to Zettler and Dasher he added, "On the cook squad, boys?" They nodded. "I see," Lamar concluded. "Then you may go too."

The boys loved Lamar, of course. He was "one of the handsomest officers in Lee's army," wrote Zettler, "and as clever and brave as he was handsome, and he was the idol of his regiment." But at that rate the regiment—and an army that was full of similar regimental officers—would always suffer from less than adequate discipline. Unfortunately, Zettler and Dasher caught up with the conscientious sentry and threatened him with dire treatment if he in future continued to take such a strict view of his duty. He promised not to.[22]

From Some Cause, Not Understood by Me

Two huge armies were gathered on the outskirts of the Confederate capital. Though both the opposing commanders were notably unaggressive, their respective governments pressed them hard to fight. From Washington, an anxious Lincoln assured McClellan, "You must act," while at Johnston's headquarters, where Jefferson Davis now resorted on an almost daily basis, the Confederate president warned his reluctant general that Richmond must not be given up without a fight and that if Johnston would not fight, Davis would find a general who would. The tense standoff outside Richmond could not continue indefinitely, and as spring began to give way to the early onset of Southern summer, the first thunders of the impending storm rumbled up from the Chickahominy swamps.

The men of the Eighth could hear the rumblings of artillery on May 31, as Johnston finally launched his counterattack in an attempt to forestall the capture of Richmond, an event that was otherwise a mere question of time. A major battle took place that day, with minor aftershocks the following morning, but the Eighth saw no action either day. For the Confederates it was one of the worst-managed major battles of the war. Partially through his own mistakes and partially through the fault of his subordinates, Johnston failed to get much of his army into the fight. The result was a drawn battle. The Confederates scored a few local successes but were repulsed in other sectors, and McClellan's host still remained poised at the very doorstep of Richmond. Only one truly significant consequence came out of the fight that Southerners were soon calling the Battle of Seven Pines, while Yankees called it Fair Oaks. Johnston received a severe wound that would keep him off duty for months to come. In need of a replacement to step immediately into an extremely difficult situation, Davis tapped his top military man, Robert E. Lee. Lee had most recently held a desk assignment as nominal commander of all Confederate forces from headquarters in Richmond. From

June 1 onward, however, he would be commander of the army that he was already beginning to style the Army of Northern Virginia. And Robert E. Lee was not afraid to fight.

A great offensive campaign cannot be launched overnight or at the mere whim of a commanding general. Much careful preparation was needed, and Lee took almost a month getting his army ready. Then on Thursday, June 26, 1862, he inaugurated his first offensive, initiating a series of battles that would come to be known as the Seven Days. Lee's plan was to destroy the smaller portion of the Union army that extended north of the Chickahominy, then sweep around the northern flank of McClellan's army, cutting his railroad supply line that ran back to his base at White House, at the head of the York River. His first blow would fall near the village of Mechanicsville. Stonewall Jackson, whom Lee had brought east after his spectacular successes in the Shenandoah Valley that spring, would fall on McClellan's right flank and then the bulk of Lee's other forces would attack the crumbling Yankee lines at Mechanicsville, just north of the Chickahominy.

That was not quite how it worked. For reasons that still remain obscure, Jackson failed to get into position, and his attack never came off. As the sun crept down the western sky, impetuous Confederate division commander Ambrose Powell Hill decided he had waited long enough and launched his troops against the unshaken Union lines at Mechanicsville. The Federals slaughtered his men as well as those of other formations that Lee hastened into battle to try to salvage the situation. Night closed down on a field covered with Confederate dead and wounded and where Union firepower still ruled supreme. Once again, the Eighth Georgia waited and listened to the roar of battle but took no part in the combat.

It was not an auspicious beginning, but in an odd sort of way it got the job done. McClellan had for some time been contemplating casting loose his York River supply line and shifting his base to the James River. Lee's aggressiveness and reports of Jackson lurking out beyond his right flank decided the matter in his mind at once. He would order his commander on the north bank of the Chickahominy to fall back a few miles and then delay the Confederates one more day while he prepared his entire army to fall back to a safe base on the James at Harrison's Landing, thirty miles or so farther away from Richmond.

Lee, of course, did not know this and would not have been satisfied anyway. His goal was not to drive McClellan away from Richmond but rather to destroy the Union army. On the following day, Friday, June 27, he planned to implement the program that had never quite come off at Mechanicsville. Jackson would hit the flank of the Federals now dug in several miles to the east behind Boatswain's Swamp, while other troops attacked head on. Again the plan degenerated into a direct assault, but this time it was successful in breaking the Union line and hastening the already planned Federal withdrawal from the north to the south bank. Conspicuous in the successful assault at what Confederates were soon calling the Battle of Gaines's Mill was a man whom the Eighth would later follow for almost a year of glorious triumphs. At Gaines's Mill, Brig. Gen. John Bell Hood stormed across the Yankee breastworks at the head of his Texas Brigade, marking himself as a man to be watched among the rising young officers of the Army of Northern Virginia.

Meanwhile, on the south bank of the Chickahominy, less than half of Lee's army faced the great mass of McClellan's directly in front of Richmond. It was a dangerous situation until Lee could sufficiently threaten McClellan's supply line north of the river to compel him to withdraw. Throughout the battles of the 26th and 27th, the Confederate forces on the south bank, including the Eighth Georgia, waited tensely for the outcome of Lee's fight north of the river, watching the rising clouds of white powder smoke and listening to the thunder of the cannons and the roar of musketry. All the while, their general officers, at least, hoped that the Federals opposite them would not attempt a direct rush at Richmond through the thin gray line left to hold them. The Yankees, of course, had no idea of doing anything of the sort and actually entertained reciprocal hopes that the Confederates would leave them alone as they made preparations and began their retreat toward Harrison's Landing.

The Eighth Georgia spent Friday the 27th in the same positions, near the Price House, just west of the New Bridge Road, that they had occupied along with the rest of Tige Anderson's brigade for almost the entire month of June. Not far to the south of their position, the New Bridge Road intersected the Nine Mile Road. Confederate artillery near them dueled with the Union guns to their front, and their division commander, Maj. Gen. David R. Jones, stood on the roof of the Price

House and directed some of the heavier guns in firing northward, over the Chickahominy, in support of the major Confederate attack then in progress at Boatswain's Swamp. That evening, Maj. Gen. John B. Magruder, commanding the southern wing of the Confederate army, south of the Chickahominy, ordered Jones to "feel" the enemy in his front by pushing forward skirmishers. To do this Jones used the brigade of Georgia politician and former Confederate secretary of state Robert Toombs, along with two regiments, the First and Ninth Georgia, from Anderson's brigade. The movement brought on a half hour or so of intense musketry along Jones's front at about sunset, but the contest remained long-range, both sides keeping well under cover, and produced few casualties. Gen. Magruder got the answer he was looking for: the Federals were still present in force in the vicinity of the Nine Mile Road south of the Chickahominy.

Saturday, June 28, dawned fair and pleasant and continued thus throughout the day. It was a day that would come to be remembered as the quietest of the Seven Days, as Lee's forces north of the Chickahominy ranged eastward along the north bank, finally ascertaining that McClellan had withdrawn all of his forces to the south side, abandoning his former supply line and destroying the stocks left in his depots. No major collision of the two armies took place that day, a circumstance highly ironic for the Eighth Georgia.[23]

On the south side of the Chickahominy, McClellan's army continued to hold its positions for one last day while wagon trains, herds of beef cattle, and all the other impedimenta of a huge army continued to move out toward Harrison's Landing. Artillery sparring continued in the Eighth's sector near the Nine Mile Road, with the Confederate gunners forcing a couple of brigades of Union infantry to pull back into a less exposed position and the Union counterbattery fire eventually forcing the Southerners to withdraw their guns. Jones wanted to do more than that. He correctly perceived that the enemy in front of him was preparing to retreat, and he was eager to strike a blow. That Saturday morning he could not find Magruder, commanding his wing of the army, so he sent a staff officer directly to Lee to request permission to launch an assault and also asking for artillery support from the north bank. As the day wore on and evening approached, Jones witnessed the effects of his artillery fire and became more anxious than ever to strike. He sent an order to Toombs to take advantage of "any positive retreat" of the enemy by moving into the Federal breastworks should the bluecoats fall back. But at this point, things began to get out of hand.

First the staff officer Jones had sent to Lee came back with word that the commanding general definitely did not desire an attack on the south bank of the Chickahominy at this time. Then the staff officer who had carried Jones's order to Toombs came back and reported that as soon as Toombs had gotten the order, he had sent an order of his own to Col. Tige Anderson, commander of Jones's other brigade, directing the latter to attack at once, with a promise that Toombs would back him up. This was such a shock to Jones that he wondered if perhaps Magruder had issued an order to Toombs without informing him. He sent to Magruder to find out, and the wing commander replied that he had ordered nothing of the sort. Learning this, Jones immediately sent an order calling off Toombs's attack, but by that time it was too late.

In fact the whole business had been Toombs's doing. A big, florid, bombastic politician, stuffed full of himself and badly overstuffed at that, Toombs fancied himself a great military man who was held back from the highest positions of command only because of Jefferson Davis's unreasonable prejudice in favor of West Point–trained men. Eventually he would do the Confederacy the enormous service of resigning from its army to show his disgust over the neglect of his talents, but for now he was a general with plenty of capacity to hurt Confederate fortunes—and Confederate soldiers.

The Union withdrawal Jones had posited as a prerequisite for any advance by Toombs had not occurred at all. Toombs may have ignorantly misunderstood Jones's order, or he may have willfully determined to win himself some military glory anyway. "I have always thought that whiskey was the incentive of this fight," a soldier of Company K recalled, and then added, "It wasn't I or the other soldiers, either, who drank the whiskey." At any rate, Toombs ordered Anderson to attack. Anderson was perplexed. "From some cause, not understood by me," he later explained, "General Toombs sent Captain Thurston to me to make the attack, and as Captain Thurston was on General Jones' staff I supposed the [previous] order had been changed, and, expecting to be supported, ordered

the Eighth and Seventh Georgia to advance." Thus on this quietest day
of the Seven Days, the Eighth was about to see its heaviest action of the
week.[24]

With the setting sun at their backs, the Seventh and Eighth
marched out into a broad field, steadily tramping toward the breastworks at the far side. Companies A, B, and K once again double-
quicked forward and fanned out into a skirmish line covering the
whole front. Behind the skirmish line, near the center of the Eighth's
main line of battle, Lt. J. M. Montgomery carried the regiment's new
flag. It was the new-pattern battle flag that the Army of Northern Virginia's regiments now carried to avoid the kind of confusion of flags
that had plagued everyone at Manassas, a square red banner with a
blue St. Andrew's cross centered on it and touching the four corners.
Along the blue arms of the cross marched thirteen stars for the thirteen states the Confederacy claimed. Now the bright banner fluttered
above Lt. Montgomery as the line strode forward through the field of
ripening wheat.

Manning the breastworks at the far side of the field were parts of
two Union regiments, the Thirty-third New York and the Forty-ninth
Pennsylvania. The Federals blazed away at the advancing Georgians.
The skirmishers had not gone fifty yards when Company A's Second
Sgt. W. Scott Hutchings took a bullet in the upper left thigh, becoming the first of many to fall that day. Lt. Moore set a bad example for
the men by stopping to aid the fallen sergeant, but the rest of the attackers pressed on. Across the field, into a skirt of woods in front of the
Union lines, through a thicket and a patch of swampy ground, and then
uphill through an open pine woods they charged, taking casualties all
the way.[25]

In Company B's skirmish line was John Krenson. He had been badly
wounded in the infamous pine thicket at Manassas the preceding summer, and the surgeons had told him his health would never permit him
to take the field again. Yet when spring rolled around in 1862 and he
heard that the Eighth was part of the army standing between the Union
host and Richmond, he had hastened to join his regiment anyway. A few
days in camp proved that the surgeons had been right about his health,
and they now issued him a discharge on the basis of disability. Yet Krenson did not want to go home on the eve of a battle, and from day to day

as the great battle for Richmond was expected momentarily, he delayed his departure. Now he got his wish and advanced once more in the ranks of his comrades, only to be shot dead in one of the first volleys, his discharge papers still in his pocket.[26]

The Northern firepower proved too much, and the attackers broke and fell back, then rallied and came on again. Again the devastating fire from the Union barricades beat them back. Col. Lamar leaped out in front of the regiment, waving his sword and calling on the men to rally. They did, but Lamar had become a conspicuous target, and presently went down, gravely wounded. As the Eighth went forward for a third attempt on the Union breastworks, Lamar waved his sword and cheered them on as they marched past where he lay. But it was no use. Federal firepower broke up this charge as it had the others.

Sam Brewer was in the thick of the charge and thought it "the hottest place" he had ever seen. "It appeared to rain lead around me," he wrote a few days later. Then a shell landed very close to him. It exploded, and he knew no more. When he awoke, the fight was over. He sat up and found that he felt no pain but that blood was flowing freely from both his ears. In the gathering darkness, he made his way safely to Confederate lines, and the only ill effects he suffered in the days that followed were that he "became very sore" and his "eyes swelled considerably."[27]

Many of the Georgians fared much worse. Those who had advanced farthest were in a predicament when the attack finally broke up; so thoroughly did the Northern bullets crisscross the field that it seemed almost suicidal even to attempt to retreat across it. Lt. Col. John Towers, sometime captain of Rome's Miller Rifles, saw no choice but to surrender and did so along with about fifteen or twenty of the men around him. The rest got back to Confederate lines as best they could, running the gauntlet of Federal fire. Somehow, Lt. Montgomery, though badly wounded, was among those who made it back to the east side of the field, and the new battle flag was saved. The young lieutenant, however, died the following day at the brigade field hospital.[28]

With Towers a prisoner and Lamar badly wounded and soon to be a prisoner as well, command of what was left of the Eighth devolved on Maj. Edward J. Magruder, who as captain had brought the Rome Light Guards to Richmond little over a year before. He had been accounted "one of the finest looking officers," but this fight had marred that somewhat. A bullet had shot away part of his nose, and another had torn into his shoulder. Refusing to leave the field, he paused only long enough to have his wounds dressed and then went immediately to work trying to get the Eighth back into some semblance of order.

The story was later told that as he went around thus, face swathed in bandages, Magruder ran into an older gentleman in a homespun suit and a broad-brimmed hat. The older man stopped him, laid his hand on Magruder's shoulder (presumably the good one), and said, "Major, you are more seriously wounded than you realize in the excitement of the moment, and you must take my carriage and go to Richmond at once to the hospital." Magruder had no time for officious civilians, and he rather brusquely told the gentleman that "he had better mind his own business." Someone nearby, seeing the exchange and recognizing the old gentleman, asked Magruder if he realized he was speaking to President Davis. Magruder said he did not and, in a scene reminiscent of Lt. Hull's encounter with Davis at Manassas the previous summer, hastily apologized to the president, explaining that command of the regiment had fallen to him and he simply had to go on. Davis told him that if his strength failed he should send for the president's carriage to take him to the hospital.[29]

The story might well be substantially true. Davis roved freely over the battlefields on all of the Seven Days, trying to help out in any way he could. He looked like an ordinary planter, well-to-do though not ostentatious, and always dignified and refined. It was just like him too not to announce his office. Cases of people failing to recognize him were common enough that he carried with him a written pass, just as an ordinary soldier might, directing sentries on the roads outside Richmond to let him go on his way to and from the army. However, Davis rode a saddle horse to the battlefield rather than taking a carriage, and so if the man who met Magruder was really the president, he must have meant that he would send for a carriage, very likely his own, in which to take the wounded officer to the hospital.

In Search of the Enemy

In fact, there proved little more for the Eighth to do that day. The order canceling the assault arrived in time to meet them returning from the slaughter that came to be called the Battle of Garnett's Farm. By the last glimmer of twilight the regiment re-formed—minus the thirteen who had been killed, sixty-three wounded, and twenty-one missing and captured—but no further action followed. Regimental adjutant Lt. Charles Harper went into Union lines under flag of truce to see if anything could be done for the many wounded there. Unfortunately, he neglected to remove his sidearm before doing so, a clear breach of the rules that govern such matters. A very tense moment occurred when, in the dim half-light, the Federals spied a revolver hanging on the hip of the Confederate officer inside their lines. Harper narrowly avoided being shot and was taken prisoner instead. "This has been a disastrous day to the 'bloody eighth,'" Melvin Dwinnell informed his readers back in Rome, and so it had. Once quiet settled down, Maj. Magruder finally retired from the field to recover from his wounds, and command of the regiment devolved on Capt. G. Oscar Dawson of Company I.

The next day, Sunday, June 29, the Eighth, along with the rest of Jones's division, lay in their camps until 10:00 A.M. and then advanced across aptly named Labor-in-Vain Swamp and through the camps the enemy had abandoned the night before. While the battle of Savage's Station raged farther to the south and east, with Lee endeavoring to cut off McClellan's retreat, the Eighth saw no action, remaining in reserve. Much of the day they marched in line of battle, uncertain of the whereabouts of the enemy and of other Confederate units and expecting any minute to receive a volley from the next line of woods. It was past nine o'clock in the evening when they received orders to march back the way they had come several miles to camp for the night. "It was raining hard, intensely dark and very muddy," wrote Melvin Dwinnell several days later, "and the men had a most disagreeable time." They finally made a very soggy camp about one o'clock the next morning.

The rain cleared off by about three o'clock, and Monday, June 30, dawned clear and bright. It was to be the climactic day of the Seven, as Lee's army had its best chance of cutting off McClellan's line of retreat back to Harrison's Landing. The two armies clashed at the Battle of Glendale, and furious fighting raged for hours. The men of the Eighth could hear the firing, and marched toward it all through an increasingly hot summer day, but did not reach the battlefield until 2:00 A.M., after eighteen hours of marching. Stragglers continued to stumble into camp throughout the night, as men who had been unable to keep up with the killing pace under the hot sun gradually caught up with the regiment.[30]

The month of July came in with more fair weather as the two armies made their last moves of the Seven Days Battles. The Union army's success in the hard-fought Battle of Glendale the day before had secured its path of retreat, and Lee was too late to win his annihilating victory by cutting off McClellan from his base. Yet he could pursue, and that he did on July 1. The real chance for profitable action was over, but Lee was loath to give up and purposed one more attack. McClellan had drawn his army into a tight, well-sited defensive position at Malvern Hill, a gentle rise with a magnificent field of fire. There he had field guns and siege artillery ranged along the line at regular fourteen-yard intervals, with solid infantry supports in reserve.

Lee's plan was to mass as much artillery as possible against the Federal position, and then if his guns succeeded in beating down the defenders' fire, his infantry would charge and carry the position. Yet Lee suffered severely during the Seven Days for lack of anything like an adequate staff. On this day as throughout the week the result was confusion, misunderstanding, and a woeful lack of coordination among Confederate units. The Eighth Georgia, having now caught up with a battlefront that had been moving rapidly eastward all week, was now about to experience some of this.

They were up and on the march again at daylight, despite their late-night tramp of the day before. As Col. Anderson put it, his brigade "again set out in search of the enemy." Their march took them almost immediately across the Glendale battlefield, where fighting had raged up until nightfall the evening before. The sight of the carnage was "heart rending and sickening in the extreme," wrote Melvin Dwinnell, but by this time the men of the Eighth were growing accustomed to such things. At any rate, they did not let it stop them from supplying themselves with ponchos, blankets, paper, envelopes, and, most of all, food, the former owners of which presumably would have no further need of such things.

After they had covered about a mile and a half, a courier met them with orders from Gen. Magruder to turn around and march back to the Darbytown Road. So back they went, but after they had marched about five miles in the opposite direction, another order from Magruder turned them right about face again and sent them marching all the way back to where the Confederate army was preparing its assault against McClellan's Malvern Hill position. Magruder now told Anderson to shelter his brigade behind a hill for the duration of the artillery barrage. Then the frustrated brigade commander got orders to move forward a bit, then farther right, then still farther right, then all the way to the far right of the army, then back to the left to his original position, "all of which orders," Anderson subsequently reported, "were executed promptly by my command over swamps, dense undergrowth, ravines, and hills."

Finally, around 4:30 P.M., the order came for the brigade to join the grand assault. Anderson advanced some distance but then halted to straighten up his line. As he did so, other troops swept on past his right, and the First, Seventh, and Eighth Georgia, thinking Anderson had given the order to resume the advance, marched off after them. The brigade never got back together during the remainder of the day's fight. Anderson remained with the Ninth and Eleventh Georgia on the Confederate right-center, while the Seventh and Eighth wound up way out on the far right of the Confederate line again.[31]

The assault that followed was one of the most disastrous of the war, the bungled result of a long chain of miscues and miscalculations that extended nearly the whole height and breadth of the Confederate chain of command that day, with plenty of blame to go around. The officers of the Army of Northern Virginia's high command were still relatively new to war and new to each other, and the best that can be said for them with reference to the Battle of Malvern Hill is that they rarely ever again performed that poorly. As always, it was the men in the ranks who had to pay the price for the errors of their superiors. Confederate troops marched out of the woods onto a long and very gradual slope that was a perfect field of fire for the massed Federal artillery at the top of the rise. The result was so gruesome it prompted Confederate general D. H. Hill to remark bitterly, "It was not war; it was murder." So thickly did fallen Rebels cover the ground that a Union officer surveying the field after the battle was horrified to note that the feeble movements of the wounded Confederates gave the ground "a peculiar crawling effect."

For once, however, the Eighth was not one of the regiments to do the largest share of the bleeding. After the disintegration of the brigade, the regiment was without orders and so never pressed home its advance into the prime killing zone. Its already badly thinned ranks lost another four killed, ten wounded, and five captured—light losses in a bloodbath like Malvern Hill but hard enough on what was left of the Eighth. The Miller Rifles, Company E, went into action with only eight, one of whom was wounded. The Rome Light Guards, Company A, took sixteen men into battle and lost two of them killed. At a range of half a mile, Monroe Phelps, "a modest young man, clever in all his ways," took an artillery shell in the abdomen and was nearly cut in two. Hugh McCullough fell at the point of the regiment's farthest advance, shot just below the eye by a Federal rifleman. He died instantly.[32]

The Malvern Hill debacle was the closing act of the Seven Days Battles. The next morning dawned cool and overcast. Rain began to fall shortly thereafter and continued heavily through a day in which temperatures did not rise much above sixty degrees Fahrenheit. The wounded soldiers, and those who were just plain tired, shivered in the damp chill as McClellan's army made the final retreat that brought it at last to the Union general's desired haven at Harrison's Landing. Lee could find no further way to hinder the Federal withdrawal and so gave up his pursuit, contenting himself, perforce, with what he had already accomplished: he had driven McClellan's host back another thirty miles or so farther from Richmond, but his own army had suffered terribly in the process, taking more casualties than it had inflicted on the Northern force.

An uneasy lull ensued between the battered contending armies in Virginia as the opposing high commands contemplated and orchestrated their next moves. The soldiers knew nothing of the counsels of those who would send them to their next encounter with the enemy and with death. They only knew or cared to know that they had accomplished their mission—they had not let the Yankees take Richmond—and the constant danger and fatigue and repeated desperate fights of the previous four months were over for the moment. As Tom Gilham of Company K explained afterward, "We had about a month's rest."[33]

And then the war went on.

CHAPTER SIX

Resistless as an Ocean Tide

A Quiet but Deep Work

"THE prospect is good for a few days, at least, of quiet and rest," wrote an obviously weary Melvin Dwinnell on July 11. "Now sweet relaxation and calm, pleasing placidity," he reveled, even though he knew "this 'good time' cannot be expected to last very long."[1]

The Peninsula Campaign was, for all practical purposes, over. McClellan's army sat in its camps at Harrison's Landing and Lee's rested in its own several miles closer to Richmond. McClellan spent his time writing dispatches of bitter recrimination to his superiors in Washington and also begging for massive reinforcements. Lee watched McClellan's still formidable army and simultaneously kept a wary eye on a growing Union threat in northern Virginia. There Lincoln had taken all of the Federal forces that had been operating in the Shenandoah Valley or covering Washington and combined them into a new Army of Virginia under Maj. Gen. John Pope. Furthermore, as Lee suspected but was not yet sure of, Lincoln was also pulling troops away from McClellan's idle encampment at Harrison's Landing, shipping them around through the Chesapeake, and forwarding them to Pope.

For the Confederate commander it was a situation fraught with extreme strategic danger. He might not know for sure which of the two opposing armies was the real threat until it was too late, or, if Pope and McClellan moved simultaneously, their two armies might become the millstones that would crush the Army of Northern Virginia between them. For the generals it was thus a season of anxious watching, but for the soldiers, of languid waiting and occasional mild curiosity about what might happen next.

"I hear nothing of any interest stirring at this time," Sam Brewer explained in a letter to his wife, "as our Army movements are done secretly." Still he could not complain about the physical aspects of his circumstances. "I am in good health and have plenty to eat and wear and nothing to do but drill a little every day." Building fieldworks and taking their turns at picket duty also occupied the soldiers during this period, but it was not, by any account, a strenuous regimen.[2]

At least, it would not have been strenuous if not for the extreme heat. An unusually wet spring had given way to an unusually dry and hot summer, with temperatures that reached the hundred-degree mark several times during July and August. "It is hot, hot, hot," complained Melvin Dwinnell, "too hot to stand, sit or lie down—so hot, in fine, that 'one feels like laying off his flesh,' as has been quaintly observed, 'and sitting in his naked bones to cool himself.'" The men just had to stand it as best they could, but it added to the languor of that summer's encampment.[3]

As welcome as the season of rest was after the exertions of the Peninsula Campaign, it had a dark side as well. It gave the men time to think, time to remember. "I have seen more in the last two weeks than I ever wish to again," wrote Sam Brewer in early July, as he recalled the battlefields of Garnett's Farm and Malvern Hill. "The whole face of the earth was covered with dead men and horses." After thirteen months of service and several glimpses of the face of battle, many of the men felt a war-weariness that no amount of ease in camp could touch. "We are in hopes peace will soon be made and we may be permitted to get home again to enjoy a peace so dearly bought," Brewer continued. "I am getting very tired of this thing and would sacrifice almost anything to have it stopped." Yet they still were not ready to accept a peace without victory and only longed for the speedy establishment of Confederate independence.

Almost worse than the war-weariness was homesickness. The soldiers spoke of men actually dying of homesickness, pining away in sadness. Perhaps a depressed mental state made them more susceptible to bodily diseases. The quiet weeks in camp after the end of the Peninsula Campaign also gave men time to think how much they missed their homes and families. Brewer once again expressed such feelings as well as any. "I sometimes get very lonely," he wrote. He would "sit and study over past scenes . . . and tears are shed thus to find myself cut off from every earthly joy." The officers were no doubt aware of the men's occasional melancholy studies, and frequently had the Eighth's highly renowned musicians serenade the camp to try to raise the men's spirits. Brewer was not moved. As he sat writing a forlorn letter to his wife he apologized for his unusually poor handwriting and noted, "Our old brass band is playing at such a rate that I am trying to turn their tunes with my pen, but they think it is very cheering to us, but not so. I had sooner hear a passel of frogs."[4]

In all of this thought, sorrow, and determination to carry on, the men had remarkably little to say about the cause for which they fought. More frequently, if they mentioned the cause at all, they merely referred to it vaguely as a righteous, glorious, and holy one, the "defense of all that is sacred or near and dear to a spirited and free people." Yet they became increasingly embittered against their enemies, for that is what war does to men's minds. Despite the fact that the Federal armies were waging a war that was restrained and civilized by the standards of most conflicts the western world had yet seen—to say nothing of ordinarily notoriously bloody civil wars—the soldiers of the Eighth, like most other Confederates and even their commanding general, came to see their foes as "vandals," "the vile Hessians," who flouted the laws of war and deserved none of its protections.[5]

During the weeks encamped near Richmond, the regiment slowly grew in numbers, recovering from the emaciated skeleton force it had been by the end of the Peninsula Campaign as sick and lightly wounded men recovered and returned to duty. "Our ranks are now rapidly filling up," Dwinnell reported. He added, however, his suspicion that not all those who had been absent had been genuinely ill. "It is lamentably true," he wrote, "that there are vastly too many men, even in our army, who 'shirk' their duty in times of great danger." He noted that sick call was always remarkably popular when heavy fighting appeared to be in the offing; some men seemed peculiarly unable to keep up on the approach march, others just wandered, and even some who were legitimately absent from the ranks had a degree of difficulty in finding the regiment again that Dwinnell considered downright suspicious. As with every regiment of the Civil War, the Eighth had its fighters and its hangers-on. Yet, in fairness, some men might face battle bravely half a dozen times but only once or twice find their resources of spirit simply unequal to carry them into or through the fight.[6]

Whatever the causes of their absence, and many were legitimate, a steady stream of recovered soldiers poured into camp. At one point in late July they were coming at a rate of twenty-five to fifty per day. Early the following month, the men rejoiced to welcome their old lieutenant colonel, John Towers, exchanged from Yankee captivity and back in command. Still, even with the returning men, Dwinnell noted, "The 'old Eighth' yet has over seven hundred names on its muster rolls, but only about four hundred in camp."

Around the beginning of August, those four hundred, along with the men of several other regiments, got a bit of excitement to enliven the otherwise boring camp routine. McClellan pushed a powerful reconnaissance probe as far forward as the old Malvern Hill battlefield. The Eighth was part of the Confederate force that advanced to counter this move. On August 5 they moved out and spent that and the next two days marching and skirmishing—and then marching some more—in the intense heat. Several members of the regiment suffered heat exhaustion, and four of them fell into enemy hands, the only casualties of the outing. "My feet," complained Sam Brewer when it was all over, "are very sore at this time as we have been on a tramp for the last three days."[7]

"What all these movements and counter movements will amount to," a puzzled Melvin Dwinnell explained to the folks back home in Rome, "we cannot divine." Through it all the soldiers simply had to guess at the larger strategic purposes that might be served by the exertions in the blazing sun or content themselves at not knowing.

Occasionally, they discerned patterns that they surmised would tell them the shape of coming movements. One of these involved Robert Toombs, who still commanded the other Georgia brigade in their division and had gotten the Eighth butchered at Garnett's Farm. The talk of the regiment on the final morning of the skirmishing and maneuvering around Malvern Hill summed it up: "There is no danger of a fight to day, for Toombs' Brigade is ahead." It was, Dwinnell confided, an indication of "the popular idea in the army of Gen. Toombs' qualities as a fighting commander." The fact was that the men thought him a pompous windbag and a poltroon in the bargain. He talked boldly, loudly, and constantly of his desire to get at the hated foe and do brave feats of arms, "but," Dwinnell concluded, "the misfortune to *him* is, *common* men cannot comprehend the reasons for some of his actions if he is *really* so very anxious to fight."

Arriving back in their camp footsore and weary after the fruitless errand to Malvern Hill and three-day waltz with the Federals there, the Floyd County boys, at least, found something to cheer them considerably. The citizens of Rome had sent another boxcar load of good things to eat, the sixth such load of the war. Carefully coached by Dwinnell's regularly published letters in the *Courier,* the Romans applied their own ingenuity as well in selecting the most desirable items and those most likely to survive the journey in good shape. The Floyd boys were very appreciative.

Meanwhile, a quiet movement was afoot among the soldiers, not merely those of the Eighth Georgia, but throughout the camps of both sides. Most of them had been raised right, in God-fearing homes where parents taught right and wrong on the basis of the Bible. Not all of the young soldiers had remained true to their early teaching during the first year of the war. Away from home for the first time, away from parents and some of the restraints of community, exposed to temptations they happily had never dreamed of back home, some had fallen into coldness and indifference toward the things of God. Some had fallen into blatant sin. It might be something like cardplaying, gambling, or Sabbathbreaking. It might be something worse. Before the war was over, twenty members of the regiment (about 1.5 percent of the total number enrolled) would be diagnosed with diseases contracted through immoral behavior. But though a Civil War soldier might transgress the moral law he had been taught as a boy, generally, if he did, he knew he was stepping over the line, and he knew God knew it.

As the months passed and the novelty of soldier life wore off, those who had enjoyed the pleasures of sin for a season, those who had merely grown indifferent, and some who had never before shown an interest in knowing God found their hearts turned toward the old ways and the peace and fulfillment many of them had once known.

"There has been a very decided change in the religious tone of the army, going on during the past six months," wrote Melvin Dwinnell. "There has been no great public demonstration in the way of revival meetings, or any thing of that sort. Yet a quiet but deep work has evidently been going on in the hearts of large numbers." He went on to note that in many regiments within the army men were holding prayer meetings every evening, and though some had made it a point to gather for evening prayers ever since joining the army, such meetings now drew much larger crowds than formerly. Outside of the prayer meetings, Dwinnell noted, "the voice of prayer is not often heard in camp," yet every day hundreds of men could be seen, in one corner of the camp or another, in silent prayer. Most of the men had Bibles, and most who had them read them daily and tried to practice what they read.[8]

One way in which this was noticeable was a marked decrease in the use of profanity, and some individuals changed so dramatically as to amaze their friends. "You never saw such a change in a boy as there is in Bob," wrote Sam Brewer to his wife regarding their friend Bob Harben. Since Harben had professed faith in Jesus Christ, Brewer wrote, he had become sober and responsible. He was also unashamed of his new faith: "I heard him pray in public last night at prayer meeting," added Brewer.

Dwinnell heartily welcomed the quiet revival. "May the good work go on," he concluded, "until not only profanity, but all other immoralities shall cease in the Confederate army, and having enlisted under the banner of Christ, every man feel a calm and holy reliance in the protection of Providence, and be willing to live or die as an all wise and just God shall determine."

Deep and Stern Convictions of Duty

"Yesterday morning at 1 o'clock the long roll beat in our brigade," Dwinnell recorded on August 14. "Tents were struck, baggage packed, and the Regiments were in line ready to march at 2 o'clock." The long period of rest was over; the armies were on the march again, and the Eighth Georgia had its part to play in the next great campaign for the control of Virginia. "The order soon came to move towards Richmond," Dwinnell added, "where we arrived just at break of day." They waited in Richmond several hours and then boarded a train for the ride to Gordonsville, where they arrived about four o'clock that afternoon.[9]

The movement of which the Eighth was now a small part was Robert E. Lee's response to the latest Federal threat in the Old Dominion. While McClellan remained in his camp at Harrison's Landing and all was quiet along the James, the Union army of John Pope gradually moved southward through the piedmont of northern Virginia, just east of the Blue Ridge. Between the two widely separated Federal armies, Lee was cornered like an animal in a trap. If he divided his outnumbered forces equally against both, he would have force enough to stop neither. Yet if he concentrated against one of them, the other might take Richmond and his supply line and then fall upon him from behind while he was engaged in front. Through several tense weeks, while the men of the Eighth rested in their camps oblivious to such developments, Lee watched Union movements seeking to discern the Federals' likely next move.

With his usual unerring skill, Lee correctly perceived that Lincoln's government was pulling troops away from McClellan to reinforce Pope. If that was true, then Lee could afford to bet that the main blow would fall in northern Virginia, and the Peninsula would now be relegated to the status of a sideshow at most. He had already dispatched Jackson to keep an eye on Polk, and as he became more certain of his enemy's intentions, he reinforced Stonewall and then prepared to join him with the remainder of his army, the corps of James Longstreet, to which the Eighth Georgia belonged. On August 9, Jackson met and defeated advance elements of Pope's army at the Battle of Cedar Mountain, and on the 13th Lee gave the orders that put the Eighth, along with the rest of Longstreet's corps, in motion.

The Eighth camped late in the afternoon of August 14 near Gordonsville, Virginia. "The pleasant oak woods in which we are," Dwinnell reported, "make a fine place for troops to rest, and it is being fully enjoyed by the vast throng around us." The men sat in little clusters and talked or else lay on their oilcloths and blankets sleeping or reading their Bibles. They remained there the next day, but that evening, August 15, orders arrived for the men to draw and cook three days' rations, a sure sign that the generals expected marching and possibly fighting.

Much to the soldiers' dismay, however, the requisite amount of food was not to be had. Instead, all they got was fresh beef and bread for one day, bacon for two, and a promise of some flour—later—to make up the deficit. Fifteen months as Confederate soldiers had taught them the value of such promises, and they feared being sent off on a hard march with insufficient food. Little could be done about that now, and the men determined to do the best they could with what rations they did have. A matter of prime concern was preserving the fresh beef, an item many soldiers disliked because it kept less well than salt pork or other cured meat and thus was often in a truly shocking state by the time they had to eat it. To avoid this, most spent a good part of the night of August 15 "jerking" the meat. "This was a novel process to many of us," Dwinnell explained, "and consists in cutting the beef into thin strips, and drying it over a fire that is not quite hot enough to cook it." This not only preserved the beef but also rendered it, in Dwinnell's opinion, "quite palatable."

Saturday, August 16, passed with no marching orders, but at eleven o'clock that night Col. Towers, now back with the regiment after his capture at Garnett's Farm and subsequent exchange, ordered the men to fall in. Several unpleasant hours followed, while Towers waited for word from the higher-ups about what to do next. When that word finally came, sometime before dawn, it was to stand down and remain in camp another twenty-four hours.

The summer before, in the early days of the war, such an order in such circumstances would not only have enraged the boys of the Eighth but driven them nearly to despair at the thought of missing a fight. They had come to have another view of the matter over the intervening year, and now Dwinnell expressed their thoughts to the folks back in Rome with disdain for any greenhorn as could feel the way they had then: "Some men when far away from the seat of war, and who have never been in a hard fought battle," he wrote, "may boast of their bravery and speak of their eagerness to meet the foe, but three or four bloody conflicts wears off this 'raw edge' and produces a dread of fields of bloody carnage and strife." They would go, all right, when ordered, not from any eagerness for the fight, but rather from "deep and stern convictions of duty," and they wanted the home folks on notice that bravery need not mean an eagerness for combat. "It is not because some men are more reckless of danger than others, that makes the difference between the brave and the cowardly," Dwinnell explained, "but it is because some men dare to do right and will do their duty."[10]

The fatigues and dangers of the campaign might be postponed, but they were not to be avoided. Marching orders soon came, and in the days that followed, the Eighth marched first one way and then another, moving together with the rest of the army as Lee stalked Pope. The Confederate general first hoped to catch and trap his opponent between the Rapidan and Rappahannock rivers, in the triangle of land just above where the former flows into the latter, but Pope was too skittish and pulled back to the north bank of the Rappahannock. Lee warily pursued, looking for an opening.

The maneuvering took the Eighth through the little Virginia village of Stevensburg on Thursday, August 21. The day was made memorable for the men of the regiment by an execution that took place in a nearby unit. The Eighth had already marched a number of miles that day when they halted for rest about noon. John Reed sent his servant, Lit, down to a nearby spring with a bucket to fetch him some water, but the black soon came running back with his bucket empty, looking badly frightened. "In the name of God, Mas John," he gasped, "don't talk of water. I had just found the spring and while I was waiting for my turn, bless God, they called a court and held a court, tried a man, and hung a man, right there, at the spring, before I could get away, to save my life."

The man whose hanging had so frightened the unwilling witness was apparently a Union spy, caught in Confederate uniform and given summary process. Lit flatly refused to go near the spring again—festooned as the scene now was with a dangling body—and so Reed got a couple of his soldiers to fetch him the bucket of water instead. His thirst at last slaked, Reed napped until the order came to fall in again and resume the march. That evening they ran out of food and had to go hungry until late the following day, when new stocks were issued. But though Friday evening brought food it also brought a heavy rainstorm, and the rain continued the following day. The men gave little heed to the inclement weather; indeed, in this sweltering summer anything that brought relief from the heat was welcome.

Our Generals Seem to Have Failed

Ultimately war meant fighting, and that too was not to be avoided much longer. Lee was looking for a way to get at Pope's army without having to stage an assault directly across the Rappahannock, and he gradually worked his way westward, farther up on that stream, probing for Pope's right flank. Pope sidled west too, trying to counter Lee's movements, and the two armies skirmished along the Rappahannock, Lee looking for an opening and Pope warding him off.

A skirmish may count little in the annals of great battles and bold feats of arms, but for the men whose lot it was to participate in one, a "skirmish" could have all the sound and fury—and stark terror—of a pitched battle. The men killed in those small probes and almost nameless encounters along the banks of the Rappahannock were just as dead as those who had fallen at Manassas, even if their families did not have the consolation of stating proudly that their loved one had fallen in the great battle. The Eighth was now bound for such a small but serious clash.

On the morning of Saturday, August 23, their orders directed them to move up in support of several batteries of Confederate artillery that were engaging Union guns on the north bank of the river near Rappahannock Station, where the Orange & Alexandria Railroad made its crossing. The Confederates also believed that the Federals had a small lodgment on the south bank here, with both artillery and infantry.

They had for days speculated that a great battle might be fought along the Rappahannock sometime soon, and now it appeared to them that the hour for such an engagement might have come. In Company I, Lt. Heard turned to John C. Reed, now commanding the company in the absence of its captain, and asked him to carry his pocketbook, so that he could take care of it in case Heard was killed. Reed pointed out that he was just as likely to be killed as Heard was. "I had not thought of that," replied the junior lieutenant, and kept his pocketbook.

The cannon were already rumbling as the Eighth, along with the rest of Anderson's brigade and another Confederate brigade, formed up and advanced in line of battle toward its assigned position. The last eight hundred yards of the advance were across an open field that seemed "fearfully smooth," with only a very flimsy fence between the advancing Rebels and the yawning muzzles of the Union guns.

It was a frightening passage but an exciting one too. "I look to the left and then to the right," remembered Reed, "and I see the line of the division as well dressed as if we were on review." The shells fell around and occasionally among the neatly dressed ranks, but they did relatively little execution. That was normal, of course, for Civil War artillery at long range, yet the guns boomed and the shells screamed with such appalling noise that even the veteran troops of the Eighth were surprised that more of them were not killed. Where shells did tear gaps in the ranks, the men closed up the line and marched on in perfect order. Recalled Read: "That line is so beautiful that I observe nearly everybody is glancing towards a flank to see it."

They reached their assigned position in support of the artillery, about 250 yards from the nearest Union guns, and lay down in line of battle. A gentle rise hid the Eighth and an adjoining regiment from the Union position, but the Federal gunners were skillful, cutting their fuses to burst just beyond the crest, showering shrapnel on the prostrate Georgians. Now and then a man was hit and carried to the rear. Company I had by far the most exposed position, suffering almost as many casualties as the other nine companies combined.[11]

Death and wounds seemed to come with bizarre randomness. Jim Brook, the oldest man in Company I, was in the act of raising himself off the ground on his hands and knees when a Union round shot, scooting low along the ground, passed between his arm and body, leaving him unharmed, but momentarily convincing his companions that it was his head they saw rolling down the hill behind him. On the other hand, another man of the same company took shelter in a deep gully at the foot of the hill and seemed to be completely safe, yet a jagged shell fragment, spinning like a boomerang, curved around the lip of the gully and smashed his thigh. Another Company I member, Hilt Dobbs, thought he had hurt the third joint of his little finger and was holding it up close to his face, examining it. All at once a Union shell passed, without exploding, and the entire finger disappeared, carried away cleanly, yet beyond the loss of his finger, Dobbs suffered no further damage.[12]

Five hours went by this way, without the Eighth or her sister regiments firing a single shot in reply. Melvin Dwinnell called it "one of the severest ordeals to which it is possible to subject even the best of troops," this being shelled and not being able to shoot back. Any moment they expected the Union infantry to charge and try to capture the Confederate guns or drive them off, but the bluecoats never went forward. Eventually it developed that they had pulled out of their south-bank enclave some hours before and were content to shell the Rebels from the north bank. Finally orders reached Col. Towers that the Confederate line was pulling back, each regiment doing its best to stay out of the way of the deadly Union fire. The Eighth got off in good order. When they reached safety and a full count was taken, it developed that a total of twenty-four men had been wounded, some very seriously but most slightly. That night they returned to the same camp they had left in the morning. The day's action may have been an ordeal for them, but in the larger picture of the campaign it was just another probe toward the river, one of half a dozen that day, establishing that Pope still held the north bank in force at that point.

Over the next couple of days they continued to shift upstream along the south bank of the Rappahannock. The Yankees were obviously doing the same along the far shore. Subsistence continued to be hand to mouth. Rations might be the standard hardtack and sowbelly one day, then only locally foraged fresh beef and green corn the next. The countryside in the valley of the Rappahannock was all too obviously picked clean of anything edible. Rail transport was just as clearly inadequate to bring up rations for the Army of Northern Virginia, and the inescapable logic of the situation was not lost on the soldiers: "The want of rations will force us forward or back soon," wrote Melvin Dwinnell.

Nor was that the worst of the situation, as it then appeared to the soldiers. As far as they could see, Pope had bested Lee and Jackson this time, gotten ahead of them, headed them off, and held them south of the Rappahannock, unable to come at his smaller army until it could be reinforced by the huge formations even then shifting up into

northern Virginia from McClellan's old position on the James. "Our
Generals seem to have been anticipated in this movement and failed,"
wrote Dwinnell. Pope was very much of the same mind. Any small
body of Confederate troops that might have managed to get across the
river beyond the Union right could, he thought, be easily dealt with.
Reinforcements from the Peninsula would soon arrive, and Pope
would be the victor in his campaign against Lee in the Virginia piedmont. As Pope—and the Confederate soldiers—had yet to learn, ap-
pearances could be deceptive, especially when it came to Lee and
Jackson.

Soldiers Must Know No Obstacles

Pope's satisfaction and the disappointment of the Confederate soldiers
were not entirely without cause. The Union general had indeed succeeded in the first phase of the campaign, denying Lee the use of a simple, short-range flanking maneuver to the west. The problem for Pope
was that he did not fully realize that his success was only the first phase
of the campaign and that Robert E. Lee was at his most dangerous when
the safe and simple solutions were denied to him.

On August 25, even as Dwinnell was writing that there seemed to be
no future in the present line of operations, Lee set in motion a new and
far more daring series of movements. Jackson, taking the smaller of the
two corps into which the Army of Northern Virginia was divided,
swung wide, far to the west of Pope's positions, and then headed north
on a turning maneuver that would take him far behind the Union army.
Jackson would threaten Pope's supply line, and then Lee, controlling
Longstreet's larger corps—including the Eighth Georgia—would fall on
the Union general when he began to fall back. It was a gambit typical
of Lee's generalship at its best: daring, fraught with danger, and promising spectacular results if successful.

The next morning, Tuesday, August 26, the Eighth pulled back from
its position near the Rappahannock so as to get the cover of woods and
hills between it and any prying Union eyes on the north bank. Then the
regiment marched westward, following the track of Jackson's corps beyond Pope's right flank. Finally they turned north again, marched to the

river, and crossed it about 5:00 P.M. They continued northward until eleven o'clock that night before making camp.

They were on the road again at eight o'clock the next morning, and marched six miles before making a brief halt for rest about one mile short of the town of Salem. There they had a bit of excitement when reports came in that the enemy had taken Salem. The brigade deployed, but after a couple of hours it developed that the only Federals in Salem were a small force of raiding cavalry, who had departed as quickly as they came. The Confederate column resumed its march and continued until late in the evening once again. When they halted on the evening of Thursday, August 27, near the village of White Plains, Virginia, the men of the Eighth were only about twenty miles from Manassas Junction, scene of their glory and great loss thirteen months before.[13]

On that same field of Manassas the following afternoon, Stonewall Jackson would initiate a second great battle, but August 28, 1862, held other action for the Eighth Georgia. The regiment took up the march again that morning at ten o'clock, in what Berrien Zettler considered "one of the hottest days I ever experienced," marching rapidly to restore the connection between the two temporarily severed wings of Lee's army. For part of the day, both Lee and Longstreet rode quite near the Eighth's position in the column, and the men stole glances of mixed curiosity and awe at the general who was already becoming legendary as commander of the Army of Northern Virginia.[14]

In the oppressive heat the rapid pace was brutal, and when the column finally halted for rest at one o'clock that afternoon, word had it that the artillery horses were giving out and had to be rested if they were to go on at all. Men sat or lay and horses stood, all panting miserably in the blazing sunshine along the turnpike.

Several members of the Eighth, however, were feeling a bit more ambitious. Two or three of them got to discussing the glories of cold buttermilk and how it was a drink ideally adapted to their current circumstances. Presently they decided to act on their deliberations and set out to walk up the road a way and see if they could find an obliging Virginia housewife who would treat them to some of the contents of her springhouse. They disappeared around the next bend in the road, but a short time later they reappeared, minus their rifles and moving at a dead run. They reported encountering more of the marauding Yankee cavalry in a village just half a mile farther on. The Federal horsemen had captured them, ascertained that they belonged to Longstreet's corps, and then released them after smashing their rifle stocks against trees.

Clearly the Federal cavalrymen were scouts, and they would bring news of Longstreet's approach to whatever sizable Union formations might be in a position to cut them off from joining Jackson. The disappointed buttermilk seekers were sent on to make their report directly to Gen. Lee, not far away, and Zettler at least believed their news was what got the column moving again shortly thereafter.

They moved more slowly at first, with skirmishers deployed out in front to warn of the enemy's presence, but once they passed the small village without encountering the foe, they resumed the previous killing pace. Out in front of them they could see Bull Run Mountain, a small mountain that ran parallel to but some miles east of the Blue Ridge. Its crest was still eight or ten miles away, and from that distance they could just make out the notch of Thoroughfare Gap, through which the Manassas Gap Railroad passed on its way to Manassas Junction and through which they would have to pass if they were to reach Jackson before converging Union forces could put Lee's widely sundered army in grave peril.[15]

They gazed ahead toward the ridge through the shimmering heat and haze as they tramped forward all the rest of that afternoon, and the sun was well down the western sky behind their backs when they reached the foot of the gap. Federal artillery near the summit of the gap took them under fire immediately, leaving no doubt as to the present ownership of that piece of Virginia real estate. Time would soon tell in what strength the Yankees held it. Orders went down the chain of command—from Lee to Longstreet to his lead division commander, D. R. Jones—to clear the gap. Jones directed his lead brigade commander, Tige Anderson, to send his lead regiment, the Ninth Georgia, straight up the road into the gap, while the rest of the brigade filed off to the left and prepared to advance in support. Toombs's brigade was coming up behind Anderson's, and Jones sent it off into the woods on the right of the road along with that of Brig. Gen. Thomas F. Drayton.

In fact, the Union troops in the gap, Brig. Gen. James B. Ricketts's division of McDowell's corps, had themselves just arrived there after a long, hard march in the hot sun, in response to the report of the Union cavalry scouts. Tired though they must have been, the Federals gave the

Ninth Georgia a warm welcome and promptly drove it back down the road. It would now be up to the remainder of Jones's division to push the Yankees out of the way. The first step was to ascertain just how far the Union line extended on either side of the turnpike. On the left of the Confederate line, Anderson ordered his regiments to send skirmishers clawing their way up the mountainside through the almost impassable tangle of thickets.[16]

In the Eighth Georgia, that duty fell to Companies A and B, the battle-scarred Rome Light Guards and Oglethorpe Light Infantry. Between the two of them they now carried only a total of thirty muskets (or rifle-muskets) forward into the thickets. Lt. Dwinnell had fallen ill that morning and was in the rear, and Lt. Robert T. Fouché led Company A. A twenty-six-year-old attorney and 1854 University of Georgia graduate from Rome, "Bob" Fouché had risen from the rank of private. As he now led the company into action he was probably still sporting the bandage around his head that was a reminder of a nearly spent shell fragment he had encountered at Rappahannock Station five days before. Leading Company B was Lt. Fred Bliss.

As the two companies started up the slope, Berrien Zettler wondered how he was going to get through the tangle of vines, briers, and scrub cedars in front of him, "but soldiers must know no obstacles," he recalled, "so I plunged in." The others did the same, and gradually their formation worked its way uphill, scrambling over boulders, crawling through the underbrush, and now and then pausing individually to catch their breath and listen for telltale sounds in the thickets ahead.

In one of these brief pauses Zettler heard distinctly the sound of canteens clanking together. Then came a man's voice: "Who's down there?" Five paces or so to Zettler's left, his comrade Stephen Baldy brought up his rifle, aiming at the point from which he judged the voice had come, but Zettler motioned to him. "Don't shoot," he said, in what he hoped was a low tone, "it may be one of our men." That was just possible, since it would have been quite natural on a day like this for any company officer, blue or gray, to detail a man to take the canteens, find a spring, and fill them. In these thickets it would be just as natural for a man to get turned around in his directions and lose track of his company.

Baldy was unconvinced. "No, I see him," he hissed back. "It's a Yankee."

The voice in the thicket spoke again: "Say, is that Company A?"

"What regiment?" Baldy shot back.

Years later when Zettler wrote down his memories of that day, he could not remember just what the man in the thicket had said. His unit was probably the 107th Pennsylvania, but whatever it was, it definitely hailed from north of the Mason-Dixon Line.

Baldy's rifle roared. Almost at the same instant a whole line of blue-coated soldiers seemed to rise out of the ground just a few feet away, simultaneously leveling their rifles. For the twinkling of an eye, Zettler found himself looking directly into the business ends of several Union weapons at near-point-blank range. He threw himself backward just as the volley crashed out and the bullets whizzed past his face as he toppled, rolled, scrambled, and tumbled back down the slope. When he emerged from the thicket at the bottom of the hill, there, right in front of him, sat Col. Anderson, who demanded to know what he had seen up there. Zettler figured he had seen about a regiment of Yankees and said so.

"Only a regiment?" countered Tige dubiously.

"That's all I had time to see," Zettler explained.

"You were frightened to death," said the brigadier in disgust, "and don't know what you saw."

Zettler thought that not quite fair, but wisely said no more. Presently another man burst out of the thicket, similarly flustered. Anderson questioned him, with the same results. By and by, Lt. Bliss too came stumbling out of the brambles.

"What's the force up there, Lieutenant?" barked Anderson.

"Well," gasped Bliss, "we came upon them very unexpectedly, and . . ."

"Yes," snapped Anderson, "and they stampeded you like they did the boys; so you know nothing. Get your men together, sir, and go back and stay there until you know something definite."

So Bliss got the company back into skirmish line and went back up the slope, each man devoutly hoping that someone else would be the first to locate the Union line. Someone did, and the men of Company B hugged the mountainside while bullets whistled over their heads long enough for them to feel they knew something definite about the Federal position, then they scrambled back down and made their reports. Only one man in the two companies, Pvt. Jim Carolan of B, paid in blood for the information thus gained. Carolan had survived a severe wound in the hip at Manassas the summer before, proving himself a tough soldier by returning to the ranks after months of difficult convalescence. This time there would be no tedious stay in hospitals for Jim Carolan. Shot through the chest, he died almost instantly.

Anderson seemed satisfied with the survivors' reports and passed along the intelligence to higher headquarters—at least a full Union brigade in position in the pass. The reaction was quick. An officer galloped up to Anderson, saluted smartly, and said, "General Longstreet's compliments, General, and he directs that you make an assault at once, that you'll be supported by his entire corps, and General Wilcox will assault in the rear." The advance began promptly, and it is no doubt a measure of how deceptive the circumstances of combat can be that even soldiers who heard the staff officer repeat Longstreet's order for a general assault nevertheless thought that only their regiment and the neighboring First Georgia were making the attack. "My heavens," exclaimed Zettler, "does he expect two little regiments to assault five?" To which another voice in the ranks of Company B replied, "He's a fool."[17]

In Company I a soldier sized up the situation and muttered, "Mount the mountain," with a roguish grin at John Reed, who now commanded the company. Reed thought his men looked worried, and he tried to encourage them, passing along the line and repeating in a low voice that the defenders, firing downhill, were sure to aim high. Meanwhile, over in Company K, Thomas Gilham thought the setting looked like descriptions he had read of the scene of the battle of Thermopylae, the mountain pass where a small number of Spartan Greeks had stoutly held off the vast forces of Xerxes the Great's Persian army in 480 B.C. To his neighbor in the ranks he remarked that he wondered which side now would play the role of the Spartans.[18]

In fact, Longstreet, under Lee's supervision, was handling the situation very wisely. His initial orders called for exactly the movement that had finally allowed Xerxes to overcome the stubborn Spartans twenty-three centuries before and half a world away: besides sending forward the main assault column of which the Eighth was a part, he also dispatched two flanking columns to turn the Union position, one by a footpath over the mountain and the other by another gap about three miles to the north. The Confederates could not afford to be stopped at this gap—it could mean the destruction of their armies—and their generals were taking no chances.[19]

"Forward," came the order, and forward went the Eighth, into vines and brush so thick they could not see ten feet in front of them. It was no parade-ground formation that climbed the slope, but somehow—and much to their own surprise—the men gradually clawed their way upward. Once again the Union volley crashed out with startlingly little warning, but Reed was much gratified to sense most of the shots passing well overhead. A brief firefight followed, with the Georgians slowly pressing forward and the foe seeming to fade away into the gathering twilight of the dense undergrowth in front of them. Then they were at the top of the pass, and the Federals were gone. They still were not quite sure how they had done it, but they had cleared Thoroughfare Gap.[20]

Berrien Zettler thought he knew why the Yankees had left. He and some of the soldiers around him had begun shouting bogus commands when they got within earshot of the Union lines. "Hold back your men there, captain!" "You boys there, go slow; wait for the flankers to get behind them!" "Hold on, men, you'll scare them off the mountain!" He felt certain that such bluffs had fooled the Yankees and driven them to retreat. After all, why else would any force have abandoned such an advantageous position?[21]

In fact, the Union retirement had far more to do with the two Confederate flanking columns and Ricketts's own lack of combativeness than with the acting abilities of Zettler and company or even the undeniable courage and prowess of the Eighth and its sister regiments. With the lack of aggressive leadership that repeatedly foiled the courage of the Army of the Potomac's soldiers, Ricketts had second thoughts about holding the gap. Receiving word of Lee's attempts to turn his position and dwelling much on how badly he was outnumbered, the Union commander chose not to attempt to counter the Confederate moves but instead to withdraw and surrender the vital pass.[22]

The men of the Eighth were happy to have it on whatever terms. They had lost two more killed and ten wounded. Of the latter, some got off fairly easy. Pvt. Dan Miller of Company A suffered a slight wound in the cheek, spent a few days in the brigade field hospital, and was back in the ranks in early September. Others fared much worse. Company G's Pvt. J. W. Lancaster had his left arm torn off by a shell, while Sgt. T. C.

Estes, of Company E, took a minié ball in the ankle. The large soft-lead slug so shattered the limb that the surgeons could do nothing for him but amputate the lower leg. For both of them, the war was over.

Still, the cost had been surprisingly low for such a vital success. The position had looked impregnable—though it was far from that—and the survival of the army depended on their success. In the anticlimax of their surprisingly easy achievement, the men of the Eighth were not quite sure how to rate their victory. Only with the passage of time did they come to understand the importance of the battle they had fought at Thoroughfare Gap. For now, as night finally settled down on Bull Run Mountain after a day that had been full of hard marching, blazing sunshine, and an adrenaline-filled scramble up a mountain slope, the men of the Eighth were happy enough just to receive the order to sleep right where they were. Tomorrow could take care of itself.

The Grandest Sight I Ever Looked Upon

Hot as the days had been of late, the nights were cool. Lt. John C. Reed, his best friend Capt. Jake Phinizy of Company K, and Lt. T. J. Bowling of the same company bunked together on the ground and shared their meager blankets as they had been doing for the past several nights. Dawn came, the morning of Friday, August 29, and they were up again, along with the rest of Longstreet's corps, and preparing to press on to join Jackson several miles to the east.

The marching order rotated routinely, and Jones's division, of which the Eighth was part, now took its place well back in the column. They had not gone far before they had tangible proof of the need for haste. Ahead of them they could hear the distant sounds of a great battle, and not long after they could see the mounting clouds of white powder smoke to the east. Jackson was heavily engaged and might be overwhelmed before the bulk of Lee's army could arrive to aid him. Grimly the soldiers strode onward through the rising heat of the morning and the sweltering afternoon.

Jackson had taken up a defensive position on the edge of the old Manassas battlefield, and the Union army of Maj. Gen. John Pope now attacked it. Pope was sadly confused by now as a result of his two weeks or so of maneuvering against Lee and Jackson. The unfortunate Union general mistakenly believed that he had Jackson trapped and was about to destroy him. In fact, Jackson was in no hurry to get away, knowing that if only Lee and Longstreet's wing of the army arrived in due time, together they could ruin the Federal commander. Remarkably, Pope, for his part, knew nothing of Longstreet's approach.

As Longstreet's wing arrived on the battlefield and began to deploy, the Eighth Georgia marched past some of the army's wagon trains parked in the road, horses hitched and facing toward the enemy. After three months of following Lee, the men had already gained a sublime confidence that they could not fail where he led. Seeing the wagons, a soldier in the ranks of Company I sang out, "Mas Robert is going to haul some of Mr. Pope's things." They marched onward, as the column left the road and marched southward toward a position on the extreme right of the Confederate line. Late in the day, two brigades of Longstreet's corps made a forced reconnaissance, and Lee watched the operation from a rise behind the lines and in plain view of the Eighth. "We all gazed at him with admiration," recalled Reed. The brief probe ended, and Lee rode off, and the men thought he looked well pleased with the way things were shaping up.[23]

It was dark before the Eighth reached its assigned position, and they lost little time stacking arms, eating, and bedding down for the night, expecting the battle to begin at dawn next day. To their surprise, however, Saturday, August 30, brought renewed heavy artillery firing, but not the expected Union assault or any movement by Lee's army. Pope, whose befuddlement was growing by the hour, now conceived the idea that Jackson was in retreat and determined to pursue him. It took him some time to get his army arranged for that purpose, but by midafternoon all was at last ready and Pope launched what will probably go down in history as the world's briefest pursuit. Jackson, of course, had gone nowhere, and Pope's brave but ill-fated soldiers crashed headlong into the same stubborn defenders and strong position that had stopped them all the previous day. Furious fighting erupted all along Jackson's line, some of it hand-to-hand, and the issue hung in the balance.

The abruptly rising roar of battle startled John Reed awake from an afternoon nap at about 3:00 P.M. The fighting he heard was the Union assault on Jackson's line, the Confederate left, but to Reed it sounded as if it came directly from in front of the Eighth's position on the Confederate right. The reason for this was that the two wings of Lee's army, Jackson's and Longstreet's, hinged together almost at right angles, with the Union army on the inside of the half-square thus formed. Pope's doomed assaulting columns were actually moving from right to left across Longstreet's front to strike Jackson's line. The battle then taking place in front of Jackson's position was at the same time equally in front of Longstreet's—and the Eighth Georgia's—as well. Almost incredibly, the hapless Union commander still refused to believe that Longstreet was anywhere near the battlefield.

As Jackson's lines wavered under the onslaught of the bulk of Pope's army, Longstreet, who had repeatedly resisted Lee's urging to open his own part of the battle, now finally deemed that the time was right to relieve the pressure on Jackson and also relieve Pope of his misconceptions about the whereabouts of the bulk of the Army of Northern Virginia. His artillery opened up a deadly enfilade fire on the advancing Federals, breaking up their assault in blood and confusion. Then he sent his infantry forward.

Hood's division struck first, led by his famous brigade of Texans. Out on the right, the men of the Eighth waited. In a treetop high above his comrades of Company I, Billy Copelan described the action to his comrades below, reporting with steadily rising excitement the Union assault, its repulse, and the Confederate counterattack. "The Texas Brigade is charging!" he cried, and described its success over the surprised and unprepared Federals. Then the order came for the Eighth to join the assault. Jones's division, advancing on the far right, initially met little resistance. They marched by the flank, double-quicking to the front much as they had in their bloody advance very near here the summer before, but this time the fighting kept well ahead of them, and for some time they had no call even to discharge their rifles.

As they advanced, Reed heard a shell coming their way but judged by the sound that it would pass well over them. Nearby, however, his friend Jake Phinizy dove to the ground. The shell sailed by, and Reed looked at his friend and laughed good-naturedly. Phinizy, though, seemed nervous, besides being embarrassed. He sprang quickly to his feet, snapping irritably at Reed, "I shall stay here as long as you," and Reed felt sorry for having laughed at him.

They drew up in line at the edge of a wood, and across the open fields in front of them they could see the Chinn House. While they waited there for orders to continue the advance, they saw Gen. John B. Hood leading his troops forward, trotting his horse along the line of his brigades and riding close enough to be heard by the men of the Eighth. "Men, I shall have you to charge that artillery," Hood was shouting. "Don't waste your fire on the infantry. If you only go close enough, they will run. Kill the horses, so that they cannot carry off the guns." Others heard him say, "Go it, boys, we'll give them more than they can attend to!" Soon Hood and his troops were lost from sight in the smoke and dust, and the Eighth took up its advance again, moving closer to the Chinn House. They were still just beyond the fringes of intense combat, and artillery fire swept the ground where they walked. Reed especially noted the canister, most deadly of Civil War artillery loads. Each round (from the most common type of cannon) consisted of twenty-seven iron balls, each about an inch in diameter. As he marched along with his company, Reed could see canister balls that, having spent most of their energy, were bounding and skittling along the ground, and the sight of them gave him an odd sensation in the shins.

As they marched, Sgt. John Leigh of Company C spotted a man hugging the ground in a shallow gully near the Eighth's line of march. Determined to rout the skulker out and get him into ranks, Leigh ran over and spoke sharply to him. To his surprise, the man, who jumped immediately to his feet, proved to be an officer with a wounded hand. That it was the officer's *right* hand that was disabled was probably a good thing for Leigh, for, apparently outraged at having a lowly sergeant impugn his courage, the injured officer immediately began making eager if not very effective efforts to get at his revolver with his left hand. Leigh lost no time getting back into ranks, and the wounded officer stalked off to the rear.

The Chinn House stood on a ridge that commanded a good view of the surrounding fields. The panorama that spread out before the men of the Eighth as they reached that vantage point now was one they would never forget. "As far as one can see on both sides," wrote John Reed years later, "our battle flags are streaming, the great [St. Andrew's] cross on each seeming to be leaping and springing forward as the color-bearer is double quicking, and our advance travels on as resistless as an ocean tide. The globular flashes of the cannon, for a moment like red suns in a fog, the momentary spots of fire blazing forth and going out along the whole front of regiments, horses in a gallop carrying our artillery forward, the men on the first line charging, cheering and firing, the enemy broken, but trying in many places to stand—this all comes back upon me as the grandest sight I ever looked upon."[24]

The Federals had defended Chinn Ridge tenaciously, all but wrecking the first wave of the Confederate assault before finally giving way. Now to D. R. Jones's division, composed of Anderson's brigade and their fellow Georgians of Toombs's brigade, fell the task of storming Henry Hill. The Widow Henry had died in the previous summer's battle, and charred ruins were all that remained of her house, yet the hill that bore her name, and that had been the scene of the famous Confederate stand of the summer before, was the last position from which the Union general could hope to save his army. If the Rebels could take Henry Hill, much of Pope's army would be trapped south of Bull Run and captured or dispersed.

At the Chinn House, Tige Anderson halted his brigade and brought them into line of battle. His horse had been shot out from under him almost at the outset of the advance, and his aide, Lt. C. C. Hardwick of the Eighth Georgia's Company B, had fallen too, badly wounded in the thigh. On foot and with no staff officer to help him, Anderson was hard put to direct his brigade. Jones, believing himself well out on the flank of the Union position, now swung his division to the left and made for the key intersection of the Warrenton Turnpike and Manassas–Sudley Road. "Division, left wheel! Division, left wheel!" was the order Berrien Zettler remembered being passed down the line from each man to his neighbor in ranks, apparently because the officers' shouts could not be heard in the fearful din of battle. Under heavy artillery fire, the men carried out the left wheel, and then waited until Jones gave Anderson the order to resume the advance.

Long-range artillery fire was not usually a big killer in the Civil War, but at this point one or more Union batteries got the Eighth's range precisely. Worse still, Jones's left wheel gave the Federal guns on Henry Hill an enfilading position. Their shells could now travel the length of the regimental line. Zettler remembered the first projectile, apparently a solid roundshot, skipping along the ground just in rear of the regimental line. Such cannonballs did not explode, but they were disconcertingly visible as they flew, bounced, or rolled across the battlefield, and lethal—or at least maiming—to as many men as might happen to get in their way in any of those modes. Artillerists liked them for the morale impact they produced among infantrymen who had to stand and watch them approach, and with the regiment lined up as it was, like tenpins for the gunners' twelve-pound iron bowling balls, the situation was an artillerist's dream.

It was a nightmare for the men of the Eighth, who had to stand and take whatever the gunners sent their way. Zettler was watching as a second round shot followed the first. With rising horror, he saw it strike the ground a few yards directly to his right, then skip upward in a black blur. Then he dropped to the ground as if hamstrung. Indeed, the cannonball had removed a pound or so of his left hamstring muscle, the flesh on the back of his leg about six inches above the knee. It also scored a shallow groove through the back of his right hamstring, as he had been just stepping forward with the right foot when it struck him. Several comrades on either side of him immediately stooped over him and asked if he felt up to being carried. He straightened his legs and, finding that no bones seemed to be broken, told them to go ahead. Hastily they unrolled the india-rubber poncho that he carried instead of a blanket, laid him on it, and carried him as quickly as they could into the shelter of a small gully about twenty yards away. Then, leaving him, they hurried back to their places in the ranks.[25]

Not everyone fared as well as Zettler, and not all the Union guns were firing solid shot. An exploding shell struck Capt. J. M. C. Hulsey of Company F, the Atlanta Grays, and blew his leg off. In Company E the scene was even more grisly. Another shell struck Pvt. J. W. Baily, blasting away his right arm. The severed limb flew up into the air, twirling over and over, and then landed just a few feet in front of John Reed, over in Company I. Neither Hulsey nor Baily would recover from his injuries. The captain died the next day; the private, three weeks later.

The order came to advance, but by now it was no longer Col. Towers who led the Eighth. He had been wounded be a shell fragment and taken to the rear. Capt. Oscar Dawson of Company I took over the command. John Reed, in turn, stepped up to the command of the company. Other companies were by now without their regular commanders as well. Aside from Company F, where Hulsey had fallen, Company A was now led by its junior second lieutenant Jim Tom Moore. Its captain, Sidney Hall, was sick in the hospital at Richmond. As for the company's other two lieutenants, Melvin Dwinnell had gone to the rear sick since two mornings ago. Bob Fouché had led the company forward at the beginning of that afternoon's advance, but in climbing a fence he had come down wrong on his ankle and thus lamed himself. Hobbling along behind the regiment, trying to catch up, he was struck down by a shell fragment.

Jones quickly realized the need to drive the Federals off Henry Hill before seizing the key intersection. He wheeled the division forty-five degrees back to the right and charged. The Eighth's line advanced down off the rise around the Chinn House, but the Federal artillery still pounded them. A single shell landing in the ranks of Company K wounded nine of the company's eighteen men and momentarily scattered the others, but the unscathed men quickly closed up their ranks and kept on.

Lt. Bowling went down, and his friends Reed and Phinizy could do nothing for him but make sure he had a canteen of water and leave him where he lay on the ground, groaning in intense pain. "There goes one of our mess," quipped Reed grimly. "Who will be the next?"

"You," Phinizy replied, and the advance went on.

The Eighth plunged forward, through the valley of Chinn Run, up the slopes of Henry Hill, and into a patch of woods and a furious close-quarters firefight with a sturdy line of U.S. Army Regulars. Capt. Dawson went down. The battle lines swayed back and forth, but neither side gave way. Later students of the battle would fault Anderson for not realizing an opportunity to turn the flank of the Union line on Henry Hill, but on foot among his men, peering through the foliage, gun smoke, and gathering dusk, Anderson never saw the opportunity that would be so plain to later historians. The Union line held till nightfall. Pope's army retreated safely, and the Federals on Henry Hill retired in good order through the gathering darkness.[26]

The surviving Georgians were not inclined to find fault with their leaders or weigh the imperfections of what was by any standard a dramatic victory. They stood where they had stopped, in a field of scattered scrub timber and saplings, and watched the last of the Union forces falling back through the twilight, still firing, but obviously leaving the field. The sun had gone down by now, and as the Georgians watched their retreating foes, the sky to their left was bathed in its afterglow. Even after all they had been through, John Reed and Jake Phinizy could exult in their army's triumph. "We should go to Washington this time," they told each other amid back-slapping and shouts of laughter. Phinizy said he was not only going to Washington, he was going to have a high old time there on all the good things to eat and drink that they would undoubtedly capture from the Yankees when they took the place. He was going to have a feast; he was going to—

Reed glanced over at his companion, who was looking after the retreating foe while he talked. Just then something with a zipping sound went "snit" through the leaves in front of them, then "dip," with a sound of muffled impact, and then zipped off through the leaves behind them. A bright spot of blood appeared on the front of Phinizy's throat—years later Reed still recalled how brilliant red it looked—then Jake toppled backward. Several of his K Company soldiers caught him—only four of them remained unwounded—and lowered him to the ground. One of them reached out with a canteen to offer his captain a drink of water. Phinizy's lips parted as though to receive the water, and then he was gone. He never made a sound after he was hit.

Reed was stunned. "For a moment," he recalled, "I was paralyzed with surprise and horror." However, there was no time for grieving. The Union artillery had unlimbered and gone into action several hundred yards farther back, and once again the air seemed thick with canister balls, skipping off the ground, buzzing angrily around their ears, thwacking into flesh and bone. The last light was fading now. Further pursuit would accomplish nothing tonight, so Anderson gave the order to pull back out of range. As the regiment marched off the field, a nearly spent canister ball struck Reed in the back of the neck. When he came to, one of his men was offering him water from a canteen.[27]

May the Lord Direct Me

The Second Battle of Manassas, as Confederates came to call it, was a great Southern victory, but the aftermath of battle was grim even when the outcome was favorable. It was about ten o'clock that night when litter bearers found Berrien Zettler and carried him to the Robinson House and set him down in front of the gate—the house itself and its yard were already jammed full of wounded men. The scene was one of chaos, as the handful of medical personnel tried to cope with the flood of misery caused by a major battle. Organization was sadly lacking from their efforts, and the result was that although in general there were serious shortages both of surgeons and of medicines, some people got more attention than they needed. During the night, three different surgeons came by and gave Zettler a dose of "an opiate of some kind." By the time the last one got to him, he was only semiconscious. Somewhat remarkably, he did eventually reawaken, but by then it was the following afternoon and it had been raining in torrents for some time.

Zettler discovered that Stephen Baldy, his companion from the slopes of Thoroughfare Gap three days before, was also there at the hospital, seriously wounded. That afternoon, a detail came with an ambulance to haul Zettler and other members of Anderson's brigade to the brigade hospital. That represented an improvement in organization and in personalized care—even a slight improvement in accommodations: instead of lying in the open air, Zettler now found himself billeted in a cow stall in a barn. The days of misery that followed tended to run together—the cow stall, an agonizing wagon ride to Warrenton, lying on the floor of a freight warehouse there, and finally transfer to a Baptist church building, where he actually had the luxury of a mattress on the floor. He survived, "rather to my surprise," as he related afterward, but Baldy, like many of the wounded, did not.

Meanwhile, his father had heard of his wound and set out for Virginia to fetch his son back home to Effingham County, Georgia. Arriving in Richmond, the sixty-four-year-old Mr. Zettler learned that the wounded of Second Manassas were at Warrenton but that the railroad no longer ran all the way to that place but stopped fifty-three miles short of it. Undeterred, he came on anyway. At the terminus of the railroad there was no chance of hiring a team of horses—both armies had long since scoured the country of quadrupeds—so he set out to walk. For company he had a number of other fathers who were on the same errand, seeking their wounded sons. They made a rest stop for one hour shortly after midnight and otherwise kept on going around the clock. They arrived in Warrenton having covered the fifty-three miles in twenty-three hours.

Even then the search was not over. The first man of whom he asked directions explained to old Mr. Zettler that there were over eighteen hundred wounded men in the town—filling all the churches, the courthouse, the schoolhouse, the railroad warehouse, and many private homes. Finding one man among all those would take weeks. The determined father paused and then asked, pointing to a church building, "Are there any in that building yonder?"

"Yes, sir, it's full," his informant replied. "You see a man's head on the floor in the preacher's door right now." It was true, the meetinghouse was so jammed full of wounded soldiers, lying on the floor, that the head of one of them could be seen just barely inside the "preacher's door," an entrance near the pulpit, which had been left open for ventilation.

"Then," said Mr. Zettler, "I'll begin my search right here, and may the Lord direct me." Resolutely he walked over to the church and up the steps to the preacher's door. The first man he looked at was the one whose head he had seen in the doorway from a distance. That man was Berrien Zettler, his only son. As Berrien later said, "It, indeed, must be true that the Lord directed him." His father got boarding for the two of them in a private home, where they stayed until Berrien was well enough to travel. Then, with a three-month furlough issued by the surgeon, they set out on the long, hard road back to Georgia. Berrien Zettler never rejoined the Eighth Georgia Regiment.[28]

Zettler's wound had been a serious one, but many of the wounds suffered by members of the Eighth at Second Manassas were far less so. The black powder that filled artillery shells in those days provided a relatively low-yield bursting charge. If a man suffered a direct hit, or something close it, he was killed outright or terribly maimed. If the shell landed just a few feet farther away, he was likely at most to catch a small piece of shrapnel at relatively low velocity, producing a wound that official records listed as "slight." A soldier with such a wound might return to duty within a matter of days, or he might be out of action for several months.

The canister ball that struck John Reed in the back of the neck never actually broke the skin, but it combined with other factors to sideline him for months. The obvious effects of his wound were a very sore neck and a very large bruise. Yet the blow seemed to affect his whole system—

severe nerve pain in his right shoulder and lowered resistance to the sickness that he had been struggling against for the past two weeks. The stress, the fatigue, the pain, the wretched diet of little besides green corn, all combined to lay him low, and when the army moved on, he found himself in a camp for sick and stragglers at Winchester.[29]

Melvin Dwinnell was there too, as were thousands of others representing all of the army's regiments. Even more serious, many of those who fell out of ranks were not present at any encampment. Straggling was becoming a serious problem. Men fell out because they lacked the physical resources to march any farther or the emotional resources to face more combat for the time being, but all too many of them were doing so these days. The fact was that although Lee was winning glorious victories and changing the whole momentum of the war in Virginia, he was also using up his army in the process.

The Eighth Georgia was no different from the rest of the Army of Northern Virginia in that respect. By the time they marched away from the plains of Manassas a second time, they numbered fewer than 150 men. Several companies had no officers left. In Company K the men held an election and chose B. F. Gilham as their new captain. Company A simply served out the campaign under the command of their first sergeant, R. Fred Hutchings, after Lt. Moore became ill and could not continue with the regiment. None of the companies was more than a corporal's guard in numbers by this time. The small band of Georgians who followed the regimental colors during the next few weeks was a pale shadow of what the regiment had once been.[30]

Two days after the fight at Manassas, Melvin Dwinnell wrote to tell his readers back in Rome that he would not be surprised to see Lee make his next move into Maryland. Indeed, that was exactly where the Rebel general was headed. Confederate hopes and the word of some pro-Southern Maryland émigrés had it that the state was only waiting for the appearance of a Confederate army to rise up and throw off the shackles of Lincoln and the abolitionists. The issue of invading Maryland had been discussed in the Confederate high command nearly a year earlier, and after Lee's great successes, the northward march might be the finishing move that many felt had been omitted after the first victory at Manassas the summer before, the blow that might end the war. In short, it seemed an opportunity too good to forgo, even if the army was all but used up.[31]

Some of the Prettiest Fighting

The Eighth Georgia Regiment marched north on September 3, crossed Goose Creek, and reached Drainsville, Virginia, near the Potomac and less than thirty miles upstream—or roughly northwest—of Washington, where Lincoln had reinstated McClellan and the Union general was busy, amid considerable civilian alarm, in getting the Federal army back into fighting trim. Turning away from the capital, the Georgians and their fellow Confederates marched upstream along roads not far from the south bank until they reached Leesburg, Virginia, the evening of September 4. Bull Run Mountain loomed up just west of town, and beyond it and out of sight was the Blue Ridge, while to the east, the Potomac curved down from the northwest in a broad bend before taking its course southeastward for Washington. This was as far as Lee meant his troops to go on the Virginia side of the river.

The Eighth, along with the rest of D. R. Jones's division, waited the following day while other units of the army used the nearby river fords. Then, on the morning of Saturday, September 6, they marched down to White's Ford and splashed through the waters of the Potomac to the Maryland shore. The river was broad here but rocky and shallow. The men of the Eighth could not help noticing the theatrics of neighboring brigade commander and Georgia politician Robert Toombs. Toombs drew his sword and rode across the river flourishing it menacingly toward the unseen hosts of Yankeedom, whose nearest outposts were many miles away from the opposite bank.

Thence their march took them toward the town of Frederick, Maryland, on the old National Road between Washington and South Mountain, a northeastward extension of the Blue Ridge, north of the Potomac. West of Frederick, the National Road climbed up and over South Mountain at Turner's Gap, then down the other side to the towns of Boonsboro and Hagerstown in aptly named Pleasant Valley, the north-of-the-Potomac extension of the Shenandoah Valley. The Eighth, along with the rest of Longstreet's troops, marched into Frederick on Sunday, September 7.[32]

For months, Confederates in Virginia and elsewhere had been singing James Ryder Randall's "Maryland, My Maryland" to the tune of "O Tannenbaum":

The despot's heel is on the shore,
Maryland, my Maryland.
His foot is at thy temple door,
Maryland, my Maryland.
Avenge the patriotic gore,
That flecked the streets of Baltimore,
And be the battle-queen of yore,
Maryland, my Maryland.

And so it continued, complaining of Lincoln's alleged disregard of civil liberties in Maryland and exhorting its pro-slavery citizens to rise and throw off the government of the Northern "despot." Southerners thought Maryland really wanted to be a Confederate state, and the Southern soldiers expected to be welcomed in Maryland as liberators.

That made the welcome they actually did get all the more discouraging. "The people in that portion of Maryland through which [we] marched were principally Union," explained Company F's Pvt. J. A. Adair a few weeks later. Not surprisingly, the Confederate soldiers noticed especially the reactions of Maryland's young women, and these females' facial expressions as the Southern soldiers marched by did not at all fit the image of the way damsels in distress were supposed to look upon the knights in shining armor who came to deliver them. Adair thought they looked "sour." Some of them actually waved small United States flags at the passing columns. On one occasion, the Eighth's band serenaded a group of Maryland ladies, playing rousing Confederate favorites, "Dixie," "The Bonnie Blue Flag," and "Maryland, My Maryland." Finally, one of the ladies, in a somewhat faltering voice, spoke up and asked if they could play "The Star-Spangled Banner." The band director pretended not to hear. The awareness that the inhabitants of Maryland did not want the Confederate version of "liberation" was a blow to the soldiers' morale.[33]

For some, at least, of the Eighth's soldiers, Maryland had much to recommend it. "We boys had a good time while in Maryland," recalled Thomas Gilham, "feasting on apples, apple butter, light bread and sweet milk." How the men fared depended a great deal on their skills in foraging, and most of the army continued to live for the most part on apples and green corn as they had been now for several weeks, tying their digestive systems in knots. Still the apples and corn were ripening with every passing day, and they were marching through a rich agricultural country previously untouched by war. For those who had managed to keep up thus far, the diet improved somewhat.[34]

They camped near Frederick until the morning of September 10, and then marched westward along the National Road, over South Mountain by Turner's Gap, through Boonsboro, Funkstown, and on to Hagerstown, arriving there with bands playing and flags waving at the heads of regiments on September 12. As they marched into town, they noticed a welcome exception to the general hostility of the populace. People lined the streets, staring grimly at the invaders, but one old gentleman stood in front of his house shouting, "Huzzah for Jeff Davis and the whole Southern Confederacy." Even the most sanguine of Confederates had to admit, however, that such instances were rare. On September 13 the Eighth rested in its camp along the Williamsport Road, just outside of town.[35]

Meanwhile, the campaign was not going quite the way Lee had anticipated. His plan was to shift westward after crossing the Potomac, open a supply line through the Shenandoah Valley, and then wait for the Union army to come out and fight him on ground of his own choosing, where he would win another resounding victory. But the Federals were not following the script. When Lee moved westward, he assumed that the Union garrison at Harpers Ferry would evacuate rather than risk being cut off. Instead, the Federals stayed put. Their presence made it impossible for Lee to establish a supply line through the Shenandoah Valley, and so they had to be removed. That task was in some ways very easy but in others very dangerous. It was easy because capturing Harpers Ferry and its garrison was as simple as placing large Confederate forces on the various heights that overlooked the town—dangerous because placing forces in those positions would mean separating them widely in a mountainous country with a large enemy army potentially approaching their rear from the direction of Washington. Lee had heard that George McClellan was once again in command of the Union Army of the Potomac and decided to bet on that general's by now well established slowness. The Confederate general divided his army and sent most of them by the necessary roundabout ways to take Harpers Ferry. Others would watch the passes of South Mountain against any signs of unwonted enterprise from McClellan, and the rest, including the Eighth Georgia, would be held in reserve around Hagerstown.

That, however, was not the end of difficulties for Lee. McClellan, under heavy political pressure to get Lee now that the latter was north of the Potomac, moved a bit more rapidly than usual. Not nearly fast enough to suit Lincoln, but definitely much faster than Lee would have liked. By September 13, while the men of the Eighth were enjoying a peaceful day in camp near Hagerstown, McClellan's troops were camping all around Frederick, on the other side of South Mountain, where the Rebels had been only a few days before. There a couple of Indiana soldiers found, at an abandoned Confederate campsite, a very curious paper. It was headed "Headquarters, Army of Northern Virginia, Special Orders, No. 191," and it happened to be the entire blueprint for Lee's daring operation against Harpers Ferry, lost apparently by a staff officer of Confederate major general Daniel Harvey Hill. Within hours it was in McClellan's hands, and the Union general had before him all the information he needed in order to catch Lee's army vulnerable and divided. All he had to do was cross South Mountain and gobble up Lee's forces piece by badly separated piece. His troops moved out next morning.

Lee at first knew nothing of the lost order, but he knew McClellan was marching west at a dangerous pace. He had to delay the Union forces at the passes of South Mountain long enough to allow his army to take Harpers Ferry and reunite to fight McClellan. He ordered Maj. Gen. James Longstreet to take his forces around Hagerstown and march back along the road they had covered just a few days before to join D. H. Hill's forces holding the passes of South Mountain.[36]

And so it was that on Sunday, September 14, when they would very much have liked another day of peaceful rest after the hard fighting and harder marching of the past few weeks, the men of the Eighth Georgia got orders to fall in for a forced march to a desperate fight. They tramped off eastward on the National Road and by late afternoon, badly fatigued after covering thirteen miles in nine hours on an unpleasantly hot day, they arrived back at Boonsboro, at the foot of Turner's Gap in South Mountain. There Longstreet had D. R. Jones detach Anderson's brigade, including the Eighth, and Thomas F. Drayton's to act with Hill's division, while his other forces took up positions nearby.

For the Eighth, the Battle of South Mountain became a miserably botched affair that, ironically, spared them almost entirely from casualties. Their brigade, Anderson's, was placed by Hill in a four-brigade provisional division under Brig. Gen. Roswell Ripley. Ripley blundered by ordering the ad hoc formation to advance before Drayton's or Anderson's brigade had got into position. Then Drayton, who was a habitual blunderer, had trouble handling his brigade. As a result, Anderson found that his own line had both flanks in the air and wisely pulled back to avoid disaster. Only the brigade's skirmishers were engaged. Elsewhere on the field, Confederate troops fared somewhat better, but by nightfall, the Yankees were in solid control of the gaps and had breached the barrier of South Mountain.[37]

Longstreet's divisions fell back westward the next day, but their stand, combined with McClellan's slowness and the rank cowardice of the Union commander at Harpers Ferry, had accomplished Lee's purpose. The garrison surrendered and Lee drew almost the whole of his army together on moderately good defensive ground just west of Antietam Creek, near the town of Sharpsburg, in time to meet McClellan. The Eighth Georgia, along with the rest of Anderson's brigade, marched with the rear guard, temporarily under the command of Brig. Gen. John B. Hood. They crossed Antietam Creek and went into position with their own division along Sharpsburg Ridge on the morning of September 15. Their position was immediately behind Confederate artillery covering the lower bridge, one of three bridges that spanned Antietam Creek in the vicinity of the battlefield. Throughout September 16, they lay in their positions while additional units of both armies came up, the Confederates taking position west of the creek and the Federals east of it. The artillerymen of both sides plied their guns energetically, thundering away at each other and targets of opportunity all the while, giving the Eighth another taste of that hardest job for Civil War infantrymen, lying out under artillery bombardment. Their gallant brigade commander strode up and down their prostrate lines throughout the whole bombardment, hands clasped behind his back, as if oblivious to the danger.[38]

That night Company F of the Eighth drew picket duty, guarding the Lower Bridge. As dawn broke on Wednesday, September 17, and their relief came, Capt. Lewis and his tiny company went in search of water to drink. They found a spring a little way back from the creek and slaked their thirst. As Joel Yarborough straightened up after drinking, he returned his rifle to his right shoulder and dropped his left hand to his side. Just then the crack of a rifle broke the morning stillness in the valley of Antietam Creek, and the bullet struck Yarbrough's left hand, making him the first member of the Eighth wounded at what Confederates would call the Battle of Sharpsburg. Yarbrough and his comrades always felt that the shot had come from a Union sharpshooter who had slipped across the creek in the darkness. At any rate, he refused to leave the regiment, staying with the colors throughout the eventful day that was just beginning.[39]

At that very hour, the real battle was opening several miles to the north, as heavy Union columns attacked the opposite end of the thin Confederate line. By 7:30 A.M., after two hours of ferocious fighting, Confederate forces on that flank were nearing the end of their tether, and the front threatened to collapse completely. Lee hastened to send what reinforcements he could, and that included Tige Anderson and his brigade, now less than five hundred strong. In these thin ranks, the Eighth Georgia numbered only 104, its companies anywhere from five to twenty men each. For the remainder of the day, Anderson's little brigade, including the even smaller Eighth Georgia, would function separately from its parent division.[40]

Anderson's brigade and several others moved north toward a terrain feature known then and after simply as the West Woods, where Union troops were imminently threatening to tear loose the Confederate left flank. As the Eighth approached the scene of the conflict about 9:30 A.M., a powerful fresh Union division under Maj. Gen. John Sedgwick was just then advancing into the West Woods to finish the job other Federals had started. The Confederate reinforcements moving up from the south now launched a counterattack that slammed into Sedgwick's vulnerable southern flank. Initially the Eighth found itself, along with the rest of Anderson's brigade, screened off from the combat by another Confederate brigade that slid into place in front of them in the confusion as elements of several divisions attempted to respond to the Union threat. Anderson's men lay down and took cover behind a rail fence that ran along the southern edge of the West Woods while Anderson figured out what to do next. After about two minutes he got the brigade to its feet again and had it file double-quick to the left about two hundred yards until it cleared out from behind the other Confederate troops. Then he faced them to the front again and with a yell and a volley they charged forward, part of a much larger Confederate assault. Sedgwick's division was deployed all wrong to receive such an attack and soon crumbled and fled. The victorious Confederates, including the Eighth, pursued about half a mile to the northwest before retiring to avoid a possible Union counterattack. The Eighth's George Aycock was much pleased with the foray. It had netted him "a fine sword and a very fine Colt's Repeater" at the expense of a Yankee captain who would not be needing them anymore.[41]

That stabilized the front in the area of the West Woods, but early in the afternoon a crisis developed farther south along the thin-spread Confederate line. Rebel troops in the Confederate center, along a stretch of farm road known as Bloody Lane, finally broke under the furious Union onslaught. The Eighth and the rest of Anderson's brigade were shifted southward to a position along the Hagerstown Pike just north of where Bloody Lane branched away from it. There once again they found a good place to shelter, crouching behind a stone wall that paralleled the pike until the moment came for the Confederate counterattack. Then they sprang over the wall and advanced a short distance, doing their part to stabilize the line at the north end of that hard-fought sector.

As the regiment was making its shift from the West Woods to the Hagerstown Pike, Dick Watters and George McGuire fell out to go and look for water. They found it and got their drink, but before they could catch up with the regiment, a bullet struck Watters in the right knee, severely wounding him. No place was safe on this battlefield. George carried his wounded comrade to the field hospital. The boys in the regiment could only wonder what had become of them. At the field hospital the surgeons decided to try to save Watters's leg and refrained from amputation. Yet there were good reasons that amputation was the standard treatment for such wounds in the Civil War. Infection followed, and three weeks later Dick Watters was dead.[42]

Back on the battlefield later that afternoon the focus of the fighting shifted still farther south, and the Confederate right, down around the Lower Bridge, was sorely threatened. Anderson's brigade received no further call to duty that day. They had done well in their two forays at restoring threatened sectors of the line. In a letter to his cousin, the Eighth's J. A. Adair boasted that the brigade "did some of the prettiest fighting on the field—such at least is said to be the case by several of our commanding Generals."[43]

Ironically, on this the bloodiest day of the war, when 11,530 Confederate soldiers were killed, wounded, or missing in action, the Eighth Georgia, thanks to its relatively brief and successful stints of heavy action as well as its sheltered positions during much of the fighting, escaped with only two killed and twenty-three wounded, five of whom subsequently died of their wounds. Still, that was more than 20 percent of the small number the Eighth had carried to the battlefield, and one of the killed was another color-bearer, S. B. Barnwell of Company B, third man to die during the war carrying the flag of the Eighth Georgia.[44]

The second night after the Battle of Sharpsburg the remnant of the Eighth Georgia crossed the Potomac with the rest of Lee's army back into Virginia. The long campaign was finally over. Lee had done wonders in those six months, discouraging the North, convincing Lincoln that the war could not be won without such drastic measures as the Emancipation Proclamation, and, most of all, raising Southern spirits as almost nothing else could have done. At the height of his success that year, his advance had seemed "resistless as an ocean tide," but it had come at a high price. The experience of the Eighth Georgia that summer was by no means unique. Of the 97,000 men whom Lee had mustered at the outset of his offensive in the Seven Days Battles the previous June, less than 20,000 now remained with the colors. The rest—dead, wounded, captured, sick, exhausted, barefoot, or emotionally unable to face combat again for the time being—were scattered across northern Virginia and western Maryland. Lee had saved the Confederacy that summer and almost won the war, but he had all but used up his army in the process. Now, as autumn began to paint the slopes of South Mountain and the Blue Ridge in scarlets and yellows, the tide of Confederate success ebbed silently away for a season.[45]

CHAPTER SEVEN

We Can Whip Any Army

Much the Worse for Wear

BY the end of October, the oaks, beeches, chestnuts, and poplars of North Georgia began to show their fall colors. Brisk nights reminded householders to look to their supplies of firewood. In Middle Georgia counties such as Meriwether, Bibb, Greene, and Pulaski, the remnants of summer warmth lingered, and residents' thoughts were on the cotton harvest, while in Savannah, far in the south by the sea, the balmy weather bore no trace of autumn. In all those various localities and many others up and down the state, Georgians that fall of 1862 also watched the news from the battlefronts.

The citizens of Rome followed the doings of their sons and brothers in the numerous companies Floyd County had sent to the various theaters of the war—in Kentucky and Tennessee, on the Georgia coast near Savannah, and in the Army of Northern Virginia, where Rome's favorite, the Eighth Georgia, contained three of them. They could read of the battles of Manassas and Sharpsburg and of the sickness and exhaustion in the ranks of their troops.

And they could try, at least, to do something about it. One good opportunity, for citizens of Rome and all the rest of Georgia too, was to support the efforts of the Georgia Relief and Hospital Association. That fall half a dozen representatives of the association arrived at the army's camps near Winchester, Virginia, where there was an acute shortage of surgeons, medicines, and hospital beds, among other things. They brought a large stock of medicines, and Dr. James Camak, of their number, personally treated more than three hundred soldiers. The other members of the party did their best to use the association's resources to provide at least food and shelter for the sick and wounded Georgians. Equally welcome was their mundane but highly practical shipment of a large amount of underwear for distribution to the Georgia troops. There otherwise was none of that vital commodity to be had in Winchester. The soldiers were lavish in their praise and thankfulness to the association and its representatives.

For the men of the Eighth Georgia, the months that followed were a period of rest and recuperation from the rigors of the Army of Northern Virginia's amazing summer campaigns. "Thank Heaven for this respite, short though it be, from the fatigue of forced marches, and the terrible excitement of battle," wrote Melvin Dwinnell in one of his regular letters to the *Rome Courier* that October. Camp life without combat or its immediate prospect was monotonous, he admitted, but just now that sort of monotony was immensely welcome to soldiers who had, over the preceding months, been called on to pour out every ounce of their physical and emotional strength. Absentees—the sick, the stragglers, and some of the returning wounded from the summer's many battles—gradually swelled the regiment's numbers, and by September 27, ten days after the desperate battle at Sharpsburg, Dwinnell could proudly report that the Eighth now mustered fully 150 men for duty, and its growth continued apace as the army's active provost guard strove to drive all stragglers back into their regiments. Men who were barefoot and had been allowed to stay behind in Winchester while the army made its foray into Maryland were now compelled to return to the ranks. "If made to march," Sanford Branch noted in a letter to his mother, they "will suffer terribly."[1]

Dwinnell had to admit that in many ways "the sight of the 'old Eighth' is now saddening." Aside from the regiment's scant numbers, its ranks presented a distinctly ragged appearance. The soldiers' clothes were "much the worse for wear," wrote Dwinnell, poor ghosts of the finery they had worn to Richmond seventeenth months before. The men were also in desperate need of new shoes. "We are getting a little clothing and a few pair of shoes," Dwinnell noted in early October, "one pair of shoes to a company at a time, and perhaps one suit of clothes." At this rate, he added, it would be a very long time before the army was sufficiently clad or shod.

Beyond that, however, and far more serious, the men themselves, like their equipment, were "much the worse for wear." Indeed, the unanimous conclusion of the Eighth's officers was that the regiment itself was wearing out. "There is such a thing as killing the life and fire of a regiment," Dwinnell explained, "long before the last man is killed." That seemed to be what was happening to the Eighth. Dwinnell figured that since the regiment's organization, 448 of its men had been lost to enemy action and another 300 to disease. In fact, he probably underestimated the losses to disease by 100 to 150. Yet the fact remained that the surviving members had marched so far, endured such hardship, and seen so many of their comrades fall in battle or waste away on sickbeds that they seemed reduced "to a half lethargic state of stolid indifference." The "fight" seemed at least temporarily drained out of them, and their officers feared for the results should they be ordered into battle again soon. To avoid this, they all signed a petition to Confederate secretary of war George W. Randolph, requesting that the Eighth be transferred to peaceful garrison duty in some quiet sector of Georgia for three or four months until it could gather and train new recruits and recover the fighting spirit that the recent campaign's hard marching and hard fighting had so seriously sapped. While the Eighth thus recuperated, its place in the Army of Northern Virginia could, the petitioning officers suggested, be filled by some regiment that was currently serving in garrison duty and had not yet gotten the chance to demonstrate its prowess in battle. Word got around, and soldiers wrote home about rumors of duty in Georgia that winter, perhaps Savannah, opined a member of that city's own Oglethorpe Light Infantry.[2]

By the time of the Second World War, such a practice—sending a shot-up unit to the rear to rest and recruit—would be routine procedure in the U.S. Army, but in this war and this army, its chances of becoming reality were precisely zero. This was Lee's army, and Lee believed that if the war was to be won at all, it would have to be won by heavy blows, struck fast and hard. He did not favor dispersing the South's meager manpower hither and yon to guard points and hold territory. Nor did he approve waiting for the enemy to seize the initiative. He therefore consistently strove to get and keep the largest possible number of troops in his army, so that he could strike the heaviest possible blows and have the greatest chance of winning the war. He never willingly approved any transfer of troops away from the Army of Northern Virginia, and in that policy the authorities in Richmond usually sustained him.

More than that, however, the Eighth Georgia could not take a furlough from the Army of Northern Virginia because if it did, every other regiment in the army would be entitled to the same treatment. The Eighth was indeed wearing down and losing its fighting edge, but in that respect it was typical of nearly all the regiments in Lee's army. The Eighth could not go home. Like dozens of other groups—shell-shocked remnants of what had once been proud regiments—it would have to stay and, if necessary, fight, because tattered and weary bands like it were all the army the Confederacy had at the moment in the most prestigious theater of the war.

The salvation of Lee's battered and weary army lay in the inert nature of its foe, Union major general George B. McClellan. Haunted by hobgoblins of his own imagining—traitors behind and innumerable hosts of Rebels before—"Little Mac," as his adoring Union soldiers called him, moved with glacial slowness that fall until Lincoln's considerable patience was finally exhausted. The president relieved McClellan of his command in early November, replacing him with Maj. Gen. Ambrose Burnside, but by that time, Lee's army had had nearly two months to recover. The time Burnside then needed to get his army in hand and undertake a campaign provided an additional month's reprieve, filling out the minimum three-month rest that the officers of the Eighth had believed their regiment needed in the first place. By the time Burnside moved that December, the Army of Northern Virginia was rested, fit, and ready.

Lee also made use of the reprieve to improve the organization of his army, easing out inept or sickly officers and promoting promising young ones. One general officer who had performed brilliantly that summer, from the great charge at Gaines's Mill during the Seven Days Battles to the desperate stand around the Dunker Church at Sharpsburg, was John Bell Hood. Anderson's brigade, including the Eighth Georgia, had operated alongside Hood or under his temporary command for a large part of the late-summer campaigning. Now, with their nominal division commander, D. R. Jones, still on the sick list and likely to stay that way, Anderson's and the other brigades of Jones's division were distributed to the other divisions of Longstreet's First Corps. One of those divisions would now be Hood's, on an official and permanent basis, and into that division went Anderson's brigade. On Monday, October 6, they paraded for their first formal review by Gen. Hood, along with the rest of the division. Tall and rangy, with blue eyes and tawny hair and beard, the thirty-one-year-old Hood looked like grim and remorseless war. Henceforth, for the rest of the conflict, the men of the Eighth Georgia would take pride in being part of Hood's division, "that body of incomparable soldiers."³

It had been a warm, dry autumn—more like summer really—with midday temperatures in the Shenandoah Valley still uncomfortably warm well into October and dust a serious irritant in camp. Then the season changed abruptly. A front moved through the area on Friday evening, October 10, and days of cold, drizzling rain followed. The problem of clothing now became acute. Capt. Scott of Company E, the Miller Rifles, set out for Floyd County to procure clothes from home for his and the other Floyd County men. Lt. Young of Company G, the Pulaski Volunteers, headed for his own unit's home in Middle Georgia on the same errand, and Lt. Shelman of Company B, the Oglethorpe Light Infantry, headed for Savannah. Melvin Dwinnell reminded the readers of the *Rome Courier* that the Confederate government was a poor and unreliable source of clothing. "The soldier's main, and almost entire dependence, is upon supplies sent him from home."⁴

In the midst of this difficult situation, the men of the Eighth had to deal with—of all things—a smallpox epidemic. The first four cases were reported in the Seventh Georgia during the first week of October, with two of three consulting surgeons agreeing that they were genuine smallpox. Then five days later the surgeons reversed themselves and decided it was only chickenpox after all. Another five days went by, several more cases appeared, and the medical men once again modified their diagnosis, this time to varioloid, a mild version of smallpox. Since no cases had yet appeared outside the Seventh, the men of the Eighth figured the smallpox scare was about over. That judgment altered slightly, however, when the number of varioloid cases in the Seventh began to multiply rapidly, and that regiment was sent off to camp some distance from the rest of the army as a quarantine measure. Several days later, and cases were cropping up in other regiments of Anderson's brigade. On October 16 the whole brigade, as well as another infected brigade, got orders to march to join the Seventh in quarantine camp, though the men of the Eighth were promised that they would not have to camp too close to the infected regiments nor come under strict quarantine rules unless the disease broke out in their camp.[5]

Quarantine camp turned out to be about fifteen miles south of Winchester, near Cedar Creek. It was definitely an out-of-the-way place, well back off the busy Valley Pike, and as they marched on ever smaller side roads toward their designated camping place, one soldier quipped that he was afraid "the road would dwindle down to a squirrel's track and go up a tree." The campsite, once reached, turned out to be pleasant enough, and the men had high hopes that in this remote area, far away from the main camps of the army, they would find it easy to obtain food in the neighborhood. In this they were disappointed. The scarcity they blamed on "speculators," who they believed had come through and bought up everything in expectation that prices would rise. In fact, this was a common myth among the Southern people, most of whom never quite seemed to understand the natural outworkings of their own government's inflationary method of financing the war. When prices skyrocketed, people felt they had to blame it on someone, some willfully evil human villain, and thus the label of "speculator" was invented. Angry, but sick to death of their army-issue diet of flour and fresh beef with very little salt, many of the soldiers paid a dollar a pound for honey, seventy-five cents a pound for bacon, and similarly outrageous prices for other items.

As for the smallpox, for the Eighth Georgia it turned out to be nothing more than a scare. The few cases in the other regiments proved mild and quickly recovered. None ever broke out in the Eighth, and the regiment's overall health was excellent.[6]

We Could Riddle Him into Doll Rags

In late October, McClellan began edging his Union army ever so slowly across the Potomac and southward into the Virginia piedmont, east of the Blue Ridge, creeping with infinite caution toward what he hoped would be a position between Lee—who was still in the Shenandoah Valley—and Richmond. By October 29 the timid Union general had most of his army on the south bank of the Potomac, and Lincoln, relieved that "Little Mac" was finally stirring, wired him to say, "I am much pleased with the movement of the Army. When you get entirely across the river let me know. What do you know of the enemy?" The operative question, however, proved to be what Lee knew of him, and the answer was that the Rebel general knew plenty. How McClellan could have imagined that he would get past the wily Virginian at such a snail's pace is a mystery. In fact, Lee recognized the Union movement and put his own army in motion to head it off.

The same day that Lincoln was telegraphing his pleasure to McClellan, the Eighth Georgia and the rest of Anderson's brigade got their orders to march east. They marched through Strasburg and Front Royal, then, as they had on their march to Manassas fifteen months before, they forded the Shenandoah. It was two and a half feet deep and ice-cold, and the rocks on its bottom were as sharp and numerous as ever. The weather was fair but rather brisk for wading. "It seemed that the water would cut our legs off," wrote a soldier of the neighboring Ninth Georgia. "I never had water to hurt me as badly in my life." They made twenty-three miles before camping for the night. Early the next morning they were on the tramp again, and to the men's dismay, their route took them across the Shenandoah a second time. This time they had to wade it at a point where it was about three hundred yards wide. Thereafter, their way led eastward over the Blue Ridge, and they would not have to worry about the Shenandoah for many months to come.[7]

The rest of the march was easier and more pleasant. They covered another seventy-four miles in the next five days. The weather remained good, the roads were sound, and the men actually found the march enjoyable despite the fatigue. They arrived in Gordonsville the evening of Monday, November 3. Two days later they moved on to Orange Court House. There they remained some days. The fringes of the two armies brushed against each other, causing skirmishes to flare up now and again. The men of the Eighth heard the firing and waited expectantly for orders to march to action. For the time being none came. What arrived instead was a formal promotion to brigadier general for Col. Anderson, who had been doing a brigadier's work for months. The men liked Anderson and were pleased with the promotion.[8]

Meanwhile, across the lines, Lincoln's disgust finally reached critical mass as he learned that McClellan had allowed Lee to outmaneuver him again. "Little Mac" was sent packing and Burnside got the call. The new commander prepared to implement a plan of his own for getting between Lee and Richmond.

The men of the Eighth knew nothing of this, of course, and turned their energies and ingenuity to getting along. A great many of them were barefoot by this time, so their corps commander suggested a way for them to improvise shoes. On November 3 he had orders read out to the troops at the regimental dress parades warning that henceforth no man would be excused from ranks for lack of shoes. Instead, he was to procure a piece of fresh beef hide at the slaughter pens where animals were butchered to feed the army. Then he should cut the rawhide to size and, as one Texan put it, "whang the moccasins on with rawhide thongs." That is, he should sew the hide around his feet, putting the hairy side inward, next to the foot, to serve in place of a sock, and thus make for himself a comfortable piece of footwear. At least, that was the theory. Advance contemplation of the obvious practical difficulties led some regiments to receive the reading of the order with shouts of laughter. The Eighth Georgia's Tom Gilham seemed to find it a fairly acceptable sort of footwear, aside from the fact that when a man finally decided to take his "shoes" off, he had to cut them off and then make a new pair the next time. Other Confederates were apparently less adept at sewing rawhide and looked as if they had each foot stuck in a twenty-pound ham.[9]

Somehow, between mending the clothes they had, getting some of their old ones shipped to them out of storage in Richmond, and drawing a few more from the quartermaster, they managed to get by without severe suffering. Old tents too came back from storage in Richmond. Melvin Dwinnell noticed that in the first few days in camp after a long march, the men rested and recovered their high spirits. Thereafter, however, the sedentary life of camp led to laziness and quarreling. The weather during the first two weeks of November was humid, close, and mild, under heavy, lowering skies, and seemed to make everyone feel slack and irritable. The men devised various ways to relieve their ennui, including the playing of rough games they had known on the schoolyard back home. One such was wrap-jackets, in which two contestants locked their left arms and then each flailed furiously at the other's back with a stout switch he held in his right hand. It had little point but to show who could "take it" the best. As Dwinnell listened to the sounds coming from a nearby match of wrap-jackets, he predicted that the combatants "will carry marks for several days to come."

Sometimes during prolonged encampments of this sort, some of the men got into trouble that resulted in courts-martial. The most common offense was "absence without leave," a milder offense than "desertion." The difference was that the soldier absent without leave intended to come back—just wanted a little more liberty than orders permitted. The prevalence of this offense demonstrated how difficult it was to make disciplined soldiers out of these independent-minded young citizens. The regimental courts-martial handed out stern sentences. A convicted offender might be sentenced "to be confined for sixty days at hard labor, wearing during this time a twelve pound ball attached to a chain to his ankle, and to forfeit two months' pay." One or two during this period were convicted of the more heinous crime of desertion; a deserter's punishment was to be branded on the left hip with the letter D, to have half of his head shaved, and to be drummed out of camp in disgrace. Minor military infractions might result in being sentenced to stand for perhaps four hours a day for thirty days on the top of a flour barrel that had been set up in some conspicuous place. It all might seem harsh to boys who had grown up in an America where government rarely molested a man who left his neighbors in peace, but this was the way of war, and, as Dwinnell pointed out, "these men would possibly have been more severely punished, if they had been tried by a general, instead of a regimental court martial."[10]

On November 19, orders came that brought a temporary end to the fun of wrap-jackets, and on the morning of November 20 the Eighth Georgia swung down the road in march column under a cold drizzling rain, through the town of Orange Court House, and then eastward on the Orange Plank Road. Plank roads had once been seen as the best in paved highways, but their one great drawback was their lack of durability. The boards that made up a plank road's continuous wooden deck would warp, break, rot, split, or just come loose. Such was now the case with the Orange Plank Road, "so dilapidated as to make it exceedingly hard to walk upon, having frequently to jump, and take long straining steps to reach from one plank to another." The twenty-one miles they covered that day should have rated as only a moderately hard march, but the poor conditions made it what Dwinnell called "the hardest our Regiment has ever made."

They continued the following day, finding the going easier as they got off the plank road. The rain continued, but the men found that the sandy soil was better able to handle the rain than the heavy clay they had left behind in Orange County. For Sanford Branch, marching in the ranks of Company B, that was little consolation. He had gotten a new pair of shoes—real shoes these, not sewed-on cowhide—just before the regiment started the march, and the long miles of walking in new shoes that were thoroughly wet had blistered his feet terribly on the first day. Now, for the second day's march, he decided to walk barefoot and carry his shoes. That too proved unsatisfactory, for the temperature was not much above freezing, and walking barefoot all day in the chilly rain and mud was a painful proposition. When for a third consecutive morning the regiment prepared to take to the road, Branch finally broke down and cut slits in the sides of his new shoes in order to ease their tightness and make them wearable on his blistered feet.[11]

The third day's march brought the Eighth at last to a position in line of battle about three miles from the town of Fredericksburg, where they made camp. It was Saturday, November 22, and rumor had it that the Yankee army was just beyond the town, on the north bank of the Rappahannock River.[12]

That rumor turned out to be true. In hopes of turning Lee's right flank, Burnside had brought his army there to cross the river and break out into the open country beyond, where Lee's supply lines would be vulnerable. Federal forces had begun arriving on the north bank opposite the picturesque little town on November 17, and the Union commander's plan might have worked save that someone forgot to bring along the pontoon bridges and delay resulted while they were brought up. On the 19th, elements of Longstreet's corps began taking up positions on the hills overlooking Fredericksburg from the south. During the days that followed, additional forces from both sides moved into position on the heights that overlooked the town from north and south. Between them lay the broad valley of the Rappahannock and the roofs and spires of Fredericksburg.

The enemy was near, and so the men were confined to their camp, ready to form up quickly for battle at the sound of a signal gun located near Lee's headquarters. Days passed, however, with no action, and the Confederates could only wait. The soldiers got opportunity to view more of the surrounding area during stints of picket duty. The Eighth's picket post was a deserted earthwork near the banks of the Rappahannock, about four miles downstream, or east, of the town of Fredericksburg. The large, stately mansions and broad, cultivated fields around them impressed the Georgians and made them feel like rustics in the presence of the kind of genteel culture they had read about in romances of the Old Dominion. A quiet kind of awe came of seeing one's stereotypes at least thus far fulfilled in reality. If they tired of looking at the houses, they could watch the river go by, 150 yards wide, clear and placid, advancing toward Chesapeake Bay with a dignity that seemed to fit the surroundings. Inland dwellers from the regiment's Middle and North Georgia companies noted with interest that the Rappahannock here rose and fell about four feet with the tide, and puzzled upcountry farm boys who had never seen an ocean wondered how the water at high tide could still be fresh.

Back in camp, the men tended to necessary tasks, rendering tallow into candles and cooking up their own homemade soap, an article that had become almost impossible to buy. The weather was frosty but dry until the last few days of November, when the clear skies gave way first to rain, then to snow, which accumulated to three inches by the 29th and showed no sign of melting soon. An extra shipment of clothes from back home arrived just then, at the best of all possible times, and the men weathered the cold with a minimum of suffering. They had become very tough, and warm clothes, sound tents, and a roaring log blaze seemed all the comfort one could ask in the snowy Virginia winter, while no military action interrupted what Dwinnell called "the monotony of passing events."

Once again, the soldiers noticed the tendency of war to devastate a region without anyone's actually wishing it so or trying to accomplish that end. This was painfully plain from the fact that the Confederate army was unavoidably destroying the Virginia farms in the area it was supposed to be protecting. An army of 75,000 men had a voracious appetite for firewood in cold weather. That commodity had not been plentiful around Fredericksburg before the army's arrival. Now local farmers claimed they were ruined because the whole of their woodlots had been cut down and consumed. Sometimes shade trees and fences went too. The surrounding area was scoured clean of foodstuffs as well, with quartermasters hauling corn as much as twenty-two miles.[13]

If the soldiers spent any of their abundant leisure time during these weeks contemplating the cause for which they were fighting, few of them bothered to write of it. An exception was Melvin Dwinnell, the newspaper editor, used to expressing his opinions in ink. To the readers back in Rome he wrote that "the voice of Providence" condemned the Union cause. To this native-born Yankee it was amazing that Lincoln and those who fought for the old flag could not seem to see that 1862's series of Union defeats in Virginia was not due to inferior generalship but to God's intervention on the side of the South. Why would the Yankees not simply admit that the Almighty fought against them and give up? In any case, Dwinnell was confident that he and his comrades could whip the Yankees again. If "Burnsides should have the hardihood to attempt to cross the river," Dwinnell wrote, "we could 'riddle him into doll rags.' " That, he hoped, might bring peace in sight. "Many think they see the 'beginning of the end of the war.' " If they won this battle, perhaps "old Abe" would give up.[14]

Safely Through Another Week

The boom of the signal cannon brought the startled soldiers out of their tents in the predawn darkness of Thursday morning, December 11. Through the cold morning fog they scrambled to take up their rifles and fall into line of battle and move up to their assigned place in the Confederate array. Then they waited. In the lingering gloom they could see little, and even as the sun rose behind the overcast somewhere out be-

yond the right flank, the growing light revealed only the thick gray boles
of the oaks, chestnuts, and beeches scattered through the woodland in
front of their line. But through the mist they could clearly hear the
growing thunder of cannon as the rival armies' artillery blasted away at
each other across the valley of the Rappahannock. The duel rumbled on
for hours.[15]

Before dawn that morning, Burnside's engineers had begun throwing
five pontoon bridges across the river at Fredericksburg. Lee countered
them with a brigade of Mississippians sharpshooting from the houses of
the town while the rest of the Confederate line waited where the high
ground began to rise up from the south side of the valley. The Mississippians' fire stopped the work on the bridges, but it also made Fredericksburg a very legitimate target for the Union artillery that was massed
battery after battery on Stafford Heights on the northern side of the valley. The Federal artillerists went to work and did their best to shoot the
army's way across the river. Bricks and boards flew and buildings smoked
and flared up into bright flames in the handsome little colonial town
while the Eighth Georgia and the rest of Lee's army on the heights to
the south could only listen, wait, and wonder.

But in the cellars of the town the Mississippians hunkered down and
held on, and when the Federal engineers dashed out onto their half-
finished bridges again, they met the same withering fire and had to give
up. Northern officers now decided they would have to clear the town
the hard way, loaded four regiments into makeshift assault boats, and sent
them into the teeth of Confederate defensive fire. The amphibious attack was successful, the pestilent Mississippians driven off, and the
bridges completed. As the day went on, Union infantry streamed across
the five spans onto the south bank of the Rappahannock, but no further
major combat occurred.

Through that day and the next, the men of the Eighth, like the rest
of Lee's army, stayed in line of battle and listened. At night they lay down
on the ground where they were and slept in line of battle too. "There
are a thousand reports about the progress of the fight," Sanford Branch
wrote his mother. "At one time we hear that the Yankees are falling back
& then we hear that we are allowing them to cross." In fact no significant action took place on Friday.[16]

Then, on the morning of Saturday, December 13, Burnside sent his army forward against the Confederate positions. The Eighth Georgia, as part of Anderson's brigade of Hood's division, was almost precisely in the center of the Confederate line. The Union assaults struck against both the right and the left but left the center untouched. Except for the regiment's skirmishers, deployed about two hundred yards ahead of the main line of battle, the Eighth saw no action with opposing infantry, though it did stand a good deal of shelling.[17]

For the skirmishers, Companies A, B, and C, the battle looked slightly different. Their advanced position put them on lower ground, out in front of the wooded ridge on which the bulk of the Confederate army was deployed. In front of them was an open field, and crossing the field, about midway between their position and the river, was the embankment of the Richmond, Fredericksburg & Potomac Railroad, behind which Federal skirmishers took cover during part of the day. To the right of the Eighth's position, about midday, Union forces scored a temporary success against troops of A. P. Hill's division but were soon driven back. The Eighth's skirmishers supported the Confederate counterattack with their long-range fire, and received the same in return. For James R. Boggs, of Company A, that return fire had fatal consequences; he was shot dead. In the same company, Sgt. George Aycock, who had picked up a Colt revolver from a dead Yankee officer back at Sharpsburg, took a bullet squarely in the head. His men carried him off the field, but he obviously could not last long. John Watson of Company C might have wondered what it was about him that attracted enemy bullets. He had returned not long before from convalescence after a severe wound at Sharpsburg. Now he was one of only three men to get hit along the skirmish line, taking a bullet in the leg that would keep him out of action for another ten months.

Back on the main battle line, the two casualties were both caused by shrapnel from bursting shells. A piece struck Company E's Henry Garrett in the head. He died two days later. R. N. Bowden, of the same company, got a piece in the ankle, ending his career as a soldier. Otherwise the regiment was virtually unscathed. They lost three men captured, soldiers who had apparently blundered into the Yankee line on obscure errands. In return, the Eighth's skirmishers gathered up some thirty-one Federal prisoners who had apparently become equally disoriented during the Union retreat from that advanced position on Hill's front. Finally,

Leopold Ottenheimer, of Company G, came up missing. The night after the battle he and several others got permission to creep forward and see if the Yankees had lost any good overcoats or full haversacks in their flight. The others came back, but Ottenheimer was never heard from again.[18]

And that was the battle of Fredericksburg for the Eighth Georgia Regiment. The soldiers could not quite believe that it was over. General Lee could not believe it was over. Yet after waiting on the battlefield throughout Sunday, December 14, Burnside started his army in retreat back across the Rappahannock. The Federals completed their withdrawal before daylight Monday morning. Lee had just won his most lopsided victory. Union casualties came to 12,653 killed, wounded, and missing; Confederate, 5,309. Burnside had made it easy for them, but in a letter home that month, Sanford Branch assured his mother, "I feel confident that we can whip any army that they can put in the field, under any leader that they can produce. I consider the Confederate army commanded by Lee, Jackson and Longstreet invincible."[19]

For the Eighth Georgia, things very quickly got back to business as usual. They returned to their old camp with its "monotonous routine of daily duties." The only out-of-the-way event during the next week was medical. To everyone's amazement, George Aycock survived, despite having his skull fractured by a Union bullet. Thanks to the long range, the shot had done no more. A surgeon removed bone splinters from the wound, and the sergeant set out on the road to recovery, even as his death was reported in the newspaper back home.

But camp life for the healthy was dull. "It is really remarkable," Melvin Dwinnell explained to his readers back home, "how soon we fall back to the same dull state of carelessness. . . . As soon as the dead and wounded of even a great battle, are removed from sight, the great mass of old soldiers exhibit no more evidences of excitement than if no unusual thing had taken place. Arms becomes their profession and fighting their occupation and they go about it very much as other men do to their customary daily duties, and when a battle is over those who come out unharmed, feel a kind of sweet satisfaction, not very unlike the enjoyment experienced by a laborer who has got successfully through some disagreeable, and perhaps long dreaded job of work."[20]

Back home it was much the same. News reports of the battle of Fredericksburg appeared in the columns of the *Rome Courier* sandwiched between items such as T. N. Poullain's offer to sell his "Valuable Plantation," 862 acres between Rome and Calhoun, with a dwelling and "the usual outbuildings," for $10,000. There was J. J. Coben's more modest offer of his storehouse and dwelling for sale, and then there was a notice from Allen J. Bell, of Hall County, Georgia, offering a reward for the return of his "runaway negroes," an announcement that the spring term at Rome Female College would open January 11, and another from Flemmon Moss: "All persons are hereby forewarned against trading with my wife Catharine L. Moss, as I will not be responsible for any contracts made by her."[21]

There was more to worry about down in Savannah. Nearby Fort Pulaski had fallen to a Union amphibious expedition in April, spreading consternation in the hometown of Company B and, to a lesser degree, throughout Georgia. Local Confederate forces succeeded, however, in holding the Yankees in their enclave around the fort, and the town of Savannah remained firmly in Rebel hands. Conscious of the threat to the coastal city, Richmond authorities set about moving the Confederate Ordnance Bureau's facilities from there to Macon.

Deep in the interior, Macon was as safe a spot as anyone could think of, notwithstanding a recent series of fires there, in which arson was suspected. The hometown of Company C soon boasted a Confederate government arsenal, armory, and the Central Laboratory of the Confederate Ordnance Bureau besides its other factories already on a war footing. Industry had never boomed like this before on the banks of the Ocmulgee. Slaves were often used in the factories as well as the cotton fields and always commanded high prices and brisk business during the war. J. B. Smith and Company advertised in the *Daily Telegraph* a "fine negro fellow 25 years old," skilled in the use of tools. On one occasion Smith and Company offered thirty-two slaves for sale at public auction and on another $2,900 for a single slave. Times were good.

Culture was also thriving in Bibb County. Plays, tableaux, and musical performances followed one after another, many of them dedicating their proceeds to various efforts to send material relief to the soldiers. The young ladies of the Wesleyan Female College performed the popular operetta *The Flower Queen,* to raise money for the Soldiers' Relief Society, and the Johnson Minstrels performed to a packed house.[22]

Life went on back in Georgia, sometimes happily, sometimes not, but for the most part, what William T. Sherman would later call "the hard hand of war" had not yet touched the homes of the Eighth's soldiers.

On Virginia's contested ground, the Georgians dealt with the cold winter weather and the ever-present boredom as best they could. Dwinnell got a pass and walked down to Fredericksburg to see the effects of the battle. He counted a total of three buildings in the whole town that had not been hit by artillery fire. "Some houses were literally torn to pieces, others had six or eight ball holes through them, and still others a less number. Here you would see where a ball had passed through a window, there through a door, in another place through the brick walls. The insides of many buildings were torn to fragments by the bursting of shells." Relatively few houses had actually burned down, but to a generation that lived and died before the great devastations of the twentieth century, all this looked bad enough. Even worse, to the seething Dwinnell, was the evidence that some of the Union soldiers, demoralized by their senseless defeat, had taken out their frustrations by vandalizing a large number of houses. It was what he expected from the "Abolitionist army."[23]

Others in the regiment managed to entertain themselves in more cheerful ways, holding mock dress parades at which outrageous general orders were read out to the snickering troops: "There will be hereafter, twelve battalion drills, before breakfast, each day, and one hundred and twenty roll calls between breakfast and dinner and in the afternoon there will be eight brigade drills, and four dress parades"—and so on in like facetious vein. The men roared with laughter, but the joke had a basis in fact: "The men do despise drilling; day after day, week in and week out," Dwinnell explained. "These exercises afford them nothing new to think about; still, in order to obey the commands, they have to keep their minds on what they are doing." The worst of it was that as far as the soldiers could see, the drill brought them no benefit. In fact, it was a key element in what made them a combat-ready unit, and it had the added benefit of keeping them out of trouble and making the boredom at least somewhat less than it otherwise would have been.[24]

Much more popular with the men was a new policy of furloughs. These were to be granted on the basis of length of continuous service with the regiment, without absence. By that standard, the very first of the coveted furloughs went to private Billy Dasher of Company B. Others came after in their turn.[25]

For those who remained in camp, there were other comforts. Several agents of the Georgia Relief and Hospital Association arrived, though they found the brigade tolerably well clothed and in little need of the extra distribution they were prepared to make. Sanford Branch got a new pair of pants from them and did the only honorable thing for the filthy old pair he had been wearing—he burned them.[26]

The association agents were an encouragement in other ways as well. One of them, a Rev. Mr. Potter of Georgia, preached to the men on Sunday, December 21. The occasion was a very meaningful one for the men, who, like many Confederate regiments, lacked a chaplain of their own at that particular point in the war and thus ordinarily got little chance to hear preaching. Especially moving was Potter's reciting at the beginning of his sermon the words of the first verse a hymn by John Newton, "Safely through another week/God has brought us on our way." Though the dangers of the most recent battle were by then eight days past, the soldiers—or many of them—"thanked our kind Heavenly Father for preserving [us] unharmed throughout the recent battles." If any of them reflected that the hymn's author had once been a slave-ship captain but had given up such employment after placing his faith in Christ, none left any record of it.[27]

The Best Place to Move From

Christmas of 1862 the men celebrated, as best they could, in camp, treating themselves to ginger cakes purchased from local citizens at the outrageous price of three for a dollar. And so another winter passed over the Georgians who had come to Virginia to fight for the Confederacy. An officer in the Eleventh Georgia, also of Anderson's brigade, wrote, "Since the fight we have fixed up quite comfortably for the winter knowing that the Yankees could not drive us from our position. So we sit quite easy under our tent flies, eat our bread and beef and smoke our pipes with the happy smile of peace for a while at least."[28]

The morning of Tuesday, January 6, 1863, dawned bright, clear, and crisp, with a thick covering of soft snow on the ground. Over in the

Texas Brigade, certain spirited young men, about four hundred in number, decided it was time to go over and have some fun with "goobers" or "goober grabbers," as they called all the Georgians and the Eleventh Georgia in particular, after that incident back in 1861 in which the Georgia boys had fallen out of ranks to attack what they thought was a field of peanuts, only to be disappointed to find that the plants were clover, with no "goober peas" among the roots. This fine morning the Texans planned to "shell out" the "goobers" of the Eleventh Georgia with snowballs, so they made plenty of snowballs and stuffed them in their haversacks in preparation.

At first the Texan assault was successful. With a Rebel Yell and a volley of snowballs they drove the Eleventh out of its camp, "pelting them unmercifully." Then, however, word of the "attack" spread to the rest of Anderson's brigade. Drummers beat the long roll in the camps of the Seventh, Eighth, and Ninth Georgia, and the "goober grabbers," a thousand strong, scrambled out of their huts, formed and deployed into line of battle, and advanced snowballing with a right good will. The Texans fell back on their camp and called out the rest of the Texas Brigade to reinforce them. The advancing Georgians could see the westerners scrambling around making snowballs and falling into ranks while a waggish captain stood on a stump and facetiously urged them on with oratorical flourishes about Napoleon's "march across the icy Alps" and allusions to Campbell's "Hohenlinden" with its line "All bloodless lay the untrodden snow." It soon was thoroughly trodden, as the two sides waded into each other again. Then Benning's Georgia Brigade came up to reinforce the "goober" side, and the Texans, despite the help of a North Carolina regiment, had to haul up the white flag. Such mock battles were not uncommon in the army this snowy winter.[29]

Not all the activities of that winter camp were pleasant. Late in January a court-martial convicted Pvt. Merry G. "Poss" Christian, of Company K, of absence without leave and cowardice in the face of the enemy, apparently at the recent battle of Fredericksburg. The court sentenced the illiterate, twenty-four-year-old farmer "to be marched up and down, in front of his regiment, at Dress Parade, under charge of a sentinel, for three successive days, with a placard on his back, inscribed in large letters, 'COWARD,' and afterwards walk a ring fifty feet in diame-

ter, under charge of a sentinel, every alternate hour, from reveille to retreat for thirty successive days, carrying a weight of fifty pounds."

The strains of war showed up in various ways. John Reed finally decided that he could no longer afford the cost of keeping Lit, his personal
servant, and so let him go. Lit, despite his hatred of danger, decided to
stay on with the company, earning his keep handsomely by means of the
numerous washing and other odd jobs that he picked up for hire from
the other soldiers.

The peaceful times in the chilly camps around Fredericksburg were
to be of surprisingly short duration for the men of two of Longstreet's
divisions, those of Hood and Maj. Gen. George Pickett. For them, orders
came February 16 to pack their excess baggage for shipment by rail. The
soldiers themselves, like infantrymen since the days of Rome and before,
would go afoot, and they would be leaving early the next morning. As
part of Hood's division, the Eighth likewise made its preparations for a
major movement.

The reason for the move was unease in Richmond about the threat
to the Confederate capital posed by the continuing Federal presence in
coastal enclaves in southern Virginia and North Carolina. With operations on the Rappahannock seemingly at a standstill for the rest of the
winter, Lee agreed to assuage Richmond's fears by dispatching Longstreet and two of his divisions to cover the capital.

The roll of drums in the camps of the two divisions woke the soldiers
an hour before dawn on the morning of February 17. Emerging from
their tents they discovered the ground covered with several inches of
snow, which was still falling thickly. It continued falling all that day on
the long marching column of soldiers moving southward from Fredericksburg, and before they made camp that night—without their tents,
which had not caught up with them yet—it had accumulated to a depth
of eight or nine inches. They set out again the next morning, and if any
of the soldiers were inclined to congratulate themselves that the snow
had stopped, the thought must have died aborning, for no sooner had
the column gotten back out onto the road than a steady, drizzling rain
set in. It rained all day, and by one soldier's estimate the mud was soon
six to twelve inches deep.

And so they continued, slogging through the mud by day, lying down
in it by night, until they reached a better stretch of road and passed

through Richmond on February 22. They camped that night south of the James River. About half an hour after the men rolled up in their blankets and lay down to sleep that night, the snow started falling again, and by morning the sleeping soldiers were only indistinct mounds in the snow. Nevertheless the mounds stirred and the soldiers shook off the snow at the beating of the drums next morning.[30]

It was of this difficult journey that Sgt. M. O. Young of the Ninth Georgia, also of Anderson's brigade, related an account regarding a soldier of the Eighth. Supposedly this man had somehow lost his voice completely during the operations around Yorktown in March and April 1862. As this mute soldier was slogging alongside his comrades on this miserable march, he slipped and fell to the ground. As he struck the ground, he let out a grunt of pain. After he had climbed to his feet again, it occurred to him that if he could grunt, he ought to be able to talk as well. So to his own surprise as well as that of his comrades, he began talking. Fearing that if he stopped talking he would once again lose the ability to do so, he continued for the rest of the day, greatly wearying the other men of his company. Who this Eighth Georgia man was, Young did not say, and at this remove in time it is impossible to say who he was or whether, indeed, his story was not a tall tale.[31]

For several weeks they camped in the vicinity of Petersburg while the high command decided what to do next. One occupation for the soldiers during this period was religious observance. An active Soldiers' Christian Association in Anderson's brigade held nightly prayer meetings, well attended and earnest. The soldiers drew up a pamphlet and had it printed, explaining the reasons for setting up the Christian Association and presenting its constitution. It explained that the men missed their regular churches back home—Methodist, Baptist, and Presbyterian—and wished for some regularly organized substitute in the army. They established the Christian Association as a sort of ad hoc church that would be "acceptable to all orthodox denominations." The members accepted the fundamental doctrines of the faith and promised to attend the meetings of the association, to obey the Ten Commandments and the specific teachings of the particular denomination to which they belonged, and also to abstain from gambling and drunkenness. If need arose and they were able, they pledged to give each other decent burials and write to the folks back home to inform them of their loss. They took the step of publishing their agreement because they wanted the people to know that even amid the "many temptations" of army life, "Christ has kept a few . . . faithful followers." More than that, God was calling sinners to Himself and increasing the number of believers even while the war continued.[32]

Indeed, the soldiers realized that God was at work in their midst. The Rev. W. C. Dunlap, who had taken over the duties as the Eighth's chaplain, wrote, "God has wonderfully blessed us of late. We have had going on in our midst a revival of religion. . . . I have held prayer-meetings in my own regiment until ten o'clock many a night, and, after closing, the brethren would all retire to the woods . . . and there, with no other covering save the open canopy of heaven, pour out their souls in humble supplication at a throne of grace, often remaining until after midnight." On March 27, a date proclaimed by President Jefferson Davis as a national day of "fasting, humiliation, and prayer," the whole brigade held a unified meeting, with generals Hood and Anderson present. The band played, and then "Brother Crumley," a roving missionary to the army camps, "preached a most appropriate sermon." Afterward once again many of the soldiers retired in small groups to the woods to hold prayer-meetings.[33]

Meanwhile the war went on. The Richmond authorities assigned Longstreet command of the Department of Southern Virginia and North Carolina, and Secretary of War James A. Seddon suggested he take his force and see if he could drive the Federals out of the southeast Virginia town of Suffolk. If the town proved too heavily fortified, Longstreet's action would at least pin the Yankees inside their stronghold, allowing Confederate authorities to sweep up large stocks of food and fodder in the southeastern counties of the state. Lee's army desperately needed such supplies, lending further appeal to the plan. Longstreet accepted it.[34]

Thus on April 8 the Eighth Georgia, along with the rest of Hood's and Pickett's divisions, marched out of its camps near Petersburg and stepped off down the road toward Suffolk, about one hundred miles to the southeast. The roads were in good shape, the terrain level, and the weather delightful. The men were full of vigor, hardened veterans, well rested, their ranks filled out by the return of last summer's wounded and sick. Spring was in the air, and the gray-clad ranks swung along jauntily, covering twenty miles a day.[35]

On April 11, Longstreet's Confederates took up their positions around the fortified Suffolk lines while the Federals pulled back into their entrenchments. The siege that followed never had much chance of success, and it was not particularly well conducted at that. Still, it accomplished the most important objective—allowing collection of supplies in southeastern Virginia.

For the men of the Eighth, the siege operations meant sniping back and forth across the lines and receiving a good shelling now and then, much like what they had experienced from Yorktown to the outskirts of Richmond one year before. J. A. "Soldier Jim" Adair wrote to the *Atlanta Southern Confederacy* to report proudly of having the Yankees penned up and making them keep their heads down with skillful sharpshooting. It was not a one-sided exchange, however, as several members of the Eighth discovered when a high-caliber shell burst in their midst, wounding five men but, almost miraculously, killing none.[36]

The Eighth's finest hour of the siege came on April 17, when Capt. John Young of Company G led a counterattack against a Union picket sortie, driving the Federals back into their fortified lines and pushing his own company out two hundred yards in advance of the rest of the Confederate picket line. The cost, however, was a severe wound to one of Company G's best men, Sgt. David G. Fleming, who would be out of action for months to come. In all, the Suffolk siege cost the Eighth a total of ten men wounded, most slightly, and one man captured. However, at least one member of the regiment died of disease during the operation.[37]

By late April the operation had accomplished about as much as could reasonably be expected, and Lee desperately wanted his troops back. On April 28 the large, powerful, and thoroughly reconditioned Army of the Potomac, now under the command of Maj. Gen. Joseph Hooker, began crossing the Rappahannock River upstream from Fredericksburg, obviously opening a new and extremely dangerous campaign. Lee urgently telegraphed Longstreet to break off the siege and rejoin the main army, but it was the evening of May 3 before Anderson's brigade took to the road as part of the general movement back toward Richmond. The march, once it started, was vigorous, but there was no longer any chance of joining Lee and Jackson for the climactic showdown with Hooker. That clash, the Battle of Chancellorsville, took place from May 1 to May 4. It was perhaps the most dazzling of Lee's victories, the ultimate collaboration of the Lee-Jackson team, but it also saw the accidental wounding of Jackson by his own men. The great Confederate chieftain died May 10, several days before the Eighth Georgia, along with the rest of Longstreet's troops, arrived on the scene, too late to aid in the defeat of Hooker.

The men of the Eighth later remembered Suffolk as almost "the best place to move from" that it was ever their misfortune to get stuck in during the war, "a wretched place" and "a detestable hole." Now they knew only that they were glad to be back with the Army of Northern Virginia and were ready to follow Marse Robert, and win inevitable victories, wherever his banners might lead them.[38]

CHAPTER EIGHT

※

A Scythe of Fire

Quit Fooling with Them

GRAY-CLAD soldiers stood shoulder to shoulder in a line of battle that stretched nearly two miles long spanning a broad, gently undulating plain of farm fields and pastures. The sun blazed down on them, and the broad expanses around them shimmered with heat. To the west, misty blue mountains spread along the horizon, fading into the haze both north and south. Sharp-voiced commands rasped out through the humid air, and the ranks of sweating soldiers wheeled crisply from one formation to another, maneuvering with the skill of what they were, battle-tested veterans. A battery of artillery galloped by in a cloud of dust and unlimbered. Sweating artillerists rammed down their loads; then eager gunners yanked the lanyards and the cannons roared and belched out huge clouds of white smoke as from the throats of the eight thousand men of Hood's gallant division rose the Rebel Yell.

Watching them from the gently rising ground in front and knolls on the flanks, scores of women gasped in admiration, clapped, and waved

The first flag of the Eighth Georgia was a copy of the Confederacy's first national flag, "The Stars and Bars." *(Courtesy of W. O. Clark)*

The Eighth Georgia's Confederate battle flag.
(Courtesy of Steven Townsend)

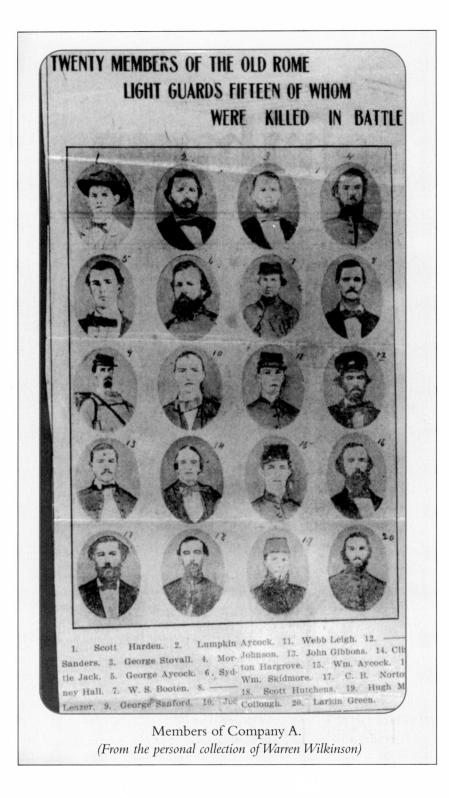

Members of Company A.
(From the personal collection of Warren Wilkinson)

Hamilton Branch, Company B, with a friend. Branch is wearing the elaborate uniform of the Oglethorpe Light Infantry.
(From the personal collection of Warren Wilkinson)

Augustus Monroe Boyd, Company E.
(Courtesy of Georgia Department of Archives and History)

William Alfred Powell, Company F, holding his
Model 1822 musket.
(Courtesy of W. F. Lenoir)

John Paulden Duke, Company H, with his wife, Irene Isabella
Orrill, of King and Queen County, Virginia, March 2, 1865.
(From the personal collection of Warren Wilkinson)

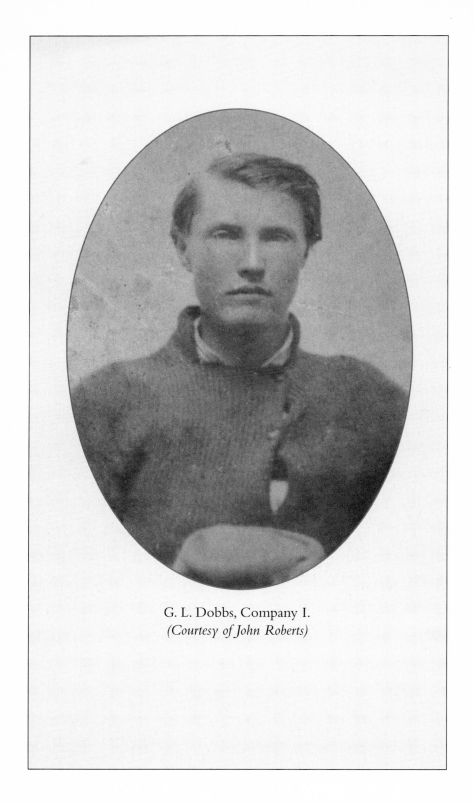

G. L. Dobbs, Company I.
(Courtesy of John Roberts)

Thomas Christian, Company K.
(Courtesy of the Library of Congress)

Jacob Phinizy,
Company K.
*(From the personal
collection of Warren
Wilkinson)*

Ezekiel Townsend,
Company I, many
years after the war.
*(Courtesy of Steven
Townsend)*

handkerchiefs and sunbonnets. This grand review of Hood's division had cost the men a great deal of exertion on this unusually hot May 27, 1863. The reviewing field was several miles' march from the various regimental camps, and a review always meant much marching about and, even worse, standing still under full field gear while the sweat ran in rivulets down faces and soaked through shirts. The sham battle with which they concluded the show was even more hard work under the hot sun, but the men figured it was worthwhile. They had typical young men's eagerness to oblige the ladies, and they had seen so few ladies for so long that this opportunity to impress them with their performance was not nearly as unwelcome as it would have been had the audience been composed of any collection of mere generals. The ladies' presence, at the invitation of the gallant Hood, made an onerous duty at least somewhat pleasing. One soldier wrote that the six-hour-long chore "was a beautiful sight to look at . . . but not in the least beautiful or pleasant to the ones who were in the review." Still, he and his comrades were willing "to suffer a little to have the curiosity of the nice ladies satisfied."[1]

The Eighth Georgia, along with the rest of Tige Anderson's brigade, Hood's division, and Longstreet's detached force, had been back with the Army of Northern Virginia for two weeks. They were strong, rested, and ready for anything. Their morale had never been higher. Their camp was several miles northeast of Orange Court House, Virginia, near Raccoon Ford on the Rapidan River. It was a pleasant camp, and the men's spirits were high. They had never believed they could actually lose the war. Since the first battle of Manassas they had considered themselves superior soldiers. Now, however, despite having missed the battle of Chancellorsville, the men of the Eighth felt the new and even greater confidence that clash had inspired in the army. They were invincible. They would as a matter of course thrash the Yankees whenever those blue-clad miscreants were foolish enough to get in their way. "Our troops are as usual alert and determined and seem to bid defiance to all the Yankee Army," a member of the regiment wrote at the time. "We have come to believe that we have got them all to kill and we are preparing for the slaughter and are going to do it right and quit fooling with them."[2]

On Tuesday, June 2, orders came to pack up, prepare rations, and be ready to march. Early on the following morning, they took to the roads. Their march took them northward, across the Rapidan and on to the town of Culpeper Court House, where they arrived on the afternoon of June 4 and went into camp. As they settled down in their new surroundings, the rumor began to make the rounds that they would soon be traveling *much* farther north, all the way across the Potomac and into the enemy's country. The prospect excited the men enormously.[3]

Lt. John Calvin Reed, recently back with the regiment after a long convalescence, stood quietly in the darkened encampment and listened to the men talking around their campfires. "You would have thought that they were just about to emerge from the wilderness and settle in the promised land," he recalled. They could leave their baggage behind and get everything they needed in Pennsylvania. They would have plenty to eat without hauling food around in their haversacks. They could get new blankets and shoes, and they would need no tents if they slept on the nice clean straw in those spacious Pennsylvania barns. True, "the federal soldiers might interfere, but what of that? They knew how to quiet the federal soldiers."

Reed also noticed another manifestation of the troops' sky-high morale. Sick men in the military hospitals, if they had strength enough to get about at all, were sneaking off and rejoining their regiments. Two such were members of his own Company I. Eyeing them skeptically, Reed noticed how weak they seemed and weighed their chances of keeping up on what promised to be a grueling campaign of marching. Still, "they begged so hard, and their eyes burned with such eagerness," that he let them stay. Remarkably, the two men actually grew stronger during the hard marches that followed, a commentary as much upon Civil War hospitals as the soldiers' eagerness for battle.[4]

The day after their arrival at Culpeper Court House, the foot soldiers were treated to an unusual spectacle. Maj. Gen. J. E. B. Stuart was also in the vicinity, headquartered just north of Culpeper at Brandy Station. Under his direct command were five brigades of the Army of Northern Virginia's cavalry, some ten thousand sabers. The colorful Stuart and his hard-riding troopers had been the scourge of the Federal cavalry in Virginia for two years, and on this June 5 they put on a show to rival that presented by Hood's division in its great review the previous week. Large numbers of civilians, men in their black stovepipe hats and ladies in their hoop skirts, as well as thousands of curious infantrymen turned out to see the cavalry go through its paces. "The horses are all in excellent condition," wrote Melvin Dwinnell, "and the men and horses are both well drilled. Their charges, in columns of squadrons, were splendid." Another Georgia soldier was equally impressed with the columns of galloping horsemen but thought the enjoyment of the show was marred somewhat by the thick clouds of dust. The recent spell of hot, dry weather had made plenty of it for the horses' hooves to kick up.

Next morning the orders went through Anderson's brigade for all five regiments to turn out promptly at 8:00 A.M. for brigade drill. The Seventh, Eighth, Ninth, and Eleventh Georgia regiments still formed the solid old core of the brigade, but the First Georgia, also known as the "Regulars," had been transferred away for service in its home state. In its place, the brigade got the big, new Fifty-ninth Georgia Regiment just before shipping out for Suffolk early that spring. Now Anderson proposed to keep up the demanding regimen of drills that made all five of his regiments crack outfits.

This time, however, the drill did not come off. They had hardly gotten started with the drill when orders came to cook three days' rations and be ready to march by noon. Eagerly the men packed up, but, in true army style, it all turned out to be a false alarm, a brief march out to the north of town and then a return to the old camps. Still the men's spirits were high. Whether they marched today, tomorrow, or the next day, they believed the army was on the move. Something big was afoot, and they were part of it. Whatever it was, "we do not expect to stop until we get into Maryland," wrote Company I's Sam Brewer, "only long enough to whip the Yankees that may come in our way."[5]

Brewer and his comrades could not know it, of course, but their marches of the past few days were in fact the opening moves of the Gettysburg Campaign. For months Lee and Jackson had quietly discussed the possibility of an ambitious campaign across the Potomac and deep into Pennsylvania as soon as the roads were dry and the army's draft animals recovered from their winter thinness. Early May had brought those conditions, but it had also brought the Army of the Potomac advancing across the Rapidan under its new commander, Maj. Gen. Joseph Hooker. The battle of Chancellorsville had repulsed Hooker but also seen the wounding of Jackson, who died May 10. Lee persevered, and gained for the scheme the backing of President Davis and the Richmond authorities in a lengthy mid-May conference. The Confederacy badly needed troops in the West, where the key Mississippi River stronghold of Vicksburg was in dire danger from Union forces under Ulysses S. Grant, but Davis and his advisers chose to stake their hopes to what Lee might be able to accomplish in Pennsylvania with his fine soldiers.

Lee made ready, and when Longstreet's two divisions returned that month from their sojourn around Suffolk, Lee did not bring them all the way to Fredericksburg, where the rest of the army was posted, but instead stationed them farther west, along the Rapidan. There they would have a head start on the westward movement that would take the army into the Shenandoah Valley to use the towering Blue Ridge to screen its northward march. The march of McLaws's division and then Hood's division to Culpeper had been the first step.

An abrupt interruption occurred on June 9. A suspicious Gen. Hooker sent his cavalry to probe what was going on south of the Rappahannock. The Federal horse soldiers surprised Stuart, whose job it was to screen the Confederate movement. The resulting Battle of Brandy Station was the largest cavalry battle of the war, involving ten thousand sabers on each side. Stuart's badly shaken troopers managed to rally by the end of the day and drive the blue-jacketed horseman back across the Rappahannock. The foray by the Federal cavalry gained Hooker some information about the location of Lee's army, though the Union commander was somewhat at a loss what to make of it. The day's fighting had also demonstrated a new prowess in the Union horse soldiers and embarrassed the redoubtable Stuart.

Alerted but not engaged in the fighting at Brandy Station, the men of the Eighth did not understand its true significance but did grumble a good bit about the fighting qualities of cavalry. Dwinnell noted that some of his fellow infantry were suggesting that "the bravery of one man is rarely sufficient to overcome the running propensies of six legs," but did his best to argue that the cavalrymen were really quite efficient—in their way. Sam Brewer was unimpressed. "I call them a perfect surplus body of men unless they can be handled in a different way from what ours is," he wrote his wife. "The real fighting must be and is done by our foot cavalry"—a reference to the Army of Northern Virginia's hard-marching infantrymen.[6]

The very next day, Maj. Gen. Richard S. Ewell's Second Corps began moving out toward the Blue Ridge, while Longstreet's First Corps continued to screen the Rappahannock in Culpeper County and Maj. Gen. A. P. Hill's Third Corps prepared to abandon the Confederate positions back around Fredericksburg and move west after the rest of the army.

The Eighth still waited in its pleasant camp amid open woodlands at a place called Poplar Grove. Confidence was as high as ever. Brewer wrote his wife that the men of the Army of Northern Virginia could not rightly be called "common soldiers." "I will say rather uncommon, for never did such live before. Take our history from the opening of the war and search it through and mark the place and page which says, the Army of Northern Virginia was beaten by the foe and you will find ten thousand to dispute it." Warming to the subject he continued, "We have evidently proven ourselves too much for the Yankees to do anything with us and I think they are beginning to feel it at home and this but drives our boys to new action, for I really believe our troops generally are more anxious to fight them now than they ever were." The men had the utmost confidence in Gen. Lee, and everything he ordered "is done with alacrity, nothing doubting."[7]

On Monday, June 15, came the turn of Longstreet's divisions to join the march toward the Blue Ridge and the Shenandoah beyond. Ewell's troops were already in contact with the Federals guarding the lower Shenandoah Valley town of Winchester. That very day, Ewell's men would crush the garrison there and move on. Back in the camps around Culpeper, the men of McLaws's and Hood's divisions fell in before dawn. The Eighth left Poplar Grove and took its place in the column. All day long the troops shuffled along under a torrid sun, while long dust clouds marked the column across mile upon mile of the Virginia piedmont. Hundreds of men were overcome by heat and fell out along the line of march. That day thirteen members of Anderson's brigade died of heat exhaustion.[8]

They camped for the night and continued the march next morning. The heat had moderated somewhat, and in the cooler temperatures the men stood the march much better this day. Indeed, the soldiers had energy enough to engage in "jesting and merriment all along the column." Shortly before they had left Culpeper, someone on Hood's staff—or it may have been Hood himself—had decided that the practice of shouting, or "hallooing," at officers who rode along the column during a march needed to stop. So orders forbidding the practice went out from division headquarters and colonels read them to the various regiments before the march began. Now, feeling buoyant in the pleasant weather, the men saw an officer riding along the column. From the ranks came a loud stage whisper: "Don't halloo at him; he's an officer." Several others took up the warning and repeated it with more volume. More and more took up the cry louder and louder, until the unfortunate officer was followed by a rolling chorus of "Don't halloo at him; he's an officer." The practice became standard in the division for the next several days. John Reed only wished that Hood would ride along the column.[9]

They crossed the Blue Ridge at Ashby's Gap, swung down the other side, and waded the Shenandoah again. That exercise was getting familiar by this time in the war. It was to become more so. At four o'clock on the afternoon of June 21, just as the troops were finally settling down in their camp for the night, word came that Union forces were again threatening to break Stuart's cavalry screen, this time several miles ahead near Snicker's Gap. If Federals moving westward seized the crest of the gap in force, they could seriously threaten Lee's army, spread out as it was over scores of miles.

So the men scrambled back to their feet, packed up again, and set off for several more miles of marching along the banks of the Shenandoah and then once again through its refreshingly cool waters, and finally, lengthening their strides and quickening the pace lest the Federals coming from the other side beat them to the top, they scrambled up the Blue Ridge to the crest at Snicker's Gap. The scare turned out to be a false alarm. The cavalry of the two sides was indeed skirmishing down on the piedmont, in the vicinity of Upperville, but Snicker's Gap was not threatened. The troops admired the view of mile upon mile of Virginia landscape lit by the slanting rays of the setting sun, then bedded down for the night on the mountaintop.

The next morning they awoke to find themselves in dense fog, a cloud actually, one of a whole sky-full that poured out rain and broke the dry spell. Fears that the rain might render the Shenandoah unfordable prompted orders for the troops to cross back to the west bank of the river. They marched another five miles on the west bank to the town of Berryville, Virginia, where they went into camp that evening.

Abolition Soil

The stay at Berryville stretched to a week as Longstreet's First Corps continued to cover the Blue Ridge gaps and the rest of the army kept moving north behind this screen. Ewell's Second Corps began crossing the Potomac even as Longstreet's troops were marching into the Shenandoah Valley, and within days Confederate troops had pressed across the Mason-Dixon Line into Pennsylvania. Panic spread through the civilian populace of Maryland and Pennsylvania, with the governors calling out the militia, citizens endeavoring to get their property—especially the four-legged variety—out of the way, and the state of Pennsylvania removing its official papers and other valuable items from the capital at Harrisburg.

The stay at Berryville was made special for the men of Company A by an interesting discovery. They were not far from where they had camped two long years before, just before marching eastward to the First Battle of Manassas. The flag of the Rome Light Guards, presented them by the ladies of Rome back when the company was preparing to leave for Virginia, had not been seen since that time. Individual companies did not carry flags in this war—colors were a regimental concern—but the men of the Light Guards, Company A, felt the loss of the banner nonetheless. Now during their June 1863 sojourn in the Valley, they somehow discovered that the flag was still safe and sound and in the faithful keeping of a local citizen, a Mr. McGuire. It was a comfort and an inspiration, after all they had been through in the past two years, to look at the flag Rome's ladies had carefully sown, with its motto, "Our liberties we prize—Our right we will maintain."[10]

The period of rest ended Wednesday, June 24. Twenty miles marching that day and as much again the next brought them to within four miles of the Potomac. They noticed as they passed through some of the towns and occasional farms along the road in this part of the country that doors and shutters were tightly shut, well ropes and pump handles removed.

Clearly the great majority of the local populace, though Virginians, were determined to give neither aid nor comfort to the Rebels.

Before bedding down for the night, they obeyed orders to cook another two days' rations, sure sign of additional hard marching—and maybe more—during the next forty-eight hours. Reveille on Friday morning, June 26, sounded at 2:00 A.M. The weary soldiers arose under the first spattering drops of an all-day drizzle, breakfasted, struck their tents, packed up, and prepared to resume the march. They were on the road again by five o'clock, and a couple of hours of marching brought them to the Potomac opposite Williamsport, Maryland. Fording the river proved remarkably easy. The great river that in the eastern portion of the Civil War separated Union from Confederate states had at this time and place no more than two and a half feet of water in its deepest parts. Splashing through it was easier than fording the Shenandoah, at which the men were by now old hands.

They splashed out of the waters on the far side, scrambled up the bank, and fell back into the long, loose, ground-eating stride that had carried them over a hundred miles of Virginia roads that month. Now, however, their boots, shoes, or bare feet were pressing the soil of Maryland, a state that claimed no allegiance to the Confederacy.

About two miles beyond the river, Hood's division column halted for a rest and had a whiskey ration issued to the troops. Such a ration was common in the Civil War at times when the troops suffered unusual labors or exposure to inclement weather. In the misguided medical thinking of that time, it was actually seen as a medicinal measure that would help preserve the soldiers' health. Possibly wading the thigh-deep Potomac and marching in a cool summer rain constituted sufficient physical strain to warrant the whiskey ration. Or possibly the sometimes irresponsible Hood saw it as a way to celebrate the crossing into enemy territory. At any rate, the men gathered around cheerful fires that were all the more cheerful because they were made of the fence rails of local farmers, who were presumably Union in sentiment. Spirits were high, and there was a good deal of laughing and horseplay.[11]

A number of the men declined to imbibe their whiskey ration, but unfortunately many of these obligingly gave their unused portion to their imbibing comrades, with the result that a number of soldiers got drunk. John Reed remembered an inebriated private tripping over his own feet and falling again and again full-length on his face. Each time he rose bruised and angry, cursing his way up and down the whole chain of command.[12]

They ate their midday meal during this halt on Maryland soil, and then at noon resumed their march, pressing ever farther north, toward the Pennsylvania line. The next few miles were on dirt road, by now reduced to appalling mud. It was miserable marching, but the men kept up well. Morale was high, straggling rare, the column well closed up and squelching ahead through the slop at a respectable pace. About four o'clock that afternoon they crossed the Pennsylvania line, denoted by a little stone marker at the side of the road. The men waved their hats and shouted themselves hoarse as wave after wave of Rebel Yells swept up and down the column, started as successive units sighted the Pennsylvania marker. Now they were on "abolition soil," as Dwinnell called it, for the first time in the war. The difference was not very noticeable—certainly not in the soil, and as for the people, they were about the same as in Maryland and the extreme lower Shenandoah Valley of Virginia, with the vast majority bitterly opposed to the rebellion.[13]

As they marched deeper into Pennsylvania that rainy afternoon, they did pass at least one undoubted supporter, a girl, looking to be about sixteen years old, standing beside the road and spiritedly singing "Maryland, My Maryland." Elsewhere, civilians fearfully kept out of sight of the invaders of their homeland, with only here and there a head peeping out between shutters to gratify curiosity about the fearsome Rebels. On one such occasion the men heard a female voice at a window above them saying, "Why, they won't hurt you. All their muskets and equipment are marked U.S.!"[14]

They bivouacked that night in a rural Pennsylvania setting, three miles from the Maryland line, four miles from the town of Greencastle, and, as Melvin Dwinnell cheerfully but incorrectly noted, forty-six from Harrisburg, the capital of Pennsylvania (the true distance was closer to sixty miles). Still, even the glib newspaperman found this long, dripping, three-state day somewhat confusing. They had literally, as one of the Eighth pointed out, eaten "breakfast in Virginia, dinner in Maryland, and supper in Pennsylvania." Scribbling his dispatch to the *Rome Courier* next morning, Dwinnell correctly gave his location as Franklin County, but incorrectly noted the state as Virginia rather than Pennsylvania. That would take some getting used to.[15]

Such as the Army Needs

Next morning the generals allowed their men "the luxury of sleeping until sun rise," and they resumed the march at seven o'clock. As the Eighth was forming up to begin the trek that day, a soldier of I Company noticed a little boy eyeing them timidly and occasionally casting a glance back at some companion not brave enough to venture into sight of the fierce Rebels. The soldier tried to speak kindly to the boy, but just then the child turned and yelled, "Jim they don't have horns."[16]

As they marched, the men grew increasingly impressed, almost amazed at the bounty of the land through which they were passing. Rich, lush fields of wheat, clover, and corn lay on either side of the road. Dozens of huge well-built barns of brick or brightly painted wood dotted the landscape. "They look as fine as churches," a Georgian observed, "and are twice as large." All in all it was "one of the richest sections of country" Melvin Dwinnell had ever seen.

One thing they did not see was four-footed beasts. The large and numerous barns and pastures obviously bespoke a substantial population of that sort, but neither horse nor cow was to be seen. The reason lay in the fact that Maj. Gen. Robert E. Rhodes's Confederate division, of Ewell's Third Corps, had already passed that way and was even then encamped near Greencastle. Lee had issued strict orders to his army against plundering. The Confederates would not "disturb citizens or private property," as Dwinnell put it, "except such as the army needs." The exception, however, encompassed more or less everything that could be eaten or ridden. Such items were, at least in theory, not to be taken by the private soldiers, but by duly ordered quartermaster officers. The Pennsylvanians would not have their goods plundered, simply impressed. The thrifty and prosperous farmers probably took little comfort in that or in the fact, which they almost certainly did not know, that the Confederate army routinely treated its own civilians the same way, and would continue to do so. In some ways, a passing army was not unlike a plague of locusts. Melvin Dwinnell was not so far from the truth when he wrote, "Private property has been respected quite as much as it would have been in our own territory."

With that exception, however, the countryside through which they marched that day continued to be the most lush and thriving farming country the Georgians had ever seen. They marched through Greencastle, a neat and pleasant little town of fifteen hundred or two thousand inhabitants. Stores were closed and shuttered. Private houses had their shutters closed too. Very few men were to be seen, but large numbers of ladies stood watching the invaders march by. Some were crying, and all bore such expressions of "dread and apprehension" as to stir feelings of pity in the marching men.

The soldiers themselves were cheerful, laughing and joking as they swung along the roads and the streets of the towns. Occasionally one of their jests would even draw a smile from the frightened and somber onlookers, but such instances were rare. At the head of the regiment waved the recovered flag of the Rome Light Guards, and the men were pleased to note that its fine appearance attracted considerable attention as they passed through the towns.

Also attracting considerable attention at such times was the Eighth's regimental band. The musicians who had thrown down their instruments and taken up muskets at First Manassas had returned to the practice of their music once the battle was over, and by this point in the war they had firmly established their reputation as one of the best bands in the Confederate army.[17]

From Greencastle, another eleven miles of marching took them to Chambersburg, seat of Franklin County and another neat and pleasant town, though larger than Greencastle, having five thousand to six thousand inhabitants. Once again as the column swung into the town the colors were uncased and the band struck up a lively tune. Once again the streets were lined with women, but these all seemed to have supplied themselves with small United States flags, which they waved in defiance of the invaders. It looked almost like a picture-perfect Fourth of July parade except that it was a week early and the flags and uniforms of the marching column in the street were all wrong. The band's repertoire was also not that of traditional Independence Day celebrations, with "The Bonnie Blue Flag" and "Dixie" replacing "Hail Columbia" and "The Star-Spangled Banner." Still, there was no denying the music was very well done. One Chambersburg woman could not believe that the backward Southerners could play such fine music and asked Lt. Reed, "The men in your band are not natives, are they?" Reed stopped, and solemnly informed the lady that in fact all of the members of the Eighth Georgia's band were Pennsylvanians who had gone to fight for the South because they believed in the justice of its cause. The Southerners had felt "it would be too hard to expose such friends to bullets" and had therefore made them all into musicians.[18]

South Carolinians in a neighboring division of Longstreet's First Corps noticed some of the Chambersburg women appealing to the Confederates' personal servants—black slaves—to make their escape and gain freedom in Pennsylvania. If any of Anderson's Georgians noticed the same phenomenon during their march through the town, they wrote nothing about it. The number of personal servants seems to have declined somewhat by this time. As a general rule, rations in Lee's army were scarce enough without having the extra mouths to feed.

Food, and many other good things, the men hoped to find in abundance in Pennsylvania, but just as Anderson's Georgians had observed the strange absence of cattle and horses from the countryside, they also noticed something missing from the towns as well, where "the Quartermasters of Rodes' Division had pressed nearly all the boots, shoes, hats and other articles suitable to the army." The Confederates would later remember with pride that they had been strictly kept from pillaging in Pennsylvania; Lee's army had more orderly ways of stripping the countryside of such private property as it might find useful.

Just beyond Chambersburg they made their camp. Sunday, June 28, 1863, the troops rested, bathed, washed clothes, and prepared and cooked another three days' rations so that they would be ready to march rapidly and continuously if called upon to do so. That day and the next the First Corps commissary and quartermaster personnel went through the nearby town, forcing their way into closed stores—breaking in if necessary—and ransacking the premises in search of useful commodities that store owners might be hiding. Since Chambersburg's merchants had already been subjected to this treatment by the Second Corps and probably at least elements of the Third, the results were not spectacular, "some flour and bacon but nothing else of any considerable value." For good measure, the Confederates tore up several miles of nearby railroad track.[19]

Augustus Brantly and his messmates in Company D managed to find a pig somewhere in the neighborhood and decided that the porker was "lost"—nothing to do, therefore, but eat it. They butchered it and somewhere managed to scrounge a kettle big enough to stew that much pork. With watering mouths they watched the simmering pot and whiffed the aroma of the pork. Then it occurred to someone that they really ought to have salt on their meat. This big a feast would require a good deal of salt, but finally they found a soldier who told them he knew where they could find a bag of salt. They agreed to give him a share of the feast in exchange for it, and, sure enough, a few minutes later he returned with a sack and poured liberally from it into the pot. Only later, upon tasting the meat, did Brantly realize that the contents of the sack had been not salt but "a sand preparation for scouring." The pork was a total loss.[20]

That same evening, Sunday, June 28, not far away, at Longstreet's headquarters, a scene was occurring that was to have immense importance for the men of the Eighth and a great many others. Spy Henry T. Harrison, employed directly by Longstreet, arrived at the latter's camp near Chambersburg with important information. The Army of the Potomac was not, as Lee had supposed, far to the south, but had crossed its namesake river and was moving rapidly northward in the wake of the Army of Northern Virginia. Longstreet took Harrison to Lee. The news was a shock to the commanding general, who had received no report of the kind from Stuart, his normally reliable source of information. Indeed, the cavalry leader had been out of touch for days, maneuvering far to the east, on the other side of the rapidly moving Union army. Convinced of the truth of Harrison's report, Lee dispatched orders for the various far-flung elements of his army to converge in south-central Pennsylvania, just east of South Mountain.[21]

For Hood's division, including the Eighth Georgia, those orders did not immediately entail any hard marching. They were near the center of the spread-out array of Confederate forces in Pennsylvania, just across South Mountain and about a day's march from the intended area of concentration. Thus on Monday, June 29, they continued resting in their pleasant camp near Chambersburg, while all across south-central Pennsylvania, from the Cumberland Valley to the banks of the Susquehanna and from Carlisle all the way down to Emmitsburg and Taneytown in Maryland, long columns of troops, some clad in blue and others in gray, toiled under the hot midsummer sun on some of the longest and hardest marches of the war. And all were making toward the same general area in lush, bucolic Adams County, Pennsylvania, just north of the Maryland line and east of South Mountain, where all the meandering roads, highways, and turnpikes just happened to converge at the little college town of Gettysburg.

Today We Shall Whip Them

On the morning of Tuesday, June 30, the Eighth Georgia, along with the rest of Anderson's brigade and Hood's division, marched eastward out of Chambersburg, an easy hike of six miles that took them to Fayetteville, in the western foothills of South Mountain. Word was that "Hooker," whom the soldiers thought still commanded the opposing army, was "coming on" and that they might "meet him in a day or two." That day they drew extra issues of food and ammunition, telltale signs that the high brass was expecting trouble.[22]

The next morning, July 1, was another leisurely one. The men rose at sunrise and were cooking rations at eight o'clock when orders came to get ready to march as soon as possible. As usual in the army, the order to hurry up was followed with the requirement of waiting, and it was midafternoon before they took up the march. The day was not hot, only mildly warm, with temperatures in the high seventies, but the atmosphere was close and the humidity oppressive. For the men toiling along a steady uphill grade under the load of weapons, ammunition, and haversacks, it was plenty warm enough. John Reed mopped his forehead and commented to a companion, "Who would have thought it was so warm in this latitude?" From the porch of a roadside house they happened to be passing just then came a woman's voice in response: "You will find it much warmer when you meet General Hooker." Reed glanced up and saw a neatly dressed lady holding several small U.S. flags and "beaming with triumph." Not to be outdone, Reed tipped his hat and replied, "If General Hooker makes it no warmer than he did at Chancellorsville, we shall not find it oppressive."[23]

The road took them through a gap in South Mountain, a wild-looking region of pine, spruce, and hardwood forests, granite outcrops, and roaring mountain streams. The shade and cool water were welcome to the marching troops on this warm and humid day. A few miles from the crest of South Mountain they passed the burned-out ruins of Caledonia Iron Works. The ironworks belonged to Republican congressman Thaddeus Stevens, a leading advocate of freedom for the slaves and vigorous prosecution of the Union war effort. To punish this political enemy, passing Confederate troops had put the torch to his ironworks, and now it was a smoldering ruin.

Down the east slope of South Mountain and across the verdant, rolling Pennsylvania countryside, the march went on and on that afternoon and evening. It was the most vexing kind of marching too. The road was clogged with most of the troops, artillery, and wagons of two of the army's three corps, and the congestion necessitated frequent stopping and waiting for those up ahead to clear the road. Darkness fell, and still they tramped along, no longer seeing the fine farms that had beguiled their journey all day. Only by the rich smells of growing things and the other smells of well-stocked barns did they know that they were passing the same kind of countryside out there beyond the rail fences that lined the pike, now invisible in the darkness.

They had covered fourteen miles by midnight, when they came to a stream known as Marsh Creek. The rest of the army was said to be near the town of Gettysburg, another four miles along this road. There had been fighting this day, but things had settled down now. Longstreet's divisions could wait until tomorrow to complete their march. Wearily the men bedded down for a few hours' sleep.

Reveille stirred the sleeping soldiers out of their blankets in the predawn darkness at 3:00 A.M. The columns formed again and they continued their march toward Gettysburg. The sun rose before them as they marched, and by the time they stopped they could see by the light of the new day the cupola of a dignified-looking building rising above the trees a mile or so in front of them. It was the cupola of the Lutheran theological seminary on the northwest side of Gettysburg. Beyond the town, they could just make out the bulge of a hill, where the Army of the Potomac was said to be awaiting them.[24]

While the Eighth and the rest of Longstreet's troops had been marching to the battlefield the day before, the first clash of the battle of Gettysburg had taken place on the rolling country north and west of the

town. Almost by accident the Confederates had found all the circumstances in their favor. More of their troops got to the battlefield in timely
fashion, and their arrivals even came from just the right points of the
compass to flank and crush the two Union corps they faced on July 1.
The defeated Federals retired through Gettysburg to the high ground
southeast of town, Cemetery Hill, which the men of the Eighth could
make out from their position across town, and Culp's Hill, out of sight
behind it. There during the night and the early hours of the following
day, the rest of the Army of the Potomac had been coming up and taking position. Lee determined to follow up his victory of July 1 by striking the enemy again the following day, and for this purpose he planned
to use the two newly arrived—and thus fresh—divisions of Longstreet's
First Corps, McLaws's and Hood's.

The men of the Eighth and their comrades in the other regiments of
the two divisions knew little of this. They had heard from other soldiers
of the great battle that had been fought the day before and of the Confederate victory. The Southern troops, they heard, had fought heroically
and successfully. Three thousand Union prisoners were said to have
been taken, and the enemy driven back three miles. All this made
Longstreet's men all but frantic to get into the fight themselves. Reed
recalled his men's "ardor" as being at a "white heat." Morale had been
astronomical for weeks and now rose to a veritable fever of eagerness
to get at the foe.[25]

Throughout the morning of July 2, Hood's and McLaws's divisions
waited along Herr Ridge, a gentle, more or less north-south landform
that lay a couple of miles west of Gettysburg. They had filed south off
the Chambersburg Pike, their approach road, at about the point where
it crossed Herr Ridge. To the east, they could see the fields fought over
in the previous day's battle, with trampled wheat, torn-down fences, and
scattered bodies of men and horses. At one point during the morning
they saw, or thought they saw, Gen. Lee, attended by several other officers, pause on the crest of Seminary Ridge, two ridges to the west of
them, and study the Union positions beyond.

The soldiers studied those positions too and the cannon that were visible on them. During the long wait, Lt. Fred Bliss of Company B wandered over to the Ninth Georgia to spend some time with his good
friend Capt. George Hillyer. Their friendship had started some months

before when Bliss had been accused of leaving the ranks without permission during one of the regiment's battles—it is not clear just which. Hillyer, as judge advocate of the court-martial, became convinced that Bliss was in fact innocent, having been forced by illness to leave his command. Hillyer's earnest arguments convinced the court, and Bliss was exonerated. Since then the two had become very close. Now, Bliss, Hillyer, and several other officers of the Ninth sat around on the grass gazing toward the Union positions. One of them gestured across at the enemy guns and spoke. "Now boys," he said, "we are going to have a great battle and a great victory today. Suppose that, by divine revelation, it were made known in a manner that we all believed it, that if some one of us would walk across that valley and up to those batteries and be blown to atoms by one of those cannon, and thus sacrificing one life instead of many the victory would be ours, is there one of us that could do it?" The chance of death was one thing; certainty of it, another. The little group of brave men grew quiet as each questioned the limits of his courage. The silence was broken by Bliss, who sat bolt upright from his previous reclining position on the grass. "Yes," the lieutenant blurted intensely, "if I could do that, I would walk straight across that valley and put my breast to one of the cannon and myself pull the lanyard." And each hoped he could do the same.[26]

The waiting finally ended shortly after noon, when orders came to fall in for a march that everyone knew at once was meant to take them into action. Excitement surged. "I never at any time in the war heard such eager wishes for instant battle," recalled Reed. Expressions of fierce satisfaction and anticipation seemed to be on every face.

The men's eagerness made the slow pace of the march all the more irritating. McLaws's division led the march, followed by Hood's. Tige Anderson's brigade was the last in Hood's column, and the Eighth next to the last in Anderson's. All of that meant that the men of the Eighth would have to put up with all the delays inherent in waiting for that much traffic to clear each obstacle or delay that might attend the road ahead of them.

Then a really serious delay occurred. They had marched over onto the west slope of Herr Ridge, out of sight of prying Union eyes on the heights east and south of Gettysburg. Their descent took them down into the valley of Marsh Creek, miles downstream from the point at which they had camped the night before. After following the creek only a short distance, however, the road they were following rose back up the western slope of the ridge, and there was the problem. Up at the head of the long column, McLaws saw that the road was about to cross over to the eastern slope and realized that once his men were on that side of the ridge, he might just as well send the Yankees a telegram spelling out the intended location of what was in fact supposed to be a surprise attack on the Union flank. He called a halt, and Longstreet rode up to confer with him about what to do next. Meanwhile, back down the column, Hood, "in his eagerness for the fray," tried to march his division around McLaws's halted column on a road that could not possibly accommodate such a stunt. The result was that he got the leading elements of his own division miserably entangled with the trailing elements of McLaws's.

At this point, Longstreet and McLaws decided that the only way to get to the position they were seeking on the Union flank without having the Yankees see them on the way would be to countermarch—turn the whole column around and go back the way they had come until they reached a place from which they could take a different route. At this point it would have made sense simply to have turned everyone right about face and marched back with the rear of the column leading. Civil War generals, however, often disliked that expedient, because they arranged their columns in just the order they wished them to arrive on the battlefield. The present was such a case, and so Longstreet issued orders for Hood's division to cool its heels while McLaws's turned around and marched past it going the other way. Then Hood's would follow.[27]

The men of the Eighth knew little of such matters, only that the march was very slow, with disgustingly frequent and lengthy halts, while the brass up at the head of the column apparently tried to straighten things out. Spirits remained high, and the men chafed to be at their foes. "These Yanks say that we whip them in Virginia because we are at home and they are away from home," one of them remarked fiercely. "Today we shall whip them at home." One of the many pauses in their march came near a house. The dwellers there had fled at the approach of a hostile army, and a number of the Georgians went inside to look around. Soon some of them were back out sporting all sorts of women's attire such as had been popular a generation or two before. Gowns, dresses, and "sky-scraping" bonnets could hardly have looked becoming on the bearded, sun-browned warriors, but their comrades roared with laughter and played along with the joke, acting the part of eager young "gallants" who sought to hug or dance with the newly appeared "belles." The ersatz females hammed it up, giggling, blushing, and peeking coyly over the tops of their turkey-tail fans, while the column of soldiers hooted, howled, and rolled on the ground in mirth.

"Fall in!" came the shouted order, and the men shed their purloined finery in the yard of the house, snatched up their rifles, and scrambled into ranks. Moments later the column stepped off again. A few minutes later, the road was empty and quiet, the troops a receding dust cloud, distant clatter of equipment and fading shouts of laughter, while the carefully treasured heirloom garments of one unnamed Pennsylvania family lay scattered and soiled across their yard.[28]

The resumed march led by small farm lanes back over Herr Ridge the way they had come, then up the Fairfield Road as if they were marching into Gettysburg. West of Seminary Ridge, however, near Willoughby Run, they turned left onto the "Ravine Road," which followed that stream. The ground was level here, trending slightly downhill, and the shade of walnuts and sycamores would have been as welcome as the cool chuckling of Willoughby Run to soldiers marching through the heat of the day. This Thursday, July 2, was just as humid as the day before and a good ten degrees warmer. The Ravine Road had the drawback of being narrow, squeezed between fencerows on either side that constricted the marching column, forced it to stretch out, and caused more delays and waiting for Anderson's men near the tail of the long column.[29]

A Splendid Line of Brave Men

As they began to draw near the place of deployment, occasional artillery fire greeted them, first sign that the maneuver planned by Lee was not working out quite as envisioned. Lee had assumed that the Union line of battle extended from Cemetery Hill southwestward along a gently upraised swell of earth that followed the route of the Emmitsburg Road. His orders to Longstreet were to get astride that road with his two divisions and drive straight up it, northeastward toward Gettysburg, rolling up the Union line as he went. It was to be a reprise of what Jackson had done to Hooker in the thickets around Chancellorsville two months before. That the Federals had spotted Longstreet's column and begun shelling it before it even got completely into position to launch its attack was a fair indication that the surprise achieved at Stonewall's last battle was not going to be repeated here.

In fact, the situation was even more complicated than that. The Union line had never run along the Emmitsburg Road as Lee supposed, or at least the Army of the Potomac's commander Maj. Gen. George C. Meade had never meant it to. From Cemetery Hill, overlooking Gettysburg, the Union position curled not southwest but due south, running directly back along a low ridge that took its name, like the hill at its end, from the town cemetery. The upper end of Cemetery Ridge was the sector of Winfield S. Hancock's Union Second Corps. The lower end, and the extreme Union left flank, belonged to Maj. Gen. Daniel Sickles's Third Corps.

Sickles was a New York Democratic politician of scandalous life and limitless ambition. The latter had led him to claw his way to political prominence in peacetime and military rank in war. The former had been conveniently overlooked by previous Army of the Potomac commander Joseph Hooker, who, apparently reckoning that character did not count, had given Sickles command of the Third Corps.

Sickles had become nervous that day about the position of his corps. This southern reach of Cemetery Ridge did not amount to much—as a ridge—and Sickles became fixated on a broad, low, lumpy, irregular patch of high ground some distance out in front of his assigned position. With the tendency of the nonmilitary mind to think that higher ground always trumped lower, Sickles decided he had to have it. In blatant disobedience of Meade's orders, the Third Corps commander took his troops out onto that rise near the Emmitsburg Road. The position was exposed, vulnerable, and much too spread out for Sickles's ten thousand or so men to defend. From a boulder field known as Devil's Den the line ran northward along Houck's Ridge, northwestward past a broad, sloping wheat field, across a wooded, stony hill, and over open fields to the big peach orchard of the Sherfy farm. Thence it ran back to the northeast along the Emmitsburg Road, making Lee's previous misconception at least partially correct. Furious when he learned of Sickles's disobedience, Meade sensed at once that Lee would make the Army of the Potomac pay for this blunder before the position could be corrected. He was right.

Thus by an ironic pair of mistakes, the Eighth Georgia would be part of a massive Confederate attack that was supposed to strike a strongly positioned Union army in the flank by surprise, but would instead strike an alerted but drastically ill-positioned foe in a frontal assault. In many ways, it would be a confused and confusing affair.

The opposition of massed Union artillery in and around the Sherfy peach orchard—soon to be *the* Peach Orchard—and on the high ground farther south announced promptly to Longstreet, Hood, McLaws, and their arriving troops the warm reception the Federals had in mind for them. Longstreet deployed McLaws's division facing toward the new Union position and, finding that the Federal line overlapped that division on the south, sent Hood's men filing off past McLaws's to take position at the far right of the Confederate line. Once arrived at their designated jumping-off points, all faced left. Their attack would now move almost straight east, rather than northeast as Lee had envisaged. It would be an attack en echelon, with the rightmost brigade going in first, then the one on its left, and so on.

Hood's four brigades were deployed in two lines. The front had Brig. Gen. Evander Law's Alabama Brigade on the right, ready to lead off the attack, and Brig. Gen. Jerome Robertson's Texas Brigade on the left. The second, or supporting, line of Hood's division was composed of the division's two Georgia brigades, Benning's (the same brigade that had once been Toombs's) on the right, behind Law, and Tige Anderson's on the left, supporting Robertson and the Texans. Anderson had four regiments available for the fight that day; from left to right they were the Ninth, Eighth, Eleventh, and Fifty-ninth. The Seventh was detached on other duty.

Twenty-four-year-old Lt. William S. Booton, of Company A, the Rome Light Guards, should really have been on other duty as well. His position as secretary to Gen. Anderson not only relieved him of all other duties but also took him away from the battle line. With the great battle obviously about to begin, Booton begged Anderson to let him rejoin his company for the duration of the fight. Anderson at first refused. Booton was a skilled and valuable officer and had no business risking his neck unnecessarily. Booton pressed his case, however, and finally prevailed. Eagerly he made his way to where Company A, Eighth Georgia, was taking its place in the brigade line.

The men of the Eighth formed up for the attack in an area known as Biesecker's Woods. Farmer Biesecker got all his firewood in this woodlot, so the dead and down timber was kept cleared out. The Biesecker cows saw to it that the leafy green underbrush was chewed away everywhere up to the level that a straining cow's mouth could reach. It was an open woodland, like most on the battlefield, and the men could see a good distance through it. About two hundred yards in front of them was the forward Confederate line, running along a fence at the eastern edge of the woods. The troops here were men of the Third Arkansas, belonging to the Texas Brigade. Just in front of them were the buildings of the Snyder farm, and beyond them, angling across the front, was the Emmitsburg Road.

The thunder of the artillery rose to a higher volume as over on the right Law's Alabama Brigade surged forward to open the attack at about four o'clock. Next, Robertson's Texans strode forward in precise order, Lone Star banners waving in the hot, humid air. Anderson's Georgians watched them go, and then moved forward to take their place at the rail fence at the front of the woodlot. Before them spread a wide expanse of farmland, pasture, and orchard, nearly half a mile across. At the far edge of this expanse rose a low ridge, the counterpart here of the one on which the Georgians now crouched. The southern end of this opposing ridge was bald, and sported a line of Union soldiers and four cannon belching fire and smoke. Woodlands cloaked the middle and northern portions of the low ridge as it sagged north toward lower ground. The Federal line must run through there someplace, for north of it, on the swell of ground along the Emmitsburg Road half a mile northeast of the Eighth's position, battery after battery of Union guns hammered away at them from the vicinity of the Peach Orchard.

The gunners were starting to get the range now, and shells were falling among the men in the tree line. A hundred yards or so to the left, over in the Ninth Georgia, a shell tore a leg off of a courier, killing him. John Reed took stock of the situation and decided that the flimsy rail fence behind which his men were lying would do them no good against incoming artillery fire. Reasoning that a shell striking the fence would be likely to drive splinters before it, into his men, he ordered Company I to clamber over the fence and lie down in front of it. At least that source of danger might be evaded.

Out in front, along the ridge, in the gap beyond the south end of it, and on the lower slopes of the smaller of two large conical hills that rose behind it, the rattle of musketry rose to a continuous searing clatter that rolled across the farmlands mingled with shouts, cheers, screams, and Rebel Yells. At the southern end of the ridge, Houck's Ridge, was that rockpile called Devil's Den, and a small triangular field bounded by stone fences and already well on its way to later notoriety as "the Slaughter Pen." Beyond them, the smaller of the two conical hills was Little Round Top (the larger, and farther south, was Round Top), and on its lower southern slopes a fierce battle was raging between Law's Alabamians and a hastily deployed Federal brigade. The Texans added their weight to the assault on the front of Little Round Top and clawed fiercely for control of Devil's Den as well. The call went back for reinforcements, and the men of the Eighth and their comrades in Anderson's brigade watched as their fellow Georgians of Benning's brigade scrambled to their feet, dressed their line, and strode forward through the bursting artillery shells toward the Slaughter Pen and Devil's Den.

In the same direction, off to the right front of the Eighth's line, Reed looked and saw about a quarter mile away a group of mounted officers moving through the division's sector. Regimental officers were going into battle on foot today, so these men had to be the staff of someone with some rank. Indeed, as Reed looked, he believed he saw the tall, rangy, tawny-bearded form of the gallant Hood himself. As Reed watched, an artillery shell seemed to burst immediately over the group. The tall figure of Hood sagged in the saddle, and the staff officers crowded around and helped him to dismount. Reed could not know it from that distance, but a piece of shrapnel had struck Hood in the left arm, wounding him severely. One thing that did appear discernible from the lines of the Eighth was that the division was going to be fighting today without its redoubtable commander.[30]

Out front, somewhere in the woods along Houck's Ridge, Robertson's Texans ran into trouble. They encountered not only hot resistance from the crest of the ridge in front of them but also a devastating flank fire from a stone wall off in the woods to their left. Robertson sent staff officers galloping off to get help, one to Longstreet, another to Benning—who, unbeknownst to Robertson, was already committed in support of Law—and a third to Anderson. Anderson was willing to help, and without waiting for word from Longstreet, he gave the order for his brigade to advance. Robertson's staff officer would accompany Anderson to show him where his brigade was needed.

It was about 5:00 P.M. as Anderson's voice boomed out so loud the whole brigade could hear him. At his order the four Georgia regiments, with the Eighth in the left-center position, rose and dressed their ranks. Then Anderson's voice rang out again above the distant roar of artillery, and the line strode forward, banners waving. They left the shadows of the woods, passed the Snyder farm buildings, and strode out into the open field. Melvin Dwinnell looked up and down the brigade line from his place in the file closers' rank of Company A and swelled with pride. "A more splendid line of brave men never moved on to deadly combat," he wrote, as he described the scene.[31]

Pride may have added luster to Dwinnell's assessment of the line, but the combat was deadly enough indeed. The guns in the Peach Orchard had them enfiladed, firing the shot down the whole length of the Georgia line, and the effect was harrowing for the gray-clad infantrymen. The danger was greatest on the left, closest to the guns, where the Ninth Georgia was marching. Casualties were already falling by the time they reached the Emmitsburg Road, just one hundred yards from the cover of the woods. A sturdy post-and-rail fence lined either side of the road, and the formation slowed and became ragged as the men clambered over these obstructions. A single shell burst felled two men. Another Confederate reached the first fence, threw his arms over it to climb it, and sagged back to the ground with his death wound. Among the first to fall was Will Booton, who could easily have avoided going into action if he had wished.

On the far side of the second fence they paused to re-form their ranks, and now they were in almost perfect enfilade for the guns in the Peach Orchard. It was a target for artillerists to dream about. Over in the Ninth, the regimental commander, Lt. Col. John C. Mounger, wanted his men back in formation quickly after they surmounted the Emmitsburg Road fences. "Boys," Mounger shouted as many of them were still clambering over, "Guide right!" Just then a shell burst immediately in front of him, killing him instantly, killing and wounding others, and blasting a hole in the fence. Dirt, fence rails, and bodies sailed through the air. Astonishingly, some of the men tossed through the air landed unhurt and got up and resumed their places in the already thinning ranks.[32]

Col. John R. Towers formed up his Eighth Georgia, and together with the other regiments of the brigade on either side, they once again took up the advance with close to parade-ground order. With the enemy cannon firing on their flank, everything that missed the Ninth Georgia came right into the Eighth. Melvin Dwinnell wrote a few days later of shells opening great gaps in the ranks and noted that "the deadly missiles were almost constantly whizzing over their heads." Yet the men closed up the awful gaps and strode on, doing their best to maintain their alignment.[33]

Near the left of the Eighth's line of battle, John Reed heard and felt a stunning explosion in the ranks just to his left. He looked in that direction and saw Sgt. Jeff Copeland, of his own Company I. Copeland's shirt glistened red with blood. To Reed's amazement, the sergeant continued to keep up with the regiment, without apparent difficulty, even as the pace quickened. Only later did Reed learn that the gore that covered Copeland came instead from Orderly Sgt. Travis Maxey. Maxey had often said that if he was to be killed during the war, he wanted to be blown to pieces and never know what had hit him. He had gotten his wish. The shell struck him squarely and then exploded. No part of his head, neck, or upper torso was ever found, and his friends identified his corpse after the battle only by the clothes he was wearing.[34]

At some point still fairly early during this advance across the open fields, the brigade went to double-quick time. It may have been the punishment from the artillery motivating Anderson, his colonels, or perhaps the men themselves to try to reduce the time of exposure. Possibly it was the sight of the Union skirmish line ahead of them. All the way from their camps below the Rapidan a month before, the men had been chafing for a chance to get at the Yankees and confident they would beat the bluecoats badly when they got that chance. Now at last they saw blue-clad soldiers in front of them, and the eagerness may well have been unbearable. Dwinnell recalled that "the men were in good spirits and bravely determined to carry all obstacles before them." The Federal skirmish line was the first.[35]

The Union skirmishers were spaced out at intervals of a few yards among the outbuildings, house, and barn of a farmer named Rose, through his orchard (not *the* Peach Orchard, which was four hundred yards to the north of the Rose farm), and along the edge of his wood-lot, Rose's Woods. They really were no obstacles to the advancing Confederates at all. They fired a few scattering shots, took a volley in return, and then fell back at a run, having fulfilled their mission of alerting their main battleline to the enemy's approach. In the intense atmosphere of battle, the sight of even the enemy's skirmishers falling back could be misinterpreted, and a number of officers and men in the advancing Confederate line made the common mistake of believing that they had just broken a major Union formation and sent its fragments fleeing in disorder. The battle rage came over them; the pace quickened, and the Rebel Yell rose from their throats.[36]

Stand Up and Fight

As they surged forward into the Rose orchard, both the fruit trees themselves and the buildings of the Rose farm, which was on their left, gave them a degree of shelter from the brutal fire of the batteries in the Peach Orchard beyond. Out of the Rose orchard they charged on the far side, across 150 yards or so of open field, and into Rose's Woods. The sudden transition from the sunlight of this scorching July day into the cool, moist greenness of the woods was startling. As eyes adjusted to the muted light they would quickly have noticed the many stones that littered the forest floor, from rocks the size of pumpkins to boulders and outcroppings the size of pianos. Visibility was about seventy-five yards.

The men stumbled forward around the mossy tree trunks and over the rocks of all sizes, feet crunching through last autumn's leaves and swishing through the lush, low undergrowth. Soon they became aware that the ground was falling away steeply in front of them. Down they plunged, still yelling, still running, sometimes scrambling, sliding on the seats of their pants, or jumping down from boulders or small ledges. There was movement in the woods and brush in front of them. Hands tightened on rifle stocks and muzzles dropped to the level before the panting, sweating men realized that what they were seeing were cattle and hogs in panic flight downhill away from this charging line of

screeching madmen. A hundred yards they ran through the woods, dropping fifty feet in elevation. They were just approaching the bottom of the
ravine. Then the woods ahead of them began to brighten with daylight
filtering through the trees and fleeting glimpses of a wide and gently rising yellow plain beyond—a field of ripening wheat, a stone fence edging it, a line of rifle muzzles coming level just along the top of the fence.

A volley exploded into their very faces, with a row of stabbing jets of
flame and a billowing cloud of sulfurous white smoke. Bullets hummed
past their ears like angry bees, smacked great clouts of bark from the
trees, ricocheted off rocks with an insane whine, and slammed into
human flesh and bone. Afterward it was impossible to remember who
went down in that first volley. There was no time to notice. The Eighth
and its sister regiments on either side returned the fire, and found themselves suddenly involved in the hottest fight of their lives. For many of
them it would be the last. The Yankees along the far edge of the woods
were determined to hold that position, and the Georgians were just as
determined to take it.

They waded forward into the fire of the Federals, firing back as they
went. Then they halted and settled down to an extended exchange of fire
with the Union battle line behind the stone wall. Melvin Dwinnell recalled several days later that they had halted on orders, probably from
Anderson. Many years afterward, John Reed thought it had been the terrain that stopped them. Just in front of them at the very bottom of the
ravine ran a sluggish little brook that the locals called Plum Run, the
west fork of Plum Run, to be exact. It meandered lazily across the broad
bottom of the ravine, just a few yards from where the woods ceased at
the stone wall and the gentle upward slope of the wheat field began, *the*
Wheat Field, as it was ever afterward to be known, one of the most
fiercely contested parcels of ground in the history of America's wars.

It was Plum Run that posed the most serious obstacle as far as Reed
was concerned. The ground for several yards on either side of its banks
was marshy, and Reed called it "a bog." He was sure that they could have
pushed on rapidly and overrun the enemy line if only that bog had not
halted their advance. On the other side of Plum Run, the commander
of the badly outnumbered Union brigade that was trying to hold this
line thought likewise. If the Confederates had charged with the bayonet,
he later wrote, his line would have been overrun. As it was, the strong

position they held gave the Federals a chance to stop the larger Confederate brigade.[37]

Even as the costly firefight continued, the Georgians kept trying to force their way across and get at the defenders. The Eighth's color-bearer, Sgt. Felix H. King, tried to wade across but mired down almost to the hips in the soft mud. As he struggled to free himself, a bullet slammed into his leg, shattering the bone and putting him on the ground to stay. Still the desperately wounded sergeant kept trying to hold up the regiment's flag. Melvin Dwinnell dashed forward and picked up the colors but was immediately hit in the left arm. Then Cpl. Manis of E Company took the flag, but moments later he too fell severely wounded. Sgt. John Andrews of Company C was the next man to take up the colors. Before the day's fighting ended, Andrews was dead, but the Eighth held on to its colors the whole time. Meanwhile, several men were hit trying to cross the bog, and one was so deep in the mud that his dead body did not fall over but remained stuck in a semi-upright position, a macabre forward outpost of the regiment.[38]

This especially boggy segment of Plum Run seemed to be the Eighth's special problem. Farther to the right, the stream angled back farther into the woods while the stone wall where the Yankees were sheltered angled farther away from the brigade's line of advance. The Eleventh Georgia, next to the Eighth on the right, crossed the creek sooner, and quite a bit farther from the opposing firing line. Some of the Eleventh, probably on that regiment's left, used the two-to-three-foot banks of Plum Run as a natural breastwork while exchanging fire with the Yankees behind the wall. Still farther to the right, the Fifty-ninth Georgia had crossed Plum Run shortly after entering Rose's Woods and then had moved up a gradual slope to strike the same Union brigade that Robertson's and Bennings's men were already fighting. That brigade's line ran at a right angle to the one the rest of Anderson's brigade was fighting.

Along the Eighth's front, the men broke ranks to take advantage of whatever cover they could find, taking shelter behind rocks and trees and firing back at the Federals along the stone wall, men of the Seventeenth Maine, who were being stubborn today. The Union line was spread so thin here that at the moment no Union regiment joined the Seventeenth on its right, the Confederate left. Instead, there was a 150-yard gap in the line between the Maine men and the remaining regiments of their small brigade, the 110th Pennsylvania and the Fifth Michigan, occupying the forward slope of a stony hill—*the* Stony Hill—just across the ravine, on the northwest side of the Wheat Field. The gap in the Union line corresponded approximately to the left of the Eighth and the right of the Ninth Georgia, but as John Reed could attest, those sectors were still taking plenty of fire from the Maine men along the stone wall and the Pennsylvanians and Michiganders on the Stony Hill. Try as they might, the Georgians could not force their way across the Plum Run slough in the teeth of this fire.

Now, just when it seemed things could not get worse for the Eighth, things did just that. Reed glanced to his left, wondering what troops were supposed to be supporting Hood's division on the left and might help them break loose these stubborn Yankees. Instead of seeing Confederates approaching from the left rear, he saw in front of the line on the left Federals marching up in fine order, banners waving. Two small regiments of bluecoats, the 115th Pennsylvania and the Eighth New Jersey, marched through the thin woods on the Stony Hill, down across the corner of the Wheat Field, and into the gap in the Union line, filling it nicely. These regiments belonged to a brigade posted farther north, beyond the Stony Hill, and had been sent down to help out in the badly threatened Wheat Field sector.

Reed, just opposite these two new regiments, saw their orderly formation halt just about seventy yards in front of him, and years later he would still remember how their rifle barrels gleamed in the sunlight. Then they fired, and "a scythe of fire leaped forth" from their guns, wrote Reed. "The air all around me turned to hissing lead." Thirty yards farther left along the Eighth's firing line, Lt. Benjamin F. Gilham of Company K had just caught sight of the new Union formation when a bullet from that volley stuck him squarely in the forehead. He threw up his arms while his knees buckled, and he seemed to sink almost slowly onto his back, while blood spouted from the wound. Capt. C. M. Ballard of Company C fell dead in the same volley, as well as many enlisted men.

The left of the Eighth and right of the Ninth now turned their fire upon the newcomers, and the fight went on. Powder smoke billowed up

in clouds and hung beneath the forest canopy, obscuring the view. The
Georgians crouched behind trees and boulders or the banks of Plum
Run itself and, peering beneath the smoke, could just make out the feet
and legs of the men in the opposing battle line. Minutes passed while
both sides went on loading and firing again and again. Then the Georgians realized that the 115th Pennsylvania and the Eighth New Jersey
were gone and assumed they had driven the regiments away. In fact, they
had pulled out on orders from higher headquarters. Still, the renewed
gap in the Union line offered an opportunity the Confederates were not
slow to seize. Once again they pushed forward. The far left of the Eighth
and most of the Ninth got across Plum Run and secured a lodgment in
a thick clump of alders beyond it, on the very edge of the Wheat Field.
Farther to the right of the Confederate line, the right wing of the Eighth
joined the Eleventh Georgia in splashing through Plum Run and surging toward the stone wall, only a few yards away.[39]

Still they could not break the Union line. The steadfast Seventeenth
Maine rose up and met the Georgians trying to vault the stone wall.
Blue and gray slugged it out across the rude stone fence with bayonets,
rifle butts, and point-blank fire. The Yankees even succeeded in grappling
a member of the Eleventh and dragging him over to their side of the
wall as a prisoner.

Meanwhile, even as they fought hand to hand along much of their
line, the Maine men responded to the Georgians in the alder thicket by
refusing their right flank. That is, they swung the right three companies
of the regiment backward like a gate on its hinge until they formed a
line at right angles to the rest of the regiment behind the stone wall. This
new line now poured its fire into the Georgians trying to push through
the gap between the stone wall and the Stony Hill. Together with the
Fifth Michigan and the 110th Pennsylvania up on the Stony Hill, the
Maine men formed a deadly crossfire that covered the gap nearly as well
as any solid line of infantry could have done. On the far left of Anderson's brigade, the Ninth Georgia now found its own flank vulnerable to
Union fire from the Stony Hill, and Anderson sent word for it to execute a maneuver similar to that just carried out by the bluecoats from
Maine, refusing its left flank to counter the threat. With all the higher-
ranking officers already down, the job fell to a captain, who found that
the noise of firing was so great he could not communicate by voice but

had to make his orders known by pantomime. Somehow he got the left flank refused.[40]

The Maine soldiers behind the stone wall simply refused to be dislodged, and frustrated men of the Eighth Georgia waded into the bog and stood full upright to try to get good shots at their crouching targets. "Stand up and fight fair!" some of the Georgians shouted. "Stand up and fight for your apple butter!" But the boys from Maine knew when they had a good thing. They crouched low, rested their rifle barrels along the top of the wall, and dropped the charging Georgians one after another.

Over in Company F, Orderly Sgt. Joel Yarbrough lay beside his friend Seth Strong. Yarbrough was the tallest man in the company and Strong the second-tallest, but they made the most of what cover they could find. They lay on their bellies to fire and rolled onto their backs to reload, trying to make the smallest targets possible. Strong had an especially good position, with a large rock just in front of his head. It was not a very big rock, so Strong got as close to it as possible, pressing his temple against it to maximize the cover it provided while peering around the side of it to find a mark to shoot at. A shell crashed down through the forest canopy above and smashed directly into Strong's rock before exploding. Fragments wounded Yarbrough and several other men nearby, but Strong never got a scratch. As the wounded men dragged themselves back from the firing line or were helped by friends, Capt. Lewis noticed that Strong still had not stirred. Stepping to his side and rolling him over, Lewis found the tall man dead, killed by the force of the shell, transmitted to his head by the rock behind which he sheltered.[41]

What battery fired the fatal shell is impossible to determine. At the top of the rise on the far side of the Wheat Field, Lt. George B. Winslow's Battery D, First New York Light Artillery, had set up shop with its six twelve-pounder smoothbore brass "Napoleon" cannon. In order to support the infantry in his front, Winslow had to fire directly over the heads of the Seventeenth Maine. Since the fuses of Civil War shells were unreliable and prone to burst early, the danger of friendly fire casualties precluded the use of shell when firing over friendly infantry. Winslow therefore stuck exclusively to solid shot, which he sent crashing through the treetops and down into Rose's Woods as rapidly as his men could ram powder and shot down the barrels of their red-hot guns.

Trees splintered over the heads of the Georgians, branches tumbled to the forest floor, and round shot smacked into the soft earth or bounded off boulders and rock outcrops. Standard artillery doctrine of the day posited that such fire would have a demoralizing effect on the infantry who were its recipients, but if any of the Georgians were even aware of it, over the earsplitting din of rifle-firing in the ravine, they left no record. The majority of the shot probably fell well behind the Confederate firing line, which was in very close quarters with the Federal troops the gunners were trying to avoid. The shell that killed Seth Strong probably came from the line of artillery extending eastward from the Peach Orchard or possibly from a Union battery recently brought into position with great difficulty on the crest of Little Round Top, to the southeast of Rose's Woods.[42]

While the enlisted men took cover as best they could, except when trying to get good shots, the officers of the Eighth stood coolly in their places just behind the firing line. John Reed leaned carelessly with his left shoulder against a small hickory tree, his weight on his right foot. Lt. Heard, also of Company I, strolled over to Reed with equal sangfroid, and the two affected a conversation with as much nonchalance as could be mustered by two men who were shouting at the top of their lungs to make themselves heard at a range of eighteen inches. Reed told Heard how he had seen Gilham fall with an obviously fatal wound, and Heard replied, "You will be killed too if you don't lie down." Reed was not about to be the first of the Eighth's officers to seek cover. "No," he demurred jauntily, "I shall only get a furlough."

The circumstances were hardly adapted for small talk, and speaking was too much effort anyway. Heard and Reed stood together watching the fight for a few moments. Suddenly Heard screamed in pain. Reed, whose eyes had been on the firing line, started to turn toward him but before his eyes could find him, Reed felt a sledgehammer blow on the inner side of his right knee. "I felt as though I had been struck with a club wielded by two hands." The force of the blow turned him back away from Heard, and he grasped the hickory sapling to keep from falling down. Looking down, he saw that his leg was bleeding profusely. It would move but would bear no weight. Seizing a rifle lying nearby on the ground to use as a crutch, Reed painfully began making his way to the rear. In his shock he did not catch sight of Heard, who was lying nearby with a serious wound in the side.

Getting to the rear was an ordeal for those who were hit. Dragging themselves, or being helped, dragged, or carried by comrades, they no longer had the activity of battle, the exhilaration of resisting the enemy, to numb their fears and became starkly aware of the swarms of bullets passing close around them. Reed felt as if every such missile were aimed directly at him. He wanted to get away quickly, but his wound and the tough, uphill terrain he had to cover limited him to a painfully slow pace. "Nothing else in the war ever tried my courage so severely" as the trip to the rear, he recalled. "I thought every step would be my last."

It was the kind of ghastly experience of which memory will tolerate little. Years later, Reed thought he had gone only about 20 yards to the rear of the firing line, but by his description he must have gotten at least as far as the Rose orchard, outside the ravine at least 150 yards away and 50 feet higher in elevation than the place where he was wounded. The lip of the ravine sheltered the ground here from the small-arms firing down along Plum Run and the edge of the Wheat Field, and a large collection of wounded Georgians had gathered under a large apple tree. Reed joined them, but shortly thereafter a shell from one of the batteries in the Peach Orchard, several hundred yards to the north, exploded in the top of the apple tree, showering the wounded with green apples. A second shot exploded lower in the branches, alarmingly close. Those wounded who could walk or who had friends to help them stirred again and struggled to get farther to the rear.

Reed made it as far as a stone fence, which he essayed to climb. His mind was, understandably, no longer quite clear, and having pushed off with his good left leg, he found that he would have to come down on his wounded right one. This he was loath to do, and so he remained straddling the fence in pitiable condition, calling for help. Up from behind the fence popped a Yankee—no doubt part of the skirmish line Anderson's brigade had overrun on its way in—who kindly helped him down and then continued helping him off toward the rear. Reed asked the bluecoat why he had been hiding, and the soldier replied that he had heard that the attacking troops belonged to Hood's division, and they took no prisoners. The Federal was appalled to learn that Reed belonged to the dreaded division, but the Confederate lieutenant soon satisfied him that Hood's men were glad to take prisoners. Thus reassured, the kindly Yankee helped Reed all the way back to a Confederate aid station. There the surgeon took a hasty look at Reed, still standing supported by his Yankee friend, and airily announced that the bullet must come out—now. Forceps in hand, he went to work, while Reed, still erect, saw the woods begin revolving around him with express-train speed. Then he blacked out entirely. A moment later he came to, his friend still supporting him, while the surgeon proudly held up a bloody bullet in his forceps. Reed got his furlough.[43]

The Valley of Death

Meanwhile, back down in the ravine along Plum Run, the Eighth Georgia, like the rest of Anderson's brigade, could get nowhere. Anderson realized that it was no use trying to fight his way into the Wheat Field without support on his left to neutralize the troops on the Stony Hill. Indeed, that hill was the key to the Wheat Field, and it could best be taken by troops advancing directly eastward against it rather than by his own men trying to claw their way up from the Plum Run Valley along the southwest side of the Wheat Field.

The Confederate troops slated to make that advance, supporting Hood's division on the left, were those of McLaws's division, which had been in position along Seminary Ridge in Biesecker's Woods even before Hood's men had reached their own starting points. McLaws should have gone forward immediately after Hood's first line became engaged. Indeed, it should have been McLaws's right brigade, six South Carolina regiments under Brig. Gen. Joseph B. Kershaw, that supported Robertson's Texans on the left. Instead, Anderson's brigade, Hood's division reserve, had to be committed early in the fight rather than saved to exploit later successes. Longstreet was with McLaws during this period and apparently delayed the latter's attack for reasons that seemed sufficient to him but that no one else has ever understood.

And so Anderson's men, unsupported, fought to a bloody standstill but could not batter their way into the Wheat Field past the outnumbered but well-sited and stubborn Federals. Anderson decided it was time for them to pull back and wait for the support of McLaws's division before making another attempt. The brigadier passed the word to his regimental commanders, or the junior officers who now led what was left of most of his regiments, and the brigade, minus the Fifty-ninth Georgia, which had been absorbed into Confederate forces attacking Houck's Ridge, pulled back to the west edge of Rose's Woods, and a brief lull ensued on this part of the battlefield.[44]

Anderson rode over to Kershaw's brigade to consult about the next attack, then hurried back to set his brigade in order. Gunfire continued to rattle steadily from skirmishers and brigades still hotly engaged farther south in Hood's sector. From the area of the Rose farm buildings, just beyond the brigade left, came the sound of the farm's bell ringing repeatedly and at odd intervals as stray bullets struck it. Anderson dismounted to walk his line as the men lay panting at the top of the ridge along the western edge of Rose's Woods. He was nearing the right of the line when he went down with a bullet in the thigh. His men carried him to the rear, out of the fight, and command of the brigade fell to Lt. Col. William Luffman of the Eleventh Georgia. By this time all four of the brigade's colonels were out of action, including the Eighth's Col. John R. Towers. Command of the regiment now fell to Capt. Dunlap Scott.

It was perhaps 5:30 or 6:00 P.M. when Kershaw finally led off the advance of McLaws's division. The South Carolinians swept across the open fields, past the Rose farm buildings and through the Plum Run Valley well upstream from the scene of the Georgians' previous fight near the Wheat Field. Then they crashed against the Union troops on the Stony Hill, the Fifth Michigan, 110th Pennsylvania, and a couple of brigades that were meant to guard the hill against an attack from the west such as this one. The Georgians of Anderson's brigade went forward at the same time, striking the Seventeenth Maine along the stone wall and from their angle adding weight to the blow against the Stony Hill.

At first it was the same nightmarish scenario they had experienced a few minutes before. The right of the Eighth was stopped cold in front of the stone wall, and the left, pushing forward once again into the alder thicket, was cut down by the vicious crossfire from the Stony Hill and the refused companies of the Seventeenth Maine. This sector was simply too strong and too well defended ever to be taken by frontal assault. Again the Georgians took shelter in Plum Run itself, using its banks as a natural trench. Many of them fell killed and wounded into the quiet, shallow waters, and soon the stream literally ran red. It was, at least initially, predominantly the blood of Anderson's Georgians that gave Plum Run its battlefield nickname: Bloody Run.

Then, however, the tide shifted for the South. Confederates on either flank of Anderson's brigade broke the logjam that held the gray advance back on this part of the field. To the right, elements of the brigades of Robertson and Benning, along with the Fifty-ninth Georgia, finally overwhelmed and crushed the Union troops holding the north end of Houck's Ridge. From this success the victorious regiments swung both south and north. To the south they cleared Houck's Ridge and Devil's Den. To the north, they drove the battered defenders toward the Wheat Field, eventually threatening to cut off the Seventeenth Maine and Winslow's Battery.

Meanwhile, to the left of Anderson's brigade, Kershaw's South Carolinians finally succeeded in clearing the Stony Hill. As the Union troops there fell back to the east, the Seventeenth Maine kept pace with them and dropped back over the crest of the Wheat Field to the field's northeastern edge, out of sight of the stone wall they had defended long and well. The yelling Georgians surged forward once more and this time swarmed over the stone wall and, for the first time, out into the Wheat Field itself.

Seldom in battle was momentum to shift more frequently or suddenly than it did here in the Wheat Field sector this evening. As the Georgians moved up through the sloping field of grain, they came under heavy and accurate artillery fire. Winslow's battery, at the top of the slope, now no longer had to worry about firing over its own infantry. It could now fire shell, and did so to good effect. The Wheat Field made a splendid field of fire. If perhaps a trifle small for artillery practice, it was certainly no place to charge uphill right into the muzzles of well-served cannon. Shaken, the Georgians scurried back to the shelter of the stone wall.

Just as quickly, the situation shifted again. Confederate pressure from the south, up Houck's Ridge, finally forced Winslow to limber up his battery and beat a hasty retreat. The guns out of the way, the Eighth Georgia and its sister regiments again scrambled over the wall and out into the Wheat Field a second time, sweeping uphill in line. They had advanced but a short way when they saw coming over the crest toward them a Union line of battle with bayonets fixed, cheering lustily. Rather than be caught in the open field, the Georgians once again fell back to the stone wall for cover. The Federals, who were none other than their old antagonists the Seventeenth Maine, stopped about halfway across the field, where the brow of the rise gave them cover against the Georgians' fire. Then the two sides went at it with rifles at 150 or 200 yards, and for the time being stability returned to the Wheat Field sector.

That stability would last only until one side or the other upped the ante by inserting more troops, and the Union side was the first to do so. All through the evening's conflict, Gen. Meade continued to feed reinforcements into the Union position, hoping to retrieve the bad situation Sickles had created. Two small brigades of the Union Fifth Corps had already been engaged on the Stony Hill, and Fifth Corps troops were backing Sickles's Third Corps elsewhere on the field. Now Meade's next wave of reinforcements arrived in the Wheat Field sector, Brig. Gen. John C. Caldwell's division of the Second Corps. The first blows fell both left and right of the Eighth Georgia. To the left, two of Caldwell's brigades pitched into Kershaw's men on the Stony Hill. To the right, another of Caldwell's brigades struck the right of Anderson's brigade, along with some of Robertson's Texans who had pushed up Houck's Ridge. Both Union drives were successful amid ferocious fighting.

Then Caldwell's fourth brigade pressed straight forward to the center of the Wheat Field, replacing the Seventeenth Maine and pouring a much greater volume of fire into the Eighth Georgia and the other regiments hunkered down behind the stone wall. The Federals fixed bayonets and charged. This time they had the advantage in numbers—about 850 men in the small brigade to about 400 to 500 (a fair estimate is all that can be made for this stage of the battle) still standing in the Eighth and Ninth Georgia and such part of the Eleventh as was not already engaged with other Union troops of Caldwell's division. Of almost equal importance, the Federals were fresh, while the Georgians had just been through two hours of some of the fiercest fighting of the war.

The Union charge swept them away from the stone wall, back across Plum Run, then pell-mell through the woods, up the far slope of the ravine, and all the way out of Rose's Woods. Back out in the cultivated fields between Farmer Rose's woods and his orchard, they finally managed to rally and re-form their line behind fencerows. The Federals were

winded by now and had suffered casualties as well. They were quite
ready to pause at the west edge of the woods.

Once again, the newly established equilibrium lasted only until one
side or the other threw in more troops. This time it was the Confederates' turn to tip the scales, as the Georgia brigades of Paul J. Semmes and
William T. Wofford, second line of McLaws's division, now moved forward to the attack. Semmes's brigade moved up directly behind what
was left of Anderson's and together they applied heavy pressure on the
Federals sheltering behind the lip of the ravine at the west edge of Rose's
Woods. Other Confederates pushed the Union line from the south,
while Kershaw rallied and along with Wofford battled again for the
Stony Hill. The Union line gave way, and for the third time in the battle the men of the Eighth, along with the other regiments, scrambled
down into the Plum Run ravine.

They retook the ground where their wounded lay, along the creek
bottom, and again ran head-on into enemy fire. Another Federal brigade,
this one from the Fifth Corps, now disputed possession of the Wheat
Field, and Semmes's and Anderson's Georgians further tinted the waters
of Bloody Run. This time, however, the Confederates had a clear advantage in numbers, with Anderson's and Semmes's brigades pressing in
from Rose's Woods and Kershaw pushing eastward from the Stony Hill.
The Federals in the Wheat Field had little chance. They headed up and
over the rise in the middle of the field and on toward the field's north
edge on the double.

Yet the Union had one more bid to make for that now badly trampled, bloodstained, corpse-strewn field of grain. A solid brigade of U.S.
Army Regulars, part of the Fifth Corps, moved into the Wheat Field
from the east and wheeled expertly across its broad expanse to face the
advancing tide of Anderson's and Semmes's men. The Eighth Georgia,
along with the other Confederate regiments, leveled their rifles and
poured a hot fire into the Federals. The key, however, as in all the fighting for the Wheat Field, was possession of the Stony Hill. Without it, the
Georgians had hammered in vain at the position a couple of hours before. Now, with the Stony Hill solidly held by Kershaw and Wofford, victory in the Wheat Field was almost easy for the Confederates, as they
possessed two sides of the trapezoid shape of the field and could defeat
any Union formation that ventured into it, including these Regulars. As

always, the Regulars retired in good order, back over the rise and out of the Wheat Field heading east.

This time the Eighth and its sister regiments followed all the way, up over the crest of the bloody Wheat Field, which so many of them had died trying to take, through a thin fringe of woods, and then out into open pastureland sloping down into a three-hundred-yard-wide valley. In the bottom of the valley was the east branch of Plum Run. On the far side of the valley, and a little to the right of the charging soldiers of the Eighth, were the bare rocky slopes of Little Round Top. Law's and Robertson's troops had been fighting hard for those slopes for nearly three hours now and had helped win for the valley of the east branch the name "Valley of Death." They could not, however, take the hill, and Union colors still waved on its crest, along an unbroken line of blue-clad troops.

Along with the other Confederate troops that had just cleared the Wheat Field—the brigades of Anderson, Semmes, Wofford, and Kershaw—the Eighth Georgia descended into the Valley of Death, firing as they went. Scattered fugitives from broken Union formations fled before them. The Georgians reached the marshy ground near the banks of the east branch of Plum Run, crossed the brook, and began to press on toward the foot of the rise, but that was as far as they got. Along the northern shoulder of Little Round Top just ahead of them stood a solid Union line of battle. This was a brigade of the Pennsylvania Reserves, one of the more famous units of the Army of the Potomac and the last uncommitted reserve of the Fifth Corps. As soon as the blue-clad fugitives were clear of their front, the Pennsylvanians poured two devastating volleys into the oncoming Confederates. Then they fixed bayonets and with a ringing "Union hurrah" they stormed down the slope and into the Valley of Death in a solid line.

Few officers were left in the Confederate line at the foot of the slope, especially in Anderson's badly shot-up brigade, but the soldiers were veterans and generally knew what needed to be done. In this case, they could clearly see what could not be done. Resistance to that advancing Yankee line was hopeless. The Confederates had already been through too much and left too many of their comrades behind. An officer of the Ninth Georgia glanced down the gray-clad line and saw dozens of battle flags, each representing a regiment, but none of them seemed to have more than about fifty men around it. Faced with the Union onslaught, the Confederate remnants turned by common consent and fell back.

They retired quickly and in no particular order back across the marshy valley, over the east fork of Plum Run, and up the slope of Houck's Ridge, but once they reached the eastern edge of the Wheat Field they quickly formed back into their ranks. Once again, as veteran soldiers, they knew almost instinctively what to do, even after three hours of the war's fiercest fighting had shredded their organizations with high casualties. Down at the southern end of Houck's Ridge, around Devil's Den, Benning's and Robertson's troops hung on, threatening the flank of the advancing Pennsylvania Reserves and finally halting the great Union counterattack and allowing the remnants of Anderson's and the other brigades to retire unmolested. Anderson's Georgians, including the Eighth, withdrew back over the Wheat Field, now a scene of unspeakable carnage, posted pickets about midfield, and pulled back into Rose's Woods and the valley of the west fork of Plum Run, where they had fought so long that evening.[45]

If attacked, the Georgians planned to use the creek bed again as a natural entrenchment, but except for some skirmishers who sparred gingerly with the Georgians out in the Wheat Field, the Federals did not come again. Presently the long, gentle twilight of a midsummer's evening in Pennsylvania gave way to night, and darkness settled down to hide the grim landscape of battle, the trampled wheat, the shell-splintered and bullet-scarred trees, and the blood-red waters of Plum Run. After the roar of battle, all seemed quiet now, despite the rattle of picket firing and the moans and cries of thousands of wounded all around.[46]

We Had Not Won

The next day, July 3, 1863, saw the climax of the battle of Gettysburg. Lee planned one more assault in hopes of gaining a great victory. Initially he hoped to use Hood's and McLaws's divisions along with Pickett's division, which had not yet seen action at Gettysburg. Longstreet informed Lee that Hood's and McLaws's divisions had been badly hurt in the fighting of July 2, and using them in the assault would leave the

Confederate right vulnerable. Lee agreed and chose two divisions of A. P. Hill's Third Corps to accompany Pickett's in the assault that was destined to become a legend known by the latter general's name.

The Eighth Georgia and the other regiments of Hood's division would thus be spared a further bleeding. That was just as well. The Eighth had moved out from Biesecker's Woods that late afternoon with thirty-six officers and 276 enlisted men. By the time they settled down for the night in Rose's Woods, 142 of the enlisted men and thirty of the officers had been shot, yielding an overall casualty rate of more than 55 percent. The other regiments that had gone into the Wheat Field with the Eighth—the Ninth and Eleventh—had suffered slightly higher percentages. The Fifty-ninth, fighting alongside the Texans and Arkansans mostly in Rose's Woods, suffered only a relatively mild 27 percent casualty rate. Still, by nightfall of July 2, almost half of the brigade's fifteen hundred men had been accounted for by wounds or death. Of those that remained, just 140 belonged to the Eighth Georgia. A fierce battle tended to reduce a regiment's numbers temporarily to an even greater degree, as some men ran out of courage and went to skulk in the rear and others simply and innocently became separated from their outfit in the immense confusion of combat. By one account, the Eighth could put just ninety-one men into line of battle on the morning of July 3.[47]

On the darkened battlefield that night the picket firing gradually died out, and only wounded could be heard. The moon rose, large and bright, and by its light soldiers of both sides as well as regularly detailed members of the two armies' "litter corps" moved about the battlefield seeking out the wounded. On this part of the field, at least, an informal and unspoken truce prevailed, and pickets held their fire when they saw dark figures moving among the crumpled forms in the no-man's-land between the lines.

Through the relative stillness of the night, they heard someone begin to sing. The men of Anderson's brigade heard the singing, and so did others farther along the Confederate front, wounded men and their helpers between the lines, and the Federals across the way. Capt. George Hillyer of the Ninth Georgia thought the voice came from somewhere between the lines and off to the brigade's left. He guessed it was a Confederate soldier of McLaws's Division. At any rate, the man had a fine, clear tenor voice and raised it now in singing the good old hymns that nearly every boy on both sides had grown up hearing from Sunday to Sunday. Hillyer thought the night grew more hushed as both sides paused to listen. He vividly remembered one of the hymns, known well to thousands of soldiers:

> Come, ye disconsolate, where e'er ye languish,
> Come to the mercy seat, fervently kneel;
> Here bring your wounded hearts, here tell your anguish;
> Earth has no sorrow that heaven cannot heal.

The singer went on through song after song, and finally sang the popular wartime number "When This Cruel War Is Over." When he finished that one, thousands of soldiers on both sides of the lines clapped and cheered. The soldiers, or most of them, finally got to sleep sometime after one o'clock that night, lying in their ranks in line of battle, and woke at dawn next morning.[48]

Theirs was a hard lot, but far more difficult was that of their wounded comrades. The wounded of the Eighth Georgia, as well as those of numerous other regiments, found themselves in a large field hospital at the farm of an unhappy Pennsylvanian named Planck, well behind Confederate lines. Sometimes it seemed as if the whole regiment was there. Col. John R. Towers had a wounded hand and Melvin Dwinnell an arm wound. Avid letter writer Sam Brewer lay there with a very severe wound in the thigh. He would die that night. Augustus Brantly, who had missed a pork dinner because of the mistake about salt back at Chambersburg, had a less serious wound, also in the thigh. Company E's Lt. Charles M. Harper was another Eighth Georgian with a severe thigh wound. It was a bad day for thigh wounds. Maybe the Federals had actually heeded their officers' admonitions to "aim low." Capt. Alexander F. Butler, of Company B, took a serious wound in the thigh, and Maj. G. O. Dawson actually had two different wounds in his right thigh. The officers, who stood throughout the fight, would have been particularly likely candidates for leg wounds.[49]

Not all wounds were leg wounds, not even among officers. Sanford Branch, who went into this battle as a lieutenant in Company B, was here at Planck's farm with a gunshot wound to the left chest. He was spitting up blood, sure sign that a lung had been hit, and no one gave him much chance of recovery. John Reed was there too, along with Lt. Heard, with whom he had been talking when both of them were hit.

Then there was Lt. Frederick Bliss, of Company B. A bullet had shattered his thigh, and that night by candlelight the surgeons amputated his leg. Less than twenty-four hours before, Bliss had told comrades that if he had the chance to win the war thereby, he would be willing to walk up to the mouth of a cannon and be blown to bits. That exact chance had not been his, but he had shown all the courage for the chances he got. Now he had little chance of living and knew it. As dawn broke on July 3, he asked Chaplain Flynn, who was standing nearby, which way the battlefield was. Flynn told him, and Bliss asked, "Won't you turn me over?" They did, turning the gravely wounded lieutenant so that his face was toward the scene of the fighting. Bliss seemed much more satisfied and remarked, "I did not wish to die with my back towards the field of battle." Yet death came neither quickly nor easily to Bliss, and he lived until the next day. He outlived Lt. J. H. Echols of Company H. Echols too had suffered the amputation of a leg, and he died on July 3. In all, more than one hundred men, from various regiments, were buried in shallow graves in the Planck apple orchard.[50]

For the men back in the ranks out in the ravine of Plum Run, July 3 brought new challenges. Fairly early in the day, Union cavalry began to harass the Confederate right flank. That sector was the responsibility of Hood's division, now commanded by Brig. Gen. Evander Law. When the badly depleted Texas Brigade, on the division's right, needed help coping with the Yankee horsemen, Law sent to Col. W. W. White, of the Seventh Georgia, who now commanded Anderson's brigade, for a regiment to reinforce the Texans. The Seventh had been detached the day before, guarding the division's wagon train. It had thus missed the bloodletting and was now the size of any two other regiments in the brigade. It also still had its colonel, something none of the other regiments did, so White took over command of the brigade. White responded to Law's call by sending the Ninth Georgia. A little later, Law sent for two more regiments, and White sent the Seventh and Eighth, still under Capt. Scott. Not long after, the rest of the brigade followed too.[51]

The distance to the extreme right flank was not far—a mile or two at most—but the day was exceedingly hot, even hotter than the one before, and the men were terribly fatigued from the previous evening's fighting. And then Ezekiel Townsend had his own private problem on this march. Clothes were not always easy to come by, and that included underclothes. Townsend had none. His outer garments sufficed to cover his nakedness, and he had certainly had no need for extra warmth in the weather that had prevailed during this campaign. However, the rough jeans cloth of his pants, during the campaign's long miles of marching in warm weather, had chafed him raw between the legs. Now the pain was so great he could barely hobble along, and so fell behind the regiment. A comrade hung back with him to help him along, though at first it seemed there was little enough he could do. As they plodded along the now empty roadway under the hot sun, it occurred to Townsend's friend that the fine dust that lay thick in the road was almost like talcum powder. He got an idea, and thus was enacted one of the strangest scenes ever witnessed (and that by only Townsend and his friend) on the eventful field of Gettysburg. Townsend made himself ready, and then his friend threw handfuls of the fine powdery dust onto the affected area until a satisfactory state of lubrication was achieved. Thus eased, Townsend set off at a good pace and soon rejoined the regiment.[52]

The cavalry fight turned out to be a small affair. Fights between infantry and cavalry usually were. The horse soldiers charged bravely enough, but in this war they could never hope to overpower the concentrated firepower of closely ranked infantry. The blue-jacketed horsemen were easily driven back with what, for cavalry, was accounted heavy casualties.

While the Georgians sparred with the Union cavalry down on the far southern end of the battlefield, events back near the center of the two contending battle lines moved toward a climax. Shortly after noon, Confederate guns opened a fierce preparatory bombardment against the Union center. This cannonade was far heavier than the one that had preceded Hood's and McLaws's assault the previous day, heavier indeed than any bombardment ever before heard on the North American continent. In the field hospital at the Planck farm, the wounded men—those who were conscious and aware of their surroundings—heard the guns and knew they signaled that another Confederate assault was about to go forward. As the thunder of the cannon continued to roll over the battlefield and the surrounding Pennsylvania countryside—fifteen minutes, half an hour, an hour—John Reed and the other Eighth

Georgians at the Planck farm "listened with breathless interest" and tense anticipation. It was 2:30 P.M., July 3, 1863. The great infantry assault that would one day be known as Pickett's Charge was about to begin. The cannonade gave way to the rattle of musketry that told the listening soldiers that the infantry fight had begun. As the noise finally began to fade away some minutes later, the direction and intensity of the sound told those at the Planck farm what was happening on the battlefield they could not see. "I perceived," John Reed recalled, "that we had not won."[53]

The Frown of Heaven

Lee perceived it too and generously told those around him it was all his fault. The Yankees also perceived it, and they stood up all along their lines and cheered, many of them chanting, "Fredericksburg! Fredericksburg!" to remind the Rebels that they had now gotten a double dose of the medicine they had given the bluecoats there. Everyone on the field knew it.

Nevertheless, Lee kept his army in position overnight. He hated admitting defeat, but there was no other choice. On July 4, he gave the order to retreat. Then at noon that day, a torrential rain began, soaking the bloodstained fields of Gettysburg and turning the dirt roads of Pennsylvania into quagmires. About the same time the rain began to fall, Confederate personnel began loading thousands of wounded men into wagons for the long haul back to Virginia. It was the middling cases that went into the wagons. The walking wounded, such as Melvin Dwinnell, would do just that—walk—all the ninety miles to Winchester, Virginia, in the lower Shenandoah Valley. The most seriously wounded would be left behind. That would mean certain capture, but to move such cases looked like certain death. In Hood's division, 515 of the 1,542 wounded were left behind, and Surgeon Thomas A. Means, of the Eleventh Georgia, remained behind to care for them.[54]

Movement in the springless army wagons, packed in tightly with other wounded men, certainly *felt* like death to those wounded men who suffered it. The train pulled out at about four o'clock that rainy afternoon, with the walking wounded slogging through the mud and rain beside the wagons as the latter jolted roughly over ruts and through mudholes. A wagon would stick fast and then the driver, often express-ing himself in language more forceful than polite, would whip his mules until the straining beasts jerked their sodden load free again with a sick-ening lurch. The wounded men inside bumped and jostled their raw wounds and broken bones against the wagons and each other and screamed in pain again and again. It was a seventeen-mile-long column of profound misery.[55]

In one wagon rode all three wounded lieutenants of the Eighth's Company I, Reed, Heard, and McClesky, along with several enlisted members of the company. Heard's suffering finally became so intense that the others decided he could go no farther, and they left him behind in Cashtown, Pennsylvania, just before the wagons started the long and rough pull over South Mountain. Heard, like those left at Planck's farm, was soon receiving medical care from his Yankee captors.

Joel Yarbrough, of Company F, had contrived to be in the column without being in a wagon, despite the severe thigh wound that made him unable to walk. Yarbrough knew some fellow Atlanta residents in one of the cavalry regiments assigned to escort the train, and he begged them to lend him a horse so that he would not have to ride in one of the wagons. The best they could do was an old mule, but the desper-ate Yarbrough was ready to take it. Afraid of being left to the Yankees and almost equally afraid of the hard boards and rough ride of the Confederate wagons, he was not going to be choosy about alternate transportation. "I will ride anything to get away," he said, and all night long he clung like grim death to the back of the mule through a steady, drizzling rain. Dr. Pettus occasionally rode alongside him to give him water to drink and be of such help as he could. Most of all, Yarbrough believed the rain helped him. "It cooled my fever and gave me strength," he recalled.[56]

Their passage through Chambersburg and Greencastle was far differ-ent from what it had been just one week before in bright sunshine with bands playing and colors unfurled. Now the creaking wagons and weary beasts and men plodded through the rain in the nighttime streets with heavy tread, sagging shoulders, and hanging heads. John Reed remem-bered a woman who showed him kindness in Greencastle, where his particular wagon happened to be when the long column made one of its halts. The kind woman dressed his wound and gave him plenty of bread, milk, and honey. He asked if she was a "Copperhead," a Southern sympathizer, but she did not say.[57]

Beyond Greencastle, the Union cavalry struck the column. In fact, the blue-jacketed troopers were striking the Confederate column all the way from Smithsburg, Maryland, back up to Caledonia Furnace, up in the pass over South Mountain east of Chambersburg, but the raid just south of Greencastle was the one that affected the wounded members of the Eighth. Reed remembered teamsters, walking wounded, and some of those in the wagons attempting to fight off the raiders. Then a regular Confederate unit escorting the train moved up and drove the Yankees off, but not before they had bagged 134 wagons and 645 prisoners. Few if any of the Eighth seem to have been lost in this debacle, though several, like Lt. Heard, had to be left along the way at places like Cashtown and, farther on, at Hagerstown, Maryland.[58]

Following by a different route, the main body of the army trudged, tired, disappointed, and, of course, soaking wet. "All night long," wrote a Texan, "the rain descended pitilessly." Off to the left, lightning flashed and flickered along the summit of South Mountain, and occasionally a brilliant flash from the clouds overhead would light up the long column of weary soldiers slogging through the yellow mud. They were still not far from Gettysburg the next day, July 5, when word passed up and down the column that Vicksburg, the great Confederate bastion on the Mississippi, had fallen, adding to the discouragement of the defeat at Gettysburg. "Every intelligent soldier knew," wrote a member of Hood's Division, "that these two events would give encouragement to the North and cast a gloom over the South."[59]

Up ahead with the wagon train, John Reed awoke from sleep to find that they had finally reached the Potomac at a place called Falling Water, but the Yankee cavalry had already been there and destroyed the pontoon bridge. The recent heavy rains had raised the river well beyond fording depth, and, in short, the Army of Northern Virginia was trapped. A single flatboat was in operation, ferrying two wagons slowly and precariously across the swollen river with each time-consuming round trip. Reed looked longingly at the hills of Virginia, looming close on the south bank of the river at this point, and reflected that it looked very much as if he was going to be made a prisoner here within sight of relative safety.

Capture appeared all the more probable when skirmish firing became audible not far to the north of them and coming closer. Presently
a Confederate cavalry officer rode up and appealed for volunteers from
the teamsters, nurses (all male, of course), and lightly wounded. In
Reed's wagon Billy Copelan, a member of his own Company I, jumped
out and went off to join the defenders. Copelan had been struck between the shoulder blades by a shell fragment. The chunk of hot metal
was not traveling all that fast by the time it hit him. It failed to pierce
the flesh but did raise a nasty contusion. As the ad hoc battalion
marched over the hill to face the foe, the men still in the wagons
cheered them, and they cheered back. Once again cavalry proved no
match for infantry, even this makeshift variety of infantry, and the
raiders were driven off. Afterward, Billy Copelan gamely continued on
to rejoin the regiment, plodding along with the other combat troops
farther back in the long column.

On July 10, J. E. B. Stuart commandeered Anderson's brigade to
blunt a particularly strong drive by Union cavalry near Funkstown,
Maryland, just southeast of Hagerstown. Col. White, still commanding
the brigade, had serious reservations about having his infantry jerked
about here and there by the famous Confederate cavalry chieftain. His
reservations grew more serious when one of Stuart's staff officers insisted on having the brigade inserted into the fight cavalry-style, deploying from column only well after they came within range of enemy
fire. As White feared, the brigade took a severe raking fire before it
could come into line, and then a battery of guns attached to the Confederate cavalry mistakenly pumped a few shells into the Georgians.
The shots landed in the Fifty-ninth, killing ten men and wounding
many more. The foe, however, turned out to be far less lethal than their
own gray-coat cavalry, and were soon driven off. The Eighth lost three
killed, five wounded, and three captured. Among the dead was Sgt.
Billy Copelan.[60]

Eventually they all made it down to the river at Falling Waters. The
rain had stopped, but a heavy mist hung over the valley of the Potomac.
From behind them came the sound of cannon and rifle fire, as the Federals harassed the rear guard. As Hood's division took its turn to cross the
rickety makeshift pontoon bridge, Gen. Lee himself sat Traveler on the
Maryland shore near the end of the bridge. One soldier thought he

looked "pale, haggard, and old" himself and the horse was splashed with mud, yet at the same time he had never appeared more noble. In a quiet, pleasant voice he told the men to form two ranks and keep to the middle of the bridge. As the Texas Brigade crossed, one of its regimental bands struck up "Dixie" from the Virginia shore. The soldiers on the bridge answered with a chorus of Rebel Yells, and, without thinking about it, fell into step. Officers shouting, "Halt! Halt! Go slow! Break the step!" managed to get that stopped before the massed vibrations of marching feet destroyed the fragile bridge that was the only lifeline to that portion of the Army of Northern Virginia that still remained on the Maryland shore. The Army of Northern Virginia might be battered, but it was not whipped. By July 14, all of its elements were safely back in the state whose name it bore.

The Eighth Georgia, along with the rest of Anderson's brigade and Hood's division, moved up the Shenandoah Valley to Bunker Hill, Virginia, and there rested nearly a week. Then they marched southeastward, over the Blue Ridge and down into the now familiar Virginia piedmont. A week of marching brought them to Culpeper Court House, Virginia, whence they had started the whole campaign scarcely one month earlier. By August 3, they were encamped near Rapidan Station, along the south side of the Rapidan River, and save for the thin ranks, missing more than half the men who should have been there, it was as if the Gettysburg Campaign had never been.[61]

But the campaign had seared its mark in the hearts and minds of the soldiers. They had thought victory close, within their grasp. They had given their supreme effort, and it had not been enough. A soldier of the Eleventh Georgia expressed the thoughts of many in Anderson's brigade and beyond when he wrote his mother, "The Armey is Broken harted. . . . They dont Care which Way the War Closes, for we have Suffered verry much."[62]

In some ways the Gettysburg Campaign broke the heart of the old Eighth Georgia Regiment and left it a shadow, almost a ghost, of its former self. Like the old soldier of the famous song, it did not die but continued thereafter to fade away under the constant abrasion of sickness, marches, and fighting. Fewer and fewer men remained in its ranks and fewer and fewer reasons remained for them to hope that their sufferings and the sacrifices of their fallen comrades would not be in vain. In some ways the history of the regiment after Gettysburg was a long nightmare procession to Appomattox. Yet the majority of those who lived and remained sound in wind and limb would continue to soldier on, against all hope as it seemed, until the bitter end.

John Reed, recalling Gettysburg more than a quarter century later and trying to explain its disappointing outcome for the Army of Northern Virginia, could only say that it "looks like the frown of Heaven."[63]

CHAPTER NINE

The Worst Part of This War

Our Times Are in His Hands

BY the time the Eighth had settled back into its camps on the Rapidan, the citizens of Georgia, from Rome to Savannah, had read of the Gettysburg Campaign in their newspapers. Readers of the *Macon Daily Telegraph* got a special report on their very own Company C, the Macon Guards, including the death in battle of Capt. Ballard and Lt. Hodgkins. The *Savannah Morning News* carried numerous reports of the casualties in Company B, the Oglethorpe Light Infantry. Sanford Branch was reported as all but certain to die. To the happy surprise of his friends and relations, he survived but could never return to duty. The subscribers of the *Rome Courier* could read Melvin Dwinnell's detailed and well-written accounts of the campaign, though his narrative became somewhat vague after the point where he was wounded in Rose's Woods on the evening of July 2. The Romans also read with intense interest the casualty reports from the three companies they had contributed to the Eighth. Like the other papers, the *Courier* tended to play down the magnitude of the defeat, assuring its readers that "our army is in a splendid condition."

The columns of news about Gettysburg appeared sandwiched between the usual advertisements that told of the persistence of almost normal life within the hard-pressed Southern states. Savannans could take note of the impending sale at auction of the Empire Salt Company, with all its stock and equipment, while the advertisements of the *Rome Courier* advised readers that Quintard Iron Works was seeking to buy scrap iron and that various parties were seeking to sell assorted plots of land, stocks of corn, gold and silver watches, sewing needles, a "fine-toned rosewood piano," and "negroes." The largest selection of slaves was definitely commanded by Mr. W. M. Ramey, who offered at private sale three girls sixteen to eighteen years old, an experienced housemaid twenty-two years of age, "one woman, 18 years old, and her child," and various other persons "all warranted to be strictly No. 1 Negroes."

The news, however, that filled the columns between such advertisements was all of war and mostly dismal. Articles told of continued Union operations against Charleston, South Carolina, though as yet, in one of the few bright spots on the general picture, the city was holding out well. The Yankees near Charleston seemed to pose a threat to Savannah too, and its citizens could read in the newspaper a proclamation from Mayor Holcombe calling on the people of Savannah to organize themselves into home defense companies.

In contrast to the good news from Charleston was the horrendous report from Vicksburg, Mississippi, which Confederate lieutenant general John C. Pemberton had surrendered to Ulysses S. Grant on July 4, along with thirty thousand Confederate troops. Port Hudson, Louisiana, surrendered a few days later, giving the Federals more prisoners and complete control of the Mississippi. Meanwhile, in Tennessee, the Union army of Maj. Gen. William S. Rosecrans maneuvered the Confederate army of Gen. Braxton Bragg almost completely out of the state. Bragg pulled his army back to Chattanooga, Tennessee, near the Georgia line and barely sixty miles north of Rome by a good highway.

The newspapers also printed proclamations from President Davis and Governor Brown calling on the people to fight on with renewed determination and warning of the dire consequences should the Yankees win. Readers could take more encouragement from the *Savannah Daily*

Morning News piece on the possibilities of British or French intervention to secure Southern independence, though, in truth, the chance of that by this time was precisely nil. Savannah readers also learned how they could send boxes of food or clothing to the soldiers in the field free of charge through the offices of the Georgia Relief and Hospital Association. Meanwhile, the *Rome Courier* sadly notified its readers of the death of Mary Booton, aged widow, on her plantation. Many believed her demise was at least hastened by news of the death her son, William S. Booton of Company A, Eighth Georgia—sometime secretary to Gen. Anderson—at Gettysburg.

Also to be found within the pages of such newspapers were ominous indications of the South's material condition: a notice of the need to pay new and higher taxes, and another apprising readers that the *Courier* had managed, with great difficulty, to find paper for printing for another week. In the South, nearly everything was becoming scarce as economic exhaustion approached.[1]

The Confederacy desperately needed a dramatic victory to turn the tide that had now set strongly against it. This need, coupled with the waning Confederate fortunes in Tennessee, prompted the Richmond authorities to make a decision that would give the Eighth Georgia Regiment a temporary change of scenery. President Davis and Secretary of War James A. Seddon, with the grudging agreement of Lee, decided to send Hood's and McLaws's divisions to Bragg in Tennessee in hopes that with these reinforcements, as well as additional troops sent from other sectors, he could save Chattanooga, along with its direct rail connection to Virginia, and at the same time win a crushing victory over Rosecrans that would reverse the momentum of the war.

The troops who were about to be called upon to perform this feat of arms had been resting quietly in their camps along the Rapidan, recovering from the strains of the past campaign. A member of the regiment could write near the end of August that since their arrival, "nothing of interest has transpired to break the dull monotony of camp life," at least by way of military operations. He reported the regiment feeling good and ready for more vigorous campaigning whenever the need might arise. "We are all enjoying ourselves finely," he wrote.

They were also experiencing a continuation of the previous spring's religious revival. "A considerable revival of religion has been going on in our Brigade for the past two or three weeks," wrote a member of the regiment. As hopes of victory in the war dimmed somewhat and the losses of battle reminded men once again of their mortality, religious interest stirred. Such interest was never far below the surface in any army of either side in this war. The nation's overwhelming Christian consensus meant that the citizen soldiers often had at least received devout upbringings. Whenever active campaigning or other pressing concerns did not interfere, many of the soldiers pursued religious interests, particularly after the initial shock of army life wore off. The months after Gettysburg were an instance of this phenomenon.

D. W. Gwin, pastor of the Rome Baptist Church, visited the Eighth and reported several well-attended meetings in the camp, with a number of men requesting prayer. The soldiers in turn liked Gwin and greatly appreciated his preaching. On Friday evening, August 21, Gwin delivered his final sermon to Anderson's brigade before departing to minister to other units of the army. For his text, he took the particularly appropriate scripture "Finally, brethren, farewell," from the apostle Paul's closing admonitions in his second letter to the church in Corinth. "Be perfect, be of good comfort, be of one mind, live in peace," the passage continued, "and the God of love and peace shall be with you." A member of the Eighth who was in attendance thought the sermon "was well timed and had a good and lasting effect on all who heard it."[2]

The religious interest was bigger than any one preacher, however, and continued after he left. A soldier of Anderson's brigade wrote home that summer, "We air having a great Rivival here in my Brigade and I am glad to See it going on. I hope it may accomplish much good and that many Sols may be converted to God." Yet another member of the brigade believed that the Christian Association had helped to spread the revival, making the Christians of the whole brigade into "one congregation," and the encampment along the Rapidan into "one long camp-meeting—a great revival season." Besides the Christian Association, the Eighth, as well as two other regiments of the brigade, had thriving "Sabbath Schools," for the religious training of the men.[3]

The increased interest in the things of God extended beyond Anderson's brigade to the rest of the army and its commander as well. Robert E. Lee had turned his thoughts to the meaning of the defeat at Gettysburg, and the month after the great battle he issued a proclamation to his troops:

> Soldiers! We have sinned against Almighty God. We have forgotten his signal mercies, and have cultivated a revengeful, haughty and boastful spirit. We have not remembered that the defenders of a just cause should be pure in His eyes; that "our times are in his hands"—and we have relied too much on our own arms for the achievement of our independence. God is our only refuge and our strength. Let us confess our many sins, and beseech Him to give us a higher courage, a purer patriotism, and more determined will; that he will convert the hearts of our enemies; that He will hasten the time when war, with its sorrows and sufferings, shall cease, and that He will give us a name and a place among the nations of the earth.

The soldiers came to much the same conclusion. God was chastening the Confederacy for the sins of its people. If they rededicated themselves to Him, perhaps He would give victory in the end. In any event, the final outcome would be in His hands.[4]

The soldiers also concerned themselves with politics during their encampment along the Rapidan. A number of men from Anderson's brigade who also hailed from Georgia's Tenth Congressional District organized a meeting to pass resolutions about current political issues. They elected the Eighth's Capt. Dunlap Scott as secretary of the meeting, and selected representatives of each company present to serve on a committee to draw up resolutions. Several men were selected from each of the Eighth's Floyd County regiments, A, E, and H. The resolutions they formulated roundly denounced the Confederate government's policy of granting draft exemptions to various civil servants, state government officials, and members of certain occupations deemed essential to the war effort. In theory, the Confederate Congress had called for the conscription of every white, male Southerner between the ages of eighteen and forty-five. In fact, there were a good many who got exemptions, from dentists to millers to shoemakers. Even at that, many modern historians believe the Confederacy may actually have *over*mobilized its potential military manpower. The soldiers, not surprisingly, did not see it that way, and consistently favored putting every last able-bodied man in the ranks with a rifle in his hands.

Most hated of all was the Confederate government's infamous "twenty-nigger rule," which stipulated that for every twenty slaves, one white man was entitled to stay home as an overseer. The law was naturally very popular among planters, who, not coincidentally, made up most of the membership of the Confederate Congress, but it was cordially loathed by the lower classes, who complained that this was "a rich man's war and a poor man's fight." The rule was also hated by all ranks of the army, who wanted the cowardly home-stayers rousted out and sent to the front.

Thus the resolutions minced no words about that or any other means used by able-bodied men to stay out of harm's way. They further called upon their brethren back home to use their votes to elect right-thinking members to Congress, and suggested in particular that the Eighth's former regimental surgeon, Dr. H. V. M. Miller, after whom the Miller Rifles, now Company E, had been named would be a good choice.

The meeting resoundingly adopted all the resolutions. Scott drew up a clean copy in proper form and sent it off to Rome, where it was published in the columns of the *Courier,* along with a nice letter from Dr. Miller, declining the honor because another candidate, already declared, seemed to fit the characteristics demanded by the soldiers.[5]

Like Old Times at Home

The orders that were to send the Eighth Georgia, along with the rest of Hood's and McLaws's divisions, on a thousand-mile odyssey came near the end of the first week of September. By that time the Federals under Rosecrans were pressing into northwestern Georgia, had forced Bragg out of Chattanooga, and some of them were as little as twenty miles from Rome. Bragg was concentrating his forces around La Fayette, Georgia, forty miles north of Rome, preparing to launch a counterblow, and there Hood's and McLaws's divisions were to repair with all possible speed.

Anderson's brigade, however, proved to be an exception. While the other eight brigades of the two divisions made for Bragg's headquarters as rapidly and directly as the Confederacy's rickety rail network would carry them, Anderson's, with its numerous troops from northwestern

Georgia, was diverted to temporary duty in Charleston, South Carolina. The citizens of Rome were sadly disappointed not to have the "glorious 8th Georgia" with them in the present crisis.[6]

The reason for the diversion to Charleston was fear on the part of the Confederate authorities that another crisis might be impending there. For some months Union forces had been making a concerted and systematic effort to take the city. When bloody assaults had failed to drive the Confederates from nearby Morris Island, the Federals had resorted to steady siege operations. By September 6, Confederate commanding general P. G. T. Beauregard saw that these would achieve success and pulled his troops off Morris Island and back to James Island. This Union success emphasized the danger to Charleston and led to the diversion of Anderson's brigade to strengthen the defenses there.

The men of the Eighth arrived September 16 and found themselves encamped in an open field on James Island, on the bank of a sort of bayou, south of the city and about a mile and a half from the wharves on the Ashley River. Their campsite offered no shade and great swarms of flies, but it did have deep, sandy soil, and they could get water—such as it was—by digging wells eight or ten feet deep. They had fresh beef, cornmeal, rice, and peas to eat, and sometimes they were able to catch some of the local fish, crabs, and oysters, though the last were of indifferent quality. They even had soap for washing, so life was definitely not all bad. Still they missed their bacon and wished they had lard for cooking, as well as vegetables, potatoes, vinegar, and flour.

They had feared that the summer heat in the low-country climate would create large amounts of sickness in the regiment, but actual numbers of sick ran only from 10 to 20 percent of those present, a reasonable figure for a Civil War regiment in camp. The most common complaint was "chills and fever," but it did not seem to be life-threatening in most cases. A heavy rain the evening of October 2 ushered in cooler temperatures and delightful weather. Since the sum of their exposure to combat during these days was listening to periodic firing of heavy guns—apparently aimed at some point remote from themselves— the duty in Charleston wound up being a virtual seaside vacation.

While the Eighth and the rest of Anderson's brigade camped in the sand and caught crabs near Charleston, the rest of Hood's division, along with Bragg's army, fought the great battle of Chickamauga, September

19 and 20, 1863. Casualty percentages rivaled those of Gettysburg in many units, and the gallant Hood himself, his arm still in a sling from his Gettysburg wound, was hit again, necessitating the amputation of a leg. The result was an indecisive Confederate victory. Bragg drove Rosecrans back to Chattanooga, but he could not destroy the Union army nor drive it farther back into Tennessee. The two battered armies, Union and Confederate, then settled down for a siege, Rosecrans grimly hanging on in Chattanooga, Bragg determined to starve him out.

The Eighth's pleasant interlude by the sea was not to last. On October 7 they were on the move again, traveling by railroad to Atlanta and then on north to the vicinity of Chattanooga. Along the route, they passed through the vicinity of the various home counties of the Eighth's component companies—B from Chatham County at the southeastern end of the state, the Middle Georgia companies from Bibb, Meriwether, Oglethorpe, Pulaski, and Greene, and finally the three Rome companies from Floyd County. A number of men took advantage of the opportunity to slip away on unauthorized leaves and visit the home folks. Most of these men were not shirkers—they just wanted to see their families— and they rejoined the regiment in a couple of days.[7]

While Anderson's brigade traveled across the state of Georgia by rail from the southeast to the northwest corner of the state, its soldiers held their regular state election. The Georgia legislature had recently passed a bill to permit Georgia troops to vote in the field in all state elections, and the men were eager to exercise their franchise in that fall's races for governor, Congress, state legislature, and various local offices. Campaigning, complete with stump speeches, had been spirited in the brigade's camps during recent days. "It really seemed like old times at home," except that unlike the prewar election rallies back home, no one got drunk. The orders to move coincided with election day, but they were not about to let that stop them and made arrangements to vote on the train. "At every wood or water station, or wherever else the train stopped the polls were opened, and some ten, twenty or thirty men voted." It was an orderly election for all that, and the results paralleled those of the civilian vote back home. Melvin Dwinnell won a seat in the Georgia legislature, drawing votes not only from the Eighth but from various other regiments that included troops from northeast Georgia. More surprising, Governor Joe Brown won reelection handily, piling up substantial majorities even among the soldiers, despite their occasionally intense dislike for him.

The regiment arrived near Chattanooga on October 9. The town of Chattanooga, comparable in size, in those days, to Gettysburg, lay on the south bank of the Tennessee River surrounded by imposing heights. To the north, across the river, rose Walden's Ridge. To the southeast lay Missionary Ridge, a long landform running southwest to northeast and rising some six hundred feet above the town. To the southwest of Chattanooga rose the dominant feature of the area, Lookout Mountain, whose broad, flat summit, rimmed by rocky cliffs, loomed more than fourteen hundred feet above the Tennessee River at its base.

Bragg had Rosecrans in a difficult situation at Chattanooga. The Confederates held Missionary Ridge and Lookout Mountain. The Union army held the town, well fortified, so that the Rebels could not hope to storm it. However, there were only two good ways to get supplies into the city, and the Confederates had them both. One way led around the north end of Missionary Ridge and then southward to Dalton and Atlanta. Rosecrans could obviously expect no succor from that direction. The other way was the gorge of the Tennessee River, west of town, where the river flowed past the foot of Lookout Mountain and then westward for several winding miles through a break in the towering Cumberland Plateau. A railroad and a tolerable wagon road led through the gorge and then beyond it to the northwest all the way up to the Union base at Nashville, but Confederate troops on Lookout Mountain and just west of it in Lookout Valley were in position to deny Rosecrans the use of those routes. Consequently, the Federals in Chattanooga had to get all their victuals by way of a perfectly execrable wagon road over Walden's Ridge. They got little enough, and were coming to very short rations by the time the Eighth Georgia and its sister regiments arrived in the area. Longstreet, who had come along in charge of Hood's and McLaws's divisions, had responsibility for the key Lookout Mountain sector, and the Eighth initially drew a position near the base of the mountain.

An informal enlisted men's truce prevailed along the picket lines during this period of the campaign, with trading and sometimes conversation taking place between opposing soldiers. The Eighth had not been in position long before its men got solid evidence that Bragg's program of starving the Yankees was having its effects. A blue-clad picket came out toward the Eighth's picket line and laid his good-quality blanket on the ground. Then he called over to the Georgians, "If you will bring and leave at this place a pone of bread, you may have the blanket," and went back to his picket post. One of the Georgians gladly enough went out and made the exchange, apparently to the satisfaction of all concerned. Later, another Federal swapped a canteen full of whiskey for a pone of bread—an unheard-of rate of exchange. Clearly there was much hunger in the Union ranks.[8]

The next few weeks passed uneventfully. The autumn rains came, making it even harder for the Federals to haul in their supplies over Walden's Ridge but also making life unpleasant for the Confederates. "We are in a complete slosh of mud," wrote a member of the Eighth, "the muddiest little coop hole that mortals ever lived in." Muddy roads inhibited Confederate supply as well, and the troops sometimes endured short rations.

The Eighth, along with the rest of Anderson's brigade, was shifted several times to differing positions in the line, even spending several days atop mighty Lookout Mountain itself. Even when stationed around the foot of the mountain, members of the regiment often made their way up to Lookout Point, from which they could gaze down fourteen hundred feet at the town of Chattanooga and the winding Tennessee River on one side, the lovely expanse of Lookout Valley on the other, and the high hills all around. The scenery was beautiful with the trees in their fall colors, but the sight of greatest interest was the view of the whole lines and camps of both armies spread out around Chattanooga.[9]

The Most Exciting Charge

In the predawn hours of October 27, Union forces crossed the Tennessee at Brown's Ferry west of Chattanooga and drove off the Confederates covering the river there. Those Southern troops belonged to Law's Alabama Brigade and were spread far too thin to hold the position. Law had asked for more manpower, and it had been available, but Longstreet had seen matters in a different light and had withheld the troops. The result of the brief action at Brown's Ferry was that the Federals at Chattanooga, now commanded by Ulysses S. Grant, were able to open a workable supply line through the Tennessee gorge and begin drawing ample rations.

Anderson's brigade, like Law's, was now part of Brig. Gen. Micah Jenkins's division, the gallant Hood having been badly wounded at Chickamauga the month before. The Eighth, along with the rest of the division, had been alerted at the time of the Brown's Ferry fight and had started on their way toward the scene of the action. Once again, Longstreet had other ideas and broke off the action, leaving the Federals in control of the key real estate. The next night, at Bragg's insistence, Longstreet was supposed to use Anderson's brigade, along with the rest of Jenkins's division and other troops in his command, to destroy the Union lodgment on the south bank of the Tennessee and once again close off the Union's conduit for supplies. Again, for reasons that seemed adequate to him at the time but have never been quite clear to anyone since, Longstreet chose another course, used only a small portion of his available troops, and accomplished nothing. The Eighth was not involved.[10]

With all hope of starving the Federals in Chattanooga now gone, Bragg had to think of something else. He decided to prepare for a broad turning movement to the east of Grant, but before he could do that he would have to eliminate the Union army of Maj. Gen. Ambrose Burnside at Knoxville, about one hundred miles northeast of Chattanooga. This he would accomplish by detaching Longstreet's corps to Knoxville, a move that would simultaneously please Robert E. Lee and the Richmond authorities by bringing these Army of Northern Virginia troops that much closer to their parent unit. Accordingly, orders went out on November 4, and Longstreet's men began a cold, wet, muddy march from their defensive positions on and around Lookout Mountain to the train station, a dozen or so miles away. Three days later the Eighth Georgia finally boarded a train bound for Sweetwater Station, well up the Tennessee River valley.

After they reached Sweetwater, the campaign continued to be a slow and disorganized event. They camped several days there, suffering intensely from cold and not enjoying very ample rations either. On November 14 they got moving again, marching northeastward up the Tennessee Valley toward Knoxville. They crossed the river on what one soldier called a "homemade pontoon" bridge, pressed on, and began skirmishing with forward elements of Burnside's force.[11]

The next day they slogged forward again, this time with Jenkins's division in the lead and its skirmishers, including a detail from the Eighth Georgia, carrying the fight to the gradually retreating enemy. In the gathering dusk they came in sight of the campfires of a large Union force at Lenoir Station, Tennessee, but halted for the night without pressing the Federals. The skirmishers were simply left in their advanced positions to serve as pickets during the night and then cover the advance when it resumed first thing in the morning. Throughout the night, John Reed later recalled, they could hear the sound of considerable activity coming from the Union camps, and then, just before daylight, they heard the loud, long whistle of a departing train. Apparently the noise the night before had been caused by the bluecoats pulling out. "Why did we not cut the railroad the day before?" Reed wondered, but no one could ever answer that question.

In the gray dawn they pressed forward again. The sector in which the Eighth Georgia's skirmishers were advancing seemed to be a series of thickets, and the men struggled through the dense brush. They had just passed into a clear area when a shot rang out and Pvt. N. J. Martin of Company H fell with a severe wound to the face and neck. The other Georgians could hear scrambling in the bushes ahead, then the sound of horses galloping away. The enemy, dismounted cavalry, had been the videttes or forward outposts of the Union army. When the Confederates approached, the Union horsemen had fired a shot—striking down Martin—and then mounted up and made their escape, alerting the Union main body of the Confederates' approach.

The sound of galloping hooves told Reed and his men that the enemy were making off, so they wasted no more time prodding slowly and cautiously through the bushes but gave chase as rapidly as they could. By breakfast time they had overrun the camp of the Union cavalry, which despite the alertness of the Federal videttes still offered rich plunder to the hungry Confederates: coffee, condensed milk, hardtack, and meat, both salt and fresh. The skirmishers stopped a few minutes for breakfast and then pressed ahead once more. The sun was just rising then, and its first rays glinted on the bayonets of the Union rear guard, retiring over a hill about a mile away, and on hilltops farther off the Confederates could see white-topped army supply wagons plodding back toward Knoxville.

Exhilarated at the prospect of striking the enemy's wagon train, the skirmishers pushed ahead still faster. The officer commanding the divisional skirmish line, Lt. Col. Thomas M. Logan of the Hampton Legion, made sure the flanks of the line advanced as rapidly as the center. Several times the Union rear guard made brief stands to delay the pursuit, but each time the left and right flanks of the Confederate skirmish line began to curl around the ends of the Union line and the Federals beat a retreat. Again and again the two forces sparred with each other, along fencerows, streams, or ridges, in woods or thickets, the Confederates fiercely enjoying the sensation of following a retreating foe, and the Federals doing what they were supposed to do by making their pursuers deploy and approach with caution.

Sometimes there was no-nonsense fighting. At one point Reed and his Eighth Georgia contingent, moving to flank the enemy, ran straight into them in an apple orchard and had a fight that within its small space and short time sounded almost as intense as a pitched battle. When the Federals once again fell back and Reed and his men followed, an old woman on the porch of a nearby cabin cheered them on: "Give it to 'em, my brave boys. They killed all my hogs last night."[12]

Pvt. Augustus Brantly, of Company D, was having a red-letter day. Trotting along a muddy road after the retreating Yankees, he saw something white lying up ahead. Upon reaching it he found it was a rasher of bacon. That, coupled with the fine breakfast, would have been enough to make this a day to be remembered, but then he and some of his comrades came upon a Union supply wagon that had apparently mired down and been abandoned by its owners. It was full of hardtack, much to the delight of Brantly and the other Georgians.[13]

Farther on, Reed led his men down a slope thickly covered with young hickory trees. At the bottom was a ditch, and in it Reed spied a solid line of bluecoats at a range of fifty yards. He ordered his own men to take cover and fall back to the top of the hill. Other Rebels joined them—the skirmish reserve moving up behind the first scouts—and again a hot firefight developed. The officer in command of all the skirmishers of Anderson's brigade was wounded, and Reed took over the duty. With the rest of the divisional skirmish line engaged to right and left, Reed had this fight all to himself. He was a general for one very small battle.

At first, it did not go well at all. His men worked their way down the slope, keeping the Federals pinned down with their fire. Then, however, as the Confederates started their final rush into the ditch, the bluecoats rose up and poured a volley into their faces. The fire was so intense it "seemed to scale the bark off of every hickory," and the skirmish line lost more men in that minute or two of destruction than it did all the rest of the day. The deadly fire drove them back again, and when Reed tried to rally them for another rush, he found they had had enough of that game.

He was just contemplating how he could work some men around to the left to flank this stubborn line of Yankees when he saw moving up from behind him "a beautiful line of infantry." It was the South Carolina brigade that had come to the division along with Gen. Jenkins, and it still bore his name. A crack unit, it represented the main Confederate battle line in this sector of the division's front. Pointing to the advancing South Carolinians, Reed asked his skirmishers if they were going to let someone else "bag our game." They were not and charged down the hill yelling like fiends. The renewed confidence and dash of the Confederate skirmishers convinced the Federals they had delayed the advance as long as was necessary here, and they hastily pulled out and fell back. For Reed, it was "the most exciting charge of my experience," surpassing Manassas, Gettysburg, and all the rest, "for it was the only one that I ever led."[14]

As the pursuit continued, not all of the Federals made their escape. Pvt. W. W. Ware, of Company E, came on two brothers, cut off from following their retreating comrades. Ware demanded their surrender, but the two bluecoats suggested that it might not be appropriate for two to surrender to one. Ware cocked his rifle and said he could make it even. That seemed to have the desired effect, and he was soon leading his prisoners to the rear. A good many of the Federals overrun by Reed's men subsequently made their escape, as no Confederates were available to escort them to the rear.

And despite the steady advance, work on the skirmish line could be dangerous even when the enemy was not making a concerted stand. Brantly was approaching a rail fence when the top rail suddenly erupted in splinters under the impact of a bullet. Brantly whirled toward the direction from which he thought the shot had come, saw some branches moving, and snapped off a shot. That evening, when he related the story to other members of the regiment who had been advancing behind him, they informed him that at the place he described they had found a dead bluecoat, shot through the back as he apparently had tried to make off after taking his shot at Brantly.[15]

Yet the day had not been as successful for the Confederates nor as disastrous to the Federals as it might have been. They were not far from Campbell's Station, Tennessee, and just near the ditch where the Union rear guard had briefly held up Reed and his men, another road joined the one on which the Federals were retreating. On that other road, McLaws's division was advancing, hoping to get in the rear of most of Burnside's army and cut it off. The bluecoats successfully evaded the trap and withdrew to Knoxville largely unscathed. Why they were able to make such an escape is another of the lingering questions of the Knoxville Campaign.

As the Federals broke contact and hastened their withdrawal to Knoxville, light faded and the day's action came to an end. John Reed lay down exhausted. "I would close my eyes," he later recalled, "only to see the blue coats scampering across the fields and through the woods before me" as his weary mind replayed the scenes of the day. It had been, he thought, "the most lively and exciting day of the war."[16]

The Sullen and Angry Expression on the Faces of Our Soldiers

And so Burnside and his troops settled down behind the formidable defense works of Knoxville, and Longstreet and his troops settled down to lay siege to them. Nearly two weeks went by while Longstreet tried to figure out how to take the city and get on with the work Bragg had assigned him. After several changes of plans, he finally decided to attack Fort Sanders, a key strongpoint on the Union perimeter.

The attack was set for the predawn hours of November 29, and Tige Anderson, now recovered from his Gettysburg wound, quietly announced it to his brigade after nightfall on the 28th. First order of business, to be carried out shortly after midnight that night, was to drive the Union skirmishers out of their advanced rifle pits. In theory this would allow the attacking column to make a shorter advance and would give Confederate skirmishers forward positions from which to sweep the Union parapets and cover the advance. Once again the duty fell to John Reed with a detachment of the Eighth, serving together with the rest of the division's skirmishers all under the command of Lt. Col. Logan.

The men took their positions and stood waiting to advance, hunched against the cold wind, stamping and shivering. At the appointed signal, the firing of Logan's pistol, they all dashed forward and took the Federal skirmishers by surprise. "Wake up, Jim, the rebels are right on us," Reed heard one of them cry out before passing them by and waving both to the rear as prisoners. Glancing down the line he saw Company I's mild-looking, soft-spoken Pvt. Bob Shedd, "the quietest and meekest man in the company," pointing his rifle down into a Union trench. "Halt," Shedd was saying in his habitual mild voice. "If you do not halt I will shoot you." A scrambling sound came from inside the trench, and Shedd's rifle roared. "Oh, my arm! My arm!" someone was moaning from inside the trench, while Shedd shook his head sadly. "I told you I would shoot if you did not halt."

The skirmishers secured the positions assigned to them and spent the rest of the night sparring with the Union skirmishers—who wanted their old positions back—and ducking artillery fire. Whatever else the morning's attack might do, it would not find the enemy unprepared.

In fact, the skirmishers' midnight action was about the last thing that went right for the Confederates in the entire operation. Reed and his company had the dubious privilege of moving back from the skirmish lines to join the rest of the regiment and take part in the main event. As they got to the assembly area they could vaguely perceive various bodies of troops moving about and getting into position. Then as the night sky changed from black to gray, they could make out the dark shape of the first attacking column moving forward on their right.

The plan was for three of McLaws's brigades to assault Fort Sanders itself, while Anderson's brigade, backed up by two more of Jenkins's brigades, attacked the Union line about one hundred yards to the left of the fort. If McLaws's men had by that time been successful in storming the fort, Anderson would wheel left to roll up the rest of the Union line. If not, he would wheel right and go into the fort from flank and rear while McLaws's men continued to threaten it in front.

The plan had a certain logic to it, but the preparations were woefully inadequate. As usual, the men in the ranks paid the price. McLaws's brigades advanced as planned but upon reaching the fort ran into snags, both literal and figurative. The Federals had built an extensive abatis, or entanglement of tree branches, in front of the fort and had also strung telegraph wire between stumps near the ground, perfect for tripping up men in the gray dawn light. Worse by far, however, was the fort's ditch. About fourteen feet wide, it was located directly outside the parapet. Faulty Confederate reconnaissance had estimated it to be only four or five feet deep. In fact, it was more like fifteen feet, vertically, from the bottom of the ditch to the top of the parapet, and the steeply sloping side of the parapet was slippery mud—except where it was frozen into a solid sheet of ice. Gen. Jenkins, a thoroughly first-rate officer, had thought the men ought to take scaling ladders or other devices for getting across the ditch and into the fort, but Longstreet and McLaws did not see it that way. Thus as McLaws's soldiers poured down into the ditch, they were almost helpless to get up the other side. They clawed and slipped and boosted one another while the defenders enfiladed the ditch with canister, held their rifles over the parapet and fired them down into the seething mass, or tossed hand grenades over into the packed ditch.

The Eighth Georgia was not supposed to be in that ditch at all. Once McLaws's brigades had started their advance, Anderson's brigade started forward as well. Then something went terribly wrong. Jenkins later explained that the colonel of one of the lead regiments veered off course to the right, taking the rest of the brigade with him. The mistake came from guiding on McLaws's troops, who, said Jenkins, were also veering badly to the right. Yet McLaws said his troops went in where they were meant to, and since his troops did get into the ditch of the fort, he was probably right. In any case, instead of striking the Union line well north of the fort, Anderson's brigade plunged straight into the ditch and into the same dilemma that had stopped McLaws's assault. Indeed, by that time, Longstreet had already given the order to recall McLaws's badly mauled brigades.

Unaware that it was by mistake that the brigade was approaching the obviously impregnable fort, John Reed thought that if he were in command, he would lead the brigade against the Yankee line somewhere off to the left, where it looked as if they might have had a chance. As it was, the prospect was ghastly. "I could see the close packed huddle of our men" in the ditch, Reed recalled, "and I became sure that we were not going to take the fort."

The scene in the ditch was incredible. Reed saw an officer of the Ninth Georgia make it to the top of the parapet by supreme athletic effort and then stand there blazing away with his revolver until a Union soldier pushed him off with a pike. Other Confederates fired through the embrasures of the guns, driving the cannoneers away from their pieces. Bullets zipped past them from the parapet and the rest of the Union line, and Southern soldiers went down one after another without being able to do much in reply. Tom Oliver, one of the best soldiers in Company I, was killed that way, and Company A's Capt. S. H. Hall fell mortally wounded with a bullet through both lungs. And through it all was the feeling of utter helplessness. "There we stood feeling extremely silly and foolish," Reed recalled. "I shall never forget the sullen and angry expression on the faces of our soldiers" when the order to retreat was given. Anderson's brigade, numbering less than a thousand men that morning, had lost 187 men killed, wounded, and captured. Thirty-three of those were from the Eighth Georgia. Among those captured was the mild-mannered Pvt. Shedd.[17]

Scarcely thirty minutes after the failed assault, Longstreet received word that Bragg had been defeated at Chattanooga three days before. He lost no time in deciding to call off the siege of Knoxville and withdraw his force northeastward, farther away from Bragg and closer to Virginia. It took several days to get the army ready to move, and on December 4 they finally marched away under a cold, steady rain. Their route took them up the valley of the Holston River, a chief tributary of the Tennessee, to Rogersville, intermittently harassed by Union cavalry. Anderson's brigade had the rearguard duty and carried on most of the battle with the pesky blue-jacketed horsemen.

It was in any case a march of misery. The weather was cold and icy, with alternating rain, sleet, and snow. The men's clothes were mostly threadbare. Many men lacked blankets, and, worst of all, a great many lacked shoes. The path of the retreating army was sometimes marked by bloody footprints in the snow. Food was scarce too, as they had to live on what they could forage off the countryside, and that was precious little.

A hard march on December 14 brought the head of the column to Bean's Station, Tennessee, where it tangled with Union forces there in an inconclusive action. The Eighth, still with the rear guard, did not get up in time to join the fight. Skirmishing continued, at one or both ends of the column, for the next several days. On December 23 they crossed the Holston River at Long's Ferry, waiting all day long while a single ferryboat worked back and forth across the river. On Christmas Eve they finally went into winter quarters near Morristown, Tennessee.

It was a brutally cold winter for the ill-clad, ill-shod troops. Despite their lack of shoes and clothing, they did picket duty, foraged, skirmished with the Yankees, and occasionally shifted to new camps a few miles in one direction or the other as military exigency seemed to demand. Boredom, cold, hunger, separation from loved ones, and the awareness of great valor and suffering apparently wasted all weighed on them through the early months of 1864.

For the first time in its history, the Eighth Georgia began to have a problem with desertion. The phenomenon had previously been negligible. A single man had deserted in the regiment's first year of service. Despite the hard marching and fighting of 1862, only two more veteran members of the Eighth had deserted that year, along with a couple of conscripts, part of a steady trickle of their sort who were sent to the regiment as replacements but had never wanted to fight this war in the first place. The third year of the war had been much the same. A conscript or two, along with a couple of hired substitutes, had left the ranks, but the veterans of the Eighth had known what they were fighting for.

The brutally disappointing late-fall campaign in East Tennessee began to change that situation in ominous ways. One member of the regiment deserted to Union lines that October, taking the oath of allegiance to the United States and receiving free transportation to the north bank of the Ohio River. For him, the war was over, and he could follow normal peacetime pursuits, subject only to the stipulation that he remain in the North for the duration of the conflict. If he was wise he probably stayed a good while longer. It was the standard deal the Union government offered to Confederate soldiers who saw the error of their ways. The following month, November 1863, four more veteran members of the Eighth, men who had joined up back in 1861, availed themselves of that offer, and in early December two members of Company H did so on the same day, apparently together. It was almost getting to be a thing a man was not ashamed of anymore.

A soldier in the Eleventh Georgia summed up the situation not only for the rest of Anderson's brigade but also for the whole of Longstreet's corps when he wrote, "We have seen the worst part of this war since we came to Tenn." And though a few might desert, the great majority stood it as best they could and longed for another springtime to lift the dark winter of their suffering and loss.[18]

CHAPTER TEN

⁊

The Raging Sea

The Battle That Most Tried My Nerves

THE long winter passed, and springtime came on at last. The snow melted, and the brooks and branches burbled along bank-full. Every oak put on a thousand little yellow-green beards of pollen, and the beeches and chestnuts shot out tiny spring-green spikes of new buds. Forsythia bloomed and the dogwoods promised well. Yet most welcome of all to the soldiers of Longstreet's corps were the orders that came April 11, 1864, calling them eastward to rejoin Robert E. Lee and his Army of Northern Virginia in its camps below the Rapidan. "We were glad when the order came," wrote Company K's Tom Gilham, "for if we had to fight we wanted to see Uncle Bob Lee about."[1]

They marched out of their stale, muddy camps and across the fresh green country side to the various stations of the Virginia & East Tennessee Railroad, where they "took the cars," as the saying was in those days, for Virginia. By April 14, Anderson's brigade was encamped near

Charlottesville, Virginia, an intermediate stop on their way to join Lee. Six days later they boarded the trains again, and a week or so of intermittent traveling brought them at last to their destination near Gordonsville. There they, like the rest of the Army of Northern Virginia, would await the movements of Ulysses S. Grant, now commanding all Union armies and making his headquarters with the Army of the Potomac, which would be under his personal supervision.

On April 29, the Eighth Georgia and all the rest of Longstreet's corps turned out in their best uniforms, looking as fine as washing, brushing, and polishing could make them, and Gen. Lee came down from his headquarters to review them there. The Eighth was now part of the division of Maj. Gen. Charles W. Field, who had replaced Jenkins in a command shake-up that winter. The new division commander was a thirty-six-year-old veteran of some of the Army of Northern Virginia's hardest battles. Beside Field's division in the broad reviewing field was that of Maj. Gen. Joseph Kershaw, who had replaced McLaws. The troops were the same, though, even if many who had once stood in their ranks were no longer present. Their review by "Uncle Bobby Lee" was a profoundly meaningful event. The field rang with the yells and cheers of the men for their commander, and neither the general nor his men were dry-eyed. It was, said one witness, almost "a military sacrament."[2]

Reviews had a practical meaning, and the soldiers knew what it was. Fighting was expected, and soon. Lee's expectation was fulfilled when on May 4, 1864, Grant crossed the Rapidan and advanced toward Lee through a region of tangled second-growth forest and dense thickets known simply as the Wilderness. The armies had met here before, one year ago almost to the day, for the Battle of Chancellorsville, but the Eighth Georgia, like the rest of Longstreet's troops, had missed it, being away on their unpleasant excursion to Suffolk at the time. For them, this would be the first encounter in those dark woods.

Only minor skirmishing occurred that first day between the Federals and elements of Richard Ewell's Second Corps of the Army of Northern Virginia. The following day, however, May 5, the battle was joined in earnest, as Lee struck hard in hopes of throwing Grant back across the Rapidan. Furious day-long fighting in the confusion of the tangled thickets of the Wilderness brought long casualty lists but no decisive results. Only Ewell's Second Corps and A. P. Hill's Third Corps were engaged for the Confederates. All that day, Longstreet's men marched from the camps around Gordonsville toward the scene of the fighting. They covered thirty miles in all and camped at 5:00 P.M. about ten miles from the battlefield. Hill's Third Corps had been having a very bad time that afternoon and evening, and Lee directed Longstreet to move up and relieve Hill first thing in the morning.

Longstreet's men were up and on the march again at 1:00 A.M., May 6, but even with as early a start as that, they did not reach the battlefield before U. S. Grant had opened the second full day of fighting. Grant sent Winfield S. Hancock's Union Second Corps booming through the thickets and right into Hill's tired, dispirited, and badly positioned troops. The Confederate line went to pieces, and Union troops swarmed up the Orange Plank Road and out into the clearing of the Widow Tapp's farm, not far from the Confederate supply wagon train. The situation looked very bad.

Lee was on Traveler at the Widow Tapp's clearing trying to rally the broken and fleeing remnants of Hill's Corps, but even the beloved commander could not get the panicked soldiers to form a line. The sixteen Confederate cannon of Lt. Col. William T. Poague's battalion, with their hardworking crews, deployed behind a low breastwork of fence rails to the left of the Orange Plank Road, and were about all the force holding the Federals back for the time being.

Longstreet's men had been on the road for several hours now, and as the light rose in the eastern sky ahead of them, so too did the rumble of battle. They all knew what lay ahead of them. Soon walking wounded began to trickle past them in ones and twos, then in larger numbers. Members of the ambulance corps carried the more seriously injured to field hospitals, which were gruesome sights for the advancing troops as they passed. Unwounded men began to appear with increasing frequency among the flocks of fugitives, until they made up the great bulk of the fleeing horde. Clearly, one or more Confederate formations had come apart in the fighting toward which Longstreet's men were marching.

In an unusual measure, Longstreet's two divisions, Field's and Kershaw's, marched side by side in the road, the head of Kershaw's column just about a hundred yards ahead of the leading soldiers of Field's. At the head of Field's division was Anderson's brigade. Marching thus near the van of the cops, the men of the Eighth were among the first to see the signs of impending defeat. Yet like their comrades in the other regiments, they pushed on steadily like the veterans they were. Tom Gilham looked at his comrades in Company K and thought he "never saw men more determined to do their whole duty." As far as he could see, the whole regiment, the whole brigade, seemed to feel the same way.[3]

"Double-quick" came the familiar order, and they trotted down the road toward the sound of the guns. They could hear the panting of their comrades around them, the thump of boots, shoes, or bare feet on the dirt roadbed, the clatter of accouterments, and rising above them all, louder and louder, the roar of artillery now growing very close. Then, up ahead, someone yelled, "Here they come!" Moments later the Georgians found the road no longer lined with fleeing men but with sweaty, powder-grimed artillerymen who dashed over from their red-hot guns, tossing their caps and shouting. "We yelled ourselves nearly dumb to cheer them as they swept by," recalled one of the gunners. Still at the double-quick, the Georgians obeyed Anderson's shouted orders, filed right out of the road, and formed line of battle. Deploying, according to orders, on the right rather than the left of the road, Anderson's men missed the heavy fighting and dramatic scenes that took place in the Widow Tapp's clearing, as Confederate troops rolled back the Union assault. Instead Anderson's men remained in reserve during the first part of that day's fighting.[4]

About ten o'clock, orders arrived for a movement. Longstreet had discovered that Hancock's left flank was vulnerable and began putting together a striking force from the troops on his own right. The striking force was to consist of three fresh brigades, Anderson's being one of them. It took time for them to get into position through the dense foliage. First they filed right until they came to a railroad cut that offered them access to Hancock's flank. Then they filed down the cut with Anderson's brigade in the lead. When they reached the desired position at about eleven o'clock that morning, all four attacking brigades faced left into line, moved out of the cut, and began to beat their way through the woods toward Hancock's vulnerable flank.

The result at first was all that Longstreet had hoped. Several Union brigades buckled quickly under the unexpected flank attack, and for about thirty minutes the Confederates seemed in a fair way to roll up

Hancock's line. Grant and his subordinates, however, rushed in Union reinforcements, and the attackers lost momentum and cohesion as they went. The assault stalled far short of doing anything like lethal damage to Hancock's corps, much less Grant's army, but Longstreet was eager to get it going again. With his staff and key subordinates he rode forward to set things in order for a renewal of the assault. At this point, however, the tangled wilderness that had hitherto helped the Confederates now worked against them. The confusion it caused led to another friendly fire incident similar to the one that had laid Jackson low in these same woods just over a year before. This time Longstreet was the victim, badly though not fatally wounded. Several key officers riding with him were killed or wounded, including the Eighth's former division commander, Brig. Gen. Micah Jenkins, killed almost instantly by a bullet in the forehead.[5]

The loss of so much of its vital leadership temporarily crippled Longstreet's corps and brought a lull of several hours in active operations, during which the two sides nevertheless continued to bushwhack each other in the gloomy forest. Then about 4:00 P.M., Lee sent Longstreet's troops forward in another attack. This time they enjoyed much less success. The Federals had dug in behind breastworks along the Brock Road and fought fiercely. Confederate losses were heavy. Anderson's brigade, in the forefront of the assault of Field's division, was able to drive the defenders back briefly on its front, but the advantage was short-lived. The Federals quickly rallied and counterattacked, driving the Georgians back and, according to one account, capturing the flag of the Eighth Georgia. The incident is somewhat obscure and may be an error. At any rate, the "Second Bunting" flag that had been presented to the Eighth on the eve of the Seven Days Battles two years before was never lost and continued with the regiment all the way to Appomattox.[6]

The fighting in the Wilderness was much different from any combat the Georgians had previously encountered. They had fought in thickets before—in the infamous pine thicket at First Manassas and on the slopes of Bull Run Mountain at Thoroughfare Gap—but in this case the entire battle was in one enormous thicket that stretched out beyond the battlefield in every direction. John Reed referred to it as "that clapper-clawing in the dark of the thick underbrush," and did not like to say much about it. Others commented on the strangeness of a fight in which they could rarely see the enemy nor more than their own company of Confederate forces either. They pressed on through the underbrush, firing in the direction from which they were taking fire.[7]

At one point Augustus Brantly burst out of a particularly thick patch of underbrush to find himself face-to-face with a Yankee. "Surrender!" shouted the badly startled Brantly, and the Federal, apparently even more startled, threw down his gun and raised his hands. At this point another Yankee stepped out of the bushes. Brantly tried the same procedure on him, but this bluecoat was made of sterner stuff. Instead of throwing down his rifle, he pointed it at Brantly and replied, "Lay down your gun!" For a few moments, which of course seemed much longer, the two armed men stared at each other over the barrels of their guns. The standoff was broken when several of Brantly's comrades from the Eighth stumbled into the tiny clearing and tipped the scales decisively in his favor. The two Yankees they sent off to the rear as prisoners.[8]

Darkness fell on the smoky woodland battlefield. Exploding shells had set the woods on fire in places, shedding a lurid light on the scenes of bloodshed and threatening to burn some of the helpless wounded left between the lines. Men scurried about in the darkness looking for friends and carrying injured men out of the way of the crackling fires. Augustus Brantly thought it had been "the battle that most tried my nerves." John Reed considered it "the hardest and best fighting ever made by our corps," and a soldier of the Seventh Georgia figured that it must have been a Confederate victory, since he saw more blue-clad corpses than gray. The other Georgians thought the same, though their own losses had been considerable—seven dead, fifty-six wounded, and eighteen captured out of a total strength of scarcely more than two hundred. Among the dead was Company B's Pierce Butler Holmes, a second lieutenant when he died and, an eternity ago back in Howard's Grove, "the first Confederate to enlist for the war." One other loss the regiment sustained, outside of combat, and noticed and grieved at least by the men of Company I: John Reed's former personal servant, Lit, died of pneumonia in the field hospital a few days after the battle.[9]

Union casualties at what would be called the Battle of the Wilderness had exceeded Confederate losses by a wide margin, but from now on such things were not going to mean very much. Unlike previous Union Commanders of the Army of the Potomac, Grant was not going to play that game. He was not driven back across the Rapidan nor deterred from further advance. He would hit fast and hard and, in his own words, "keep moving on."

It Was a Butchery

Grant next moved around Lee's right flank and struck for the key crossroads at Spotsylvania Court House, hoping to cut Lee off from Richmond. It was close, but Lee just succeeded in blocking him. Both armies dug in extensively, and Grant hammered at Lee's lines to see if they would give way.

The Eighth Georgia found itself posted near the left of the Confederate line at Spotsylvania. On May 10, Union soldiers of Gouvernor K. Warren's Fifth Corps attacked. The Eighth was ready. They were situated in a narrow field, only about seventy-five yards wide, and Col. Towers gave his company commanders strict orders to have their men fire in volley; first rank, on one knee, would fire in one volley, second rank, firing over their comrades' heads, in another. There was to be no wasting of ammunition. The men were to aim low, and they were not to fire until the enemy reached the far edge of the field, virtually point-blank range.

About four o'clock in the afternoon Warren's men came on. The Georgians waited until the Yankees reached "the deadline" at the far edge of the field. Then up and down the Eighth's trenches came the voices of the company commanders: "Rear rank, ready; aim; fire!" A sheet of flame leaped out of the leveled muzzles in the direction of the advancing foe. "Load!" came the company commanders' final order after the carnage of the first point-blank volley, the company commanders orders rang out again: "Front rank, ready; aim; fire!" Again the Eighth's line blazed out at the attackers. Again came the captains' voices—"Load!"—and ramrods clanked in rifle barrels. The Union attack broke up and sifted back in retreat. They came back, though, again and again. One soldier of the Eighth thought he counted eleven separate attacks that day, but it was hard to say for sure.

By the tail end of the assault, the blue-clad infantry was not showing much eagerness to press home attacks against the stoutly manned Confederate trenches. They seemed to have discerned the phenomenon of "the deadline," and whole formations of them wisely went to ground just beyond it, despite the urging of their officers, and contented themselves with keeping up a desultory harassing fire against the Georgians in the trenches.

About 5:00 P.M. a more successful assault carried the Federals all the way into the lines of the neighboring Texas Brigade. Defenders and attackers fought with bayonets and clubbed muskets. Soon, however, Confederate reinforcements moved up from the rear and reestablished the line.

May 11 passed with minor skirmishing, and May 12 saw a massive Union assault on Ewell's Second Corps lines, leading to twenty-four hours of the most intense fighting of the war. The Eighth Georgia, however, was not even a spectator to the bloody conflict, which from their position off at the left end of the line they could hear but not see. Two assaults struck Anderson's lines that morning—Grant's way of making sure they sent no help to Ewell's hard-pressed sector—and the Federals fought their way into the Confederate trenches and fought there hand to hand for several minutes before being driven back with heavy losses.

Still, the Battle of Spotsylvania had been relatively easy on the Eighth Georgia, costing it scarcely a dozen casualties, and only two of those killed outright. It had been the first time in the regiment's history that it had had the privilege of fighting a pitched battle from behind breastworks. The effects of those long piles of earth and logs were dramatic and the low casualties a sharp contrast to the Eighth's heavy losses in the Wilderness. What remained of the Eighth after Spotsylvania was not much larger than any one of the ten companies that had originally left Georgia to form the regiment back in 1861.

After the battle was over and the Federals had pulled out of their positions opposite the Eighth, John Reed, now captain of Company I since the death of Capt. T. J. Blackwell at the Wilderness, walked out to survey the battleground. The scene he found was appalling. The Union dead lay thick along "the deadline," and in one place Reed counted eleven bodies touching each other. "It was a butchery that made me sick to look upon," he recalled years later.[10]

Finding that he could make no progress by frontal assaults, Grant tried flank movements again, sidling around Lee's right. Lee responded, and the two armies sidestepped southeastward across the Virginia piedmont, sometimes a few hundred yards in a day, sometimes a dozen miles. Occasionally there was threat of serious fighting, as at the crossings of the North Anna River, where the Confederate position was so strong that Tom Gilham of the Eighth fervently hoped Grant would attack, but the Union general was too cagey. Sometimes serious fighting really did erupt, as at Haw's Shop, where Robert Tuggle, a new recruit just arrived to join Company K, fired off sixty rounds of ammunition alongside his new comrades during his first two hours as a soldier. Always there was skirmishing and cannonading. Grant never succeeded in his goal of cutting Lee off from Richmond, but in order to block him Lee had to keep falling back closer and closer to the city. The soldiers of both sides entrenched themselves now at every opportunity. For the men of the Eighth Georgia the month of May went by in a blur of marching, digging, and skirmishing all in the midst of pervasive filth, ankle-deep dust, blazing sun, and scant rations.[11]

By the first of June they reached Cold Harbor, on the ground fought over during the Seven Days Battles two years before and just a few miles outside of Richmond. Lee had run out of room to retreat, but Grant had also run out of room to maneuver. So the Union general tried a massive frontal assault. On June 3 the Eighth was one of many, many Confederate regiments that experienced one of their easiest major battles. From the almost complete safety of their trenches they mowed down the advancing Federals like grass before a scythe. Across the whole width of the battle front, the Army of the Potomac lost seven thousand men in the space of an hour, a butchery far worse than that which had sickened John Reed back at Spotsylvania. Confederate casualties were negligible. The Eighth's share of the loss was two men wounded.

After Cold Harbor the Eighth, and the rest of Lee's army, got a few days' rest. Grant remained quiet in his trenches, and two weeks went by. Only at the end of that period did Lee realize that for the past couple of days, Grant had not been in those trenches. Instead the Union commander had stolen a march on his foe, had slipped around the Confederate right again, and was threatening the vital city of Petersburg, Virginia, directly south of Richmond. If Petersburg fell, Richmond was lost. Lee reacted by dispatching his first Corps, now commanded by Lt. Gen. Richard Anderson (no relation to Tige). The rest of the army would follow. As part of the First Corps the Eighth, along with the rest of Field's division, marched hard and skirmished sharply with Union troops between Richmond and Petersburg.[12]

"It was fight all day and march all night," recalled a member of the Eighth, "but we were stimulated with the hope that we would defeat the enemy, and that would end the struggle." By the narrowest of margins, Lee, aided by Confederate troops under P. G. T. Beauregard already stationed south of Richmond, succeeded in blocking Grant's move. That, however, was far from being the end of the war, as many Southerners had fondly hoped. Instead, there was nothing left now for the stubborn Union general but to settle down for a siege of Petersburg and Richmond. There was nothing for Lee and his men but to settle down to stand that siege as long as they could.[13]

As Befits One of the Eighth Georgia

The Eighth had experienced a taste of siege warfare on the Peninsula two years before, and the campaign of the past month and a half had been fought primarily in trenches, but Petersburg surpassed all that had gone before. In dry weather the trenches were ovens and the dust was everywhere. In wet weather they were pigpens. The fire of enemy sharpshooters made it as much as a man's life was worth to raise his head above the top of the breastworks or even to peek out of the firing slits, between logs, that were built into the parapet. "During the day we had to stick close to cover," John Reed wrote, "rarely ever having any opportunity to stand erect."

Much of life was lived in "bomb-proofs," underground bunkers that were safe against anything but a direct hit by the largest shells. Aside from relative safety, a bomb-proof offered all the comforts and amenities of living in a hole in the ground with a number of other men as dirty as oneself. The big events of the day were the arrivals of enemy shells, high arching mortar shells that dropped down from the sky and the "straight shells," as the men called them, the work of conventional cannon with more or less flat trajectories. The arrival of such deadly messengers was not anticipated with pleasure, but at least it did relieve the boredom.

One night the Union artillerists were particularly active, lobbing mortar shells into the Eighth's sector of the line at intervals of anywhere from a few minutes to a few seconds. Sam Sharyer of Company F took the whole business in a jocular vein, hooting and shouting in derision of the gunners' aim as each shell came over. Other members of the regiment were clearly not enjoying the bombardment nearly as much. Finally, about midnight, Sam declared that "he would not be deprived any longer of his natural rest." With that, he marched out of the trench and set up his pup tent in a nice sandy spot some yards to the rear. Within a short time he was sound asleep, and his comrades back in the trench could hear him snoring.

Everyone else was dozing too when at about 2:00 A.M. they were all brought painfully wide awake by the whistling of a descending mortar shell. They had slept through others, but this one was different. With the practiced ears of veteran soldiers, they knew this one was going to be close—very close. It landed a few yards from Sharyer's tent and, with fuse still sputtering, bounced and rolled right in. Sharyer came out the other end of the tent at a pretty good pace, laughing hysterically and yelling that "he would have no such messmate." No sooner was he clear than the ground shook with a heavy explosion. When the smoke drifted away, a crater remained where the tent had stood, while shreds of cotton fabric slowly floated back to earth.[14]

Not everyone could take the life in the trenches with the same humor as Sharyer, and morale sagged. What bothered the men was not only the hardships they had to endure but also the sense that now, at last, their cause might truly be hopeless. Tom Gilham had been away from the regiment because of sickness and returned in mid-July, a month into the siege. He was shocked at the low spirits of his comrades. "Up to the time that I had left in June, 1864," he wrote, "our boys were cheerful and hopeful, but when I returned to the regiment at Petersburg their countenances were changed to sadness—for we felt that all was lost." Still they were determined to do their duty to the bitter end and leave the final result to God.[15]

All the regiment's cooking was done by men detailed for that purpose at a special camp they set up about a mile behind the lines. Then, usually at night, some lucky member or members of the cook detail would get the unenviable and highly dangerous duty of carrying the rations up to the men in the front-line trenches. One day John Reed decided he wanted to eat a meal in peace for a change. Securing the necessary permission, he crept out of his trench and made his way, rushing from one cover to the next, until he felt safe from Union sharpshooters.

As he walked along toward the cooks' camp, he fell in with Col. Towers, who kept his horse back at the cooks' camp and was going to check on the beast. They arrived there and were enjoying a relatively peaceful meal when they were startled by the sound of a loud slap nearby. Looking in the direction from which the sound had come, they saw that the colonel's horse was obviously in pain. Upon investigation they found that it had been struck in the shoulder by a bullet, breaking a bone. The shot had undoubtedly been fired by a Union sharpshooter at some target in the Confederate trenches. Aimed a bit too high, it had carried a mile to the rear with lethal force. The soldiers had grown fatalistic about such events and had a saying that "when a bullet came so far it was bound to strike a live object." In fact, several cooks were indeed wounded or killed during the course of the siege by bullets that traveled that far to strike them.

About the end of July, the Eighth just missed having the dubious privilege of being the object of Grant's next offensive. Coal miners in a Pennsylvania regiment had dug a long tunnel reaching all the way under Confederate lines. Under a key Rebel strongpoint the Pennsylvanians placed several tons of powder. As soon as the fort was blown sky-high, the Union plan called for several bluecoat divisions to press through the gap in Confederate lines and roll up Lee's army. The Eighth almost gained the distinction of becoming in this manner some of the Confederacy's first airborne troops, but a shift of assignments a few days before the Union assault took the Eighth to another sector and left the duty on top of the great mine to other troops. The July 30 Battle of the Crater, as the Union assault was called, was another failure for the Federals, though it did blow up a regiment of South Carolinians in the first blast. "Somehow I have always regretted that we missed that wild morning," John Reed wrote years later.[16]

The Eighth's new position was on the north bank of the James River directly in front of Richmond. They were on some of the same ground they had marched and fought over during the Peninsula Campaign, not far from the battlefield of Malvern Hill. The regiment's sector fell in a stretch of wooded and swampy ground. Company K was deployed as pickets a couple of hundred yards in front of the main line of trenches on August 14 when a heavy Union probe struck that part of the line. Company K was hit hard. Capt. T. J. Bowling took a bullet in the face, just below the eyes, and another in the right shoulder. Jim Floyd was struck in the foot, and Robert Tuggle, the company's last recruit, suffered a slight wound in the right shoulder. Several others were captured.

The unwounded survivors scampered back to the main trench, and one of them mentioned that he had seen Bowling go down. Tom Rollins was a member of the litter corps and also a messmate of Bowling's. Excitedly he asked where Bowling lay. A soldier who had seen the captain fall pointed out to Rollins a large tree in the woods about 150 yards away. "He is just a few feet to the right of that tree," the man explained, but remonstrated that it was certain death to try to get to him. The Yankees had the area covered. "Then they will have to hit me on the wing," Rollins replied. "After I reach the tree the grass will hide me and him. There is no use for the litter corps but to bring off the wounded." He paused to make sure he was looking at the right tree, then jumped up and sprinted for the spot amid a fusillade of enemy fire. As he neared the tree, his comrades back in the trench saw him drop into the grass. Tense moments passed, and then they saw him come scrabbling along low to the ground, below the tops of the grass stems, in something between a crawl and a trot, the wounded captain on his back. He had not been hit, nor had the captain suffered further injury. Bowling actually recovered, though he was never able to return to duty.[17]

Back in the trenches the men of the Eighth fought off intermittent Federal thrusts all day. That afternoon, Company I became engaged in a duel with a Union battery about eight hundred yards away. The first shell penetrated clear through the top of their trench's parapet and landed inside, its fuse still lit. A quick-thinking soldier snatched it up and heaved it over the parapet. Everyone ducked down into the trench, and the shell exploded harmlessly. A minute or two later, however, the whole process was repeated in another part of the company. Realizing that sooner or later a shell was going to burst with deadly effect, Capt. Reed decided to engage the battery even though it was clearly well beyond the theoretical effective range of his men's Enfield rifles. Estimating the distance himself and ordering his men to set their sights as he specified, he gradually ranged in on the battery, correcting his estimates by spotting the dust kicked up by successive volleys. To his great satisfaction, he finally succeeded in getting the range and forcing the battery to limber to the rear and withdraw.

The Union presence in front of the Georgians' lines continued to increase throughout the following day, August 15. That night John Reed sat up smoking his pipe in a pine thicket behind the lines, enjoying a respite from sharpshooters. Lt. J. W. Culpepper of Company D joined him and took out his own pipe. As Reed recalled, "we were soon puffing away sociably." Culpepper was reputed the handsomest lieutenant in the regiment and had a very pleasant personality withal. Reed was dismayed to hear what his friend had to say this night. Culpepper said that from Company D's position over on the regimental right one could see much more of the Union preparations than were visible from Reed's position with Company I on the left. They were going to have a fight the next day, Culpepper continued. "And it came into my mind that I shall be killed. I shall be killed instantaneously." Soldiers took these premonitions seriously. The ones that failed were forgotten and the ones borne out were remembered, until they seemed uncannily reliable. Reed tried to cheer his friend up, but given that he believed Culpepper's death to be imminent, he was not much help. The lieutenant spoke of his mother, and as he rose to go back to his company he added, "I shall not try to dodge the death that I know is coming. I shall fall as befits one of the Eighth Georgia."

The next day the Federals did indeed renew their attack in large numbers and supported by a heavy artillery bombardment. Several Confederate brigades to the left of Tige Anderson's, as well as the left of Anderson's brigade itself, broke under the onslaught. Tige pulled the Eighth and one other regiment out of line and launched them to the left to try to recoup the situation there. The regiment maneuvered with the practiced skill of veterans, despite the bursting shells all around them. A round exploded in the midst of Company K, wounding half a dozen men, but Lt. Tom Gilham, commanding the company now since Bowlings was gone, kept the unwounded men moving forward.[18]

The regiment took up a position along a rail fence and exchanged fire with enemy troops in a cornfield in front of them. It was a hot fight for a while, but soon they were joined by Law's and Benning's brigades, coming up to help plug the gap, as well as remnants of the shattered units that had been overrun. As they gained the ascendancy over their foes, the impulse to charge was almost universal. John Reed thought it was a private who finally shouted, "Over the fence and charge!" They did it, and the Rebel Yell rose above the roar of battle as they swept the Union line out of the cornfield. Dashing along at the head of his company, Reed saw out of the corner of his eye his friend Lt. Culpepper leading his own company, well out in front of the men, sword in one hand, cap in the other. Then Culpepper was down, and the surging Confederate battle line rushed on.[19]

They were most of the rest of the day fighting their way back into the positions that had been lost in the initial Union attack. The troops fought with veteran skill that required little direction on the part of officers. Each man knew what to do, and the line advanced by short rushes, in open order, rather than in parade-ground formation. For the first time that day they encountered black Union troops, as well as the usual all-white units. "Our boys went mad when they found they had to fight Negroes," Gilham recalled.[20]

Late in the day the Eighth was involved in an effort to retake a house occupied by the Federals. The Union troops had solid control of the Confederate trenches they had taken that morning but not much more—except the house, a key position several hundred yards from the trenches. After several unsuccessful attempts to take the building, members of several Confederate regiments charged the structure simultaneously from different sides. John Reed led the dash for the house from his side, and right beside him was Sam Sharyer, who had laughed at the Federal shells. They were only a few steps from the house when Sharyer was hit and fell without a groan. Reed and the others pressed on and helped take the building, closing out the day's fighting.

Afterward Reed walked back to check on his friends. Sharyer was hit in the abdomen, a hopeless case. Culpepper had been struck in the forehead. Someone had cleaned him up by the time Reed got back to him, and he thought the lieutenant still the handsomest man in the regiment.[21]

A Secret Whisper

After the Battle of Fussell's Mill, as it was called, the Eighth was shifted back to the south bank of the James as part of Lee's effort to counter a lunge by Grant's forces for the Weldon Railroad at Reams' Station. For this action Tige Anderson's brigade was temporarily attached to Hill's Third Corps and launched at Union Troops threatening Lee's vital supply lines to North Carolina and points south. The action was a spectacular Confederate victory. The Union formation they attacked, the once formidable Second Corps, was now largely composed of men whose enlistments were nearly up or else drafted men who did not want to be there in the first place. They offered relatively weak resistance and were routed.

The Yankees lost several cannon, and one of them, at least, was taken by the Eighth. Ezekiel Townsend had friends in the artillery and knew what to do with cannon. Discovering that the gun was still loaded, he got some of his comrades to help him turn it around and fire it at the retreating enemy. The result was unexpected. Union batteries farther on returned the fire vigorously, some of their shots sailing over Townsend and his extemporized gun crew and landing near Confederate batteries back in the rear. They, in turn, interpreted this fire as having come from Townsend's captured cannon, having seen the smoke from his shot but not being close enough to tell which way the gun was pointed. Accordingly, they too favored the Eighth with a bombardment. The perplexed Townsend, crouching behind a large oak tree, called out, "Well, this is the first fight I was ever in, when I did not know which side of the tree to take."[22]

The siege continued along much the same pattern—weeks of boredom and constant danger in the trenches punctuated by desperate fights to block another of Grant's many bids for the upper hand. In late September and early October the scene of action was once again the north bank of the James, and once again Field's division was called upon to supply a portion of Lee's striking force. This time, however, the results were quite the opposite of those at Reams' Station. A counterattack was planned in order to recover some advantageous ground that Grant had taken. Several brigades were involved and careful timing was important. Anderson neglected to explain the plan of attack to his colonels, some of whom became confused and moved to attack the enemy prematurely. Lee's delicate plan was thrown into disarray, and the result was a confused and disjointed attack that the Federals easily repulsed.

Tom Gilham took a bad wound to the arm in this attack, and had to have the limb amputated afterward. John Zuber, also of Company K, was shot through the head and died shortly afterward. Gilham considered him the best man in the company. "If there ever was a soldier without a fault John Zuber was the man," Gilham wrote years later. "He was a pure Christian soldier." Jim Tom Moore, who had gone off to war as first sergeant of the Rome Light Guards—and a brand-new bridegroom—three years before, was captain of Company A in this fight. He received a severe gunshot wound in the hip, plus flesh wounds in the left arm, chest, throat, jaw, and scalp. He would live, but for him the war was over. Pvt. Sam Stephens, twenty-year-old "mischief-man" of Company G who back in 1861 burst Hawkinsville's old cannon to summon the members of the Pulaski Volunteers, here suffered his sixth and final wound of the war, a minié ball in the right thigh. The result was amputation, and Sam was out of the war, though he lived another half century afterward. In all, the Eighth suffered six killed, seventeen wounded, and two captured in the debacle known as the Battle of Chaffin's Farm, probably about a quarter of the regiment's strength by that time.[23]

Gradually the autumn passed into winter, and the cold weather and muddy roads of that season in Virginia brought a close to further active maneuvering. The troops settled into winter quarters in rude shacks conglomerated out of logs, sticks, mud, and such tents as they had, graced with chimneys made of barrels. Yet the siege went on with its danger and death. Clothes were scant and threadbare, food never adequate. Morale sank lower and lower. With the cessation of active campaigning, the men had time, as one of them put it, to "grieve over our lost cause, for we were satisfied that the fates were against us."[24]

The news from home was worst of all. The Yankees had been there. Rome fell on May 18, while the Eighth had been busy fighting at Spotsylvania. Retreating Confederate forces burned the bridge over the Oostanaula and hauled away the machinery of the Etowah Iron Works. They would have done the same with that of the Noble Brothers & Company Iron Works, one of only fifteen private foundries in the South to manufacture cannon for the Confederacy. Unable to remove the machinery, the gray-clad troops tried to wreck it but failed at that too. The Yankees would handle that task for them, burning the factory and blowing up the smokestacks after sending the machinery away to the North. Meanwhile, before Union troops moved into the town,

Confederate stragglers, former slaves, and renegade citizen had broken into houses and looted and vandalized over $100,000 worth of property. Finally, the Union army arrived and raised the Stars and Stripes over the courthouse.

The Federals requisitioned abandoned houses and other buildings as barracks and hospitals. They also confiscated large amounts of foodstuffs, but on the whole behaved with shocking decency and restraint. Contrary to Confederate propaganda, the Yankees respected the persons and the personal property (food and draft animals excepted) of the inhabitants. No one was assaulted—or even insulted—but for the men of the Eighth far away in Virginia, that was not the point, or at least not all of it. The problem was not what the Yankees were doing there but that they were there at all, not that the Federals were without mercy but that the Georgia civilians were at their mercy. Men, in this case those of companies A, E, and H, who had told themselves through more than three years of terrible war that they were fighting to protect their homes, their firesides, and, most of all, their womenfolk, now had to wonder what the point was in further resistance.[25]

Atlanta's turn came in September. By mid-July, Sherman's army was on the outskirts, throwing shells into the garrisoned and defended city. Then, at the beginning of September, the Confederate army, commanded by the Eighth's former division commander John B. Hood, could hold on no longer and had to retreat southward. With that the homes of Company F, the Fulton Grays, were behind Union lines. Sherman sensibly ordered noncombatants out of the city, still very much a potential battle zone, but the forced evacuation was a hardship for the citizens, some of them no doubt the families of Company F men.

In November, Sherman and his army marched out of Atlanta headed southeast, toward the homes of Company I in Greene County. To the surprise of many, Sherman veered away to the east of Macon, much to the relief of the families of Company C, but his army scored a path through the middle of the state all the way to Savannah, which he took shortly before Christmas. It was not that Sherman's men were everywhere nor that their depredations were extreme—the real danger to personal safety came from renegades and deserters of both armies who haunted the region where neither side had firm control. What ate at the hearts of Georgia soldiers in Virginia was that their families were coping with turbulent and possibly dangerous times back home and they were not there to protect them.

Desertions picked up again. After things had settled down in winter quarters early in 1864, desertions had dropped back to their previous negligible rate. Once the military campaigns opened that May, however—the one the Eighth was fighting in Virginia and the one their families were facing back in Georgia—they had increased dramatically, reaching the same rate they had the preceding autumn in East Tennessee. From June to November 1864, members of the Eighth deserted at a rate of more than two soldiers per month. With the active maneuver over and the army pinned into a hopeless defense against Grant's siege of Richmond, December 1864 saw that rate more than double.

The division had to keep up a strong picket line in front, lest it be surprised by a Union assault, yet an ever increasing trickle of soldiers took advantage of picket duty to desert to the enemy. On December 9 a member of Company A and one from Company B took advantage of a scouting patrol on the Darbytown Road to make good their escapes. The following February 14, two members of Company I went over together, and three days later no fewer than four members of Company E went into Union lines together. Just under a month later, on March 16, Company H had its own four-man desertion, and four days later another member of that company deserted along with a Company C soldier. By the end of March 1865, the total of those members of the regiment who had crossed the lines and taken the oath of allegiance since the previous December 1 had reached seventeen, a significant portion (probably about 20 percent) of the badly depleted regiment's potential manpower.

Confederate officers feared that men would also try sneaking off and making their way home without going over to the enemy, and to prevent this, the division maintained a second picket line in the *rear* of its trenches, just as strong as the one in front and entirely manned by specially picked soldiers, to try to apprehend such would-be deserters. Officers staged meetings to whip up the soldiers' Confederate patriotism, with fiery stump speeches from such skilled and admired officer-politicians as Brig. Gen. Henry Lewis Benning, of their sister brigade. Yet, as Reed had to admit, "the picket line in the rear, the meetings and the speeches were all for naught. A secret whisper, audible to the soldier alone, but trumpeting in his ear so loudly that he could hear nothing else, called him to go to his suffering mother, wife or children; and at last he would steal away."

Yet Reed was mistaken in thinking that the men were leaving in order to go directly to their families back in Georgia. While existing records make it difficult to determine with certainty when a man deserted and made his way directly home, they are sufficient to rule out that possibility in all but a very small handful of cases. The startling fact therefore emerges that the overwhelming majority of Eighth Georgia soldiers who deserted did so by going directly to the enemy and taking the oath of allegiance.

Who were these men and why did they go? The strongest factor in determining whether an Eighth Georgia soldier deserted (aside from status as a conscript in a few cases) was whether the Federals had visited or occupied his home county. Men from occupied or visited counties deserted at a rate almost fifteen times higher than those who knew their home environs to be unbesmirched by the tread of Yankee boots. Interestingly, men from towns—Atlanta, Macon, Savannah, and especially Rome—deserted at significantly higher rates than those from the more rural scenes of Greene, Oglethrope, Pulaski, and Meriwether counties, even taking into account factors of Yankee occupation. Pulaski County's Company G lost not a single man to desertion throughout the entire war, and save for a couple of conscripts, Oglethorpe's Company K could make the same claim. Not without reason have military writers since the ancient Romans maintained that "sturdy peasant lads" make the best soldiers.

The fact that these soldiers went straight into Union lines tells something of their motivation. By choosing that course they would not be home any time soon, to protect and care for their families, yet they would run vastly less risk of being apprehended by Confederate authorities and, very probably, put before a firing squad. It stands to reason, then, that they did not believe their families to be in imminent mortal danger either from hunger or from the hand of the enemy, and certainly did not believe their presence at home could have availed anything against the occupying Union armies. Yet the presence of Northern troops in their home districts made meaningless the concept of fighting to defend hearth and family. That concept had brought most of the men into the ranks and kept them there through hard years of conflict. Once that concept was gone, many men found they had little left for which to fight. Ultimately, in the Eighth Georgia, the soldier who deserted was opting to ensure his own survival, and eventual return to his family, rather than continue to risk life and limb in a war he now believed was senseless. The deserter was making his own separate peace, but the majority of those still able to fight would soldier on to the bitter end.[26]

I Will Be in My Place

Spring found the Eighth Georgia, or what was left of it, still holding its lines on the north bank of the James east of Richmond. They had no warning that anything was amiss until orders came on April 2 to pull out of their trenches and withdraw to the west, through Richmond. Information was hard to get, but something told them that this would be their last time as Confederate soldiers to march through Richmond as the Confederate capital. The weeping citizens, who lined the streets to see them go, seemed to know as much. Reed stopped and asked an old man and from him learned for the first time that Lee had suffered a serious disaster south of the James and was evacuating both Petersburg and Richmond. They took the cars in Richmond one last time and rode down to Petersburg to join the rest of the army in its desperate retreat westward.

Marching reinvigorated them. They were out of the accursed trenches and bomb-proofs and most of all they were out on the open roads of Virginia, roads that had always led them to victory in every other springtime of the war. Perhaps they would evade Grant, join the small Confederate army of Joseph Johnston in North Carolina, and still snatch victory out of the jaws of defeat.

They marched without food the first several days, while constant skirmishing went on at the flanks and rear of the column. When rations were finally issued at Farmville, Virginia, on Friday, April 7, the Yankees were on them again before John Reed could finish baking his corn pone. He burned his mouth bolting the hot dough as the regiment and one other double-quicked to the scene of the threatened Federal breakthrough. They deployed in a field dotted with scraggly pine saplings and charged toward the advancing foe. One last time the high-pitched wail of the Rebel Yell, first heard at Manassas so long ago, rose from their throats. One last time the Eighth Georgia was charging, firing, loading, and driving back its enemies. It was hand-to-hand in many parts of the line, and the Eighth's color-bearer even knocked down an opposing soldier with his flagstaff. Then almost as quickly as it started the fight was over. The Federals fell back, and, for the moment, the army's rear was safe again.

Pvt. Henry Alonzo Smith, of Company A, had enlisted as a musician but long since been diverted to more practical duties. Physically unequal to the rigors of frontline service, he had usually drawn assignment as a clerk at some rear-area headquarters. That had been his duty up until the evacuation of Richmond, five days before. Now everyone was in the ranks again, and Smith received a wound that resulted in the amputation of his right arm. Robert Tuggle, the last recruit to Company K, now had the added distinction of being the last man hit in the company, taking a bullet in the left arm. Company E's John Hill also had a distinction at Farmville. He was the regiment's only fatality in that action and the last member of the Eighth Georgia to die in battle.

The retreat went on. All day Saturday the remnants of the Eighth, and of the rest of the army, trudged wearily onward toward a place called Appomattox Court House, where more rations were supposed to be found. They camped just short of the place that night.

Next morning, Sunday, April 9, 1865, they were up again very early and stumbling forward all but numbed with fatigue and hunger. Up ahead, out of sight beyond a hill, they heard a flare-up of musketry, then silence, but the awareness of the presence of the enemy near the army's forward elements meant less right now than the quest for food. They were not too faint to give a rousing chorus of Rebel Yells for Gen. Lee as he galloped toward the front in his full dress uniform; they would always have strength enough to cheer their beloved commander. Then they spied nearby a Confederate teamster feeding corn to his team. They converged on the spot. Capt. Charles Harper of Company E scrabbled about in the mud and managed to scrounge up a respectable number of grains of parched corn, which he ate with relish. John Reed did even better, persuading the teamster to part with a small portion of his supply and carrying it off to share with his company.

Just as he got back to the regiment he heard one of his men say that the army had been surrendered. Reed flew into a rage and threatened to cut the man's head off. Soon they fell out to rest beside the road, and Reed sat munching parched corn—his men said they were not hungry. Col. Towers walked up and called Reed aside. Reed noticed that Towers was weeping—profusely. The colonel said that Lee had surrendered. Just then Reed saw a Federal officer galloping by with a white flag. There was no longer any room for doubt. The next few minutes—or perhaps it was hours—were a blur of grief. "The screams, curses, sobs and wailing around me made me forget myself," remembered Reed. The grief of his comrades was like "the raging sea." Sgt. J. W. Leigh was nearby, "one of the truest of the regiment," a man who never seemed to lose his confidence in victory. Now "he fell down and bellowed. He seemed to cough out great mouthfuls of bitterness, and his tears were the largest I ever saw fall."[27]

Thursday morning, April 13, as arranged in the surrender agreement, Field's division—or Hood's as they still liked to call themselves—marched out to stack their arms and receive their paroles, last of Lee's divisions to do so. The division and its constituent units dissolved there and then, and the Eighth Georgia Regiment was no more. They never surrendered the battle flag they had received back on the eve of the Seven Days. Lt. Col. Magruder hid it on his person and so took it home with him to Rome, where he used it as a cradle quilt to cover his baby son. The men of the Eighth, just over one hundred of them, made their way back to their homes in twos and threes, or alone, by whatever means of transportation they could manage, mostly on foot.[28]

"It was all over but the empty sleeves and wooden legs," wrote Tom Gilham, "and thousands of the bravest men that the country afforded, whose bones are now bleaching on the hills of Virginia." The bitterness was great, but time could heal even this wound, or at least dull its ache, and by 1876 John Reed could write that it was good that the Union had been preserved. Yet time's passage also lit the prewar years in memory's golden glow, and Reed, an old man in 1888, wrote in rapturous terms of the Old South that was gone—of tall cotton, fat hogs and cattle, lush corn, neat, prosperous, bountiful plantations, brave and cultured masters, and happy, contented slaves. It was not a picture with photographic accuracy, but it was a fair reflection of the vision of a society and culture that had moved thousands of Georgia boys to fight through four long years of war. The Old South of Reed's memories may have been in part a dream, but it was a dream for which soldiers fought and many of them died.[29]

As the old man who had once followed the flag of the Eighth Georgia finished writing his memoirs and thought back longingly to those days that would never come again, he reflected that perhaps he might see them once more after all. "What I have just said was behind me," the aged Reed explained, "has of late become prospect, and it beckons with inexpressible charm. . . . I cherish the hope that when a good Confederate like I was dies, he will go back to the Old South, and live his long lost life over and over. I will never tire of any detail. And when Hood's division marches, camps, or fights, I will be in my place in that body of incomparable soldiers. I do not now see how we can endure to act over our surrender."[30]

APPENDIX

COMPANY LETTERS, NAMES, AND COUNTIES

Company Letter	Company Name	Home County (Town)
A	Rome Light Guards	Floyd (Rome)
B	Oglethorpe Light Infantry	Chatham (Savannah)
C	Macon Guards	Bibb (Macon)
D	Echols Guards	Meriwether (Echols)
E	Miller Rifles	Floyd (Rome)
F	Atlanta Grays	Fulton (Atlanta)
G	Pulaski Volunteers	Pulaski
H	Floyd Infantry	Floyd (Rome)
I	Stephens Light Guards	Greene
K	Oglethorpe Rifles	Oglethorpe

OFFICERS AT THE FIRST BATTLE OF MANASSAS

Field and Staff
   Col. Francis S. Bartow (commanding brigade)
   Lt. Col. William M. Gardner (commanding regiment)
   Maj. Thomas L. Cooper
   Adjutant 1st Lt. John L. Branch
   Surgeon H. V. M. Miller
   Commissary Capt. George C. Norton
Company A
   Capt. E. J. Magruder
   1st Lt. S. H. Hall
   2nd Lt. Melvin Dwinnell
   Jr. 2nd Lt. G. R. Lumpkin
Company B
   Capt. Joseph J. West
   1st Lt. Hamilton Couper
   2nd Lt. A. F. Butler

Company C
    Capt. Lucius M. Lamar
    1st Lt. Matthew Ross
    2nd Lt. E. A. Wilcox
    Jr. 2nd Lt. H. B. Findley
    Jr. 2nd Lt. T. G. Hodgkins
Company D
    Capt. C. W. Howard
    1st Lt. H. E. Malone
    2nd Lt. E. C. Mobley
Company E
    Capt. John R. Towers
    1st Lt. Edward W. Hall
    2nd Lt. Dunlap S. Scott
    Jr. 2nd Lt. Armistead R. Harper
Company F
    Capt. James T. Lewis
    1st Lt. Seymour B. Love
    2nd Lt. Jennings M. C. Hulsey
    Jr. 2nd Lt. Bartley M. Smith
Company G
    Capt. T. D. Lawrence Ryan
    1st Lt. George W. Carruthers
    2nd Lt. William Charles Dougherty
    Jr. 2nd Lt. Simeon W. Taylor
Company H
    Capt. John Frederic Cooper
    1st Lt. Mark E. Cooper
    2nd Lt. John H. Reece
    Jr. 2nd Lt. Robert W. Echols
Company I
    Capt. George O. Dawson
    1st Lt. Thomas J. Blackwell
    2nd Lt. John C. Reed
    Jr. 2nd Lt. William H. Clark
Company K
    Capt. George Lumpkin
    1st Lt. Jacob Phinizy
    2nd Lt. Nathaniel H. Hunter
    Jr. 2nd Lt. William R. Wright

OFFICERS AT THE OUTSET OF THE 1862 CAMPAIGN

Field and Staff
  Col. Lucius M. Lamar
  Lt. Col. John R. Towers
  Maj. E. J. Magruder
  Adjutant 1st Lt. William F. Shellman
  Commissary Capt. George C. Norton
  Quartermaster Capt. E. A. Wilcox
Company A
  Capt. Sidney H. Hall
  1st Lt. Melvin Dwinnell
  2nd Lt. James T. Moore
Company B
  Capt. A. F. Butler
  1st Lt. Frederick Bliss
Company C
  Capt. C. M. Ballard
  1st Lt. T. G. Hodgkins
  2nd Lt. James H. Fields
Company D
  Capt. H. E. Malone
  1st Lt. R. J. Trammell
Company E
  Capt. Dunlap S. Scott
Company F
  Capt. James T. Lewis
  1st Lt. Seymour B. Love
  2nd Lt. Jennings M. C. Hulsey
  Jr. 2nd Lt. James W. Smith
Company G
  Capt. T. D. Lawrence Ryan
  1st Lt. John A. Young
  2nd Lt. Alexander Pipkin
Company H
  Capt. George N. Yarbrough
Company I
  Capt. George O. Dawson
  1st Lt. Thomas J. Blackwell
  2nd Lt. John C. Reed
  Jr. 2nd Lt. William H. Clark
Company K
  Capt. Jacob Phinizy
  2nd Lt. Thornberry J. Bowling
  Jr. 2nd Lt. William R. Wright

OFFICERS AT GETTYSBURG

Field and Staff
    Col. John R. Towers
    Lt. Col. E. J. Magruder
    Maj. George O. Dawson
    Adjutant 1st Lt. William F. Shellman
    Commissary Capt. George C. Norton
    Quartermaster Capt. E. A. Wilcox
Company A
    Capt. Sidney H. Hall
    1st Lt. Melvin Dwinnell
    2nd Lt. James T. Moore
Company B
    Capt. A. F. Butler
    1st Lt. Frederick Bliss
    2nd Lt. Sanford Branch
Company C
    Capt. C. M. Ballard
    1st Lt. T. G. Hodgkins
    2nd Lt. James H. Fields
    Jr. 2nd Lt. Amos Brantly
Company D
    Capt. H. E. Malone
    1st Lt. R. J. Trammell
Company E
    Capt. Dunlap S. Scott
Company F
    2nd Lt. James A. Adair
Company G
    Capt. John A. Young
Company H
    Capt. George N. Yarbrough
    1st. Lt. J. P. Duke
Company I
    Capt. Thomas J. Blackwell
    1st Lt. John C. Reed
Company K
    Capt. Thornberry J. Bowling
    2nd Lt. B. A. Christopher

OFFICERS AT THE OUTSET OF THE 1864 CAMPAIGN

Field and Staff
    Col. John R. Towers
    Lt. Col. E. J. Magruder
    Adjutant 1st Lt. William F. Shellman
    Commissary Capt. George C. Norton
    Quartermaster Capt. E. A. Wilcox
Company A
    Capt. James T. Moore
    2nd Lt. R. F. Hutchings
Company B
    None
Company C
    2nd Lt. Fred Walker
    Jr. 2nd Lt. E. P. Taylor
Company D
    None
Company E
    Capt. Dunlap S. Scott
Company F
    2nd Lt. James A. Adair
Company G
    None
Company H
    Capt. J. P. Duke
    1st Lt. Joseph Johnson
Company I
    Capt. Thomas J. Blackwell
    1st Lt. John C. Reed
Company K
    Capt. Thornberry J. Bowling
    2nd Lt. B. A. Christopher

OFFICERS AT THE CLOSE OF THE WAR

Field and Staff
  Col. John R. Towers
  Lt. Col. E. J. Magruder
  Adjutant 1st Lt. Amos W. Brantley
  Commissary Capt. George C. Norton
  Quartermaster Capt. E. A. Wilcox
Company A
  Capt. James T. Moore (in hospital, Augusta, Ga.)
  2nd Lt. R. F. Hutchings
Company B
  None
Company C
  2nd Lt. Fred Walker
  Jr. 2nd Lt. E. P. Taylor
Company D
  None
Company E
  Capt. Dunlap S. Scott
Company F
  2nd Lt. James A. Adair
Company G
  None
Company H
  Capt. J. P. Duke
  1st Lt. Joseph Johnson
Company I
  Capt. John C. Reed
Company K
  1st Lt. B. A. Christopher

CHAIN OF COMMAND

At First Manassas
    Army of the Shenandoah (Gen. Joseph E. Johnston)
      Second Brigade (Col. Francis S. Bartow)
      Eighth Georgia Regiment (Lt. Col. William M. Gardner)

In the Peninsula Campaign
    Army of Northern Virginia (Gen. Joseph E. Johnston; Gen. Robert E. Lee)
      Magruder's Command (Maj. Gen. John B. Magruder)
      First Division (Brig. Gen. David R. Jones)
        Third Brigade (Col. George T. Anderson)
        Eighth Georgia Regiment (Col. Lucius M. Lamar; Maj. E. J. Magruder)

In the Second Manassas Campaign
    Army of Northern Virginia (Gen. Robert E. Lee)
      Right Wing (Lt. Gen. James Longstreet)
      Jones's Division (Maj. Gen. David R. Jones)
      Jones's Brigade (Col. George T. Anderson)
      Eighth Georgia Regiment (Lt. Col. John R. Towers)

In the Gettysburg Campaign
    Army of Northern Virginia (Gen. Robert E. Lee)
      First Corps (Lt. Gen. James Longstreet)
      Hood's Division (Maj. Gen. John B. Hood)
      Anderson's Brigade (Brig. Gen. George T. Anderson)
      Eighth Georgia Regiment (Col. John R. Towers)

In 1864 and 1865
    Army of Northern Virginia (Gen. Robert E. Lee)
      First Corps (Lt. Gen. James Longstreet; Lt. Gen. Richard Anderson)
      Hood's Division (Maj. Gen. Charles W. Field)
      Anderson's Brigade (Brig. Gen. George T. Anderson)
      Eighth Georgia Regiment (Col. John R. Towers)

NOTES

Chapter 1: In Defense of Southern Rights

1. *Rome Courier*, July 21, 1863.

2. Roger D. Aycock, *All Roads Lead to Rome* (Roswell, Ga.: W. H. Wolfe Associates, 1981), 11, 39–40, 62–64, 66.

3. Compiled Service Records of Confederate Soldiers Who Served in Organizations from the State of Georgia, 8th Regiment Georgia Volunteer Infantry, National Archives, Microcopy 266, Reels 562–67; *Rome Courier*, 1861–1863 passim.

4. *Rome Courier*, Jan. 18, 1861.

5. Compiled Service Records; Aycock, *All Roads Lead to Rome*, 72; *Rome Courier*, Jan. 29, March 1, 1861; H. H. Wimpee, "A Boy's Recollection of the Civil War at Rome, Ga.," United Daughters of the Confederacy Collection, Floyd County, Georgia, Drawer 65, Box 54, Georgia Department of Archives and History; George S. Barnsley Diary, Barnsley Papers, Southern Historical Collection, University of North Carolina Library, Chapel Hill, Acc. No. 1521, pp. 6–8.

6. Wimpee, "A Boy's Recollection of the Civil War at Rome, Ga."

7. *Rome Courier*, April 16, 1861; U.S. War Department, *War of the Rebellion: A Compilation of the Official Records of the Union and Confederate Armies*, 128 vols. (Washington, D.C.: Government Printing Office, 1881–1901), Ser. 4, vol. 1, p. 217. Hereinafter cited as *OR*.

8. *Rome Courier*, April 16, 1861.

9. Ibid., April 30, 1861.

10. Ibid., April 30 and May 10, 1861.

11. Ibid., April 23 and May 17, 1861; Compiled Service Records.

12. *Rome Courier*, May 23, 1861; Aycock, *All Roads Lead to Rome*, 72.

13. Compiled Service Records.

14. Ibid.; Robert M. Reilly, *U.S. Military Small Arms 1816–1865*, (Baton Rouge, La.: Eagle Press, 1970) 33–34; *OR*, Ser. 4, vol. 1, p. 292.

15. *OR*, Ser. 1, vol. 52, pt. 2, p. 97.

16. *Rome Courier*, May 23, 1861.

17. Compiled Service Records; *Rome Courier*, May 23, 1861.

18. *Rome Courier*, May 31, 1861.

19. Robert Manson Myers, ed., *The Children of Pride: A True Story of Georgia and the Civil War* (New Haven, Conn.: Yale University Press, 1972), 690.

20. Editors of Time-Life Books, *Echoes of Glory: Arms and Equipment of the Union* (Alexandria, Va.: Time-Life Books, 1991), 95; *Rome Tribune*, n.d., but c. 1900; Aycock, *All Roads Lead to Rome*, 71; *Rome Courier*, May 28, 1861.

21. Aycock, *All Roads Lead to Rome*, 71.

22. Compiled Service Records; *Rome Courier*, May 28, 1861.

23. U.S. War Department, *The Official Military Atlas of the Civil War* (New York: Fairfax Press, 1983), p. 19, map 1; Robert W. Waitt Jr., *Confederate Military Hospitals in Richmond*, Official Publication #22, Richmond Civil War Centennial Committee, Richmond, Virginia, 1964, 31; *Rome Courier*, June 6, 1861.

24. Editors of Time-Life Books, *Echoes of Glory*, 88.

25. Lindsey P. Henderson, *The Oglethorpe Light Infantry: A Military History, Co. B,* Confederate War Series (Savannah, Civil War Centennial Commission, 1961), 1–2, 9; Kenneth Coleman and Charles Stephen Gurr, eds. *Dictionary of Georgia Biography* (Athens, Ga.: University of Georgia Press, 1983), 64–65.

26. William C. Davis, *A Government of Our Own: The Making of the Confederacy* (New York: Free Press, 1994).

27. Berrien M. Zettler, *War Stories and School-day Incidents for the Children* (New York: Neale, 1912), 43–44.

28. Henderson, *The Oglethorpe Light Infantry,* 9–17; Compiled Service Records; *Savannah Daily Morning News,* May 22, 1861; Derek Smith, "Bayard of the Confederacy," *Georgia Journal* 11 (Spring 1991): 7; W. S. Rockwell, *The Oglethorpe Light Infantry of Savannah in Peace and War: A Brief Sketch of Its Two Companies* (Savannah, Ga.: J. H. Est, 1984), 10.

29. "Georgia State Arms and Accoutrement Issues 1860–1861," Georgia Department of Archives and History, Atlanta; editors of Time-Life Books, *Echoes of Glory,* 30–31, 31–32.

30. Zettler, *War Stories,* 44–45.

31. Compiled Service Records.

32. Ibid.; Zettler, *War Stories,* 44–45; Hamilton Branch to his mother, May 25, 1861, Margaret Branch Sexton Collection, Ms. 25, Hargrett Library Special Collections, University of Georgia, Athens; Emory M. Thomas, *The Confederate State of Richmond: A Biography of the Capital* (Austin, Tex.: University of Texas Press, 1971), 22.

33. Compiled Service Records; *Official Military Atlas,* p. 19, map 1.

34. Compiled Service Records; editors of Time-Life Books, *Echoes of Glory: Arms and Equipment of the Confederacy,* 190.

35. Excerpts from an Autobiography of Joel S. Yarbrough, Georgia Department of Archives and History, Civil War Manuscripts, Drawer 283, Box 45; editors of Time-Life Books, *Echoes of Glory,* 32–33.

36. Compiled Service Records; *Hawkinsville Dispatch,* Aug. 10, 1879, p. 3; *Hawkinsville Dispatch and News,* n.d. but post-1907; Virginia Speer Harris and Hawkinsville Chapter, Daughters of the American Revolution, *History of Pulaski and Bleckly Counties,* Georgia, 1808–1956, 2 vols. (Macon, Ga.: J. W. Burke Co., 1957–1958), 1:971–972; untitled history of Company G plus roster, "Confederate Veteran" Papers, Perkins Library, Duke University.

37. Richard W. Iobst, *Civil War Macon: The History of a Confederate City* (Macon, Ga.: Mercer University Press, 1999), 5–6.

38. Ibid., 23–25

39. Ibid., 26–30

40. Ibid., 66.

41. William H. Maxey to his father, Sept. 5, 1861, Ms. 529, Hargrett Library Special Collections.

42. Arthur F. Raper, *Tenants of the Almighty* (New York: Macmillan, 1943), 32–33.

43. John C. Reed manuscript, Alabama Department of Archives and History, Montgomery, pp. 6–10.

44. Compiled Service Records.

45. Barnsley diary.

46. Compiled Service Records.

47. John C. Waugh, *The Class of 1846: From West Point to Appomattox: Stonewall Jackson, George McClellan, and Their Brothers* (New York: Warner Books, 1994); Compiled Service Records.

48. John L. Martin to his mother, May 30, 1861, Georgia Department of Archives and History, Civil War Miscellany, Drawer 283, Box 33.

49. Ibid.; Zettler, *War Stories,* 45–46; William H. Maxey to his father, June 2, 1861.

50. John L. Martin to his mother, May 30, 1861.

51. Ibid,; *Atlanta Journal,* Feb. 2, 1901.

52. *Rome Courier,* June 11, 1861.

53. *OR,* Ser. 1, vol. 51, pt. 2, p. 128.

54. *Rome Courier,* June 11, 1861.

Chapter 2: To Belong to the Southern Army

1. Hamilton Branch to his mother, June 4, 1861, Margaret Branch Sexton Collection, Ms. 25, Hargrett Library Special Collections, University of Georgia, Athens.

2. *Rome Courier,* June 11 and 13, 1861; Compiled Service Records of Confederate Soldiers Who Served in Organizations from the South of Georgia, 8th Regiment Georgia Volunteer Infantry, National Archives Microcopy 266, Reels 562–67; Melvin Dwinnell to his parents, July 13, 1861, Georgia Department of Archives and History, Civil War Miscellany, Drawer 283, box 24; Hamilton Branch to his mother, June 10, 1861; Berrien M. Zettler, *War Stories and School-day Incidents for the Children* (New York: Neale, 1912), 47–48.

3. Zettler, *War Stories,* 47–48.

4. *Rome Courier,* June 25, 1861; John Branch to his mother, June 14, 1861, Margaret Branch Sexton Collection, Ms. 25, Hargrett Library Special Collections, University of Georgia, Athens.

5. Jeffery Lash, *Destroyer of the Iron Horse: General Joseph E. Johnston and Confederate Rail Transport, 1861–1865* (Kent, Ohio: Kent State University Press, 1991), 15–17; *Rome Courier,* June 25 and 28, 1861.

6. *Rome Courier,* June 25 and 28, 1861.

7. James Pope Martin to his parents, June 19, 1861, in William H. Davidson, *Brooks of Honey and Butter: Plantations and People of Meriwether County Georgia,* 2 vols. (Alexander City, Ala.: Outlook Publishing Co., 1971), 2:121–22.

8. Sanford Branch to his mother, June 27, 1861, Margaret Branch Sexton Collection, Ms. 25, Hargrett Library Special Collections, University of Georgia, Athens.

9. *Rome Courier,* June 28, 1861; U. S War Department, *War of the Rebellion: A Compilation of the Official Records of the Union and Confederate Armies,* 128 vols. (Washington, D.C.: Government Printing Office, 1881–1901), Ser. 1 vol. 2, p. 470.

10. *Rome Courier,* June 28, 1861; Sanford Branch to his mother, June 27, 1861; Richard P. Watters to his sister, June 18, 1861, Georgia Department of Archives and History, Civil War Miscellany, Drawer 9, Box 77.

11. Zettler, *War Stories,* 49–51.

12. Hamilton Branch to his mother, June 20, 1861.

13. W. B. Dasher reminiscences, Georgia Department of Archives and History, Civil War Miscellany, Drawer 283, Box 22.

14. Sanford Branch to his mother, June 27, 1861.

15. John C. Reed manuscript, Alabama Department of Archives and History, Montgomery pp. 12–13.

16. Leonidas Howell to his grandparents, July 28, 1861, Howell Family Papers, Georgia Department of Archives and History, Civil War Miscellany, Drawer 283, Box 28.

17. *Rome Courier,* June 28, 1861.

18. Cornelia McDonald, *A Diary with Reminiscences of the War and Refugee Life in the Shenandoah Valley, 1861–1865* (Nashville: Cullom and Gertner Co., 1934), 19–20.

19. *Hawkinsville Dispatch,* July 17, 1879.

20. Reed manuscript, pp. 10–12.

21. *Rome Courier,* July 2, 1861.

22. Ibid., July 16, 1861; John Branch to his mother, July 14, 1861.

23. Sanford Branch to his mother, July 8, 1861.

24. John Branch to his mother, July 14, 1861; *Rome Courier,* July 25, 1861.

25. *Rome Courier,* July 26, 1861.

26. Ibid., Aug. 8, 1861, and July 7, 1863.

27. Ibid., Aug. 8, 1861; Henry C. Harper diary, Confederate Miscellany, I-b, Special Collections, Emory University, Atlanta, p. 8.

Chapter 3: Never Give Up the Field

1. *Savannah Republican,* July 29, 1861; Berrien M. Zettler, *War Stories and School-day Incidents for the Children* (New York: Neale, 1912), 52; *Richmond Dispatch,* July 29, 1861.
2. *Rome Weekly Courier,* Aug. 2, 1861; John C. Reed manuscript, Alabama Department of Archives and History, Montgomery, p. 15; *Savannah Republican,* July 29, 1861; R. H. Cole to his mother, July 24, 1861, in *Savannah Morning News,* July 31, 1861.
3. Zettler, *War Stories,* 52; Reed manuscript, p. 15; R. H. Cole to his mother, July 24, 1861.
4. William C. Davis, *Battle at Bull Run: A History of the First Major Campaign of the Civil War* (Garden City, N.Y.: Doubleday, 1977), 134–35.
5. Ibid., 132–34.
6. Ibid., 127–31.
7. R. H. Cole to his mother, July 24, 1861; Zettler, *War Stories,* 52–53.
8. Thomas D. Gilham, "Oglethorpe Rifles: A Full History of This Celebrated Company," in n.a., *This They Remembered* (Columbus, Ga.: Brentwood University Press, 1986), 44.
9. Zettler, *War Stories,* 53; James B. Grant to his mother, July 22, 1861, in *Augusta Daily Constitutionalist,* Aug. 3, 1861; R. H. Cole to his mother, July 24, 1861.
10. R. H. Cole to his mother, July 24, 1861.
11. Gilham, "Oglethorpe Rifles," 44–45.
12. Zettler, *War Stories,* 55.
13. Reed manuscript, p. 15; R. H. Cole to his mother, July 24, 1861; *Atlanta Journal,* Feb. 2, 1901.
14. Reed manuscript, p. 15; *Atlanta Journal,* Feb. 2, 1901.
15. Zettler, *War Stories,* 55–56.
16. Reed manuscript, p. 15; R. H. Cole to his mother, July 24, 1861.
17. Jeffrey Lash, *Destroyer of the Iron Horse: General Joseph E. Johnston and Confederate Rail Transport, 1861–1865* (Kent, Ohio: Kent State University Press, 1991), 15–17; R. H. Cole to his mother, July 24, 1861.
18. R. H. Cole to his mother, July 24, 1861; Zettler, *War Stories,* 58.
19. Ibid.
20. *Rome Weekly Courier,* Aug. 2, 1861; R. H. Cole to his mother, July 24, 1861.
21. Zettler, *War Stories,* 59.
22. *Rome Weekly Courier,* Aug. 2, 1861; R. H. Cole to his mother, July 24, 1861.
23. W. H. Maxey to his father, July 26, 1861, Hargrett Library Special Collections, University of Georgia, Ms. 529; R. P. Watters to his sister, July 28, 1861, Georgia Department of Archives and History, Civil War Manuscripts, Drawer 9, Box 77.
24. Zettler, *War Stories,* 60–61.
25. Davis, *Battle at Bull Run,* 168–70.
26. Ibid., 159–68.
27. Zettler, *War Stories,* 61; Davis, *Battle at Bull Run,* 170–77.
28. Excerpts from an Autobiography of Joel S. Yarbrough, Georgia Department of Archives and History, Civil War Miscellany, Drawer 283, Box 45; Louise C. Murphy, "My UDC Ancestor—Simeon Fletcher Culpepper," Georgia Department of Archives and History, Civil War Miscellany, Drawer 283, Box 22.
29. Thomas Lowndes Wragg to his father, July 23, 1861, Library of Congress, Miscellaneous Manuscript Collection, Container 257; Vardy P. Sisson reminiscences in *Atlanta Journal,* Feb. 2, 1901; Hamilton Branch to his mother, July 23, 1861, in Edward G. Longacre, "Three Brothers Face Their Baptism of Battle, July 1861," *Georgia Historical Quarterly* 61 (1977): 164; Reed manuscript, p. 16; Davis, *Battle at Bull Run,* 177; Zettler, *War Stories,* 61.

30. Reed manuscript, p. 15.

31. Ibid., p. 16; Yarborough autobiography.

32. Reed manuscript, pp. 16–17; Gilham, "Oglethorpe Rifles," 45.

33. Zettler, *War Stories,* 62; George S. Barnsley diary, Barnsley Papers, Southern Historical Collection, University of North Carolina Library, Chapel Hill, Acc. No. 1521.

34. *Atlanta Journal,* Feb. 2, 1861; Zettler, *War Stories,* 63; James B. Grant to his mother, July 22, 1861, in *Augusta Daily Constitutionalist,* Aug. 3, 1861.

35. Zettler, *War Stories,* 62–64; Barnsley diary.

36. Zettler, *War Stories,* 64; *Hawkinsville Dispatch,* July 17, 1879.

37. Reed manuscript, p. 17; R. H. Cole to his mother, July 24, 1861; *Atlanta Journal,* Feb. 2, 1901; Barnsley diary.

38. Barnsley diary; Reed manuscript, p. 17.

39. *Atlanta Journal,* clipping, n.d.

40. Zettler, *War Stories,* 64; Davis, *Battle at Bull Run,* 178.

41. Zettler, *War Stories,* 64–65; *Atlanta Journal,* Feb. 2, 1901.

42. Reed manuscript, p. 19.

43. Ibid.; Barnsley diary.

44. Hamilton Branch to his mother, July 25, 1861, in Edward G. Longacre, "Three Brothers Face Their Baptism of Battle, July 1861," *Georgia Historical Quarterly* 61 (1977): 165–66.

45. Reed manuscript, p. 20.

46. Ibid., pp. 19–20.

47. Barnsley diary.

48. Reed manuscript, p. 20.

49. Thomas Lowndes Wragg to his father, July 23, 1861.

50. Reed manuscript, p. 20; James B. Grant to his mother, July 21, 1861; James Pope Martin to his family, Aug. 6, 1861, in William H. Davidson, *Brooks of Honey and Butter: Plantations and People of Meriwether County, Georgia* (Alexander City, Ala.: Outlook Publishing Company, 1971), 128–29.

51. Reed manuscript, p. 20; Murphy, "My UDC Ancestor"; *Atlanta Daily Intelligencer,* Aug. 18, 1861; James Pope Martin to his family, Aug. 6, 1861.

52. George M. Battey Jr., *A History of Rome and Floyd County* (Atlanta: Webb and Vary Co., 1922); *Rome Weekly Courier,* Aug. 6, 1861; James Pope Martin to his family, Aug. 6, 1861, in Davidson, *Brooks of Honey and Butter,* 127.

53. James B. Grant to his mother, July 22, 1861; Zettler, *War Stories,* 66; *Atlanta Daily Intelligencer,* Aug. 18, 1861.

54. *Atlanta Journal,* clipping, n.d.

55. Barnsley diary.

56. Reed manuscript, p. 21.

57. Yarbrough autobiography; S. B. Love to "Dear C.," July 24, 1861, in *Atlanta Daily Intelligencer,* Aug. 1, 1861.

58. James B. Grant to his mother, July 21, 1861.

59. Thomas Lowndes Wragg to his father, Aug. 7, 1861.

60. Sanford W. Branch to his mother, July 26, 1861; Hamilton Branch to his mother, July 23, 1861, in Longacre, "Three Brothers," 164–68.

61. *Atlanta Southern Confederacy,* July 28, 1861; *Atlanta Daily Intelligencer,* Aug. 18, 1861; Reed manuscript, p. 22.

62. Barnsley diary.

63. Zettler, *War Stories,* 66–67.

64. Rome United Daughters of the Confederacy, "The First Battle of Manassas," n.d.; Barnsley diary.

65. Barnsley diary.

66. *Atlanta Daily Intelligencer,* Aug. 18, 1861. However, the report of the Sixty-ninth's senior surviving (noncaptured) officer, Capt. James Kelly, states: "Acting Lieutenant-Colonel Haggerty was

killed by a Louisiana zouave, whom he pursued as the latter was on his retreat with his regiment into the woods." U.S. War Department, *War of the Rebellion: A Compilation of the Official Records of the Union and Confederate Armies,* 128 vols. (Washington, D.C.: Government Printing Office, 1881–1901), Ser. 1, vol. 2, p. 372. The report of William T. Sherman, however, adds circumstances that tend to support the claim that it was a soldier of the Eighth, not a Louisiana Zouave, who shot Haggerty: "Advancing slowly and cautiously with the head of the column, to give time for the regiments in succession to close up their ranks, we first encountered a party of the enemy retreating along a cluster of pines. Lieutenant-Colonel Haggerty, of the Sixty-ninth, without orders, rode out and endeavored to intercept their retreat. One of the enemy, in full view, at short range, shot Haggerty, and he fell dead from his horse. The Sixty-ninth opened fire upon this party, which was returned."

67. Reed manuscript, p. 23.

68. James H. Cooper to his sister, July 25, 1861, in James E. Bagwell, "James Hamilton Cooper, Georgia Rice Planter" (Ph.D. dissertation, University of Southern Mississippi, 1978).

69. *Hawkinsville Dispatch,* July 10, 1879; Reed manuscript, p. 24.

70. Zettler, *War Stories,* 67.

71. *Savannah Republican,* July 29, 1861.

72. Reed manuscript, p. 24; James B. Grant to his mother, July 22, 1861.

73. *Atlanta Daily Intelligencer,* Aug. 18, 1861.

74. James B. Grant to his mother, July 22, 1861; Barnsley diary.

75. Barnsley diary; Zettler, *War Stories,* 70.

76. *Savannah Republican,* July 29, 1861; *Richmond Dispatch,* July 29, 1861; Zettler, *War Stories,* 69.

77. Reed manuscript, pp. 25–26.

78. *Savannah Republican,* July 29, 1861; *Richmond Dispatch,* July 29, 1861.

79. Barnsley diary.

80. Ibid.; Reed manuscript, p. 27.

81. Barnsley diary.

82. James B. Grant to his mother, July 22, 1861; Addison R. Tinsley to his father, July 24, 1861, in *Savannah Morning News,* July 30, 1861; *Savannah Republican,* July 29, 1861.

83. Yarbrough autobiography.

84. Letter signed "Upson," July 27, 1861, United Daughters of the Confederacy, Rome, Georgia; Charles M. Harper reminiscences, United Daughters of the Confederacy, Rome, Georgia.

85. James B. Grant to his mother, July 22, 1861; Yarbrough autobiography; *Savannah Republican,* July 29, 1861.

86. Reed manuscript, p. 28.

87. *Georgia Weekly Telegraph* (Macon), Oct. 11, 1861.

88. Barnsley diary.

89. *Georgia Weekly Telegraph* (Macon), Oct. 11, 1861.

90. Barnsley diary.

91. Reed manuscript, p. 29.

92. William W. Bennett, *A Narrative of the Great Revival in the Southern Armies During the Late Civil War Between the States of the Federal Union* (Philadelphia: Claxton, Remsen & Haffelfinger, 1877), 133.

93. Charles H. Smith, *Bill Arp from the Uncivil War to Date* (Atlanta: Hudgins Publishing, 1903), 41–42.

94. Ibid., 42.

95. Zettler, *War Stories,* 71–72.

Chapter 4: All Quiet Along the Potomac

1. George S. Barnsley diary, Barnsley Papers, Southern Historical Collection, University of North Carolina, Chapel Hill, Acc. No. 1521.

2. James Pope Martin to his family, July 26 and Aug. 6, 1861, in William H. Davidson, *Brooks of Honey and Butter: Plantations and People of Meriwether County, Georgia* (Alexander City, Ala.: Outlook Publishing Company, 1971), 127–29.

3. *Augusta Daily Constitutionalist,* July 30, 1861; James Pope Martin to his family, July 26, 1861, in Davidson, *Brooks of Honey and Butter,* 127; Excerpts from an Autobiography of Joel S. Yarbrough, Georgia Department of Archives and History, Civil War Miscellany, Drawer 283, Box 45.

4. R. H. Cole to his mother, July 24, 1861, in *Savannah Morning News,* July 31, 1861; James B. Grant to his mother, July 22, 1861, in *Augusta Daily Constitutionalist,* Aug. 3, 1861.

5. Frederick H. Dyer, *A Compendium of the War of the Rebellion,* 3 vols. (New York: T. Yoseloff, 1959), 3:895. U.S. War Department, *War of the Rebellion: A Compilation of the Official Records of the Union and Confederate Armies,* 128 vols. (Washington, D.C.: Government Printing Office, 1881-1901), Ser. 1, vol. 2, p. 477. Hereinafter cited as *OR.*

6. Richard P. Watters to his sister, July 28, 1861, Georgia Department of Archives and History, Civil War Miscellany, Drawer 9, Box 77; *Rome Courier,* Aug. 6, 1861.

7. *Hawkinsville Dispatch,* July 24, 1879; Berrien M. Zettler, *War Stories and School-Day Incidents for the Children* (New York: Neale, 1912), 73.

8. *Hawkinsville Dispatch,* July 24, 1879; James B. Grant to his mother, July 22, 1861.

9. *Augusta Daily Constitutionalist,* Aug. 17, 1861; Reuben S. Norton diary, quoted in Wade Banister Gassman, "A History of Rome and Floyd County, Georgia, in the Civil War" (master's thesis, Emory University, 1966); Thomas Lowndes Wragg to "Perrie," July 31, 1861, Library of Congress, Miscellaneous Manuscript Collection, Container 257; Yarbrough autobiography.

10. Richard P. Watters to his sister, July 28, 1861.

11. Yarbrough autobiography; *Rome Weekly Courier,* Aug. 6, 1861; *Atlanta Southern Confederacy,* Aug. 6, 1861.

12. Derek Smith, "Bayard of the Confederacy," *Georgia Journal* 11 (Spring 1991): 11.

13. William W. Bennett, *A Narrative of the Great Revival in the Southern Armies During the Late Civil War Between the States of the Federal Union* (Philadelphia: Clayton, Remsen & Haffelfinger, 1877), 110.

14. James B. Grant to his mother, July 22, 1861.

15. Barnsley diary.

16. John Jones to Rev. and Mrs. C. C. Jones, July 31, 1861, in Robert Manson Myers, ed., *The Children of Pride: A True Story of Georgia and the Civil War* (New Haven, Conn.: Yale University Press, 1972), 726.

17. "War's First Harvest," Georgia Department of Archives and History, Civil War Miscellany, Drawer 283, Box 27.

18. *Savannah Morning News,* July 24, 1861.

19. John C. Reed manuscript, Alabama Department of Archives and History, Montgomery, p. 34; *Georgia Weekly Telegraph* (Macon), Oct. 11, 1861.

20. *Hawkinsville Dispatch,* July 24, 1879; Reed manuscript, p. 34; Samuel J. G. Brewer to his wife, Aug. 26, 1861, in H. Candler Thaxton, ed., *My Dear Wife from Your Devoted Husband: Letters from a Rebel Soldier to His Wife* (Warrington, Fla.: privately printed, 1968).

21. Richard P. Watters to his brother, July 31, 1861, Georgia Department of Archives and History, Civil War Miscellany, Drawer 9, Box 77; Thomas Lowndes Wragg to "Perrie," July 31, 1861.

22. A. D. Craver to James Martin, Sept. 6, 1861, in Davidson, *Brooks of Honey and Butter,* 132; Barnsley diary; *Hawkinsville Dispatch,* July 24, 1879; Richard P. Watters to his sister, Aug. 28, 1861.

23. Richard P. Watters to his sister, Aug. 28 and Oct. 12, 1861; Samuel J. G. Brewer to his wife, Sept. 1, 1861, in Thaxton, *My Dear Wife.*

24. Samuel J. G. Brewer to his wife, Aug. 2, 1861, in Thaxton, *My Dear Wife*; Richard P. Watters to his brother, Sept. 3, 1861; James Pope Martin to his parents, Aug. 6, 1861, in Davidson, *Brooks of Honey and Butter,* 129.

25. Sanford Branch to his mother, July 26, Sept. ? and Sept. 1, 1861, Margaret Branch Sexton

Collection, Ms. 25, Hargrett Library Special Collections, University of Georgia, Athens; *Atlanta Southern Confederacy*, Aug. 6, 1861.

26. James Pope Martin to his parents, July 28 and Aug. 6, 1861, in Davidson, *Brooks of Honey and Butter*, 127–28.

27. John Jones to Rev. and Mrs. C. C. Jones, July 31, 1861, and John Jones to Col. William Maxwell and Rev. D. L. Buttolph, Oct. 4, 1861, in Myers, *Children of Pride*, 726–61; James Pope Martin to his parents, Aug. 6, 1861, in Davidson, *Brooks of Honey and Butter*, 128.

28. James Pope Martin to his mother, Aug. 19, 1861, in Davidson, *Brooks of Honey and Butter*, 130.

29. Robert E. L. Krick, "Francis Stebbins Bartow," National Park Service—Manassas National Battlefield Park website, www.nps.gov/mana/potpourri/people/bartow.htm.

30. Undated clipping of the *Savannah Republican* in Barnsley diary.

31. Richard P. Watters to his sister, Aug. 28, 1861.

32. *OR*, Ser. 1, vol. 5, p. 778; Richard P. Watters to his brother, Sept. 13, 1861.

33. *Hawkinsville Dispatch*, July 10, 1879; Richard P. Watters to his brother, Sept. 18, 1861, and to his sister, Oct. 9, 1861. Reed manuscript, p. 34.

34. Thomas Lowndes Wragg to his father, n.d. (ca. Sept. 9, 1861); Richard P. Watters to his brother, Oct. 3, 1861.

35. Richard P. Watters to his brother, Sept. 18, 1861.

36. Zettler, *War Stories*, 75–76.

37. Richard P. Watters to his brother, Sept. 18, 1861.

38. *OR*, Ser. 1, vol. 5, pp. 882–83.

39. Richard P. Watters to his sister, Oct. 9, 1861.

40. Richard P. Watters to his sister, Dec. 8, 1861.

41. Bennett, *Narrative of the Great Revival*, 133–36.

42. *Atlanta Daily Intelligencer*, Oct. 29, 1861.

43. *Atlanta Journal*, Aug. 17, 1901; Samuel J. G. Brewer to his wife, Dec. 27, 1861, in Thaxton, *My Dear Wife*, 39; Thomas L. Wragg to his father, Dec. 26, 1861.

44. Samuel J. G. Brewer to his wife, Dec. 27, 1861, Jan. 12 and 29, Feb. 16 and 18, 1862, in Thaxton, *My Dear Wife*, 39–48.

Chapter 5: We Must Not Let the Yankees Take Richmond

1. Richard P. Watters to his sister, March 1, 1862, Georgia Department of Archives and History, Civil War Miscellany, Drawer 9, Box 77.

2. Hamilton Branch to his mother, March 17 and April 7, 1862, Margaret Branch Sexton Collection, Ms. 25, Hargrett Library Special Collections, University of Georgia, Athens; *Rome Courier*, April 8, 1862.

3. *Rome Courier*, April 24, 1862; Hamilton Branch to his mother, April 9, 1862.

4. *Rome Courier*, April 22, 1862; Hamilton Branch to his mother, April 11, 12, and 14, 1862.

5. Berrien M. Zettler, *War Stories and School-day Incidents for the Children* (New York: Neale, 1912), 83–84; Val C. Giles, *Rags and Hope: The Recollections of Val C. Giles, Four Years with Hood's Brigade, Fourth Texas Infantry, 1861–1865*, Mary Lasswell, ed. (New York: Coward-McCann, 1961), 117–18.

6. *Rome Courier*, April 22, 1862; Hamilton Branch to his mother, April 14 and 15, 1862.

7. Zettler, *War Stories*, 84–86; *Rome Courier*, May 1, 1862.

8. *Richmond Dispatch*, May 23, 1862; Zettler, *War Stories*, 84–85; John C. Reed manuscript, Alabama Department of Archives and History, Montgomery, p. 42.

9. Zettler, *War Stories*, 84–86; B. M. Zettler, "Magruder Peninsula Campaign," *Confederate Veteran* 8 (1900):197; Hamilton Branch to his mother, April 17, 1862; U.S. War Department, *War of the Rebellion: A Compilation of the Official Records of the Union and Confederate Armies*, 128 vols. (Wash-

ington D.C.: Government Printing Office, 1881–1901), Ser. 1, vol. 11, pt. 1, p. 407. Hereinafter cited as *OR*.

10. Zettler, *War Stories,* 86–87; *Atlanta Constitution,* April 10 and 17, 1887; *OR,* Ser. 1, vol. 11, pt. 1, pp. 407–8, 420; Reed manuscript, pp. 34–35.

11. *Hawkinsville Dispatch,* July 24, 1879.

12. *Rome Courier,* May 1, 1862; *Hawkinsville Dispatch,* July 24, 1879; *Atlanta Constitution,* April 10, 1887; Reed manuscript, p. 35.

13. *Hawkinsville Dispatch,* July 24, 1879.

14. Reed manuscript, p. 36.

15. *Atlanta Constitution,* April 10, 1887; *Rome Courier,* April 1, 1862.

16. *Rome Courier,* April 1, 1862; Thomas D. Gilham, "Oglethorpe Rifles: A Full History of This Celebrated Company," in n.a., *This They Remembered* (Columbus, Ga.: Brentwood University Press, 1986), 49.

17. *Rome Courier,* May 27, June 5, and July 4, 1862.

18. Reed manuscript, p. 38.

19. Tom Hodgkins to "Mollie," July 17, 1862, Georgia Department of Archives and History, Civil War Miscellany, Drawer 283, Box 28.

20. *Hawkinsville Dispatch,* July 24, 1879; *Southern Historical Society Papers,* 28 (1900): 293; *Rome Courier,* July 4, 1862.

21. Zettler, *War Stories,* 95–96.

22. Ibid., 89–94.

23. William J. Miller, " 'Weather Still Execrable': Climatological Notes on the Peninsula Campaign, March through August 1862," in *The Peninsula Campaign of 1862: Yorktown to the Seven Days,* 3 vols. (Campbell, Calif.: Savas, 1997), 3:187.

24. *OR,* Ser. 1, vol. 11, pt. 2, pp. 662, 690, 706.

25. *Rome Courier,* July 8, 1862.

26. Berrien M. Zettler, "Can't Leave If the Battle Is to Begin," *Confederate Veteran* 9 (1901): 114–15.

27. Samuel J. G. Brewer to his wife, in H. Candler Thaxton, ed., *My Dear Wife from Your Devoted Husband: Letters from a Rebel Soldier to His Wife* (Warrington, Fla.: privately printed, 1968), 57.

28. *Third Annual Report of the State Historian of New York, 1897* (New York: Wynkoop Hallenbeck Crawford, 1898), 23–32; Stephen W. Sears, *To the Gates of Richmond: The Peninsula Campaign* (New York: Ticknor & Fields, 1992), 258–59; *OR,* Ser. 1, vol. 11, pt. 2, p. 706; E. J. Magruder to John R. Towers, January 19, 1888, private collection of Zack Waters, Rome, Georgia.

29. "E. J. Magruder" manuscript, United Daughters of the Confederacy Rome–Floyd County Public Library Special Collection.

30. *OR,* Ser. 1, vol. 11, pt. 2, p. 707; Miller, " 'Weather Still Execrable,' " 3:187–88; *Rome Courier,* July 8 and 25, 1862.

31. *OR,* Ser. 1, vol. 11, pt. 2, p. 707–8; Miller, " 'Weather Still Execrable,' " 3:187–88.

32. *Rome Courier,* July 8, 1862.

33. Miller, " 'Weather Still Execrable,' " 3:188; Gilham, "Oglethorpe Rifles," 49.

Chapter 6: Resistless as an Ocean Tide

1. *Rome Courier,* July 17, 1862.

2. Samuel J. G. Brewer to his wife, in H. Candler Thaxton, ed., *My Dear Wife from Your Devoted Husband: Letters from a Rebel Soldier to His Wife* (Warrington, Fla.: privately printed, 1968), 63; *Rome Courier,* Aug. 13, 1862.

3. *Rome Courier,* July 26 and Aug. 13, 1862.

4. Samuel J. G. Brewer to his wife, in Thaxton, *My Dear Wife,* 59–63.

5. *Rome Courier,* April 22 and Aug. 19, 1862.

6. Ibid., July 17, 24, and 25, 1862.

7. Ibid., July 26 and Aug. 13 and 19, 1862; Samuel J. G. Brewer to his wife, in Thaxton, *My Dear Wife,* 65.

8. *Rome Courier,* Aug. 19 and 22, 1862; Compiled Service Records of Confederate Soldiers Who Served in Organizations from the State of Georgia, 8th Regiment Georgia Volunteer Infantry, Microcopy 226–66, National Archives.

9. *Rome Courier,* Aug. 22, 1862; Samuel J. G. Brewer to his wife, in Thaxton, *My Dear Wife,* 68.

10. *Rome Courier,* Aug. 19, 1862.

11. Ibid., Sept. 12, 1862; John C. Reed manuscript, Alabama Department of Archives and History, Montgomery, 45–47; U.S. War Department, *War of the Rebellion: A Compilation of the Official Records of the Union and Confederate Armies,* 128 vols. (Washington, D.C.: Government Printing Office, 1881–1901), Ser. 1, vol. 12, pt. 1, p. 62. Hereinafter cited as *OR.*

12. Reed manuscript, pp. 48–49.

13. *Rome Courier,* Sept. 11 and 12, 1862; *OR,* Ser. 1, vol. 12, pt. 1, pp. 58, 62, 564.

14. *Rome Courier,* Sept. 9, 1862; Berrien M. Zettler, *War Stories and School-day Incidents for the Children* (New York: Neale, 1912), 97–98.

15. Zettler, *War Stories,* 98–99.

16. *OR,* Ser. 1, vol. 12, pt. 1, pp. 384, 386, 564, 579.

17. Zettler, *War Stories,* 103–5.

18. Reed manuscript, p. 49; Thomas D. Gilham, "Oglethorpe Rifles: A Full History of This Celebrated Company," in n.a., *This They Remembered* (Columbus, Ga.: Brentwood University Press, 1986), 49.

19. *OR,* Ser. 1, vol. 12, pt. 1, p. 564.

20. Reed manuscript, pp. 49–50.

21. Zettler, *War Stories,* 104–6.

22. *OR,* Ser. 1, vol. 12, pt. 2, pp. 384, 386, 564, 579.

23. Reed manuscript, p. 50; *OR,* Ser. 1, vol. 12, pt. 2, 557–58, 565, 579–80.

24. Reed manuscript, pp. 51–52; Zettler, *War Stories,* 107.

25. John J. Hennessy, *Return to Bull Run: The Campaign and Battle of Second Manassas* (New York: Simon & Schuster, 1993), 407–12; *OR,* Ser. 1, vol. 12, pt. 2, p. 595; Zettler, *War Stories,* 107–8.

26. Hennessy, *Return to Bull Run,* 462; *OR,* Ser. 1, vol. 12, pt. 2, p. 595; *Rome Courier,* Sept. 9, 1862; Reed manuscript, p. 53.

27. Reed manuscript, p. 53; *OR,* Ser. 1, vol. 12, pt. 2, pp. 558, 595.

28. Zettler, *War Stories,* 109–16.

29. Reed manuscript, p. 54.

30. Gilham, "Oglethorpe Rifles," p. 49; *Rome Courier,* Oct. 10, 1862.

31. *Rome Courier,* Sept. 9, 1862.

32. *OR,* Ser. 1, vol. 19, pt. 1, pp. 839, 885–86; Gilham, "Oglethorpe Rifles," 50.

33. *Atlanta Southern Confederacy,* October 3, 1862; *Rome Courier,* Oct. 9, 1862.

34. Gilham, "Oglethorpe Rifles," 50.

35. *OR,* Ser. 1, vol. 19, pt. 1, pp. 839, 885–86; *Rome Courier,* Oct. 9, 1862.

36. See Steven E. Woodworth, *Davis and Lee at War* (Lawrence: University Press of Kansas, 1995).

37. *OR,* Ser. 1, vol. 19, pt. 1, pp. 839, 885–86, 909; Douglas Southall Freeman, *Lee's Lieutenants: A Study in Command,* 3 vols. (New York: Scribner's, 1943), 2:166–83.

38. *OR,* Ser. 1, vol. 19, pt. 1, pp. 839–40, 885–86, 909; John Michael Priest, *Antietam: The Soldiers' Battle* (New York: Oxford University Press, 1993; originally published 1989), 9.

39. Excerpts from an Autobiography of Joel S. Yarbrough, Georgia Department of Archives and History, Civil War Miscellany, Drawer 283, Box 45.

40. Gilham, "Oglethorpe Rifles," 50; *Rome Courier,* Oct. 10, 1862.

41. *OR,* Ser. 1, vol. 19, pt. 1, pp. 840, 909; Priest, *Antietam,* 117–21; *Atlanta Southern Confederacy,* Oct. 3, 1862; George L. Aycock to Joseph Watters, Sept. 22, 1862, Georgia Department of Archives and History, Civil War Miscellany, Drawer 9, Box 77.

42. George L. Aycock to Joseph Watters, Sept. 22, 1862; *Rome Courier,* Oct. 24, 1862.

43. *Atlanta Southern Confederacy,* Oct. 3, 1862.

44. Priest, *Antietam,* 331; W. B. Dasher reminiscences, Georgia Department of Archives and History, Civil War Miscellany, Drawer 283, Box 22.

45. Priest, *Antietam,* 31. Regarding the effect of Lee's victories on Confederate civilian and military morale, see Gary W. Gallagher, *The Confederate War* (New York: Oxford University Press, 1997).

Chapter 7: We Can Whip Any Army

1. *Rome Courier,* Oct. 9 and 24, 1862; Sanford Branch to his mother, Sept. 20, 1862, Margaret Branch Sexton Collection, Ms. 25, Hargrett Library Special Collections, University of Georgia, Athens; Thomas D. Gilham, "Oglethorpe Rifles: A Full History of This Celebrated Company," in n.a., *This They Remembered* (Columbus, Ga.: Brentwood University Press, 1986), 51.

2. *Rome Courier,* Oct. 9, 1862; Sanford Branch to his mother, Sept. 20, 1862.

3. Gilham, "Oglethorpe Rifles," 51; *Rome Courier,* Oct. 24, 1862; John C. Reed manuscript, Alabama Department of Archives and History, Montgomery, p. 194.

4. *Rome Courier,* Nov. 4 and 20, 1862.

5. Ibid., Oct. 24, 30, and 31, 1862

6. Ibid., Nov. 7, 1862; Gilham, "Oglethorpe Rifles," 51.

7. *Rome Courier,* Nov. 20, 1862; H. C. Kendrick to "Dear Father and Family," Nov. 3, 1862, Kendrick Papers, #397-Z, Southern Historical Collection, University of North Carolina Library, Chapel Hill.

8. *Rome Courier,* Nov. 20, 1862.

9. Gilham, "Oglethorpe Rifles," 51; Val C. Giles, *Rags and Hope: The Recollections of Val C. Giles, Four Years with Hood's Brigade, Fourth Texas Infantry, 1861–1965,* Mary Lasswell, ed. (New York Coward-McCann, 1961), 137–38.

10. *Rome Courier,* Nov. 25 and Dec. 5, 1862

11. *Rome Courier,* Dec. 5, 1862; Sanford Branch to his mother, Nov. 27, 1862.

12. *Rome Courier,* Dec. 5, 1862.

13. Ibid., Dec. 12 and 19, 1862.

14. Ibid., Dec. 5, 1862.

15. Ibid., Dec. 19, 1862.

16. Sanford Branch to his mother, Dec. 12, 1862.

17. W. B. Dasher reminiscences, Georgia Department of Archives and History, Civil War Miscellany, Drawer 283, Box 22.

18. *Rome Courier,* Dec. 19, 1862; Sanford Branch to his mother, Dec. 17, 1862; *Hawkinsville Dispatch,* July 27, 1879.

19. Sanford Branch to his mother, Dec. 25, 1862.

20. *Rome Courier.* Dec. 26, 1862, and Jan. 10, 1863.

21. Ibid., Dec. 26, 1862, and Jan. 1, 1863.

22. Richard W. Iobst, *Civil War Macon: The History of a Confederate City* (Macon, Ga.: Mercer University Press, 1999), 85–103, 145–271.

23. *Rome Courier,* Jan. 1, 1863.

24. Ibid., Jan. 10, 1863.

25. W. B. Dasher reminiscences.

26. Sanford Branch to his mother, Dec. 25, 1862.

27. *Rome Courier,* Jan. 10, 1863.

28. Sanford Branch to his mother, Dec. 25, 1862; *Rome Courier,* Jan. 16, 1863; John David Wilson, "George Thomas Anderson's Rebel Brigade: A Military History, 1861–1865" (Ph.D. dissertation, Emory University, 1977), 126.

29. Giles, *Rags and Hope,* 168–70.

30. Jeffry D. Wert, *General James Longstreet: The Confederacy's Most Controversial Soldier—A Biography* (New York: Simon & Schuster, 1993), 228–29; H. C. Kendrick to his father, Feb. 23, 1863.

31. M. O. Young, "History of the First Brigade," handwritten manuscript, Georgia Department of Archives and History.

32. H. C. Kendrick to his father, March 9, 1863; William W. Bennett, *A Narrative of the Great Revival in the Southern Armies During the Late Civil War Between the States of the Federal Union* (Philadelphia: Claxton, Remsen & Haffelfinger, 1877), 252–54.

33. Bennett, *Narrative of the Great Revival,* 254–55.

34. Wert, *Longstreet,* 233–35; U. S. War Department, *War of the Rebellion: A Compilation of the Official Records of the Union and Confederate Armies,* 128 vols. (Washington, D.C.: Government Printing Office, 1881–1901), Ser. 1, vol. 18, p. 871.

35. *Atlanta Southern Confederacy.* April 29, 1863.

36. Ibid., April 23 and May 14, 1863.

37. Ibid., May 1, 1863.

38. Gilham, "Oglethorpe Rifles," 52.

Chapter 8: A Scythe of Fire

1. Samuel J. G. Brewer to his wife, in H. Candler Thaxton, ed., *My Dear Wife from Your Devoted Husband: Letters from a Rebel Soldier to His Wife* (Warrington, Fla.: privately published, 1968), 125–26; Travis Hudson, "Soldier Boys in Gray: A History of the 59th Georgia Volunteer Infantry Regiment," *Atlanta Historical Society Journal* 23 (Spring 1979): 45; H. E. Kendrick to "Dear Father and Sister," May 28, 1863, Kendrick Papers, #397-Z, Southern Historical Collection, University of North Carolina Library, Chapel Hill.

2. *Rome Courier,* June 16, 1863; Hudson, "Soldier Boys in Gray," 46.

3. H. E. Kendrick to his mother, June 6, 1863.

4. John C. Reed manuscript, Alabama Department of Archives and History, Montgomery, p. 57.

5. *Rome Courier,* June 16, 1863; H. E. Kendrick to his mother, June 6, 1863.

6. *Rome Courier,* June 22, 1863; Samuel J. G. Brewer to his wife, 129–30.

7. Samuel J. G. Brewer to his wife, in Thaxton, *My Dear Wife,* 129–30.

8. M. O. Young, "History of the First Brigade," handwritten manuscript, Georgia Department of Archives and History.

9. Reed manuscript, p. 63.

10. H. E. Kendrick to "Dear Father & family," June 21, 1863; *Rome Courier,* July 7, 1863.

11. *Rome Courier,* July 21, 1863.

12. Young, "History of the First Brigade"; Reed manuscript, p. 67.

13. Val C. Giles, *Rags and Hope: The Recollections of Val C. Giles, Four Years with Hood's Brigade, Fourth Texas Infantry, 1861–1865,* Mary Lasswell, ed. (New York: Coward-McCann, 1961), 175, 177; *Rome Courier,* July 21, 1863.

14. Reed manuscript, p. 68; Hudson, "Soldier Boys in Gray," 52.

15. Dr. Augustus Henry Brantly, interview in UDC Bound Typescripts, vol. 11, p. 149, Department of Archives and History; *Rome Courier,* July 21, 1863.

16. *Rome Courier,* July 21, 1863; Reed manuscript, p. 69.

17. *Rome Courier,* July 21, 1863.

18. Reed manuscript, p. 72.

19. *Rome Courier,* July 21, 1863.

20. Brantly interview, vol. 11, pp. 149–55.

21. U.S. War Department, *War of the Rebellion: A Compilation of the Official Records of the Union and Confederate Armies,* 128 vols. (Washington D. C.: Government Printing Office, 1881–1901), Ser. 1, vol. 27, pt. 2, p. 358; Ser. 4, vol. 1. Hereinafter cited as *OR.*

22. *Rome Courier,* July 21, 1863; Hudson, "Soldier Boys in Gray," 53.

23. Reed manuscript, p. 75.

24. OR, Ser. 1, vol. 27, pt. 2, pp. 358; *Rome Courier,* July 21, 1863.

25. *Rome Courier,* July 21, 1863; Reed manuscript, p. 78.

26. Address given by Judge George Hillyer, Atlanta, Aug. 2, 1904, printed in the *Walton* (county) *Tribune.*

27. Harry W. Pfanz, *Gettysburg: The Second Day* (Chapel Hill: University of North Carolina Press, 1987), 118–21.

28. Reed manuscript, p. 80.

29. Pfanz, *Gettysburg: The Second Day,* 121.

30. Reed manuscript, p. 86.

31. *Rome Courier,* July 21, 1863.

32. M. O. Young, "History of the First Brigade."

33. *Rome Courier,* July 21, 1863.

34. Reed manuscript, p. 89.

35. *Rome Courier,* July 21, 1863; Pfanz, *Gettysburg: The Second Day,* 175–76.

36. Hillyer address.

37. Reed manuscript, p. 94; Pfanz, *Gettysburg: The Second Day,* 253.

38. Reed manuscript, p. 97; E. J. Magruder to John Towers, Jan. 19, 1888, private collection of Zack Waters, Rome, Georgia.

39. Reed manuscript, p. 100; Pfanz, *Gettysburg: The Second Day,* 247–51; Hillyer address; *Rome Courier,* July 21, 1863.

40. Hillyer address.

41. Excerpts from an Autobiography of Joel S. Yarbrough, Georgia Department of Archives and History, Civil War Miscellany, Drawer 283, Box 45.

42. Pfanz, *Gettysburg: The Second Day,* 250.

43. Reed manuscript, p. 104–6.

44. Pfanz, *Gettysburg: The Second Day,* 251–52.

45. Ibid., 394–401; Hillyer address.

46. Hillyer address.

47. Jay Jorgensen, "Anderson Attacks the Wheatfield," *Gettysburg Magazine,* No. 14, pp. 64–76. Hudson, "Soldier Boys in Gray," 62.

48. Hillyer address.

49. *Savannah Daily Morning News,* July 11 and 20, 1863.

50. Hillyer address; *Rome Courier,* July 21, 1863.

51. *OR,* Ser. 1, vol. 27, pt. 2, p. 397.

52. Written statement of Steven Townsend, grandson of Ezekiel Townsend, in author's possession.

53. Reed manuscript, p. 115.

54. *Rome Courier,* July 21, 1863.

55. Hudson, "Soldier Boys in Gray," 62–63.

56. Yarbrough autobiography.

57. Reed manuscript, p. 122.

58. Hudson, "Soldier Boys in Gray," 64.

59. Giles, *Rags and Hope,* 188–90.

60. *OR,* Ser. 1, vol. 27, pt. 2, p. 398; Reed manuscript, p. 124.

61. Hudson, "Soldier Boys in Gray," 66.

62. Quoted in "George Thomas Anderson's Rebel Brigade: A Military History, 1861–1865" (Ph.D. dissertation, Emory University, 1977), 159.

63. Reed manuscript, p. 127.

Chapter 9: The Worst Part of This War

1. *Macon Daily Telegraph,* Aug. 1, 1863; *Savannah Daily Morning News,* July 15, 18, 20, and 21, 1863; *Rome Courier,* July 21 and Sept. 7, 1863.

2. *Rome Courier,* Aug. 27 and Sept. 7, 1863; first soldier quoted in John David Wilson, "George Thomas Anderson's Rebel Brigade: A Military History, 1861–1865" (Ph.D. dissertation, Emory University, 1977), 161.

3. First soldier quoted in Wilson, "George Thomas Anderson's Rebel Brigade," p. 161; second soldier in William W. Bennett, *A Narrative of the Great Revival in the Southern Armies During the Late Civil War Between the States of the Federal Union* (Philadelphia: Claxton, Remsen & Haffelfinger, 1877), 330–31.

4. *Rome Courier,* Sept. 1, 1863.

5. Ibid., Sept. 3, 1863.

6. Ibid., Sept. 15 and 19, 1863.

7. Ibid., Oct. 13 and 15, 1863.

8. Ibid., Oct. 15 and 17, 1863.

9. Ibid., Oct. 20 and 22, 1863.

10. For a more complete account of these events see Steven E. Woodworth, *Six Armies in Tennessee: The Chickamauga and Chattanooga Campaigns* (Lincoln: University of Nebraska Press, 1998).

11. Travis Hudson, "The Charleston and Knoxville Campaigns: History of the 59th Georgia Infantry Volunteer Regiment, Part II," *Atlanta Historical Society Journal* 25 (Fall 1981): 51–53.

12. John C. Reed manuscript, Alabama Department of Archives and History, Montgomery, p. 139.

13. Hudson, "Charleston and Knoxville Campaigns," 53.

14. Reed manuscript, p. 140.

15. Hudson, "Charleston and Knoxville Campaigns," 53.

16. Reed manuscript, p. 140; U.S. War Department, *War of the Rebellion: A Compilation of the Official Records of the Union and Confederate Armies,* 128 vols. (Washington, D. C.: Government Printing Office, 1881–1901), Ser. 1, vol. 31, pt. 1, p. 458 Hereinafter cited as OR.

17. *OR,* Ser. 1, vol. 31, pt. 1, pp. 461, 490, 528–29; Reed manuscript, p. 144.

18. Hudson, "Charleston and Knoxville Campaigns," 54–65; *Hawkinsville Dispatch,* July 31, 1879; Thomas D. Gilham, "Oglethorpe Rifles: A Full History of This Celebrated Company," in n.a., *This They Remembered* (Columbus, Ga.: Brentwood University Press, 1986), 54–55; Compiled Service Records of Confederate Soldiers Who Served in Organizations from the State of Georgia, 8th Regiment Georgia Volunteer Infantry, Microcopy 226–66, National Archives; John A. Everett to his mother, No. 24, 1863, File #58, letter #86–2, Emory University Special Collections.

Chapter 10: The Raging Sea

1. Travis Hudson, "The Wilderness to Cold Harbor: A History of the 59th Georgia Volunteer Infantry Regiment, Part III," *Journal of the Atlanta Historical Society* 26 (Winter 1982-83): 19-20; Thomas D. Gilham, "Oglethorpe Rifles: A Full History of This Celebrated Company," in n.a., *This They Remembered* (Columbus, Ga.: Brentwood University Press, 1986), 55.

2. Hudson, "The Wilderness to Cold Harbor," 19-20; John David Wilson, "George Thomas Anderson's Rebel Brigade: A Military History, 1861-1865" (Ph.D. dissertation, Emory University, 1977), 180-83; *Hawkinsville Dispatch,* July 31, 1879.

3. Gilham, "Oglethorpe Rifles," 55.

4. Gordon C. Rhea, *The Battle of the Wilderness, May 5–6, 1864* (Baton Rouge: Louisiana State University Press, 1994), 297–99; Hudson, "Wilderness to Cold Harbor," 21–22; Robert K. Krick, " 'Lee to the Rear,' the Texans Cried," in Gary W. Gallagher, ed., *The Wilderness Campaign* (Chapel

Hill: University of North Carolina Press, 1997), 173; Noah Andre Trudeau, *Bloody Roads South: The Wilderness to Cold Harbor, May–June 1864* (Boston: Little, Brown, 1989), 90.

5. Robert E. L. Krick, " 'Like a Duck on a June Bug': James Longstreet's Flank Attack, May 6, 1864," in Gary W. Gallagher, ed., *Wilderness Campaign,* 236–51.

6. Hudson, "Wilderness to Cold Harbor," 23.

7. John C. Reed manuscript, Alabama Department of Archives and History, Montgomery, p. 155.

8. Hudson, "Wilderness to Cold Harbor," 22.

9. Ibid., 23; Reed manuscript, p. 158.

10. Reed manuscript, p. 158.

11. Gilham, "Oglethorpe Rifles," 56–57.

12. Travis Hudson, "Cold Harbor to Richmond: A History of the 59th Georgia Volunteer Infantry Regiment, Part IV," *Journal of the Atlanta Historical Society* 27 (Fall 1983): 31–34.

13. Gilham, "Oglethorpe Rifles," 57.

14. Reed manuscript, p. 162.

15. Gilham, "Oglethorpe Rifles," 57.

16. Reed manuscript, p. 163.

17. Gilham, "Oglethorpe Rifles," 58; Reed manuscript, p. 164.

18. Gilham, "Oglethorpe Rifles," 58.

19. Reed manuscript, p. 167.

20. Gilham, "Oglethorpe Rifles," 58.

21. Reed manuscript, p. 167.

22. Hudson, "Cold Harbor to Richmond," 40–41; Reed manuscript, p. 169.

23. Hudson, "Cold Harbor to Richmond," 41; Gilham, "Oglethorpe Rifles," 58, 63.

24. Gilham, "Oglethorpe Rifles," 58.

25. Wade Banister Gassman, "A History of Rome and Floyd County, Georgia, in the Civil War" (master's thesis, Emory University, 1966), 115–17.

26. Reed manuscript; Compiled Service Records of Confederate Soldiers Who Served in Organizations from the State of Georgia, 8th Regiment Georgia Volunteer Infantry, Microcopy 226–66, National Archives.

27. Reed manuscript, p. 178; Charles M. Harper reminiscences, United Daughters of the Confederacy, Rome, Georgia.

28. R. A. Brock, *The Appomattox Roster* (New York: Antiquarian Press, 1962), 97–99.

29. Gilham, "Oglethorpe Rifles," 61; Reed manuscript, p. 192.

30. Reed manuscript, p. 194.

INDEX

Army of the Potomac, U.S., 168, 182, 210,
215, 225, 227, 228, 232, 233, 291
Army of Virginia, U.S., 150
Atlanta Daily Intelligencer, 115
Atlanta Grays, *see* Company F
Atlanta Hook and Ladder Fire Company,
97
Atlanta Southern Confederacy, 97, 210
Aycock, George, 186, 201, 202
Aycock, William, 124

Babcock, J. W., 22
Baily, J. W., 174
Baker, Bob, 73–74
Baldy, Stephen, 165–66, 177
Ballard, C. M., 241, 263
Barber, Thomas J., 103
Barnsley, George S., 5, 25–26, 42
at First Manassas, 63, 65, 67, 68–69, 72,
75–76, 81–85, 87, 88, 90, 91
illness of, 102
in Manassas aftermath, 92–93, 98–99
Barnwell, S. B., 187
Bartow, Francis Stebbins, 14, 20, 28, 38,
93, 114
background of, 14
battlefield monument of, 106–7
becomes brigade commander, 43–44
becomes regimental commander, 26
death of, 84
fame of, 106
at First Manassas, 60–61, 62, 66–67,
69–70, 75, 78–81, 83–84
at Fort Pulaski, 14–15
funeral of, 97–98
in march to Manassas, 52, 58–59
speechmaking by, 16–18
Bartow's Brass Band, 65, 72, 89
Beardon, Andy, 97
Beardon, Maj., 97
Beauregard, P. G. T., 47, 50, 52–53,
58–61, 80, 94–95, 101, 104, 109,
112, 115, 119, 269, 292
Eighth Georgia saluted by, 83, 99–100
Bee, Barnard, 61, 62, 66–67, 80, 83, 106
Beers, Ethel Lynn, 113
Bell, Allen J., 203
Benning, Henry Lewis, 236, 301
Benning's brigade, C.S., 206, 233, 236,
240, 252, 296
Bibb County, Ga., 22, 188, 203, 270
Biesecker (farmer), 234

Black, John J., 5
Blackburn's Ford, 53
Blackwell, Thomas J., 24, 290
Bliss, Frederick, 165, 166, 228–29, 255
Bloody Run, *see* Plum Run
Boggs, James R., 201
"Bonnie Blue Flag, The" (song), 181, 223
Booton, Mary, 265
Booton, William S., 233–34, 236, 265
Borck, Julius, 8
Bowden, R. N., 201
Bowling, T. J., 169, 175, 295, 296
Bragg, Braxton, 264, 265, 268, 269, 270,
271–72, 273, 288
Branch, Charlotte, 107
Branch, Hamilton, 32, 41, 42, 62, 94, 107,
120, 121
Branch, John, 35, 42, 47–48, 96, 104, 107
death of, 74
Branch, Sanford, 42, 48, 74, 104, 107,
189, 197, 200, 202, 205, 263
wounded, 254–55
Brandy Station, Battle of, 216
Brantly, Augustus, 225, 254, 275, 276–77,
288
Brennan, Peter, 77
Brewer, Samuel, 103, 116, 143, 151–53,
155, 215, 216–17, 254
Brightwell, J. H., 126–28, 131
Brimstone (Gardner's horse), 63, 64
Brook, Jim, 160
Brown, John, 22, 28, 36
Brown, Joseph E., 4, 6, 20, 264
personality of, 7
reelection of, 270–71
Rome Light Guard addressed by, 7–8
weapons order of, 10, 17, 19, 24,
32–33
Brown's Ferry, Battle of, 272–73
"buck and ball," 73
Bull Run, First Battle of, *see* Manassas,
First Battle of
Bull Run, Second Battle of, *see* Manassas,
Second Battle of
Burnside, Ambrose, 191, 195, 197,
200–201, 273, 274, 277
Butler, Alexander F., 254
Butler, George, 73, 96
Butler "Van Guards," 21

Caldwell, John C., 249
Caledonia Iron Works, 227

tents, 9
Texas, 4
Texas Brigade, C.S., 139, 171, 261
 at Gettysburg, 233–36, 246, 247, 249,
  255
 in snowball fight with Georgia
  Brigade, 205–6
 at Spotsylvania, 290
Third Arkansas Regiment, C.S., 234
Third Corps, C.S., *see* Hill's Third Corps,
 C.S.
Third Corps, U.S., 232, 249
Third Vermont Regiment, U.S., 125–26
Thirty-third New York Regiment, U.S.,
 142
Thoroughfare Gap, Battle of, 164–69
 casualties in, 168–69
Thurston, Capt., 141
Toombs, Robert, 106, 141, 153, 164, 173,
 180, 233
 soldiers' view of, 154
Towers, John R., 6, 8, 10, 13, 32–33, 143,
 153, 157, 161, 174, 237, 247, 254,
 294, 305
Townsend, Ezekiel, 256, 298
Traveler (Lee's horse), 260, 285
Tuggle, Robert, 291, 295, 304
"twenty-nigger rule," 268
typhoid fever, 45, 105–6

Valley of Death, 251
Vicksburg, siege of, 216, 259, 264
Virginia, 4, 31
Virginia, University of, 99
"volunteer company," 4–5

wages, 134–35
Walker, Leroy Pope, 28, 32
Ward, Mrs. George A., 13
War Department, C.S., 8, 107
Ware, W. W., 276
Warren, Gouverneur K., 289
Watson, John, 201
Watters, Richard, 38–39, 97, 102, 103,
 107–8, 110, 119, 186
Webb, John, 39–41
Wesleyan Female College, 203
West, Joseph J., 74
Wheat Field, 239, 241
 fight for, 246, 248–52

"When This Cruel War Is Over" (song),
 254
White, W. W., 255, 260
Wilcox, E. A., 116
Wilcox, Gen., 167
Wilderness, Battle of the, 284–89
Wilderness Campaign, 284–92
 Battle of Cold Harbor in, 291
 Battle of Spotsylvania Court House in,
  289–90
 Battle of the Wilderness in, 284–89
 Haw's Shop fight in, 291
 maneuver to Petersburg front in, 291–92
Williams, John D., 45
Williamson, James Potter, 26
Winchester encampment, *see*
 Hollingsworth Grove
Winslow, George B., 243, 248
Wofford, William T., 250
Wofford's brigade, C.S., 250–51
Wragg, Thomas Lowndes, 69–70, 74, 110,
 115–16
wrap-jackets (game), 196

Yarbrough, Joel, 73, 85, 94, 97, 243, 258
 wounded, 185
Yarbrough, Lewis G., 97
Yarrington, Mr. and Mrs. W. W., 135–36
Yorktown, siege of, 127–31
Young, John A., 192, 210
Young, M. O., 208

Zettler, Berrien M., 26, 27, 34, 163, 164
 cherry picking incident and, 134
 at Dam Number One, 125–26
 at First Manassas, 62–64, 72, 76, 79–80,
  91
 furloughed, 178
 in honeycomb episode, 39–41
 joins Oglethorpe Lights, 15–16
 in march and train ride to Manassas,
  52–55, 58–59
 on picket duty, 111
 in Richmond excursion, 135–37
 at Second Manassas, 173–74, 177–78
 at Thoroughfare Gap, 165–68
 wounded, 174, 177–78
Zettler, Mr., 177–78
"Zouave drill," 27, 72
Zuber, John, 299